CONTRIBUTIONS TO EXTENSION THEORY OF TOPOLOGICAL STRUCTURES

CONTRIBUTIONS TO EXTENSION THEORY OF TOPOLOGICAL STRUCTURES

Internationale Spezialtagung für Erweiterungstheorie Topologischer Strukturen und deren Anwendungen, 1st

Proceedings of the Symposium
held in Berlin, August 14—19, 1967

Scientific Editors:
J. FLACHSMEYER, H. POPPE, F. TERPE

VEB DEUTSCHER VERLAG DER WISSENSCHAFTEN · BERLIN 1969

ES 19 B 3

Dieses Werk wird in Amerika (einschließlich Kanada), Afrika, Australien und Indien als Lizenzausgabe durch Academic Press, New York, verbreitet
Printed in the German Democratic Republic
Lizenz-Nr. 206 · 435/97/69
Schutzumschlag: Hartwig Hoeftmann
Gesamtherstellung: VEB Druckhaus „Maxim Gorki", Altenburg

Berichtigungen

Seite	Zeile	statt	lies
18	4 v. u.	(1956)	(1951)
30	11 v. u.	$X_a{}'$	$X_{a'}$
95	13 v. o.	$: t A t$	$: t A$
95	14 v. o.	$\cdot X$	$t X$
96	5 v. o.	$t f t\ {}^1 Y_1$	$t f t^{-1} Y_1$
103	15 v. u.	$\mathcal{U} x$	$\mathcal{U}_X$
164	12 v. o.	$A_2 \supset A$	$A_1 \supset A$
198	16 v. o.	$\square'(\varphi)\ \varphi/A$	$\square'(\varphi) = \varphi/A$
200	16 v. o.	sup	$\sup_n$
200	17 v. o.	$\sum^n$	$\sum$
252	18 v. u.	$R^{N(s', \sigma\lambda)}$	$R^{N(s', \sigma, \lambda)}$
260	9 v. o.	$\mu r(T)$	$\mu_r(T)$

VORWORT

Vom 14. bis 19. August 1967 fand in Berlin die I. Internationale Spezialtagung für Erweiterungstheorie topologischer Strukturen und deren Anwendungen statt. Veranstaltet wurde diese Tagung vom Institut für Reine Mathematik der Deutschen Akademie der Wissenschaften zu Berlin mit Unterstützung der Mathematischen Gesellschaft der DDR. Dieses Symposium war Herrn Prof. Dr. W. Rinow, Leiter der Forschungsgruppe für Topologie am Institut für Reine Mathematik der DAW zu Berlin und Leiter der Sektion Mathematik an der Ernst-Moritz-Arndt-Universität Greifswald, anläßlich seines 60. Geburtstages gewidmet.

Die Erweiterungstheorie topologischer Strukturen ist gegenwärtig ein wichtiges Spezialgebiet in der topologischen Forschung und findet bedeutende Anwendungen in zahlreichen Gebieten der Mathematik, wie zum Beispiel in der Funktionalanalysis, Funktionentheorie und Potentialtheorie. Dementsprechend ist die Anzahl der Arbeiten, die sich mit Erweiterungstheorie befassen, in den letzten Jahren beträchtlich angestiegen. Es schien daher wohl begründet zu sein, über dieses Gebiet eine Spezialtagung durchzuführen, und der intensive persönliche Kontakt mit namhaften Fachkollegen überzeugte die Veranstalter von der Nützlichkeit einer solchen Tagung. Das wissenschaftliche Ziel dieser Tagung bestand darin, eine Übersicht über die wesentlichen Aktivitäten auf dem Gebiet der topologischen Erweiterungstheorie zusammenzutragen und einheitliche Gesichtspunkte für die weitere gemeinsame internationale Forschungsarbeit herauszustellen.

Die große internationale Beteiligung an dieser Tagung mit so scharf umrissenem Thema war für die Veranstalter eine erfreuliche Überraschung. Von den insgesamt teilnehmenden 97 Wissenschaftlern kamen 53 aus dem Ausland, und zwar aus Bulgarien, ČSSR, Frankreich, Holland, Italien, Japan, Kanada, Polen, UdSSR, Ungarn und den USA. Es wurden 60 wissenschaftliche Vorträge gehalten. Die meisten Vorträge beschäftigten sich mit intern topologischen Fragen der Erweiterungstheorie. In einigen Vorträgen kam die Verbindung der topologischen Erweiterungstheorie mit uniformen Strukturen zum Ausdruck. Ferner wurden algebraische und ordnungstheoretische Fragen der Erweiterungstheorie behandelt. Auch wurden Anwendungen der Erweiterungstheorie in Funktionalanalysis, Funktionentheorie und Potentialtheorie erörtert. Einige Vorträge hatten nicht speziell die Erweiterungstheorie zum Gegenstand.

Die Veranstalter sind über den allgemeinen Wunsch erfreut, diesem Symposium ein weiteres mit der gleichen Themenstellung folgen zu lassen. Dieser Sammelband, der fast alle auf der Tagung gehaltenen Vorträge enthält, möge die weiteren Untersuchungen stimulieren!

Wir danken den Vortragenden für die Bereitstellung der Manuskripte und ihre Mitarbeit bei der Korrektur sowie dem VEB Deutscher Verlag der Wissenschaften für die Herausgabe des Bandes.

Greifswald, im Januar 1969 — Die Herausgeber

INHALT

WALLMAN COMPACT AND REALCOMPACT SPACES

RICHARD A. ALÒ (Pittsburgh, Pa./U.S.A.)
and HARVEY L. SHAPIRO (University Park, Pa./U.S.A.)

1. Introduction

In [4], ORRIN FRINK introduced a method of providing Hausdorff compactifications for Tichonov spaces. For a normal base $\mathscr{Z}$ of a Tichonov (completely regular T_1) space, he constructed the space $\omega(\mathscr{Z})$ of all $\mathscr{Z}$-ultrafilters. By choosing different normal bases $\mathscr{Z}$ for a non-compact Tichonov space X, one may obtain different Hausdorff compactifications $\omega(\mathscr{Z})$ of X. These compactifications are often referred to as Wallman-type or Frink-type compactifications. FRINK raised the question as to whether every Hausdorff compactification is obtainable in this manner. Several authors have given affirmative answers to this question for several important compactifications. In the first part of this paper we summarize the results that we have obtained in this direction. In Theorem 3.2 we give necessary and sufficient conditions for a Hausdorff compactification to be a Frink-type compactification. These are given in terms of conditions imposed on the normal base $\mathscr{Z}$. As an application we show, in an easy manner, that several compactifications are of the Wallman-type. We next consider another approach to the solution of FRINK's problem. We consider a normal base $\mathscr{Z}(Y)$ associated with the Hausdorff compactification Y of the space X. In Theorem 3.3 we give sufficient conditions on the base $\mathscr{Z}(Y)$, for the family $\mathscr{Z}(X)$ of intersections of X with the members of $\mathscr{Z}(Y)$ to be a normal base on X. We also give sufficient conditions for Y to be homeomorphic to $\omega(\mathscr{Z}(X))$. We omit the proofs which appear in [1] and [2].

Finally we consider realcompact spaces. The theory of realcompact spaces is in many ways analogous to the theory of compact spaces. To a very large extent the realcompact spaces play the same role in the theory of $C(X)$ (the ring of continuous real valued functions on a Tichonov topological space X) that the compact spaces do in the theory of $C^*(X)$ (that subring of $C(X)$ consisting of the bounded functions). Since compact spaces have pleasant properties, their study has led to the study of compactifications. Usually a compactification of a space can give interesting and worthwhile information about the space itself. For example, ORRIN FRINK (see [4]) used a compactification to show that every T_1 space with a normal base is a completely regular T_1 space. Since realcompact spaces and compact spaces play similar roles, a study of realcompactifications is also worthwhile. We use a variation of FRINK's notion of normal base to construct realcompactifications of Tichonov spaces.

2. Definitions and elementary results

A family $\mathscr{Z}$ of subsets of a nonempty set X is a *ring* of sets if it is closed under finite unions and finite intersections. It is said to be a *delta ring* if it is a ring that is also closed under countable intersections. If X is a T_1-topological space, then $\mathscr{Z}$ is said to be *disjunctive* if for any closed set F and for any point x not in F there is a Z of $\mathscr{Z}$ that contains x and is disjoint from F; $\mathscr{Z}$ is said to be *normal* if any two disjoint members A and B of $\mathscr{Z}$ are subsets respectively of disjoint complements C' and D' of members of $\mathscr{Z}$. The family $\mathscr{Z}$ is *complement generated* if for every member Z of $\mathscr{Z}$ there is a sequence of complements $(C_n')_{n\in N}$ of members of $\mathscr{Z}$ such that Z is their intersection.

The family $\mathscr{Z}$ is a *normal base* for the T_1-topological space X if it is a disjunctive normal ring of sets that also forms a base for the closed subsets of X. It is a *strong normal base* if it is complement generated. It is a *strong delta normal base* if it is a normal base that is also a delta ring and complement generated. If $\mathscr{Z}$ is a collection of subsets of the superspace Y of X, we say that $\mathscr{Z}$ is *space separating* (*with respect to* X) if whenever a member Z of $\mathscr{Z}$ is disjoint from the subspace X there is K in $\mathscr{Z}$ that is disjoint from Z and that contains X; we say that X is $\mathscr{Z}$*-dense* in Y if $\mathrm{cl}_Y\,(X \cap Z) = Z$ for all Z in $\mathscr{Z} \subset 2^Y$.

Note that many examples of strong delta normal bases exist. One of the most important is the collection of all zero-sets of a Tichonov space. Gillman and Jerison in [5] have shown that this family is a delta ring, that it is complement generated and that it satisfies the requirements for a normal base. Thus every Tichonov space has a strong delta normal base. A topological space is called *perfectly normal* if it is normal and if each closed subset is a G_δ. Thus in every perfectly normal space the family of closed subsets is a strong delta normal base.

A proper subset of a ring of sets $\mathscr{Z}$ is called a $\mathscr{Z}$*-filter* if it is closed under finite intersections and contains every superset in $\mathscr{Z}$ of each of its members. We also assume that no $\mathscr{Z}$-filter contains the empty set. A $\mathscr{Z}$*-ultrafilter* is a maximal $\mathscr{Z}$-filter. (In [3], a theory of $\mathscr{Z}$-filters is given.)

A subfamily $\mathscr{F}$ of $\mathscr{Z}$ is said to have the *countable intersection property* (c.i.p.) if any countable subcollection of $\mathscr{Z}$ has a nonempty intersection. If $\mathscr{Z}$ is taken to be the collection of all zero-sets (a zero-set is the set of all points x such that $f(x) = 0$ for a continuous real valued function f defined on the space), then X is said to be *realcompact* if every $\mathscr{Z}$-ultrafilter with the c.i.p. has a nonempty intersection. Thus every compact space is realcompact since a $\mathscr{Z}$-filter is a collection of closed sets with the finite intersection property. A *realcompactification* of a topological space X is a realcompact space Y which contains X densely.

In studying realcompact spaces the following notion is very useful. A nonempty subset A of X is said to be *Q-closed* in X if for every point p not in A there is a G_δ set G that contains p and is disjoint from A. The *Q-closure* of a nonempty subset A of X (denoted by $\mathrm{cl}_Q\, A$) is the set of points p in X such that every G_δ set G containing p meets A. In general the Q-closure of a set need not be closed. Indeed, the Q-closure of any open interval of the real line is the open interval. However, the Q-closure of a set always contains the set and is contained in the ordinary closure of the set. S.G. Mrówka in [6] has shown the following two theorems which signals the importance of this notion.

Theorem 2.1. *Every Q-closed subset of a realcompact space is realcompact.*

Theorem 2.2. *A topological space X is realcompact if and only if it is Q-closed in the Stone-Čech compactification, βX, of X.*

As a corollary to these theorems we observe that:

Corollary 2.3. *X is realcompact if and only if it is Q-closed in some compactification of X.*

Necessity of the condition is obvious by the second theorem above. On the other hand, since every compact space is realcompact, the first theorem shows that the condition is also sufficient.

3. Wallman-type compactifications

We now turn to the study of the Frink compactification question. Frink compactified a Tichonov space X by utilizing the set $\omega(\mathscr{Z})$ of all $\mathscr{Z}$-ultrafilters for some normal base $\mathscr{Z}$ on X. He obtained a compact Hausdorff topology for $\omega(\mathscr{Z})$ by assigning to each Z in $\mathscr{Z}$ the set Z^ω of all $\mathscr{F}$ in $\omega(\mathscr{Z})$ that contain Z. The collection $\mathscr{Z}^\omega$ of all Z^ω for Z in $\mathscr{Z}$ served as a base for the closed sets in $\omega(\mathscr{Z})$. Each x in X is represented in $\omega(\mathscr{Z})$, since the set $\varphi(x)$ of all Z in $\mathscr{Z}$ that contain x is a member of $\omega(\mathscr{Z})$. Through this map φ, X is homeomorphic to a dense subset of $\omega(\mathscr{Z})$.

Equivalently a base for the open sets can be defined. For each U contained in X such that the complement of U, U', is a member of $\mathscr{Z}$, assign the set U^ω of all $\mathscr{F}$ in $\omega(\mathscr{Z})$ for which there is some Z in $\mathscr{F}$ that is contained in U. This collection of sets U^ω is an open base for the same topology on X. We can now state the following results.

Theorem 3.1. *Let Y be a Hausdorff compactification of a T_1 space X, let g be the embedding of X into Y, and let $\mathscr{Z}$ be a normal base on X that satisfies the following property:*

(P) *For each y in Y and each neighborhood V of y there is a Z in $\mathscr{Z}$ such that $y \in \operatorname{cl} g(Z) \subset V$ and $\operatorname{cl} g(Z)$ is a neighborhood of y.*

Then there is a (closed) continuous map f of $\omega(\mathscr{Z})$ onto Y such that f agrees with g on X.

Theorem 3.2. *Let Y be a Hausdorff compactification of X. Then Y is homeomorphic to a Wallman-type compactification of X if and only if X has a normal base $\mathscr{Z}$ that satisfies:*

(a) $\operatorname{cl}_Y(A \cap B) = \operatorname{cl}_Y A \cap \operatorname{cl}_Y B$ *for all A, B in $\mathscr{Z}$.*

(b) *For each y in Y and each neighborhood V of y there is a Z in $\mathscr{Z}$ such that y is in $\operatorname{cl}_Y Z \subset V$.*

If Y is the Alexandroff one point compactification of a locally compact Hausdorff space X, then a normal base $\mathscr{Z}$ for X is the collection of zero sets of those continuous functions on X that are constant on the complement of some compact subset of X. That for this $\mathscr{Z}$, $\omega(\mathscr{Z})$ is homeomorphic to Y, follows immediately from our Theorem 3.2. Using Theorem 3.2 we can also show that any Hausdorff compactification of X that gives rise to a proximity that has a productive base (see Njastad [7]) can be obtained as a Wallman space $\omega(\mathscr{Z})$. Theorem 3.2 gives a very simple proof of this fact since we take as our normal base $\mathscr{Z}$ finite unions of members of the productive base for the proximity. It is immediately seen that $\mathscr{Z}$ satisfies the conditions of our Theorem. (See Alò and Shapiro [1].)

Now we turn to the study of when normal bases for a space Y are hereditary to subspaces X.

Theorem 3.3. *Suppose that X is a subspace of Y and that $\mathscr{Z}(Y)$ is a normal base on Y. If $\mathscr{Z}(Y)$ is space separating then the trace $\mathscr{Z}(X)$ of $\mathscr{Z}(Y)$ with X is a normal base on X.*

In trying to show that a normal base for a space Y is hereditary to subspaces X, it is the property of normality which produces the most difficulty. As with normal spaces, the property that a family of subsets is a normal family is not hereditary. It is interesting however, that if the subspace X is a member of the normal base for the space Y, then the normality of the family is inherited. This is given in the following corollary of our theorem.

Corollary 3.4. *If X is a subspace of a space Y and if $\mathscr{Z}(Y)$ is a normal base for Y which contains X then the trace $\mathscr{Z}(X)$ of $\mathscr{Z}(Y)$ with X is a normal base for X.*

Corollary 3.5. *Suppose that X is a dense subspace of Y and that $\mathscr{Z}$(X) is a normal base for Y. If X is $\mathscr{Z}(Y)$-dense in Y then the trace $\mathscr{Z}(X)$ is a normal base on X.*

Corollary 3.6. *If X is a compact closed subset of a normal (not necessarily T_1) space Y and if $\mathscr{Z}(Y)$ is a normal base on Y, then the trace $\mathscr{Z}(X)$ is a normal base on X.*

Theorem 3.7. *Let Y be a Hausdorff compactification of a space X and let $\mathscr{Z}(Y)$ be a normal base for Y. If X is $\mathscr{Z}(Y)$-dense in Y, then Y is homeomorphic to a space $\omega(\mathscr{Z}(X))$ where $\mathscr{Z}(X)$ is the trace of $\mathscr{Z}(Y)$ in X.*

If a subspace X is dense in a space Y then every nonempty regular closed set in Y will meet X. Thus Theorem 3.7 shows that every Hausdorff compactification Y which has a normal base that is also regular is a compactification in the sense of FRINK of each of its dense subspaces. In particular, the closed real interval has this property. To conclude this section we give some applications of Theorem 3.7.

Theorem 3.8. *Every zero dimensional Hausdorff compactification is a Frink type compactification of each of its dense subspaces.*

Theorem 3.9. *The compact Hausdorff space Q which is the arbitrary product of closed real intervals is a Frink type compactification of each of its dense subspaces.*

Theorem 3.10. *Every compact Hausdorff space Y is a Frink type compactification of each of its dense pseudocompact (and therefore countably compact and sequentially compact) subspaces X.*

4. Wallman-type realcompactifications

We now let $\mathscr{Z}$ be any strong delta normal base on a Tichonov space X. For our realcompactification of X we consider the subspace $\varrho(\mathscr{Z})$ of $\omega(\mathscr{Z})$ which consists of all $\mathscr{Z}$-ultrafilters with the c.i.p. A base for the closed subsets of this subspace topology will be the collection of subsets Z^{ϱ} of all $\mathscr{F}$ in $\varrho(\mathscr{Z})$ that contain Z. The sets $\varphi(x)$ defined above are also members of $\varrho(\mathscr{Z})$. Thus X is homeomorphic to a dense subset of $\varrho(\mathscr{Z})$ via the map φ.

In [3], ALÒ and SHAPIRO have given some basic properties of this space. In particular the following lemma, which will be needed in the next theorem, is proved there.

Lemma. *Let $\mathscr{L}$ be a delta ring of sets which is a base for the closed subsets of the topological space X and let $\mathscr{F}$ be a $\mathscr{L}$-ultrafilter with the c.i.p. If $(A_n)_{n\in N}$ is a sequence of sets in $\mathscr{F}$, then the intersection A of the sets A_n is in $\mathscr{F}$.*

Theorem 4.1. *Let $\mathscr{L}$ be a strong delta normal base of a Tichonov space X. Then X is homeomorphic to a dense subspace of a realcompact space $\varrho(\mathscr{L})$.*

Proof. The theorem will follow from the Corollary 2.3, if we show that $\varrho(\mathscr{L})$ is Q-closed in its Frink-type compactification $\omega(\mathscr{L})$. Let $\mathscr{F}$ be any member of $\omega(\mathscr{L})$ that does not have the c.i.p. and let $(Z_i)_{i\in N}$ be a collection of subsets of $\mathscr{F}$ such that their intersection Z is empty. Since $\mathscr{L}$ is a strong delta normal base, each Z_i is generated by a sequence of open subsets $(A_{i,n})_{n\in N}$ whose complements are in $\mathscr{L}$. Let G be the intersection of the basic open sets $(A_{i,n}{}^{\omega})_{i,\,n\in N}$. Since Z_i is contained in $A_{i,n}$ for each n, the G_δ set G contains $\mathscr{F}$. On the other hand by the lemma no $\mathscr{L}$-ultrafilter with the c.i.p. can be contained in G. Hence G does not meet $\varrho(\mathscr{L})$ and therefore $\varrho(\mathscr{L})$ s Q-closed in $\omega(\mathscr{L})$. This completes the proof.

Corollary 4.2. *If $\mathscr{L}$ is the strong delta normal base of all zero sets of a Tichonov space X, then $\varrho(\mathscr{L})$ is precisely the Hewitt realcompactification νX.*

Theorem 4.3. *If $\mathscr{L}$ is a strong delta normal base on a Tichonov space X, then $\varrho(\mathscr{L})$ is the Q-closure of $\varphi(X)$ in $\omega(\mathscr{L})$.*

Proof. If $\mathscr{F}$ is any element of $\omega(\mathscr{L})$ without the c.i.p., then the proof of Theorem 3 exhibits a G_δ set G that contains $\mathscr{F}$ and misses $\varrho(\mathscr{L})$. Therefore G misses the subset $\varphi(X)$ of $\varrho(\mathscr{L})$. Hence the Q-closure of $\varphi(X)$ in $\omega(\mathscr{L})$ is contained in $\varrho(\mathscr{L})$. To show the other direction it is sufficient to consider only G_δ sets G which are the intersection of basic open sets $A_n{}^{\omega}$ where the complement of A_n is in $\mathscr{L}$. If G is such a set which contains a member $\mathscr{F}$ of $\varrho(\mathscr{L})$ then for each n there is a Z_n in $\mathscr{L}$ such that $Z_n \subset A_n{}^{\omega}$. Since $\mathscr{F} \in \varrho(\mathscr{L})$, we can choose an x in the intersection of the Z_n. Then $\varphi(x)$ is in the intersection of G and $\varphi(X)$ and therefore $\varrho(\mathscr{L})$ is contained in the Q-closure of $\varphi(X)$ in $\omega(\mathscr{L})$. This completes the proof of the theorem.

Since the Q-closure of a set is Q-closed, Theorem 4.1 can be deduced from Theorem 4.3 using Theorem 2.1. However our approach above is justified by the importance of the construction.

In considering strong delta normal bases in realcompact spaces the following example is interesting. Let X be a discrete space of cardinality c (or any uncountable discrete space with non-measurable cardinal [see GILLMAN and JERISON [5], p. 163]). Let $\mathscr{L}_1$ be the collection of all subsets A of X such that A or the complement of A, A', is at most countable. It is easy to verify that $\mathscr{L}_1$ is a strong delta normal base. Now $\varrho(\mathscr{L}_1)$ is not equal to $\varphi(X)$ for there is member $\mathscr{F}$ of $\varrho(\mathscr{L}_1)$ that is not in $\varphi(X)$. In fact let $\mathscr{F}$ be the $\mathscr{L}_1$-filter that is the collection of all subsets of X whose complement is at most countable. It is a $\mathscr{L}_1$-ultrafilter since the complement Z' of Z is in $\mathscr{F}$ for any member Z of a filter containing $\mathscr{F}$ where Z is not in $\mathscr{F}$. If $(Z_n)_{n=1}^{\infty}$ is any sequence of sets in $\mathscr{F}$, then their common intersection Z is not empty since the complement of Z is at most countable and hence not equal to X. This shows that $\mathscr{F}$ has the countable intersection property. Finally $X - \{x\}$ is in $\mathscr{F}$ for each x in X and the common intersection of these sets is empty. It follows that the intersection of all the sets Z in $\mathscr{F}$ is empty. Thus $\mathscr{F}$ is not in $\varphi(X)$.

Another interesting example is to consider the same space X with the strong delta normal base $\mathscr{L}_2$ of all subsets of X. It is clear that $\varrho(\mathscr{L}_2) = \nu X = \varphi(X)$ by Corollary 4.2 and by the fact that X is realcompact if and only if $X = \nu X$ (see GILLMAN and JERISON [5], p. 116). Hence, in this case we have $\mathscr{Z}_1$ a subfamily of $\mathscr{Z}_2$ and $\varrho(\mathscr{Z}_2)$ is, homeomorphically, a proper subset of $\varrho(\mathscr{Z}_1)$.

Thus, in general, for subfamilies of the collection of all zero sets of a realcompact space X, $\varrho(\mathscr{Z})$ is not homeomorphic to X. Also different strong delta normal bases on a space X give different realcompactifications of the space. The question immediately arises as to whether every realcompactification of a space can be obtained in this manner. That is if Y is a realcompactification of a Tichonov space X, does there exist a strong delta normal base $\mathscr{Z}$ on X such that Y is homeomorphic to $\varrho(\mathscr{Z})$?

In closing, we consider the following condition on a delta normal base $\mathscr{Z}$.

(Q) If $Z_1 \supset Z_2 \supset \ldots \supset Z_n \supset \ldots$ is a nested sequence of members of $\mathscr{Z}$ then there is a sequence $(A_n)_{n \in N}$ of complements of members of $\mathscr{Z}$ such that $Z_n \subset A_n \subset \subset Z_{n-1}$ for each n.

If we replace the condition of complement generated in our strong normal base by condition (Q), similar results can be obtained. That is Theorem 4.1, Corollary 4.2, and Theorem 4.3 can be obtained for delta normal bases satisfying condition (Q).

References

[1] R. A. ALÒ and H. L. SHAPIRO, A note on compactifications and semi-normal spaces, Australian J. Math. 8 (1968), 102—108.
[2] R. A. ALÒ and H. L. SHAPIRO, Normal bases and compactifications, Math. Annalen **175** (1968), 337—340.
[3] R. A. ALÒ and H. L. SHAPIRO, Z-realcompactifications and normal bases (Australian J. Math.).
[4] O. FRINK, Compactifications and semi normal spaces, Amer. J. Math. **86** (1964), 602—607.
[5] L. GILLMAN and M. JERISON, Rings of continuous functions, Princeton 1960.
[6] S. G. MRÓWKA, Some properties of Q-spaces, Bull. Acad. Polon. Sci., Cl. III, **5** (1957), 947— 950, LXXX.
[7] O. NJASTAD, On Wallman-type compactifications, Math. Z. **91** (1966), 267—276.

ON RESIDUAL PROPERTIES OF CERTAIN SEMIGROUPS

L. W. ANDERSON and R. P. HUNTER (University Park, Pa./U.S.A.)

Following the usual terminology, we shall say that a semigroup S has a property $\mathscr{P}$ residually if any two points of S can be separated by some congruence $\sim$ such that $S/\sim$ has property $\mathscr{P}$. Since some of the properties with which we shall be dealing are not hereditary, it is convenient to say that S has a property $\mathscr{P}$ subresidually, if any two points can be separated with a homomorphism into some semigroup having property $\mathscr{P}$.

The properties with which we will be particularly interested are finiteness and compactness. Some remarks concerning terminology are probably in order. Now a group G is residually finite if and only if it is algebraically embeddable in a zero dimensional compact group. This is immediate from well known facts about compact groups. It follows from a result of NUMAKURA [21] that the above statement holds with "group" replaced by "semigroup". A group is sub-residually compact if and only if it is embeddable in a compact group, if and only if it is maximally almost periodic in the sense of VON NEUMANN [13]. Perhaps the first examples of abstract groups which were not embeddable in some compact group were those of VON NEUMANN and WIGNER [14]. Thus there exist abstract semigroups which are not embeddable (algebraically) in some compact semigroup. Another example, quite important from our standpoint, is the bicyclic semigroup. The subgroups and associated Schutzenberger groups of this semigroup are all trivial. Here we see that the question for semigroups can not be reduced to the corresponding question for its subgroups since the bicyclic semigroup can not be embedded even in a stable semigroup [3].

The following proposition, while hardly difficult will provide us with a number of examples.

Proposition 1. *Let G be a finitely generated group. Then G is sub-residually compact if and only if it is residually finite.*

Let $g \in G$, $g \neq 1$, and suppose that G is embedded in the compact group T. By the Peter-Weyl theorem there exists a closed normal subgroup N, $g \notin N$, such that T/N is a subgroup of a unitary group $U(k)$ for some k. Thus $G/G \cap N$ is a finitely generated matrix group and by a result of MALCEV [22] is residually finite.

Using the above remark one can establish the existence of a two generator, one relator group which is not maximally almost periodic. In [19] it is shown that the group $\langle a, b;\, a^{-1}b^2a = b^3\rangle$ is not Hopfian and hence not residually finite. It follows that this group cannot be sub-residually compact using Proposition 1.

It is also perhaps of interest to note that the group $G = \langle a, b; a^{-1}ba = b^2\rangle$ is residually finite but cannot be embedded in a compact Lie group. (As FLUCH [9] has shown, if G were a subgroup of some unitary group, the relation $a^{-1}ba = b^2$ would imply $b^k = 1$ for some k. However, by the Freiheitssatz [15], the subgroup generated by b in G is free.)

For the convenience of the reader we recall some classical definitions. (Here S^1 denotes S with identity adjoined if necessary.)

The Green relations, definable in any semigroup S are as follows (see, for example, [7]):

$$a \equiv b(\mathscr{L}) \qquad S^1a = S^1b$$

$$a \equiv b(\mathscr{R}) \qquad aS^1 = bS^1$$

$$a \equiv b(\mathscr{F}) \qquad S^1aS^1 = S^1bS^1$$

$$\mathscr{H} = \mathscr{L} \cap \mathscr{R} \qquad \mathscr{D} = \mathscr{L} \circ \mathscr{R} (= \mathscr{R} \circ \mathscr{L}).$$

The notion of stability has been introduced in [16] as an algebraic analogue of compactness. It will be particularly useful in our context. A semigroup S is called stable if for any $a, b \in S$ one has

$$Sa \subset Sab \to Sa = Sab \tag{1}$$

$$aS \subset baS \to aS = baS. \tag{2}$$

Among the most natural semigroups to be considered in terms of residual properties are perhaps the simple semigroups. As we shall see this question gives rise to two distinct problems in the case of stability. The completely simple case will be considered separately. The second case, dealing with $\mathscr{D}$-triviality seems to be more formidable.

A semigroup is called completely simple if it is simple (has no proper ideal) and contains a primitive idempotent. The idempotent e is primitive if eSe has no idempotent save e. This class of semigroup is rather well known (see again [5]).

Proposition 2. *Let S be a simple subsemigroup of a stable semigroup T. If S contains an idempotent, it is completely simple. If S contains no idempotent, the $\mathscr{D}$-classes of S are degenerate.*

Proof. If S contains an idempotent which is not primitive, then S contains a copy of the bicyclic semigroup. But this is impossible since the bicyclic semigroup admists no stable embeddings. Now suppose S contains no idempotents and a non degenerate $\mathscr{D}$-class. Since S is simple, it is entirely contained in some $\mathscr{F}$-class of T. From the fact that T is stable we know that this $\mathscr{F}$-class is necessarily a $\mathscr{D}$-class, D, of T and D is regular. Now S contains a non-trivial $\mathscr{D}$-class, hence S must contain a non-trivial $\mathscr{L}$- or $\mathscr{R}$-class. Assuming the latter we have that there is an element $a \in S$ such that $a \in aS = aS^2$, i.e. $a = abb'$ for some $b, b' \in S$. For $t \in T$, let R_t and L_t denote the $\mathscr{R}$- and $\mathscr{L}$-classes in T which contain t. Since T is stable and a, b and ab belong to D we have $ab \in L_b \cap R_a$ [5]. Thus by GREEN's theorem [7] we have $(L_{ab})b' = (L_b)b' = L_a$ and so $bb' \in L_a$. Now if $x \in L_a$ there $x = ta$ for some $t \in T^1$ so $xbb' = tabb' = ta = x$. Thus we have $(bb')bb' = bb'$ which is impossible since S contains no idempotent.

Corollary. *Let S be a left simple semigroup having no proper homomorphic images. Then either S is a group or S has no idempotent and no non-constant homomorphism into a stable semigroup.* (In particular, $\hat{S}$ is degenerate, see [2]).

Proof. If S has an idempotent then S is the direct product of a group and a left zero semigroup. The latter is therefore trivial. If S has no idempotent then there remains only to show that S cannot be embedded in a stable semigroup. By Proposition 2 if S had such an embedding $\mathscr{D}$ would be trivial.

The existence of semigroups which are left simple and having no proper homomorphic images has been well established. (See for example [11].)

The Baer-Levi semigroups which are right cancellative and right simple also furnish examples. Specifically let S be the set of all one to one mappings α of X into itself such that $X - \alpha(X)$ is infinite and X is countable (see [11]). Later on we shall contruct a $\mathscr{D}$-trivial simple semigroup which is a subsemigroup of a compact group. At this point however let us note the following example of an unstable subsemigroup of a zero dimensional compact group. As Green [7] has remarked the semigroup S generated by a, b, c, d, x, y subject to $axb = y$ and $cyd = x$ is such that $x \equiv y(\mathscr{F})$ but $x \not\equiv y(\mathscr{D})$. There is a natural image of S in the group generated by the same generators and relations. The latter, however, is free since we may eliminate successively as follows:

$$\langle a, b, c, d, x, y : axb = y, cyd = x\rangle$$
$$\langle a, b, c, d, x : caxbd = x\rangle$$
$$\langle a, b, c, d, x : c = xd^{-1}b^{-1}x^{-1}a^{-1}\rangle$$
$$\langle a, b, d, x : \qquad\qquad \rangle$$

The image of S is thus in a free group and is therefore residually finite.

The bicyclic semigroup furnishes us with a $\mathscr{D}$-simple semigroup, having degenerate subgroups, and which is not residually finite or even residually stable. As we shall see even in the case of a completely simple semigroup the finiteness of the subgroup will not insure residual finiteness for the semigroup. However one has the following

Proposition 3. *Let S be a completely 0-simple semigroup. If the structural group eSe, $e^2 = e$, is residually finite and if $S/\mathscr{L}$ (or $S/\mathscr{R}$) is finite then S is residually finite.*

Proof. Suppose $x, y \in S$ and x and y do not belong to the same maximal subgroup of S. Then x is not $\mathscr{R}$-equivalent to y or x is not $\mathscr{L}$-equivalent to γ. Suppose the former case obtains. The natural mapping of S onto $S/\mathscr{R}$ is a homomorphism and $S/\mathscr{R}$ is a left trivial semigroup. Now consider the two point set [0, 1] endowed with left trivial multiplication. Map $S/\mathscr{R}$ onto [0, 1] by $R_x \to 1$, $R_z \to 0$, $R_x \neq R_z$. This is clearly a homomorphism distinguishing R_x and R_y. Now the composition maps S homomorphically onto $\{0, 1\}$ distinguishing x and y. Now suppose x and y are contained in the same maximal subgroup G of S. First, recall that G is isomorphic to eSe and S is isomorphic to $G \times I \times \Lambda$ where multiplication is given by (g, i, λ) $(g', i', \lambda') = (gp(i', \lambda) g', i, \lambda')$ where p: $I \times \Lambda \to G$ is a function and I is $S/\mathscr{R}$, Λ is $S/\mathscr{L}$. Since G is residually finite, there is a homomorphism Π: $G \to F$ where F is finite group and $\Pi(x) \neq \Pi(y)$. Now let q: $I \times \Lambda \to F^0$ be given by $q = \Pi^0 p$ then $F^0 \times I \times \Lambda$ is completely simple semigroup where multiplication is given by $(f, i, \lambda)(f', i', \lambda') = (f\, q(i', \lambda)\, f', i, \lambda')$ and the function $\overline{\Pi^0}$: $G \times I \times \lambda \to F^0 \times \times I \times \lambda$ defined by $\Pi^0(g, i, \lambda) = (\Pi^0(g), i, \lambda)$ is a homomorphism such that $\overline{\Pi^0}(x) \neq$

$\neq \Pi^0(g)$. We now define a congruence, $\sim$, upon $F^0 \times I \times \Lambda$ by $(f, i, \lambda) \sim (f', i', \lambda')$ if $f = f'$, $i = i'$ and $q_{i\lambda} = q_{i\lambda'}$ for all $i \in I$. By a result of TAMURA [12] $\sim$ is a congruence. One easily sees that $(F^0 \times I \times \Lambda)/\sim$ is a finite semigroup distinguishing x and y.

To see that a finiteness condition is necessary in Proposition 3, consider the example: Let G be a non-trivial finite simple group and let $I = \Lambda =$ the positive integers. Define p: $I \times \Lambda \to G$ by $p(1, \lambda) = p(i, 1) = e$ all $i \in I$, $\lambda \in \Lambda$ $p(n, n) = e$, and for $m \neq n$, $m \neq 1$, $n \neq 1$ let $p(m, n)$ be any element of G other than e. Now if

$$f\colon (G, I, \Lambda, p) \to (G^*, I^*, \Lambda^*, p^*)$$

is an epimorphism and if G^* is not trivial then $G = G^*$, since G is simple. Further $I = I^*$ and $\Lambda = \Lambda^*$ since no two rows nor columns in the matrix (p_{ij}) coincide. Finally, we note that in a finitely generated completely simple semigroup S, both $S/\mathscr{L}$ and $S/\mathscr{R}$ are finite.

Proposition 4. *Let S be a regular semigroup such that each $\Gamma(H)$ is residually finite and each $D/\mathscr{H}$ is finite. Then S is residually finite.*

Since S is regular given x and y in S there is a Schutzenberger representation $s \to M(s)$ such that $M(x) \neq M(y)$. Since each D has a finite number of $\mathscr{H}$-classes it follows that under $s \to M(s)$ the semigroup is represented by finite matrices over some $\Gamma(H)^0$. Clearly $\Gamma(H)^0$ is residually finite. It follows that there is a

$$s \to M'(s)$$

representation by finite row monomial (or column monomial) matrices over $\Gamma(H/N)^0$, where N is an appropriate normal subgroup of finite index in $\Gamma(H)$ such that $M'(x) \neq M'(y)$.

Corollary. *Let S be an inverse semigroup which is the union of groups. If each subgroup of S is residual finite then so is S.*

References

[1] L. W. ANDERSON and R. P. HUNTER, Sur les espaces fibrés, Bull. Acad. Polon. Sci., Ser. Math., **12** (1964), 249—252.

[2] L. W. ANDERSON and R. P. HUNTER, Residual properties of certain semigroups (to appear).

[3] L. W. ANDERSON and R. P. HUNTER, Some results on stability in semigroups, Trans. Amer. Math. Soc. **117** (1965), 521—529.

[4] P. HOLM, On the Bohr compactification, Math. Annalen **156** (1964), 34—36.

[5] A. H. CLIFFORD and G. B. PRESTON, The algebraic theory of semigroups, Math. Surveys No. 7, Amer. Math. Soc., Providence R. I. 1961.

[6] R. CROISOT, Sur les équivalences bilatères, J. Math. pures et appl. **36** (1957), 373—417.

[7] J. A. GREEN, On the structure of semigroups, Ann. Math. **54** (1956), 163—172.

[8] S. BALCERZYK and J. MYCIELSKI, On the existence of free subgroups in topological groups, Bull. Acad. Polon. Sci., Ser. Math., **4** (1956), 415.

[9] W. FLUCH, Maximal-Fastperiodizität von Gruppen, I, Math. Scand. **16** (1965), 148—158.

[10] G. Thierrin, Contribution à la théorie des équivalences, Bull. Soc. Math. France **83** (1955), 103—159.

[11] M. Teissier, Sur les semi-groupes admettant l'existence du quotient d'un côté, C. R. Acad. Sci. Paris **232** (1951), 1120—1122.

[12] T. Tamura, Decompositions of a completely simple semigroup, Osaka Math. J. **12** (1960), 269—275.

[13] J. von Neumann, Almost periodic functions on groups, I, Trans. Amer. Math. Soc. **36** (1934), 445—492.

[14] J. von Neumann and E. Wigner, Minimally almost periodic groups, Ann. Math. **41** (1940), 746—750.

[15] W. Magnus, Das Identitätsproblem für Gruppen mit einer definierenden Relation, Math. Annalen **106** (1932), 295—307.

[16] R. J. Koch and A. D. Wallace, Stability in semigroups, Duke Math. J. **24** (1951), 193—196.

[17] Z. Frolík, The topological product of two pseudo compact spaces, Czechoslovak Math. J. **10** (1960), 339—349.

[18] W. Maak, Fastperiodische Funktionen auf Halbgruppen, Acta Math. **87** (1952), 33—57.

[19] G. Baumslag and D. Solitar, Some two-generator one-relator non-Hopfian groups, Bull. Amer. Math. Soc. **68** (1962), 199—201.

[20] L. W. Anderson and R. P. Hunter, Homomorphisms and dimension, Math. Annalen **147** (1962), 248—268.

[21] K. Numakura, Theorems on compact totally disconnected semigroups and lattices, Proc. Amer. Math. Soc. **8** (1957), 623—626.

[22] A. I. Malcev, On the faithful representation of infinite groups by matrices (russ.), Mat. Sbornik (N. S.) **8** (1940), 405—421.

ON THE COMPACTIFICATION OF CERTAIN SEMIGROUPS

L. W. Anderson and R. P. Hunter (University Park, Pa./U.S.A.)

Following Holm [4], we define the Bohr compactification of a semigroup S as a pair $(\sigma, \hat{S})$ where $\sigma: S \to \hat{S}$ is a dense representation and $\hat{S}$ is a compact semigroup having the property that the diagram

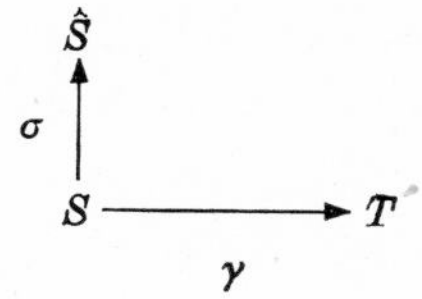

where γ is a dense representation of S in the compact semigroup T, completes to the diagram

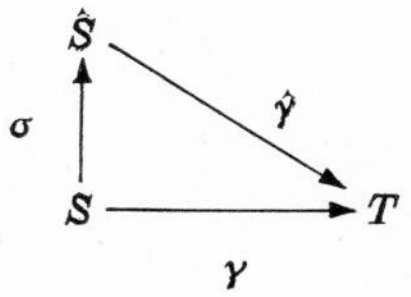

where $\hat{\gamma}$ is a continuous epimorphism. As Holm has shown, $\hat{S}$, may be viewed as the separated completion of S with respect to the finest uniform structure $\mathcal{U}$ which is precompact, compatible with the multiplication in S, and defines a topology coarser than the initial topology on S.

The problem of the compactification of a semigroup S is clearly connected with that of its residual properties in a number of ways (see [2]). For example, S is subresidually compact if and only if σ is a faithful (monomorphic) representation. And S is residually finite if and only if no two distinct points of S are sent into the same component of $\hat{S}$ under σ. Indeed, suppose x and y are two fixed but arbitrary points of S. If $\sigma(x)$ and $\sigma(y)$ lie in different componente of $\hat{S}$, form the decomposition $\sim$ which identifies each component. Then $S/\sim$ is a totally disconnected compact semigroup and is therefore residually finite, so that x and y can be separated with a homomorphism onto a finite semigroup. On the other hand, if x and y can be so separated than $\sigma(x)$ and $\sigma(y)$ clearly can not lie on the same component of $\hat{S}$ because of the factorization property of $\hat{S}$.

This note will be closely connected with [2] since we shall consider in more detail the problem of the compactification of a completely simple semigroup. In that note we saw that S need not be residually finite even though the structural group was a cyclic group of order **2**.

Let S be a semi lattice which is totally ordered under the usual idempotent partial order ($e \leqq f$ if and only if $ef = fe = e$). It can be shown without difficulty that $\hat{S}$ is also a totally ordered semi lattice. Moreover $\hat{S}$ is totally disconnected for if C were a non-degenerate component of $\hat{S}$ it must be an arc. It would then follow that C has a non vacous interior. Hence some pair of points of $\hat{S}$ must be sent into the component C under the homomorphism σ. As we have seen this is impossible since S is residually finite.

Let S be the unit interval under the multiplication min (x, y) and having the discrete topology, and let T be the same semigroup but with the usual topology. Since the Bohr compactification $\hat{S}$ is zero dimensional one may note that a curious consequence of the Bohr compactification is the existence of dimension raising homomorphisms. (For a more involved discussion of this theory see [20].)

In [18], Maak extends almost periodic compactification to semigroups by proving that an almost periodic function on a semigroup can be approximated appropriately by unitary representations. Thus, the Maak compactification of a semigroup S clearly will not often co-incide with the Bohr compactification since the former is always a group. Now let S be a semigroup and α a dense representation of S into the compact group G. Since two points of S can be separated by a homomorphism into a compact group if and only if they can be separated by an almost periodic function we have the commutative diagram where S_M denotes the maximal almost periodic group belonging to S, in the sense of Maak [18]:

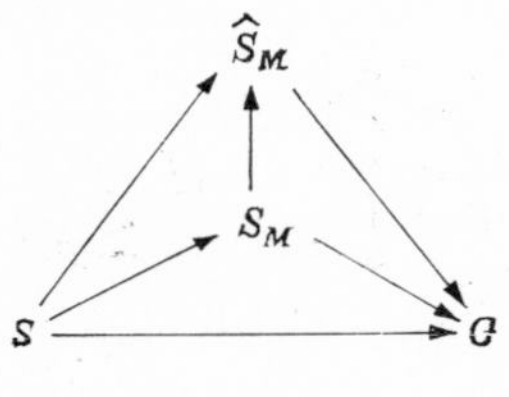

Following Thierrin [10] we shall call a semigroup S a homogroup if it has an ideal K which is a subgroup. It is to be noted that K is necessarily a minimal ideal. A compact semigroup will become a homogroup if, for example, its idempotents commute. If S is a homogroup and e the identity of its minimal ideal K then $x \to xe$ is a retracting homomorphism of S onto K.

Proposition 1. *Let S have the property that if $f: S \to T$ is a homomorphism into a compact semigroup T then the closure of $f(S)$ is a homogroup. (This is the case, for example, if S is abelian, normal, or is itself a homogroup.) Then the Maak compactification is the minimal ideal of the Bohr compactification. That is to say* $\hat{S}_M = \operatorname{Ker}(\hat{S})$.

We recall that a semigroup S has a group G as maximal group image if any homomorphism of S onto a group T factors through G:

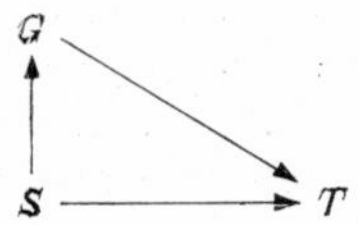

A given S need not have a maximal group image. However, a completely simple semigroup has such an image [5].

Proposition 2. *Let S be a semigroup having a maximal group image G. Then $\hat{G}$ coincides with the Maak compactification of S if and only if S has the property that each homomorphic image of S in a compact group is a group.*

We now fix our attention on the completely simple semigroup. We recall again a number of pertinent facts: A completely simple semigroup S can be characterized as a four-tuple (X, Y, G, p). Here X and Y are respectively left and right trivial semigroups, G is a group and p is a function from $X \times Y$ to G. The multiplication is given by $(x, y, g)(\bar{x}, \bar{y}, \bar{g}) = (x, \bar{y}, gp(\bar{x}, y)\bar{g})$. The sets X and Y are, in point of fact, the quotient semigroups $S/\mathscr{L}$ and $S/\mathscr{R}$. The structural group G is taken as H_e for any idempotent e. These are all mutually isomorphic. It is well known and not difficult to see that a homomorphic image of a completely simple semigroup is again completely simple and a compact semigroup which contains a dense completely simple subsemigroup is again completely simple. The above characterization of a completely simple semigroup carries over in the appropriate manner, to the compact case. The group in this case is compact, the quotient semigroups $S/\mathscr{L}$ and $S/\mathscr{R}$ are compact, and the sandwich function $p: S/\mathscr{L} \times S/\mathscr{R} \to H_e$ is continuous. One further item of importance is that the cannonical mappings $S \to S/\mathscr{L}$ and $S \to S/\mathscr{R}$ are open. (This can be noted by an analysis of the decomposition. In fact if D is a $\mathscr{D}$-class of a compact semigroup then the cannonical maps $D \to D/\mathscr{L}$ and $D \to D/\mathscr{R}$ are open [1].)

Let us consider the nature of the Bohr compactification $\hat{S}$ of a completely simple semigroup S. First of all we assert that if $\hat{S} = (X', Y', G', p')$ is the representation according to Rees of $\hat{S}$ as a four-tuple then we must have $X' = \beta(X)$ and $Y' = \beta(Y)$. (Here, $\beta(T)$ is the Stone-Čech compactification of T). To see this note that $S/\mathscr{L}$ is a left trivial semigroup so that any continuous mapping f of $S/\mathscr{L}$ to any compact space T can be viewed as a continuous homomorphism by endowing T with the left trivial multiplication. By the nature of the Bohr compactification, the following diagram commutes:

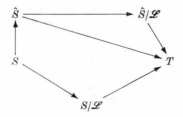

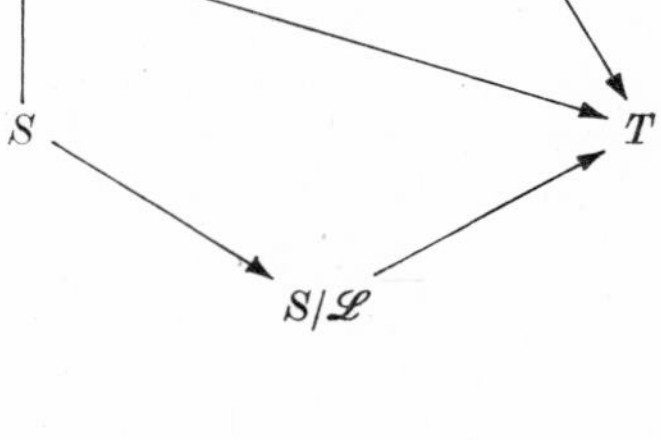

Thus $\hat{S}/\mathscr{L}$ is, by uniqueness, $\beta(X) = \beta(S/\mathscr{L})$. Likewise $\beta(Y) = \beta(S/\mathscr{R}) = \hat{S}/\mathscr{R}$. Furthermore G' is a compact group having a dense continuous homomorphic image of G. Now G' is, of course, a homomorphic of $\hat{G}$ and it may be proper.

Let us consider the following question. Given a dense representation $G \to G'$ when can the sandwich function p be "extended" to $\beta(X) \times \beta(Y)$. This, of course, includes the question of when the subresidual compactness of G extends to that of S. Otherwise said when can one complete the diagram below:

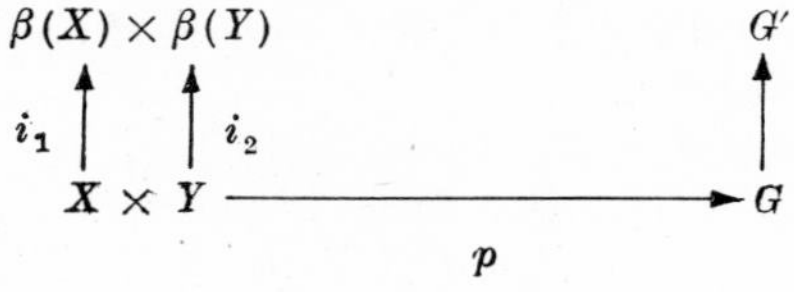

where i_1 and i_2 are canonical maps. To this end we establish the following proposition which will give us a criterion for the subresidual compactness of certain completely simple semigroups.

Lemma. *Let X, Y completely regular T_2, C compact T_2, $f: X \times Y \to C$ continuous. Then f has a continuous extension to $\beta X \times \beta Y$ if V an entourage on C implies there are open sets $U_1, \ldots, U_n$ in X and open sets $V_1, \ldots, V_n$ in Y such that $\{U_i \times V_i\}$ covers $X \times Y$ and if x and y are in $U_i \times V_i$ $(i = 1, \ldots, n)$ then $(f(x), f(y)) \in V$.*

Proof. If f has a continuous extension, say $\hat{f}$, to $\beta X \times \beta Y$ then $\hat{f}$ is uniformily continuous and the condition follows. To prove the condition is also sufficient, recall the theorem of Frolík [17].

$f: X \times Y \to I\,(= [0, 1])$ has a continuous extension to $\beta X \times \beta Y$ iff $\varepsilon > 0$ implies there is $U_1 \times V_1$, $U_2 \times V_2, \ldots, U_n \times V_n$ a cover of $X \times Y$ (U_i open in X, V_i open in Y) such that $x, y \in U_i \times V_i$ implies $|f(x) - f(y)| < \varepsilon$. Now let $g: C \to I$ be any continuous function. We will show that gof satisfies the condition of Frolík, hence, has an extension $g\hat{o}f$, to $\beta X \times \beta Y$. Let $\varepsilon > 0$, then since g is uniformily continuous, there is an entourage V in C such that $(x, y) \in V$ implies $|f(x) - f(y)| < \varepsilon$. Now for V we have a cover $\{U_i \times V_i\}$ of $X \times Y$ with open sets such that $x, y \in U_i \times V_i$ implies $(f(x), f(y)) \in V$ thus $|gof(x) - gof(y)| < \varepsilon$. Now let $e: C \to I^{C(C,I)}$ be the evaluation map and define

$$\hat{f}: \beta X \times \beta Y \to e(C)$$

by

$$\hat{f}(x)(g) = g\hat{o}f(x).$$

$\hat{f}$ is clearly continuous since gof is continuous and for $x \in X \times Y$, $\hat{f}(x)(g) = g\hat{o}f(x) = gof(x) = f(x)(g)$ hence $\hat{f}\,|X \times Y = eof$.

We observe that $S = (X, Y, G, \lambda)$ is subresidually compact iff there is a compact group G^1 with G dense in G^1 and an extension $\bar{\lambda}: \beta X \times \beta Y \to G^1$ of λ, i.e. if λ: $X \times Y \to G^1$ satisfies the conditions of the lemma.

Finally, we note that if $S = (X, Y, G, \lambda)$ and $S^1 = (X, Y, G, \lambda^1)$ are isomorphic, both are subresidually compact if either one is.

Example 1. Let L be a left trivial semigroup. (That is to say, multiplication is $xy = x$ for all x, y). It is clear that the Stone-Čech compactification $\beta(L)$ coincides with L. Note that any function from L to a compact space X can be viewed as a homomorphism enclosing X with the left trivial multiplication. The same statements hold for $L \times L$ so that

$$\beta(L \times L) = \widehat{L \times L}.$$

Suppose that the set for L is, say, the set of integers. It is well known that $\beta(L) \times \times \beta(L)$ and $\beta(L \times L)$ do not coincide. Thus Bohr cmpactification does not commute with cartesian products even in the finite case. The same remarks can be made by using a zero trivial semigroup (i.e. all products equal to some fixed element). This example will then be abelian.

Example 2. The semigroup S of (2×2)-matrices

$$\begin{pmatrix} x & y \\ 0 & 1 \end{pmatrix}$$

where x and y are positive integers. The semigroup S is not algebraically embeddable in a compact group. To see this one has only to note that in S

$$\begin{pmatrix} N & 1 \\ 0 & 1 \end{pmatrix} \begin{pmatrix} 1 & 1 \\ 0 & 1 \end{pmatrix} = \begin{pmatrix} 1 & 1 \\ 0 & 1 \end{pmatrix}^N \begin{pmatrix} N & 1 \\ 0 & 1 \end{pmatrix}.$$

From [14], it follows that $\begin{pmatrix} 1 & 1 \\ 0 & 1 \end{pmatrix}$ could not be separated from the identity with a unitary representation.

It should be noted however that S is residually finite nil. To see this one has only to examine the Rees quotients of certain ideals.

Example 3. The semigroup S of (2×2)-matrices

$$\begin{pmatrix} x & y \\ 0 & 1 \end{pmatrix}$$

where x and y are positive rational is not subresidually compact. (It is however embeddable in a locally compact connected group.) To see that S is not a subsemigroup of a compact semigroup suppose on the contrary that it were. Since S is simple it follows that $\bar{S}$ is completely simple. The natural mapping $\bar{S} \to \bar{S}/\mathscr{L}$ defines a homomorphism onto a right trivial semigroup. It follows readily that the homomorphism must be constant on the matrices of the form

$$\begin{pmatrix} 1 & a \\ 0 & 1 \end{pmatrix}$$

and from this that it must be constant on all of S. In the same way the map $\bar{S} \to \bar{S}/\mathscr{R}$ is trivial so that $\bar{S}$ is contained in a single $\mathscr{H}$-class and is thus a group. From the previous example it is immediate that this is impossible.

Example 4. The bicyclic semigroup $\mathscr{C}(p, q)$. We recall that $\mathscr{C}(p, q)$ is defined as the semigroup on two generators p and q subject to the relation $pq =$ identity $- 1$. (For a detailed description of this semigroup, see [5].) Now $\mathscr{C}(p, q)$ has $Z =$ the integers as maximal group image. Moreover any proper homomorphic image of $\mathscr{C}(p, q)$ is a cyclic group. Finally $\mathscr{C}(p, q)$ cannot be embedded in a compact semigroup. Now let T be a compact semigroup and γ a dense representation of $\mathscr{C}(p, q)$

into T. From what has been said above, it follows that there is a commutative diagram

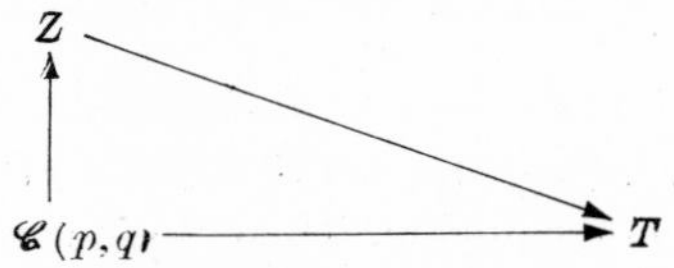

where Z denotes the integers. This diagram extends to

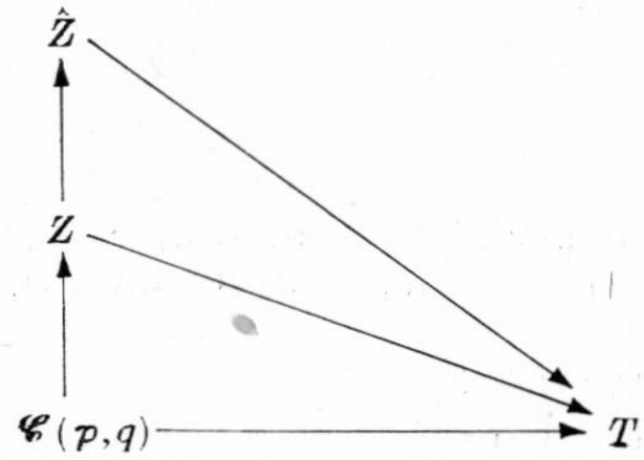

and by the uniqueness of the compacifictation we see that $\hat{\mathscr{C}}(p, q) = \check{Z}$.

References

[1] L. W. ANDERSON and R. P. HUNTER, Sur les espaces fibrés, Bull. Acad. Polon. Sci., Ser. Math., **12** (1964), 249—252.

[2] L. W. ANDERSON and R. P. HUNTER, Residual properties of certain semigroups (to appear).

[3] L. W. ANDERSON and R. P. HUNTER, Some results on stability in semigroups, Trans. Amer. Math. Soc. **117** (1965), 521—529.

[4] P. HOLM, On the Bohr compactification, Math. Annalen **156** (1964), 34—36.

[5] A. H. CLIFFORD and G. B. PRESTON, The algebraic theory of semigroups, Math. Surveys No. 7, Amer. Math. Soc., Providence R. I. 1961.

[6] R. CROISOT, Sur les équivalences bilatères, J. Math. pures et appl. **36** (1957), 373—417.

[7] J. A. GREEN, On the structure of semigroups, Ann. Math. **54** (1951), 163—172.

[8] S. BALCERZYK and J. MYCIELSKI, On the existence of free subgroups in topological groups, Bull. Acad. Polon. Sci., Ser. Math., **4** (1956), 415.

[9] W. FLUCH, Maximal-Fastperiodizität von Gruppen, I, Math. Scand. **16** (1965), 148—158.

[10] G. THIERRIN, Contribution à la théorie des équivalences, Bull. Soc. Math. France **83** (1955), 103—159.

[11] M. TEISSIER, Sur les demi-groupes admettant l'existence du quotient d'un côté, C. R. Acad. Sci. Paris **232** (1951), 1120—1122.

[12] T. TAMURA, Decompositions of a completely simple semigroup, Osaka Math. J. **12** (1960), 269—275.

[13] J. VON NEUMANN, Almost periodic functions on groups, I, Trans. Amer. Math., Soc. **36** (1934), 445—492.

[14] J. VON NEUMANN and E. WIGNER, Minimally almost periodic groups, Ann. Math. **41** (1940), 746—750.

[15] W. MAGNUS, Das Identitätsproblem für Gruppen mit einer definierenden Relation, Math. Annalen **106** (1932), 295—307.

[16] R. J. Koch and A. D. Wallace, Stability in semigroups, Duke Math. J. **24** (1951), 193–196.
[17] Z. Frolík, The topological product of two pseudo compact spaces, Czechoslovak Math. J. **10** (1960), 339–349.
[18] W. Maak, Fastperiodische Funktionen auf Halbgruppen, Acta Math. **87** (1952), 33–57.
[19] G. Baumslag and D. Solitar, Some two-generator one-relator non-Hopfian groups, Bull. Amer. Math. Soc. **68** (1962), 199–201.
[20] L. W. Anderson and R. P. Hunter, Homomorphisms and dimension, Math. Annalen **147** (1962), 248–268.
[21] K. Numakura, Theorems on compact totally disconnected semigroups and lattices, Proc. Amer. Math. Soc. 8 (1957), 623–626.
[22] A. I. Malcev, On the faithful representation of infinite groups by matrices (russ.), Mat. Sbornik (N. S.) 8 (1940), 405–421.

FRAMES AND COMPACTIFICATIONS

B. BANASCHEWSKI (Hamilton/Can.)

Introduction

A complete lattice in which the (binary) meet operation distributes over arbitrary joins is called a *frame*. Particular examples of frames are, of course, the topologies on a set, and certain statements about topological spaces can, in fact, be regarded as consequences of appropriate statements about frames [5]. The aim of this paper is to consider compactifications in this manner.

Associated with any frame $\mathfrak{v}$ is the space F whose points are the proper filters $\mathfrak{x} \subseteq \mathfrak{v}$ and whose topology is generated by the sets $F_a = \{\mathfrak{x} \mid a \in \mathfrak{x} \in F\}$, $a \in \mathfrak{v}$. We shall call F the *filter space of* $\mathfrak{v}$ and, generally, the subspaces of F *filter spaces in* $\mathfrak{v}$. For any such space X, the topology is then generated by the sets $X_a = X \cap F_a$, $a \in \mathfrak{v}$; its closure operator Γ_X, incidentally, is given by $\Gamma_X A = \{\mathfrak{x} \mid \mathfrak{x} \subseteq \bigcup \mathfrak{a} (\mathfrak{a} \in A), \mathfrak{x} \in X\}$.

Compactifications of continuous images of a topological space X are here shown to be representable by certain filter spaces in the topology $\mathfrak{D}$ of X, and a general study is then made of the filter spaces of this type in an arbitrary frame.[1])

1. Filter spaces in topologies

In order to show that filter spaces in frames are closely connected with extensions of topological spaces we make the following observation regarding T_0-spaces X and Y and the topology $\mathfrak{D}$ of X:

Proposition 1. *For any continuous mapping $f\colon X \to Y$ such that Y is a strict extension of $f(X)$, the mapping φ which associates with each $y \in Y$ the filter in $\mathfrak{D}$ generated by the $f^{-1}(U)$, U any open neighbourhood of y, is an embedding of Y into the filter space of $\mathfrak{D}$.*

From this one readily obtains the following three assertions, the first and second by restricting the hypotheses on f, the third by using the first in the general case.

[1]) Support from the National Research Council of Canada making participation in this symposium possible is gratefully acknowledged.

Corollary 1. *The mapping* $\nu\colon x \leadsto \mathfrak{D}(x) = \{U \mid x \in U \in \mathfrak{D}\}$ *embeds* X *into the filter space of* $\mathfrak{D}$.

Corollary 2. *If* Y *is a strict extension of* X *then the mapping which associates with each* $y \in Y$ *its trace filter on* X, *i.e. the filter in* $\mathfrak{D}$ *consisting of all* $U \cap X$, U *any open neighbourhood of* y, *embeds* Y *into the filter space of* $\mathfrak{D}$, *its restriction to* X *being* ν.

Corollary 3. *The mapping* $\nu(X) \to \varphi(Y)$ *given by* $\mathfrak{D}(x) \leadsto \varphi(f(x))$ *is continuous.*

In the case of Hausdorff spaces, this last described mapping is in fact purely set theoretically determined, for then every $\mathfrak{D}(x)$ contains exactly one member of $\varphi(Y)$, namely $\varphi(f(x))$.

With the same notations as above one has, in a more restricted situation:

Proposition 2. *If* Y *is compact Hausdorff then its image under the embedding* φ *has the following properties:* (1) *Every maximal filter in* $\mathfrak{D}$ *contains exactly one member of* $\varphi(Y)$, *and* (2) $\bigcap \varphi(y)$ $(y \in Y) = \{E\}$.

Later it will result from considerations in the more general setting of frames that any filter space in $\mathfrak{D}$ with these two properties is of the type $\varphi(Y)$.

2. Mappings between filter spaces in a frame

For any filter spaces X and Y in a frame $\mathfrak{o}$, let $X \lhd Y$ (X is covered by Y) mean that each $\mathfrak{x} \in X$ is contained in some $\mathfrak{y} \in Y$ and each $\mathfrak{y} \in Y$ contains exactly one $\mathfrak{x} \in X$. This is equivalent to the condition that the set $\{(\mathfrak{y}, \mathfrak{x}) \mid \mathfrak{y} \in Y,\ \mathfrak{x} \in X,\ \mathfrak{y} \supseteqq \mathfrak{x}\}$ be a mapping from Y to X. Given $X \lhd Y$, this mapping will be called the *natural mapping* $Y \to X$. It is of particular interest to know when this might turn out to be continuous, and the considerations below will lead to a condition which ensures this.

The following notations will be used for arbitrary frames: For any $a \in \mathfrak{o}$, let $a' = \bigvee b (a \wedge b = 0)$ be the largest element of $\mathfrak{o}$ disjoint from a. For any subsets $\mathfrak{x}$ and $\mathfrak{y}$ of $\mathfrak{o}$, let $\mathfrak{x} * \mathfrak{y}$ mean that $a \wedge b \neq 0$ for all $a \in \mathfrak{x}$ and $b \in \mathfrak{y}$, and $a * \mathfrak{y}$ for $a \in \mathfrak{o}$ and $\mathfrak{y} \subseteqq \mathfrak{o}$ that $\{a\} * \mathfrak{y}$. If $\mathfrak{x} * \mathfrak{y}$ then $\mathfrak{x}$ and $\mathfrak{y}$ are called *compatible*, otherwise *incompatible*. For any subset X of the filter space F of $\mathfrak{o}$ and any $a \in \mathfrak{o}$, put $X^a = \{\mathfrak{x} \mid a * \mathfrak{x} \in X\}$.

One now has, for any $X \subseteqq F$:

Lemma 1. (i) *If* $a \leqq b$ *then* $X^a \subseteqq X^b$ *for any* a *and* b *in* $\mathfrak{o}$. (ii) $X^a = X - X_{a'}$ *for any* $a \in \mathfrak{o}$. (iii) *For any* $\mathfrak{x} \in X$, $\bigcap X^a (a \in \mathfrak{x}) = \{\mathfrak{z} \mid \mathfrak{x} * \mathfrak{z} \in X\}$.

Since one also has $X_a \subseteqq X^a$ for all $a \in \mathfrak{o}$, one obtains with the aid of this lemma:

Proposition 3. *If* X *is compact Hausdorff and any two distinct members of* X *are incompatible then, for each* Y *such that* $Y \rhd X$ *the natural mapping* $Y \to X$ *is continuous.*

A similar observation, not needed in the present context, is that the natural mapping $Y \to X$, for $Y \rhd X$, is continuous if X is a regular, dense subspace of F. Both these results follow from the fact that, in either case, the hypothesis on X ensures that the sets X^a, $a \in \mathfrak{x}$, generate the neighbourhood filter of $\mathfrak{x}$ in X.

3. A particular set of filter spaces in a frame

Motivated by Proposition 2 we now consider the set $\mathfrak{K}$ of all compact Hausdorff filter spaces X of a frame $\mathfrak{o}$ for which the following conditions hold:
(K1) Every maximal filter in $\mathfrak{o}$ contains exactly one $\mathfrak{x} \in X$.
(K2) $\bigcap \mathfrak{x}(\mathfrak{x} \in X) = \{e\}$, e the unit of $\mathfrak{o}$.
The first condition is equivalent to $X \lhd M$, M the space of *maximal* filters in $\mathfrak{o}$. We note that $\mathfrak{K}$ is never empty since $\{\{e\}\}$ belongs to it, but that M, though compact Hausdorff and satisfying (K1), need not belong to $\mathfrak{K}$.

One readily sees that the relation $\lhd$ determines a partial order on $\mathfrak{K}$, and that for any $X, Y \in \mathfrak{K}$ with $X \lhd Y$ the natural mapping $Y \to X$ is continuous, the latter being an immediate consequence of Proposition 3. Further properties of $\mathfrak{K}$ with respect to $\lhd$ could be established directly at this point, but it is more convenient to delay this until later, and we turn to properties of the individual $X \in \mathfrak{K}$.

For elements $a, b \in \mathfrak{o}$ we put $a \ll b$ iff $b \vee a' = e$, and we call a filter $\mathfrak{x}$ *regular* iff for each $a \in \mathfrak{x}$ there exists a $b \in \mathfrak{x}$ such that $b \ll a$. It is clear that in a topology $\mathfrak{O}$ the corresponding relation is that of *regular inclusion*, given for $U, V \in \mathfrak{O}$ by $\Gamma U \subseteq V$, Γ the closure operator determined by $\mathfrak{O}$, since the largest $W \in \mathfrak{O}$ disjoint from U is the complement of ΓU. Here we have:

Proposition 4. *For each* $X \in \mathfrak{K}$, *all members of* X *are regular filters.*

The proof of this employs the fact that $\bigcap \mathfrak{x}(\mathfrak{x} \in X) = \{e\}$ in an essential way; for other compact Hausdorff subspaces of F, e.g. M, this proposition need not hold [2].

A filter $\mathfrak{p} \in F$ is, as usual, called *prime* iff $a \vee b \in \mathfrak{p}$ implies that $a \in \mathfrak{p}$ or $b \in \mathfrak{p}$. Examples of prime filters are, of course, the maximal filters. A prime filter compatible with a regular filter must contain the regular filter, and hence one obtains for the set $P \subseteq F$, of all prime filters:

Corollary. *For any* $X \in \mathfrak{K}$, $X \lhd P$.

In particular, for any subspace S of P and any $X \in \mathfrak{K}$, the restriction of the natural mapping $P \to X$ to S is continuous; moreover, if S is dense in F then its image in X is dense in X. This together with the fact that, for a topology $\mathfrak{O}$, the filters $\mathfrak{O}(x)$ are prime, provides the converse of Proposition 2.

4. Description of $\mathfrak{K}$ by relations on the frame

On a frame $\mathfrak{o}$ we now consider the set $\mathfrak{R}$ of binary relations R which have the following properties for any elements a, b, x, y of $\mathfrak{o}$:

(R0) oRo and eRe.
(R1) If aRb then $a \ll b$.
(R2) If aRb, $x \leq a$, and $b \leq y$ then xRy.
(R3) If aRx and aRy then $aRx \wedge y$.
(R4) If aRx and bRx then $a \vee bRx$.
(R5) If aRb then $b'Ra'$.
(R6) If aRb then there exists an x such that aRx, xRb.

In the particular case of topologies, these relations are what FREUDENTHAL introduced as *normal D-systems* [6], elsewhere referred to as *relations of completely regular inclusion* [3]. Such relations always exist, the set of all pairs (o, x) and (x, e), $x \in \mathfrak{v}$, being one, and in fact the smallest one, of this type.

For any such relation R, a filter $\mathfrak{x} \in F$ is called an *R-filter* iff for each $a \in \mathfrak{x}$ there exists a $b \in \mathfrak{x}$ such that bRa. With the notation $R(\mathfrak{x}) = \{a \mid bRa$ for some $b \in \mathfrak{x}\}$ this then means $\mathfrak{x} = R(\mathfrak{x})$. Also, one readily sees that, for any $\mathfrak{x} \in F$, $R(\mathfrak{x})$ is an R-filter, and hence the largest R-filter $\mathfrak{y} \subseteqq \mathfrak{x}$, and that the maximal R-filters are exactly the $R(\mathfrak{m})$, $\mathfrak{m}$ maximal in F. Furthermore, one has

Proposition 5. *For each* $R \in \mathfrak{R}$, *the space* $M(R)$ *of all maximal R-filters belongs to* $\mathfrak{K}$.

Conversely, for any $X \in \mathfrak{K}$, we define a relation R_X by saying that aR_Xb iff $X^a \subseteqq X_b$, and obtain

Proposition 6. *For each* $X \in \mathfrak{K}$, R_X *belongs to* $\mathfrak{R}$ *and* $M(R_X) = X$.

In addition, one observes that, for R and S in $\mathfrak{R}$, $R \subseteqq S$ implies $M(R) \lhd M(S)$; similarly, for X and Y in $\mathfrak{K}$, $X \lhd Y$ implies $R_X \subseteqq R_Y$; and finally $R \subseteqq R_{M(R)}$ for each $R \in \mathfrak{R}$.

5. Generation of relations belonging to $\mathfrak{R}$

To begin with, let R be a binary relation on an arbitrary set E. We call R *cotransitive* iff aRb implies that there exists a c such that aRc and cRb; in terms of relational composition, this means $R \subseteqq R \circ R$, i.e. the dual of transitivity. Our aim is to derive a specific cotransitive relation from any given transitive R as follows:

An *R-chain* is a sequence $\sigma = (x_1, \ldots, x_n)$ where $x_i R x_{i+1}$ for all $i = 1, \ldots, n-1$. If σ and τ are R-chains, σ is said to *refine* τ (notation: $\sigma < \tau$) iff $\sigma = (x_1, \ldots, x_n)$, $\tau = (y_1, \ldots, y_m)$ where $x_1 = y_1$, $x_n = y_m$, and $y_j = x_{j'}$, $y_{j+1} = x_{j''}$ with $j'' > j' + 1$ for all $j = 2, \ldots, m-1$. The relation R^* is defined by the condition that aR^*b holds iff there exists a decrasing sequence $\sigma_0 > \sigma_1 > \ldots$ of R-chains such that $\sigma_0 = (a, b)$. Concerning this new relation one has:

Lemma 2. R^* *is cotransitive and is, in fact, the largest cotransitive relation* $S \subseteqq R$.

In view of this, R^* will be called the *cotransitive kernel* of R. The interest in this concept lies in the following result concerning relations on a frame $\mathfrak{v}$:

Proposition 7. *For any transitive relation on* $\mathfrak{v}$ *satisfying* (R0) *to* (R5) *the cotransitive kernel belongs to* $\mathfrak{R}$.

Considering in particular the relation $\ll$ on $\mathfrak{v}$ one immediately obtains:

Corollary 1. $\mathfrak{R}$ *has a largest member, namely the cotransitive kernel* $\ll^*$ *of the relation* $\ll$, *and consequently* $\mathfrak{K}$ *has a maximum in the sense of* $\lhd$.

Also, from the fact that the conditions (R0) to (R5) are retained under arbitrary intersections, and from the correspondence between $\mathfrak{K}$ and $\mathfrak{R}$ described in the previous section, one derives:

Corollary 2. $\mathfrak{K}$, *partially ordered by* $\lhd$, *is a complete lattice.*

If the frame considered is the topology $\mathfrak{O}$ of a space X and hence the relation $\ll$ is regular inclusion, the cotransitive kernel of the latter is the relation which holds for $U, V \in \mathfrak{O}$ iff U and $X - V$ are completely separated [4]. It follows from this that the space $M(\ll^*)$ is a generalization of ALEXANDROFF's description of the Stone-Čech compactification [1].

We conclude this paper with a result concerning frames which expresses the equivalence of complete regularity and compactifiability for T_0-spaces.

A frame $\mathfrak{o}$ will be called *completely regular* iff $a = \bigvee b (b \ll^* a)$ for each $a \in \mathfrak{o}$. A filter $\mathfrak{x} \in F$ is called *completely prime* if, for any family (a_α) in $\mathfrak{o}$, $\bigvee a_\alpha \in x$ implies $a_\alpha \in x$ for some α. A set $X \subseteqq F$ is said to *separate* $\mathfrak{o}$ iff $X_a = X_b$ implies $a = b$.

Now, let C be the space of all completely prime filters in $\mathfrak{o}$ and K the largest member of $\mathfrak{K}$. Then one has:

Proposition 8. *If* $\mathfrak{o}$ *is completely regular then* $C \subseteqq K$. *Conversely, if* C *separates* $\mathfrak{o}$ *and* $C \subseteqq K$ *then* $\mathfrak{o}$ *is completely regular.*

The topological theorem in question is obtained from this by the added observation that filters of open neighbourhoods of points are, in fact, completely prime.

References

[1] P. ALEXANDROFF, Bikompakte Erweiterungen topologischer Räume, Mat. Sbornik (N. S.) **5** (1939), 420—429.

[2] B. BANASCHEWSKI, On the Katětov and Stone-Čech extensions, Canadian Math. Bull. **2** (1959), 1—4.

[3] B. BANASCHEWSKI, Extensions of topological spaces, Canadian Math. Bull. **7** (1964), 1—22.

[4] B. BANASCHEWSKI and J.-M. MARANDA, Proximity functions, Math. Nachr. **23** (1961), 1—37.

[5] C. H. DOWKER and DONA PAPERT, On Urysohn's lemma, Proc. Second Symposium on General Topology, Prague 1966.

[6] H. FREUDENTHAL, Neuaufbau der Endentheorie, Ann. Math. **43** (1942), 261—279.

A TOPOLOGY FOR GENERAL BINARY SYSTEMS[1])

T. N. Bhargava and Sigrid E. Ohm[2]) (Kent, O./U.S.A.)

A halfgroupoid is a very general algebraic system consisting of a nonvoid set on which is defined a binary operation, meeting only the requirement of closure, for none or some or all of the possible pairs of elements in the set. In case the operation is defined for all pairs of elements in the set, the system is called a groupoid. The theory of groupoids, which is rather recent, has been investigated by several people, notably Birkhoff [2], Borůvka [3], Bruck [4], and Doyle and Warne [5]. Topological groupoids have been considered mainly by Šulka [9], and Warne [10]. Finally Hanson [6] has studied in his doctoral dissertation connections between binary systems (groupoids) and admissible topologies. However no study of the properties of halfgroupoids seems to have been made; possibly because of the extremely general structure of a halfgroupoid. That these halfgroupoids have some interesting properties was shown by Ohm [8]. In this paper our object is to present a study of an ideal topology associated with halfgroupoids, and to show an interesting connection between such an ideal topology and the digraph topology obtained by Bhargava and Ahlborn [1] in a study of topological properties of directed graphs.

1. Halfgroupoids

A nonvoid subset S of a halfgroupoid H is called a subhalfgroupoid if and only if $S \cdot S \subset S$. A nonvoid subset A of a halfgroupoid H is called an antihalfgroupoid if and only if $A \cdot A \subset \bar{A}$ where $\bar{A}$ denotes the complement of set A.

A left (right) ideal for a halfgroupoid H is a subset $I_L(I_R) \subset H$ such that $H \cdot I_L (I_R) \subset I_L(I_R)$. A two-sided ideal is a subset $I \subset H$ which is both a left and a right ideal. A point ideal is any ideal consisting of a single element. The empty set is considered a trivial ideal, either left, right, or two-sided.

Let $a, b \in H$; then a is a right factor of b and b is a left multiple of a, denoted by a/b, if there exists an element $c \in H$ such that $c \cdot a = b$. An element $a \in H$ is prime if the set of right factors of a is the empty set or $\{a\}$ itself. An element which is not prime is called composite. An element $a \in H$ for which $a \cdot a = a$ is called an idempotent element. An element $a \in H$ is a right zero element if for all $b \in H$, $b \cdot a = a$. An element $a \in H$ is a right unit element if for all $b \in H$, $b \cdot a = b$.

---

[1]) Prepared under a NASA Research Grant No. NsG-568 at Kent State University.

[2]) Now at Purdue University.

Definitions corresponding to right ideals or two-sided ideals can be made in an obvious manner but are not given here because throughout this paper we limit ourselves to left ideals only.

2. The *L*-topology

Let $\mathscr{I}_L, \mathscr{I}_R, \mathscr{I}_T$ be the families of all left, right, and two-sided ideals respectively for a halfgroupoid H.

Theorem 2.1. *The family $\mathscr{I}_L$ (or $\mathscr{I}_R$, or $\mathscr{I}_T$) constitutes a topology with the property of completely additive closure.*

Remark 2.1. The family of all possible left, right, and two-sided ideals does not, in general, constitute a topology. For example, for the halfgroupoid H defined by

$$H = \begin{array}{c|ccc} & a & b & c \\ \hline a & a & c & a \\ b & c & - & c \\ c & c & b & c \end{array}$$

the family of all possible ideals, left, right or two-sided, is $\{\emptyset, H, \{a, c\}, \{b, c\}\}$ but $\{a, c\} \cap \{b, c\} = \{c\} \notin \mathscr{I}_L$ or $\mathscr{I}_R$. However $\mathscr{I}_L \cup \mathscr{I}_R$ taken as a subbase does give us a topology.

Remark 2.2. Two halfgroupoids with same elements but different operations may have identical left ideal topologies. For example

$$H_1 = \begin{array}{c|cccc} & a & b & c & d \\ \hline a & - & c & c & d \\ b & c & b & - & - \\ c & - & a & c & a \\ d & b & - & - & b \end{array} \qquad H_2 = \begin{array}{c|cccc} & a & b & c & d \\ \hline a & b & - & c & a \\ b & - & a & c & d \\ c & b & c & - & - \\ d & b & c & - & c \end{array}$$

have exactly same topologies.

Throughout the rest of this paper we call the left ideal topology $\mathscr{I}_L$ as L-topology and denote it simply by $\mathscr{I}$. An element I_L of $\mathscr{I}_L$ is denoted simply as I.

Theorem 2.2. *The topological space $(H, \mathscr{I})$ is connected if, and only if, there does not exist an I in $\mathscr{I}$ such that $\bar{I}$ is a subhalfgroupoid and $(I \cdot \bar{I}) \cap I = \emptyset$.*

Theorem 2.3. *The topological space $(H, \mathscr{I})$ satisfies T_0 if, and only if, for every a in H there exists a point ideal I_a in $\mathscr{I}$ such that for all b, distinct from a, b is not a right factor of a.*

Proof. Let a belong to H. If a is a right zero element, then $H \cdot \{a\} \subset \{a\}$, so that $\{a\}$ is a point ideal. If a is not a right zero element and there exists some I_a in $\mathscr{I}$ containing no right factor of a and no other element except a, then I_a is a point ideal.

If I_a does contain an element $b \neq a$, then $I_a \cap \overline{\{a\}}$ also contains b but not a and is therefore an open set in $\mathscr{I}$. Thus in every case T_0 is satisfied.

Conversely, suppose the condition is not met, i.e. for some right nonzero a in H the point ideals I_a in $\mathscr{I}$ contain at least one more element, other than a, which is a right factor of a. Then $\cap \{I_a\}$ contains some element $b \neq a$, where b is such that b/a. Since b/a, there exists an x in H such that $x \cdot b = a$ so that a belongs to $H \cdot I_b$ for any arbitrary I_b in $\mathscr{I}$; but $H \cdot I_b \subset I_b$ so that a belongs to every I_b. Hence $(H, \mathscr{I})$ does not satisfy axiom T_0.

Remark 2.3. For the halfgroupoid

$H =$

	a	b	c
a	a	b	c
b	a	c	b
c	a	b	c

the topological space $(H, \mathscr{I})$ does not satisfy T_0.

Theorem 2.4. *The topological space $(H, \mathscr{I})$ satisfies T_1 if, and only if, every elemen of H is a point ideal; or equivalently if, and only if, every element of H is a right zero element.*

Remark 2.4. Let

$H_1 =$

	a	b	c
a	a	b	c
b	a	b	b
c	a	b	c

, $H_2 =$

	a	b	c
a	a	b	c
b	a	b	c
c	a	b	c

Then $(H_1, \mathscr{I})$ satisfies T_0 but not T_1; and $(H_2, \mathscr{I})$ satisfies T_1.

Remark 2.5. The topological space $(H, \mathscr{I})$ is completely characterized by the conditions of Theorem 2.4, so that all the other separation axioms T_i $(i > 1)$ imply T_1.

3. Continuity of operation

Following is a rather strong sufficient condition for the binary operation in a half groupoid H to be continuous:

Theorem 3.1. *If every composite element c of a halfgroupoid H is such that every right factor b of c belongs to every point ideal I_c containing c then the binary operation in H is continuous under the L-topology.*

Proof. Let a, b, c be any arbitrary elements in H such that $a \cdot b = c$. If $b = c$, then $I_a \cdot I_c \subset I_c$ for every I_a and I_c in $\mathscr{I}$. If $b \neq c$, then c is composite and b belongs to every I_c in $\mathscr{I}$. Thus b belongs to $I_b \cap I_c$ for every I_b, I_c in $\mathscr{I}$. Let $I_b \cap I_c = I_b'$; then $I_a I_b' \subset I_b' \subset I_c$.

Remark 3.1. That the above condition is not necessary is shown by the following example:

$$H = \begin{array}{c|ccc} & a & b & c \\ \hline a & b & - & a \\ b & - & - & b \\ c & a & b & - \end{array}\,, \qquad \mathscr{I} = \{\emptyset, H, \{b\}, \{a, b\}\}.$$

The operation is continuous with respect to L-topology $\mathscr{I}$; and $a \cdot a = b$, i.e. a/b; $\bigcap \{I_b\} = \{b\}$ so that $a \notin \bigcap \{I_b\}$.

As a matter of fact something much stronger is true: Let H be a halfgroupoid on k elements for which the L-topology fails to give continuity. Then there exist a, b in H such that $a \cdot b = c$, and $I_a \cdot I_b \not\subset I_c$. Let $H' = H \cup \{x\}$, $x \in H$. We define a halfgroupoid on H' by defining the operation in H' to be precisely that of H. Hence all elements of $H \subset H'$ have the same minimal left ideals as in H. Thus for each $k \geqq 3$ there exist halfgroupoids for which the minimal left ideals do not yield continuous operations.

Remark 3.2. The continuity of operation in $\mathscr{I}$ can be, however, achieved by modifying the original operation in the following way: Let the operation be defined in such a manner that if a, b belong to H, and I_a, I_b are minimal left ideals containing a and b respectively, then $I_a \cdot I_b \subset I_{ab}$, whenever $a \cdot b$ is defined, and $I_{a \cdot b}$ is the minimal left ideal containing $a \cdot b$.

4. A connection with digraphs

A digraph (directed graph) $\Gamma(A, E)$ consists of a set A and a subset E of the cartesian product $A \times A$. The points of A are called as vertices and the elements of E as diedges.

Definition 4.1. The digraph topology $\mathscr{T}$ on $\Gamma(A, E)$ is the family of all subsets $B \subset A$ such that $(\bar{B} \times B) \cap E = \emptyset$. That is, the set $B \subset A$ is open under $\mathscr{T}$ if there are no edges in E which emanate from subset $\bar{B}$ and terminate in subset B (Bhargava and Ahlborn [1]).

It has been shown in [1] that the mapping of the set of all possible digraphs, on a fixed set A, onto the set of all digraph topologies is a many-to-one correspondence. This, as we have seen earlier in this paper, is also true of the mapping of the set of all possible halfgroupoids, on a fixed set A, onto the set of all L-topologies.

Let $\mathscr{H}$ be the class of all halfgroupoids on a fixed set A, and let $\mathscr{D}$ be the class of all digraphs on the same set A. Mappings between $\mathscr{H}$ and $\mathscr{D}$ can be constructed such that under these mappings the set $\mathscr{H}(\mathscr{I}) = \{H \in \mathscr{H}\colon \mathscr{I}$ is the L-topology on $H\}$ corresponds to the set $\mathscr{D}(\mathscr{T}) = \{D \in \mathscr{D}\colon \mathscr{T}$ is the digraph topology $D\}$, where $\mathscr{I}$ and $\mathscr{T}$ are identical topologies.

First of all we note that a binary operation defined for a set A can be considered as a set F of ordered triples, that is $\emptyset \subset F \subset A \times A \times A$; in terms of our original definition we have $F = \{((a, b), c)\colon a \cdot b = c \text{ in } H\}$. Let (A, F) denote a halfgroupoid on A with binary operation F, and let (A, E) denote a digraph on set A. Then

$$\mathscr{H} = \{(A, F)\colon \emptyset \subset F \subset A \times A \times A;\ \ F = \{((a, b), c)\colon a \cdot b = c \text{ in } A\}\},$$

and

$$\mathscr{D} = \{(A, E)\colon \emptyset \subset E \subset A \times A;\ \ E = \{(a, b)\colon a, b \in A\}\}.$$

Let $\Phi\colon \mathscr{H} \xrightarrow{\text{into}} D$, such that $\Phi(H, F) = (H, E)$ where $E = \{(c, b)\colon\ ((x, b), c) \in F\}$.

Let $\Phi'\colon \mathscr{D} \xrightarrow{\text{into}} H$, such that $\Phi'(H, E) = (H, F)$ where $F = \{((c, b), c)\colon\ (c, b) \in E\}$.

The following theorem shows that these mappings Φ and Φ', both of which are many-to-one, establish, in a certain sense, a topological correspondence between halfgroupoids and digraphs in such a manner that the L-topology is exactly the same as the digraph topology.

Theorem 4.1. *Let* $\Phi\colon \mathscr{H} \xrightarrow{\text{into}} \mathscr{D}$, $\Phi'\colon \mathscr{D} \xrightarrow{\text{into}} \mathscr{H}$, $\mathscr{H}(\mathscr{I})$, *and* $\mathscr{D}(\mathscr{T})$ *be defined as above. Then* $\Phi(\mathscr{H}(\mathscr{I})) = \mathscr{D}(\mathscr{T})$ *and* $\Phi'(\mathscr{D}(\mathscr{T})) = \mathscr{H}(\mathscr{I})$.

The proof of this theorem is quite simple and straightforward, but a little lengthy, and hence is omitted. It may be found in Ohm [8], which also contains some other details and relevant results.

Acknowledgements. We are most grateful to Professor P. H. Doyle of Michigan State University for several useful discussions and suggestions which have resulted in improvement of this paper.

References

[1] T. N. Bhargava and T. J. Ahlborn, On digraph topology, Acta Math. **19** (1968), 47—52.
[2] G. Birkhoff, Lattice theory, Amer. Math. Soc. Coll. Publ. No. 25 (1948).
[3] O. Borůvka, Grundlagen der Gruppoid- und Gruppentheorie, Berlin 1960.
[4] R. H. Bruck, A survey of binary systems, Berlin-Göttingen-Heidelberg 1958.
[5] P. H. Doyle and R. J. Warne, Some properties of groupoids, Amer. Math. Monthly **70** (1963), 1051—1057.
[6] J. R. Hanson, Connections between binary systems and admissible topologies, A Ph. D. Thesis, Virginia Polytechnic Institute 1965.
[7] J. L. Kelley, General topology, Princeton N. J. 1955.
[8] Sigrid E. Ohm, Some topological properties of halfgroupoids, A Master's Thesis, Kent State University 1964.
[9] R. Šulka, Topological groupoids, Mat.-Fyz. Časopis Slovensk. Akad. Vied. **5** (1955), 10—21.
[10] R. J. Warne, Connected ordered topological groupoids with idempotent endpoints, Publ. Math. Debrecen **8** (1961), 143—146.

SCHREIERSCHE GRUPPENERWEITERUNGEN UND DIE ERWEITERUNGSTHEORIE TOPOLOGISCHER GRUPPEN

HELMUT BOSECK (Greifswald)

Eine Gruppe G heißt *Schreiersche Erweiterungsgruppe* der Gruppe G_0' mit der Gruppe G_1': $G = \{G_0', G_1'\}$, wenn in G ein zu G_0' isomorpher Normalteiler G_0 existiert, so daß die Faktorgruppe G/G_0' zu G_1' isomorph ist [7].

Diese Definition läßt sich unmittelbar auf topologische Gruppen übertragen, wenn man das Wort „Gruppe" durch „topologische Gruppe", das Wort „Normalteiler" durch „abgeschlossenen Normalteiler" und das Wort „isomorph" durch „isomorph und homöomorph" ersetzt.

Unter der *Erweiterungstheorie topologischer Gruppen* verstehen wir die Frage nach den Kompaktifizierungen topologischer Gruppen [8].

Eine *Kompaktifizierung* (K, α) der topologischen Gruppe G besteht aus einer kompakten topologischen Gruppe K und einem stetigen Homomorphismus α von G auf eine dichte Teilmenge von K: $K = \overline{\alpha(G)}$.

Ist die topologische Gruppe $G = \{G_0', G_1'\}$ eine Schreiersche Erweiterungsgruppe der topologischen Gruppe G_0' mit der topologischen Gruppe G_1', so definiert jede Kompaktifizierung (K, α) von G auf naheliegende Weise eine Kompaktifizierung (K_0', α_0') der topologischen Gruppe G_0' und eine Kompaktifizierung (K_1', α_1') der topologischen Gruppe G_1'. Die kompakte topologische Gruppe K_0' ist dabei isomorph und homöomorph zur abgeschlossenen Hülle K_0 des Bildes von G_0 bei dem stetigen Homomorphismus α von G in K und die kompakte topologische Gruppe K_1' ist isomorph und homöomorph zur Faktorgruppe K/K_0: $K_0' \cong K_0 = \overline{\alpha(G_0)}$, $K_1' \cong K/K_0$. Die kompakte topologische Gruppe K der gegebenen Kompaktifizierung von G ist also eine Schreiersche Erweiterungsgruppe der kompakten topologischen Gruppe K_0' aus einer Kompaktifizierung von G_0' mit der kompakten topologischen Gruppe K_1' aus einer Kompaktifizierung der topologischen Gruppe G_1'.

Es entsteht die folgende Frage:

Gegeben sei eine topologische Gruppe $G = \{G_0', G_1'\}$, die eine Schreiersche Erweiterungsgruppe der topologischen Gruppe G_0' mit der topologischen Gruppe G_1' ist. Es sei ferner eine Kompaktifizierung (K_0', α_0') der topologischen Gruppe G_0' und eine Kompaktifizierung (K_1', α_1') der topologischen Gruppe G_1' gegeben. Unter welchen Bedingungen existiert eine Schreiersche Erweiterungsgruppe $K = \{K_0', K_1'\}$ der kompakten topologischen Gruppe K_0' mit der kompakten topologischen Gruppe K_1', die in einer Kompaktifizierung (K, α) der topologischen Gruppe G vorkommt?

Eine Antwort auf diese Frage ist unter anderem deshalb von Interesse, da einerseits jede topologische Gruppe als Schreiersche Erweiterungsgruppe einer zusammenhängenden topologischen Gruppe, der Zusammenhangskomponente des Einselementes, mit einer total-unzusammenhängenden Gruppe aufgefaßt werden kann, andererseits die Frage nach der Existenz isomorpher Kompaktifizierungen für zusammenhängende topologische Gruppen durch den bekannten Satz von FREUDENTHAL beantwortet ist [5].

Die topologische Gruppe $G = \{G_0', G_1'\}$ sei eine Schreiersche Erweiterungsgruppe der topologischen Gruppe G_0' mit der topologischen Gruppe G_1'. Wir betrachten zunächst die folgenden Abbildungen, die die algebraische Struktur von G als Schreiersche Erweiterungsgruppe bestimmen:

(a) Es sei φ eine Repräsentantenabbildung; d.h., φ sei eine Abbildung von G_1' in G, deren Bild ein Repräsentantensystem für die Faktorgruppe G/G_0 ist. O.B.d.A. nehmen wir an, daß $\varphi(e_1') = e$ ist.

(b) Es sei q das zugehörige Faktorensystem; d.h., q sei diejenige Abbildung von $G_1' \times G_1'$ in G_0, die durch folgende Gleichung gegeben wird:

$$\varphi(x_1') \cdot \varphi(y_1') = \varphi(x_1' y_1')\, q(x_1', y_1'), \quad x_1', y_1' \in G_1'.$$

(c) Es sei σ das zugehörige Automorphismensystem; d.h., für $a_1' \in G_1'$ und $x_0' \in G_0$ sei die Abbildung σ von $G_1' \times G_0'$ in G_0 definiert durch

$$\sigma(a_1', x_0') = (\varphi(a_1'))^{-1}\, x_0(\varphi(a_1'));$$

dabei ist $x_0 \in G_0$ das Element, das dem Element x_0' bei dem Isomorphismus zwischen G_0' und G_0 entspricht.

Die auf den Gruppen G, G_0' und G_1' gegebenen Topologien bezeichnen wir mit τ, τ_0' und τ_1'. Ferner bezeichne τ_0 die Einschränkung der Topologie τ auf den Normalteiler G_0, in der G_0 homöomorph zu G_0' ist. Sind (K_0', α_0') und (K_1', α_1') gegebene Kompaktifizierungen der Gruppen G_0' und G_1', so werden durch diese Kompaktifizierungen auf den Gruppen G_0' und G_1' neue, total beschränkte Topologien definiert, die wir mit $\tau_0'^{(\alpha)}$ und $\tau_1'^{(\alpha)}$ bezeichnen und die wegen der Stetigkeit der Homomorphismen α_0' und α_1' schwächer sind als die ursprünglichen Topologien. Schließlich bezeichne $\tau_0^{(\alpha)}$ die durch Übertragung der Topologie $\tau_0'^{(\alpha)}$ von G_0' auf G_0 erklärte Topologie.

Sind die folgenden Bedingungen erfüllt:

1. Es gibt eine $\tau_1'^{(\alpha)}$-offene e_1'-Umgebung $U_1'^{(\alpha)}$ in G_1', so daß φ eine auf $U_1^{(\alpha)}$ stetige Abbildung bezüglich der Topologien τ_1' und τ ist;
2. das Faktorensystem q ist in (e_1', e_1') stetig bezüglich der Topologien $\tau_1'^{(\alpha)} \times \tau_1'^{(\alpha)}$ und $\tau_0^{(\alpha)}$;
3. das Automorphismensystem σ ist stetig bezüglich der Topologien $\tau_1'^{(\alpha)} \times \tau_0'^{(\alpha)}$ und $\tau_0^{(\alpha)}$,

so läßt sich auf der Schreierschen Erweiterungsgruppe G eine total-beschränkte Topologie $\tau^{(\alpha)}$ so erklären, daß $\tau^{(\alpha)}$ schwächer als die gegebene Topologie τ ist, auf G_0 mit $\tau_0^{(\alpha)}$ übereinstimmt und die Faktorgruppe G/G_0 in der durch $\tau^{(\alpha)}$ induzierten Topologie zu G_1' in der Topologie $\tau_1'^{(\alpha)}$ homöomorph ist. Die Vervollständigung von G in der Topologie $\tau^{(\alpha)}$ ist eine kompakte topologische Gruppe K, in die G stetig und homomorph abgebildet werden kann und die als Schreiersche Erweiterungsgruppe der kompakten topologischen Gruppe K_0' mit der kompakten topologischen Gruppe K_1' nachgewiesen werden kann.

Die oben angegebene Bedingung 1 ist schärfer als die Forderung, daß die Gruppe G als topologischer Raum ein Hauptfaserbündel über G_1' mit G_0' als Faser und Strukturgruppe sei. Ist G_1' eine kompakte topologische Gruppe, so ist die Bedingung 1 zu der eben genannten Forderung äquivalent.

Die Bedingung 1 impliziert, daß die konstruierte kompakte Gruppe K nicht nur Schreiersche Erweiterungsgruppe der kompakten topologischen Gruppe K_0' mit der kompakten topologischen Gruppe K_1', sondern darüber hinaus ein Hauptfaserbündel über K_1' mit K_0' als Faser und als Strukturgruppe ist.

Ferner läßt sich zeigen, daß der stetige Homomorphismus α von G in die kompakte topologische Gruppe K dann und nur dann ein stetiger Isomorphismus ist, wenn dies für die gegebenen Abbildungen α_0' und α_1' gilt.

Literatur

[1] E. M. Alfsen and P. Holm, A note on compact representations and almost periodicity in topological groups, Math. Scand. **10** (1962), 127—136.

[2] H. Boseck, Über die Einlagerung topologischer Gruppen in kompakte, Archivum Math. (Brno) **2** (1966), 127—139.

[3] H. Boseck, Two classes of almost periodic functions on topological T_0-groups, Proc. Second Symposium on General Topology, Prague 1966.

[4] H. Boseck, Über den Zusammenhang zwischen den Kompaktifizierungen einer topologischen Gruppe und den Kompaktifizierungen ihrer Normalteiler und Faktorgruppen (erscheint in Math. Nachr.).

[5] H. Freudenthal, Topologische Gruppen mit genügend vielen fastperiodischen Funktionen, Ann. Math. **37** (1936), 57—77.

[6] P. S. Mostert, Local cross sections in locally compact groups, Bull. Amer. Math. Soc. **59** (1953), 645—649.

[7] O. Schreier, Über die Erweiterung von Gruppen, I: Monatshefte Math. und Phys. **34** (1926), 165—180; II: Abh. Math. Sem. Hamburg **4** (1926), 321—346.

[8] A. Weil, L'intégration dans les groupes topologiques et ses applications, Act. Sci. et Ind. No. 869, Paris 1940.

MANNIGFALTIGKEITEN ALS KOMPAKTIFIZIERUNGEN DER OFFENEN VOLLKUGEL

H. G. BOTHE (Greifswald)

Es sollen Kompaktifizierungen der n-dimensionalen offenen Vollkugel O^n untersucht werden, bei denen der kompaktifizierende Raum K eine Mannigfaltigkeit und das Adjunkt $K - O^n = L$ eine Teilmannigfaltigkeit von K ist. Der uninteressante Fall $n = 1$ sei ausgeschlossen. Da O^n in K dicht liegt, müssen K und L zusammenhängend sein, und die Dimension m von L ist kleiner als die Dimension n von K ($K = K^n$, $L = L^m$). Es soll hier untersucht werden, welche Mannigfaltigkeiten K^n, L^m hierbei auftreten können.

Ist M^m eine geschlossene Teilmannigfaltigkeit der Mannigfaltigkeit N^n, so verstehen wir unter einer Normalumgebung von M^m in N^n eine abgeschlossene Umgebung U von M^m in N^n zusammen mit einer Retraktion $p: U \to M^m$, bei der U zum Raum eines Faserbündels über M^m mit der abgeschlossenen $(n - m)$-dimensionalen Vollkugel V^{n-m} als Faser und der orthogonalen Gruppe als Strukturgruppe wird. Eine solche Normalumgebung heißt trivial, falls sie ein Produktbündel darstellt.

Es seien $L^m \subset K^n$ Mannigfaltigkeiten der oben betrachteten Art. Wir unte-r suchen zunächst den Fall, daß K^n einen nicht leeren Rand ∂K^n besitzt. Man sieht sofort, daß dann L^m mit ∂K^n zusammenfallen muß. Über die Möglichkeiten für K^n gibt der folgende Satz Auskunft:

Satz 1. *Ist $n \neq 4, 5$, so ist K^n eine n-Zelle (d. h. zu V^n homöomorph). Ist $n = 4, 5$, so ist ∂K^n eine $(n - 1)$-dimensionale Homotopiesphäre, und man kann K^n so in den n-dimensionalen euklidischen Raum E^n einbetten, daß ∂K^n in E^n eine triviale Normalumgebung besitzt und K^n gerade die abgeschlossene Hülle der beschränkten Komponente von $E^n - \partial K^n$ wird.*

Beweis. Wir dürfen $n > 2$ voraussetzen. Nach M. BROWN [4] gibt es einen Homöomorphismus f von $\partial K^n \times [0, 1)$ auf eine offene Umgebung von ∂K^n in K^n mit $f(x, 0) = x$. Man konstruiert damit leicht einen Homöomorphismus g von K^n auf $K^n - f\left(\partial K^n \times \left[0, \frac{1}{2}\right)\right) = K'^n$. Dabei gilt $g(\partial K^n) = \partial K'^n = f\left(\partial K^n \times \frac{1}{2}\right)$. Ist h ein Homöomorphismus von $\operatorname{Int}(K^n)$ auf E^n, so ist $hg: K^n \to E^n$ eine Einbettung, bei der $hg(\partial K^n)$ eine triviale Normalumgebung besitzt und bei der $hg(K^n)$ mit der abgeschlossenen Hülle der beschränkten Komponente von $E^n - hg(\partial K^n)$ übereinstimmt. Es ist nicht schwer, zu beweisen, daß für $1 \leqq i \leqq n - 2$ die Homotopiegruppen $\pi_i(\partial K^n)$ trivial sind, so daß ∂K^n tatsächlich eine Homotopiesphäre sein muß. Man bemerke hierzu, daß jede Abbildung $\tau: S^i \to \partial K^n$ in K^n nullhomotop ist und daß man wegen $i \leqq n - 2$ diese Homotopie in die Menge ∂K^n schieben kann. Ist ∂K^n eine Sphäre (was für die Dimensionen, in denen die Poincarésche Vermutung bewiesen ist, also für $n - 1 \neq 3, 4$ sicher stimmt), so ist $hg(\partial K^n)$ eine in E^n flache $(n - 1)$-dimensionale Sphäre. Wir können also ein bekanntes Ergebnis von M. Brown [3] anwenden und erhalten, daß die abgeschlossene Hülle der beschränkten Komponente von $E^n - hg(\partial K^n)$ und damit auch K^n eine n-Zelle sein muß.

Komplizierter wird die Situation, wenn wir K^n als randlos voraussetzen. Wir wollen in diesem Fall, dem wir uns jetzt zuwenden, annehmen, daß L^m in gewissem Sinne glatt in K^n liegt, womit wir meinen, daß L^m eine geschlossene Teilmannigfaltigkeit von K^n ist, die in K^n eine Normalumgebung besitzt. Diese Voraussetzung ist sicher dann erfüllt, wenn man K^n eine Differentialstruktur aufprägen kann, bei der L^m eine differenzierbare Teilmannigfaltigkeit wird. Zunächst geben wir ein Verfahren an, nach dem man derartige Mannigfaltigkeiten (d. h. geschlossene Mannigfaltigkeiten $L^m \subset K^n$, bei denen L^m eine Normalumgebung besitzt und $K^n - L^m$ in K^n dicht und zu O^n homöomorph ist) konstruieren kann.

Es sei V^n die n-dimensionale abgeschlossene Vollkugel mit der Randsphäre S^{n-1}. Weiter sei $p: S^{n-1} \to L^m$ eine Faserung über einer geschlossenen Mannigfaltigkeit L^m mit typischer Faser S^{n-m-1} und der orthogonalen Gruppe als Strukturgruppe. Mit Z bezeichnen wir den Abbildungszylinder von p. Z ist also eine Mannigfaltigkeit mit dem Rand S^{n-1}, die L^m als Teilmannigfaltigkeit enthält, und Z selbst mit der Fortsetzung von p auf Z ist Normalumgebung von L^m in Z. Die Vereinigung $K^n = V^n \cup Z$ wird also eine geschlossene Mannigfaltigkeit mit der Teilmannigfaltigkeit L^m, wobei L^m die Normalumgebung Z besitzt und $K^n - L^m$ zu $K^n - Z$ und damit zu $V^n - S^{n-1}$ d. h. zu O^n homöomorph ist.

Die bekannten Faserungen von Sphären durch Sphären (siehe etwa [7], S. 105ff.) liefern die folgenden Mannigfaltigkeiten $L^m \subset K^n$.:

(1) $K^n = S^n$, L^m einpunktig $(m = 0)$;

(2) $K^n = RP^n$ (n-dimensionaler reeller projektiver Raum), $L^m = RP^{n-1} = (n - 1)$-dimensionale Hyperebene von RP^n;

(3) $K^{2n} = CP^n$ (n-dimensionaler komplexer projektiver Raum), $L^m = CP^{n-1} =$ Hyperebene von CP^n (der reellen Dimension $m = 2n - 2$);

(4) $K^{4n} = QP^n$ (n-dimensionaler projektiver Raum über den Quaternionen), $L^m = QP^{n-1} =$ Hyperebene von QP^n (der reellen Dimension $m = 4n - 4$);

(5) ein Paar $L^m \subset K^n$ mit $n = 16$, $m = 8$ und $L^m = S^8$.

Der folgende Satz sagt aus, daß man im Fall $n \neq 4, 5$ mit dieser Methode der Sphärenfaserung alle Paare $L^m \subset K^n$ erhält.

Satz 2. *Ist $n \neq 4, 5$ und K^n eine geschlossene Mannigfaltigkeit mit der geschlossenen Teilmannigfaltigkeit L^m $(m < n)$, die in K^n eine Normalumgebung besitzt und für die $K^n - L^m$ zu O^n homöomorph ist, so erhält man die Mannigfaltigkeiten K^n, L^m auf die oben beschriebene Weise mittels einer Faserung $p: S^{n-1} \to L^m$.*

Beweis. Es sei $p: U \to L^m$ eine Normalumgebung von L^m in K^n. Man darf dabei voraussetzen, daß der Rand ∂U von U lokal flach in K^n liegt (falls das nicht von vornherein der Fall ist, ziehe man U ein wenig zusammen). Aus $K^n - L^m \approx O^n$ folgt $K^n - U \approx O^n$, so daß $(K^n - U) \cup \partial U$ eine Kompaktifizierung von O^n darstellt, wie sie in Satz 1 betrachtet wurde. Es ist also $(K^n - U) \cup \partial U \approx V^n$ eine n-Zelle mit der $(n - 1)$-dimensionalen Randsphäre $\partial U = S^{n-1}$, die durch

$p|_{S^{n-1}}: S^{n-1} \to L^m$ in $(n-m-1)$-dimensionale Sphären gefasert wird. Die Normalumgebung U kann man als Abbildungszylinder von $p|_{S^{n-1}}$ ansehen, und K^n entsteht, indem man an $(K^n - U) \cup \partial U \approx V^n$ diesen Abbildungszylinder U längs $\partial U = S^{n-1}$ anheftet.

Aus dem Beweis ergibt sich, daß man in den Fällen $n = 4, 5$ alle Paare K^n, L^m auf die folgende Weise erhalten kann: Man betrachte eine $(n-1)$-dimensionale Homotopiesphäre H^{n-1}, die mit einer trivialen Normalumgebung in E^n so eingebettet ist, daß die beschränkte Komponente C von $E^n - H^{n-1}$ zu O^n homöomorph ist. Nun suche man eine Faserung $p: H^{n-1} \to L^m$ mit der typischen Faser S^{n-m-1} und der orthogonalen Gruppe als Strukturgruppe. Vereinigt man die abgeschlossene Hülle von C mit dem Abbildungszylinder von p, so erhält man K^n.

Ist die Poincarésche Vermutung auch in den Dimensionen 3 und 4 richtig, so gilt der Satz 2 also ohne die Dimensionsbeschränkung.

Der Satz 2 gestattet es, die bekannten Ergebnisse über die Nichtexistenz von Faserungen von Sphären durch Sphären anzuwenden, um die Möglichkeiten für die Mannigfaltigkeiten K^n, L^m einzuschränken. Zunächst folgt aus [2], daß für die Dimensionen n, m nur die folgenden Fälle in Frage kommen: n beliebig, $m = 0$; n beliebig, $m = n - 1$; $n \equiv 0 \pmod 2$, $m = n - 2$; $n \equiv 0 \pmod 4$, $m = n - 4$; $n = 2^k$, $m = 2^{k-1}$. (Die Fälle $n = 4, 5$ bedürfen hier eines besonderen Beweises!) Ist $n = 2m$, so erkennt man aus der exakten Bündelsequenz von $p: S^{n-1} \to L^m$, daß L^m eine Homotopiesphäre (für $m \neq 4$ also eine Sphäre) sein muß. Hiermit kann man noch die Fälle $n = 2^k$, $m = 2^{k-1}$ für $k > 4$ ausschließen. Ist nämlich K^{2^k}, $L^{2^{k-1}}$ ein Paar der betrachteten Art, so erhalten wir eine Faserung $p: S^{2^k - 1} \to S^{2^{k-1}}$ mit $S^{2^{k-1}-1}$ als typischer Faser. Da eine solche Abbildung p die Hopfsche Invariante 1 haben muß, für $k > 4$ aber keine Abbildung $S^{2^k-1} \to S^{2^{k-1}}$ mit der Hopfschen Invariante 1 existiert (siehe [1]), muß $k \leq 4$ sein.

Es stellt sich die naheliegende Frage, ob außer den in den Beispielen (1) bis (5) angegebenenen noch weitere Paare K^n, L^m existieren. In diesem Zusammenhang sei der Fall $m = n - 1$ betrachtet. Man erhält die Paare K^n, L^{n-1}, indem man auf der Randsphäre S^{n-1} von V^n die Identifizierungen $x = f(x)$ vornimmt, wo f eine fixpunktfreie Involution von S^{n-1} ist (das folgt aus Satz 2). Nach [6] gibt es eine solche Involution, die zudem (bei der üblichen Triangulierung von V^n) stückweise linear ist, bei der aber die aus S^{n-1} bei der Identifizierung $x = f(x)$ hervorgehende Mannigfaltigkeit in der Kategorie der stückweise linearen Mannigfaltigkeiten und der stückweise linearen Abbildungen nicht zu RP^{n-1} isomorph ist $(n > 5)$. Falls also für einen projektiven Raum RP^m $(m \geqq 5)$ die kombinatorische Hauptvermutung zutrifft, so gibt es ein Paar K^n, L^{n-1} mit $L^{n-1} \not\approx RP^{n-1}$.

Auf jeden Fall kann man für die Mannigfaltigkeiten K^n, L^m viele Einschränkungen herleiten, und man erhält auch Resultate darüber, inwieweit die Struktur von K^n die von L^m und die Struktur von L^m die von K^n beeinflußt. Es soll hierauf jedoch nicht eingegangen werden.

Schließlich noch eine Bemerkung zu den Paaren K^n, L^m, bei denen L^m keine Normalumgebung in K^n besitzt. Die bekannten Beispiele von wilden Einbettungen von Mannigfaltigkeiten in Mannigfaltigkeiten (siehe z. B. [5]) zeigen, daß solche Paare tatsächlich existieren. In diesem Zusammenhang sei die folgende Frage gestellt: Gibt es zu jedem solchen wilden Paar K^n, L^m ein zahmes Paar K'^n, L'^m, für das K'^n zu K^n und L'^m zu L^m homöomorph ist?

Literatur

[1] J. F. Adams, On the non-existence of elements of Hopf invariant one, Ann. Math. **72** (1960), 20—104.
[2] J. Adem, Relations on iterated reduced powers, Proc. Nat. Acad. Sci. **39** (1953), 636—638.
[3] M. Brown, A proof of the generalized Schoenflies Theorem, Bull. Amer. Math. Soc. **66** (1960), 74—76.
[4] M. Brown, Locally flat imbeddings of topological manifolds, Ann. Math. **75** (1962), 331—341.
[5] R. H. Fox and E. Artin, Some wild cells and spheres in three-dimensional space, Ann. Math. **49** (1948), 979—990.
[6] M. W. Hirsch and J. Milnor, Some curious involutions of spheres, Bull. Amer. Math. Soc. **70** (1964), 372—377.
[7] N. Steenrod, The topology of fibre bundles, Princeton 1951.

ON COMPACTNESS IN UNIFORM SPACES[1])

SALVATORE CIAMPA (Pisa)

In a previous paper the author gave a characterization of completeness of a uniform space in terms of convergence of the Cauchy nets defined on the directed set $\mathscr{K}$, $\mathscr{K}$ being a base for the uniformity of the space.

Now a similar characterization for compactness and total boundedness is sought. To solve these problems two concepts of equivalence between nets are defined:

Given a uniform space $(T, \mathscr{K})$, $\mathscr{K}$ being a base of uniformity, the nets λ, μ in T are said (a)-*equivalent* if and only if they have the same adherence points; they are said (b)-*equivalent* if and only if there exists $F \in \mathscr{K}$ such that for every $x \in T$ and every $E \in \mathscr{K}$, if $E \subset F$ then "λ is eventually in $E(x)$" is equivalent to "μ is eventually in $E(x)$", where $E(x)$ is the set of all those $y \in T$ such that $(x, y) \in E$.

Then a net is defined to be (a)-*maximal* whenever it is (a)-equivalent to each of its own subnets; the net is defined (b)-*maximal* whenever it is uniformly (b)-equivalent to each of its own subnets (here uniformly means that there is only one $F \in \mathscr{K}$ which is good for all subnets).

With these definitions it is true that:

A. *In the uniform space* $(T, \mathscr{K})$ *the following propositions are equivalent*

A. 1. *the space* T *is compact*;

A. 2. *every* (a)-*maximal net in* T *converges*;

A. 3. *every net in* T *defined on the ordered set* $N \times \mathscr{K}$ *(with the product order) where* N *is the ordered set of positive integers and* $\mathscr{K}$ *is ordered by inclusion, converges if it is* (a)-*maximal.*

B. *In the uniform space* $(T, \mathscr{K})$ *the following propositions are equivalent*

B. 1. *the space* T *is totally bounded*;

B. 2. *every* (b)-*maximal net in* T *enjoyes the Cauchy property*;

B. 3. *every* (b)-*maximal sequence in* T *enjoyes the Cauchy property.*

C. *If* T *is a uniform space and* $\mathscr{K}$ *is its whole uniformity, then total boundedness of* T *is equivalent to the following condition: every* (b)-*maximal sequence converges and falls eventually in the set of its convergence points.*

---

[1]) The paper related to this communication appeared in the Rend. Sem. Mat. Univ. Padova, **39** (1967), 72—85.

ERWEITERUNG, KOMPAKTIFIZIERUNG UND VERVOLLSTÄNDIGUNG SYNTOPOGENER RÄUME

ÁKOS CSÁSZÁR (Budapest)

In [1] wurde der Begriff der syntopogenen Struktur als gemeinsame Verallgemeinerung von Topologien, uniformen Strukturen und Berührungsstrukturen eingeführt. Eine *syntopogene Struktur* $\mathcal{S}$ auf der Menge E ist eine gewisse Bedingungen erfüllende Klasse von *topogenen Ordnungen*, d. h. von einigen einfachen Axiomen genügenden transitiven Relationen zwischen den Teilmengen von E. In einem topologischen Raum E bildet z. B. die einzige, durch

$$A < B \Leftrightarrow A \subset \operatorname{int} B$$

definierte topogene Ordnung $<$ eine die Topologie eindeutig bestimmende syntopogene Struktur $\{<\}$. Ähnlicherweise ist für eine Berührungsrelation δ die durch

$$A < B \Leftrightarrow A \not\delta E - B$$

definierte Relation $<$ eine topogene Ordnung, und $\{<\}$ ist wiederum eine syntopogene Struktur. Ist $\mathfrak{U}$ eine aus symmetrischen Nachbarschaften bestehende Basis für eine uniforme Struktur, so bilden die durch

$$A <_U B \Leftrightarrow U(A) \subset B \qquad (U \in \mathfrak{U})$$

definierten topogenen Ordnungen $<_U$ eine syntopogene Struktur. Für weitere Einzelheiten sei auf [1] hingewiesen.

In [2] und [3] wurde ein allgemeines Verfahren zur Übertragung von syntopogenen Strukturen ausgearbeitet. Mit Hilfe dieses Verfahrens entsteht die folgende Methode der Erweiterung von syntopogenen Räumen.

Es sei jedem Element x einer Menge $E' \supset E$ ein Filter $\mathfrak{s}(x)$ in E zugeordnet; für $x \in E$ sei speziell $\mathfrak{s}(x)$ mit dem Grundfilter $\mathfrak{g}(x) = \{X : x \in X \subset E\}$ identisch. Für $X \subset E$ sei

$$h(X) = \{x : x \in E', X \in \mathfrak{s}(x)\}$$

gesetzt. Ist nun $<$ eine halbtopogene Ordnung ([1], S. 25) auf E, so ist die durch

$$A' <^s B' \Leftrightarrow \text{es gibt } A, B \text{ mit } A < B, \quad A' \subset h(A), h(B) \subset B'$$

definierte Relation $<^s$ eine halbtopogene Ordnung auf E' mit $<^s|E = <$ ([1], S. 66). Ist $\mathscr{S}$ eine syntopogene Struktur auf E, so ist

$$\mathscr{S}^s = \{<^{sq} : < \in \mathscr{S}\}$$

([1], S. 31) eine syntopogene Struktur auf E' mit $\mathscr{S}^s|E = \mathscr{S}$, und E ist in $[E', \mathscr{S}^s]$ dicht ([1], S. 211). Somit ist $[E', \mathscr{S}^s]$ eine *Erweiterung* von $[E, \mathscr{S}]$.

Sind die Filter $\mathfrak{s}(x)$ für $x \in E' - E$ in $[E, \mathscr{S}]$ rund ([1], S. 240), so ist $\mathfrak{s}(x)$ mit der Spur $\mathfrak{v}(x)$ $(\cap)$ E ([1], S. 205) in E des Umgebungsfilters $\mathfrak{v}(x)$ von $x \in E' - E$ in bezug auf $[E', \mathscr{S}^s]$ ([1], S. 206) identisch, und wenn noch die Filter $\mathfrak{s}(x)$ für $x \in E' - E$ in bezug auf $[E, \mathscr{S}]$ nichtkonvergent ([1], S. 206) sind und aus $x, y \in E' - E$, $x \neq y$ immer $\mathfrak{s}(x) \neq \mathfrak{s}(y)$ folgt, ist $[E', \mathscr{S}^s]$ bis auf E relativ separiert ([1], S. 241).

Sind die Filter $\mathfrak{s}(x)$ in $[E, \mathscr{S}]$ komprimiert ([1], S. 216), so ist E sogar in $[E', \mathscr{S}^{ss}]$ ([1], S. 36) dicht, und wenn die Filter $\mathfrak{s}(x)$ in $[E, \mathscr{S}]$ Cauchy-Filter ([1], S. 212) sind, ist E sogar in $[E', \mathscr{S}^{ssb}]$ ([1], S. 49) dicht. Es sei noch bemerkt, daß die komprimierten runden Filter mit den maximalen runden Filtern zusammenfallen.

Ist umgekehrt $[E', \mathscr{S}']$ eine beliebige Erweiterung von $[E, \mathscr{S}]$, d. h., ist $\mathscr{S}'$ eine syntopogene Struktur auf $E' \supset E$ mit $\mathscr{S}'|E = \mathscr{S}$ und ist E in $[E', \mathscr{S}']$ dicht, so sei $\mathfrak{v}(x)$ für $x \in E' - E$ der Umgebungsfilter von x, $\mathfrak{s}(x) = E$ $(\cap)$ $\mathfrak{v}(x)$ die Spur von $\mathfrak{v}(x)$, und es werde für $x \in E$ wiederum $\mathfrak{s}(x) = \mathfrak{g}(x)$ gesetzt. Dann ist $\mathfrak{s}(x)$ für $x \in E' - E$ in bezug auf $\mathscr{S}$ rund, und $\mathscr{S}'^{tp}$ ist feiner als $\mathscr{S}^{stp}$ ([1], S. 83, 41, 23).

Ist $[E', \mathscr{S}']$ eine solche Erweiterung von $[E, \mathscr{S}]$, daß E in $[E', \mathscr{S}'^s]$ dicht ist, und setzt man $\mathfrak{s}(x) = \mathfrak{v}'(x)$ $(\cap)$ E für $x \in E' - E$, wobei $\mathfrak{v}'(x)$ den Umgebungsfilter von x in bezug auf $\mathscr{S}'^s$ bezeichnet, so sind diese Filter $\mathfrak{s}(x)$ $(x \in E' - E)$ komprimierte, runde Filter in $[E, \mathscr{S}^s]$, und $\mathscr{S}'^s$ ist feiner als $\mathscr{S}^{ss}$; weiterhin kann man hier $\mathscr{S}'^s$ durch $\mathscr{S}'^{sb}$, $\mathscr{S}^s$ durch $\mathscr{S}^{sb}$ ersetzen und „Cauchy-Filter" statt „komprimiert" sagen.

In [4] wurde das oben geschilderte Erweiterungsverfahren auf die Theorie der doppelten Kompaktifizierung von syntopogenen Räumen angewendet. Dabei versteht man unter einer *doppelten Kompaktifizierung* des syntopogenen Raumes $[E, \mathscr{S}]$ eine Erweiterung $[E', \mathscr{S}']$ von $[E, \mathscr{S}]$ mit der Eigenschaft, daß $\mathscr{S}'$ doppelt kompakt, d. h. $\mathscr{S}'^s$ kompakt ([1], S. 222, 229), E dicht in $[E', \mathscr{S}'^s]$ und außerdem $\mathscr{S}'$ relativ separiert bis auf E ist. Zu einer solchen Erweiterung gelangt man, wenn $\mathfrak{s}(x)$ den Elementen $x \in E' - E$ eineindeutig die in bezug auf $\mathscr{S}^s$ runden, komprimierten, nichtkonvergenten Filter zuordnet und dann der Raum $[E', \mathscr{S}^s]$ gebildet wird. Zwei doppelte Kompaktifizierungen desselben Raumes $[E, \mathscr{S}]$ lassen sich durch einen die Punkte von E festhaltenden Isomorphismus ([1], S. 117) aufeinander abbilden.

Als Spezialfall erhält man daraus den Satz von Ju. M. Smirnov ([5]) über die Kompaktifizierung von Berührungsräumen. Allgemeiner kann man den Satz von Smirnov über die Kompaktifizierung von vollständig regulären Räumen folgendermaßen verallgemeinern. Eine syntopogene Struktur $\mathscr{S}$ heiße *symmetrisierbar*, wenn $\mathscr{S} = \mathscr{S}_0{}^p$ mit einer geeigneten symmetrischen ([1], S. 71) syntopogenen Struktur $\mathscr{S}_0$ ist. Unter *Kompaktifizierung* eines symmetrisierbaren syntopogenen Raumes $[E, \mathscr{S}]$ versteht man eine solche Erweiterung $[E', \mathscr{S}']$ von $[E, \mathscr{S}]$, daß $\mathscr{S}'$ symmetrisierbar, kompakt und bis auf E relativ separiert ist. Nun erhält man alle Kompaktifizierungen des symmetrisierbaren Raumes $[E, \mathscr{S}]$, wenn man alle symmetrischen syntopogenen Strukturen $\mathscr{S}_i$ $(i \in I)$ mit $\mathscr{S}_i{}^p = \mathscr{S}$ betrachtet und die doppelten Kompaktifizierungen $[E_i', \mathscr{S}_i{}^s]$ von $[E, \mathscr{S}_i]$ bildet; dann ergeben die Räume $[E_i', \mathscr{S}_i'{}^p]$ alle Kompaktifizierungen von $[E, \mathscr{S}]$. Insbesondere ist $\mathscr{S}_i$ genau dann feiner als $\mathscr{S}_j$, wenn E_j' ein $(\mathscr{S}_i'{}^p, \mathscr{S}_j'{}^p)$-stetiges ([1], S. 116) Bild von E_i' unter einer die Punkte von E festhaltenden

Abbildung ist, und $\mathscr{S}_i \sim \mathscr{S}_j$ ([1], S. 24] besteht genau dann, wenn $[E_i', \mathscr{S}_i'^p]$ und $[E_j', \mathscr{S}_j'^p]$ mit Hilfe eines die Punkte von E festhaltenden Isomorphismus aufeinander abbildbar sind. Unter den Strukturen $\mathscr{S}_i$ befindet sich eine feinste $\mathscr{S}_0$ mit der Eigenschaft, daß jede $(\mathscr{S}, \mathscr{S}'')$-stetige Abbildung $f: E \to E''$, wobei $[E'', \mathscr{S}'']$ symmetrisierbar und kompakt ist, sich $(\mathscr{S}_0'^p, \mathscr{S}'')$-stetig auf E_0' fortsetzen läßt.

Die obigen Ergebnisse ermöglichen es, die Theorie der doppelten Vervollständigung aus ihnen herzuleiten. Dabei heißt die Erweiterung $[E'', \mathscr{S}'']$ von $[E, \mathscr{S}]$ eine *doppelte Vervollständigung*, wenn $\mathscr{S}''$ doppelt vollständig, d. h. $\mathscr{S}''^s$ vollständig ([1], S. 219, 221), E dicht in $[E'', \mathscr{S}''^{sb}]$ und $\mathscr{S}''$ bis auf E relativ separiert ist. Ist nun $[E', \mathscr{S}']$ eine doppelte Kompaktifizierung von $[E, \mathscr{S}]$ und bezeichnet man mit E'' die abgeschlossene Hülle von E in bezug auf $\mathscr{S}'^{sb}$, so ist $[E'', \mathscr{S}' | E'']$ eine doppelte Vervollständigung von $[E, \mathscr{S}]$; wird insbesondere $\mathscr{S}'$ in der Form $\mathscr{S}^{\mathfrak{s}}$ mit Hilfe der in bezug auf $\mathscr{S}^s$ runden, komprimierten Filter dargestellt, so besteht E'' aus denjenigen Punkten von E', für die $\mathfrak{s}(x)$ in bezug auf $\mathscr{S}^{sb}$ rund und ein Cauchy-Filter ist. Jede andere doppelte Vervollständigung von $[E, \mathscr{S}]$ erhält man daraus mit Hilfe eines die Punkte von E festhaltenden Isomorphismus.

Es ist zu beachten, daß die speziellen Eigenschaften eines syntopogenen Raumes bei der doppelten Kompaktifizierung im allgemeinen verlorengehen. Zwar läßt ein einfacher ([1], S. 72) oder symmetrischer syntopogener Raum immer eine ebensolche doppelte Kompaktifizierung zu, aber ein biperfekter ([1], S. 72) Raum $[E, \mathscr{S}]$ besitzt im allgemeinen keine biperfekte doppelte Kompaktifizierung; eine solche existiert genau dann, wenn $\mathscr{S}$ total beschränkt ([1], S. 330) ist, und dann fallen die doppelten Kompaktifizierungen mit den doppelten Vervollständigungen zusammen.

Ebenso besitzt ein perfekter ([1], S. 71) syntopogener Raum im allgemeinen keine perfekte doppelte Kompaktifizierung. Es sei z. B. $\mathscr{T}$ einfach und perfekt (also eine Topologie) auf E. Eine doppelte Kompaktifizierung von $[E, \mathscr{T}]$ wird folgendermaßen erhalten. Es sei $\mathfrak{R}$ der kleinste, die $\mathscr{T}$-offenen und $\mathscr{T}$-abgeschlossenen Mengen enthaltende Ring; ein Filter in E mit einer Basis aus $\mathfrak{R}$ werde ein $\mathfrak{R}$-*Filter* und ein maximaler $\mathfrak{R}$-Filter ein *Ultra-*$\mathfrak{R}$*-Filter* genannt. *Triviale* Ultra-$\mathfrak{R}$-Filter sind diejenigen mit einer Basis aus Mengen der Gestalt $V \cap \overline{\{x\}}$, wobei $x \in E$ und V die Umgebungen von x durchläuft; die anderen Ultra-$\mathfrak{R}$-Filter heißen *nicht-trivial*. Nun seien zu den Elementen von $E' - E$ durch $\mathfrak{s}(x)$ die nicht-trivialen Ultra-$\mathfrak{R}$-Filter eineindeutig zugeordnet, für $x \in E$ setze man wiederum $\mathfrak{s}(x) = \mathfrak{g}(x)$. Dann ist $[E', \mathscr{T}^{\mathfrak{s}}]$ eine doppelte Kompaktifizierung von $[E, \mathscr{T}]$, wobei die einzige topogene Ordnung $<^{\mathfrak{s}}$ von $\mathscr{T}^{\mathfrak{s}}$ durch

$$A' <^{\mathfrak{s}} B' \Leftrightarrow \text{es gibt eine } \mathscr{T}\text{-offene Menge } G \text{ mit } A' \subset h(G) \subset B'$$

definiert wird.

$\mathscr{T}^{\mathfrak{s}}$ ist im allgemeinen keine Topologie, aber $[E', \mathscr{T}^{\mathfrak{s}p}]$ ist ein kompakter topologischer Erweiterungsraum von $[E, \mathscr{T}]$. Ist speziell $[E, \mathscr{T}]$ ein T_1-Raum (oder allgemeiner „schwach regulär", d. h., jede Umgebung eines Punktes enthält die abgeschlossene Hülle desselben Punktes), so ist die Wallmansche Erweiterung von $[E, \mathscr{T}]$ ein Unterraum von $[E', \mathscr{T}^{\mathfrak{s}p}]$, und zwar besteht ihre Grundmenge außer aus den Punkten von E noch aus denjenigen $x \in E' - E$, für die der Filter $\mathfrak{s}(x)$ ultraabgeschlossen ist.

Literatur

[1] Á. Császár, Grundlagen der allgemeinen Topologie, Budapest und Leipzig, 1963.
[2] Á. Cszászár, Transposition de structures syntopogènes, Ann. Univ. Budapest., Sect. Math., **6** (1963), 55—70.
[3] Á. Császár, Contributions à la transposition de structures syntopogènes, Ann. Univ. Budapest., Sect. Math., **9** (1966), 27—43.
[4] Á. Császár, Double compactification d'espaces syntopogènes, Ann. Univ. Budapest., Sect. Math., **7** (1964), 3—11.
[5] Ju. M. Smirnov, O prostranstvach blizosti (russ.), Mat. Sbornik (N. S.) **31** (1952), 543—574.

ÜBER DIE ÄQUIVALENZ VON ERWEITERUNGEN[1])

F. Danzig (Greifswald)

Zwei Erweiterungen γX und δX eines topologischen Raumes X heißen bekanntlich *gleich*, in Zeichen $\gamma X = \delta X$, wenn es einen Homöomorphismus φ von γX auf δX gibt mit $\varphi(x) = x$ für alle $x \in X$. Der Raum X bleibt also bei der Abbildung φ punktweise fest. Die Erweiterungen γX und δX mögen *äquivalent* heißen, abgekürzt γX äqu δX, wenn es einen Homöomorphismus φ von γX auf δX gibt mit $\varphi(X) = X$. Der Raum X bleibt also hierbei nur als Ganzes erhalten.

Natürlich folgt aus $\gamma X = \delta X$

$$\gamma X \text{ äqu } \delta X.$$

Wir fragen, wann auch aus γX äqu δX

$$\gamma X = \delta X$$

folgt. Wir werden dafür einige hinreichende Bedingungen angeben.

Zunächst sei γX eine Hausdorffsche Kompaktifizierung von X. Die zu γX gehörige präkompakte uniforme Struktur von X bezeichnen wir mit $\mathcal{U}_\gamma(X)$ und betrachten sie im Sinne von Tukey als System von Überdeckungen.

1. *Gilt γX äqu δX, ist γX Hausdorffsche Kompaktifizierung und ist jeder Homöomorphismus von X auf sich ein uniformer Isomorphismus von $\mathcal{U}_\gamma(X)$ auf sich, so folgt $\gamma X = \delta X$.*

Beweis. Mit γX ist auch δX Hausdorffsche Kompaktifizierung. γX äqu δX gilt genau dann, wenn $\mathcal{U}_\gamma(X)$ und $\mathcal{U}_\delta(X)$ uniform isomorph sind. Der uniforme Isomorphismus sei φ. Ist $\alpha \in \mathcal{U}_\gamma(X)$, so $\varphi^{-1}(\alpha) \in \mathcal{U}_\delta(X)$ und daher $\alpha = \varphi(\varphi^{-1}(\alpha)) \in \mathcal{U}_\delta(X)$. Ist $\beta \in \mathcal{U}_\delta(X)$, so $\varphi^{-1}(\beta) \in \mathcal{U}_\gamma(X)$ und daher auch $\beta = \varphi(\varphi^{-1}(\beta)) \in \mathcal{U}_\gamma(X)$. Also $\mathcal{U}_\gamma(X) = \mathcal{U}_\delta(X)$, daher $\gamma X = \delta X$.

Aus dem Beweis fließt zugleich das folgende Resultat über beliebige uniforme Strukturen $\mathcal{U}(X)$ und $\mathcal{V}(X)$ eines vollständig regulären Raumes X.

2. *Sind $\mathcal{U}(X)$ und $\mathcal{V}(X)$ uniform isomorph und ist jeder Homöomorphismus von X auf sich ein uniformer Isomorphismus von $\mathcal{U}(X)$ auf sich, so ist $\mathcal{U}(X) = \mathcal{V}(X)$.*

---

[1]) Diese Arbeit enthält einen Teil der Ergebnisse der Dissertation des Verfassers, Greifswald 1967. Dem Referenten Prof. Dr. W. Rinow ist der Verfasser zu Dank verpflichtet.

Die Bedingung von Nr. 1 können wir auch mit Hilfe stetiger Funktionen ausdrücken. $C^*(X)$ sei die Banach-Algebra aller beschränkten stetigen reellen Funktionen auf X. Es sei

$$C_\gamma^*(X) = \{f : f \in C^*(X),\ f \text{ hat Fortsetzung in } C^*(\gamma X)\}.$$

$C_\gamma^*(X)$ ist die zu γX gehörige vollständig reguläre Banach-Unteralgebra mit Einselement von $C^*(X)$.

3. *Ist γX Hausdorffsche Kompaktifizierung und ist für jeden Homöomorphismus φ von X auf sich mit $f \in C_\gamma^*(X)$ stets auch $f \circ \varphi \in C_\gamma^*(X)$, so folgt aus* γX äqu δX

$$\gamma X = \delta X.$$

Beweis. $\mathcal{U}_\gamma(X)$ ist eine schwache uniforme Struktur. Ist $\alpha \in \mathcal{U}_\gamma(X)$, so existieren daher endlich viele $f_i \in C_\gamma^*(X)$ und $\varepsilon_i > 0$, $(i = 1, \ldots, n)$, so daß $\alpha > \bigwedge_{i=1}^{n} f_i^{-1}(\alpha_{\varepsilon_i})$, wobei α_{ε_i} ε_i-Überdeckung von R ist, bestehend aus den ε_i-Umgebungen der Punkte von R. Es folgt $\varphi(\alpha) > \bigwedge_{i=1}^{n} (f_i \circ \varphi^{-1})^{-1}(\alpha_{\varepsilon_i})$. Wegen $f_i \circ \varphi^{-1} \in C_\gamma^*(X)$ ist $\varphi(\alpha) \in \mathcal{U}_\gamma(X)$. Die Struktur $\mathcal{U}_\gamma(X)$ hat also die Eigenschaft von Nr. 1.

Wir zeigen noch, daß auch umgekehrt aus der Bedingung von Nr. 1 die von Nr. 3 folgt. Ist nämlich $f \in C_\gamma^*(X)$, α_ε eine ε-Überdeckung von R und φ ein Homöomorphismus von X auf sich, so ist $f^{-1}(\alpha_\varepsilon) \in \mathcal{U}_\gamma(X)$ und daher

$$(f \circ \varphi)^{-1}(\alpha_\varepsilon) = \varphi^{-1}(f^{-1}(\alpha_\varepsilon)) \in \mathcal{U}_\gamma(X), \text{ also } f \circ \varphi \in C_\gamma^*(X).$$

Die Bedingung von Nr. 3 ist speziell für die Stone-Čech-Erweiterung βX erfüllt.

4. *Ist* βX äqu δX, *so auch* $\beta X = \delta X$.

Als nächstes betrachten wir den Fall einer Shanin-Kompaktifizierung $\omega_{\mathfrak{A}} X$ eines beliebigen topologischen Raumes X, wobei $\mathfrak{A}$ eine Basis der abgeschlossenen Mengen ist, die die leere Menge und mit je zwei Mengen auch ihren Durchschnitt und ihre Vereinigung enthält (siehe Shanin [4]). Wir brauchen das folgende Ergebnis von Shanin:

Ist δX eine Kompaktifizierung von X, so gilt $\omega_{\mathfrak{A}} X = \delta X$ genau dann, wenn

(1) $\{\overline{A}^{\delta X} : A \in \mathfrak{A}\}$ eine abgeschlossene Basis von δX ist,

(2) $\overline{\bigcap_{i=1}^{n} A_i}^{\delta X} = \bigcap_{i=1}^{n} \overline{A_i}^{\delta X}$ gilt für je endlich viele $A_1, \ldots, A_n$ aus $\mathfrak{A}$

und

(3) $\{x\} \in \mathfrak{F}(\delta X)$ ist für $x \in \delta X - X$.

5. *Ist $\varphi(\mathfrak{A}) = \mathfrak{A}$ für jeden Homöomorphismus φ von X auf sich, so folgt aus* $\omega_{\mathfrak{A}} X$ äqu δX

$$\omega_{\mathfrak{A}} X = \delta X.$$

Beweis. φ sei Homöomorphismus von $\omega_{\mathfrak{A}} X$ auf δX mit $\varphi(X) = X$. (1), (2) und (3) sind für $\omega_{\mathfrak{A}} X$ erfüllt, wegen $\varphi(\mathfrak{A}) = \mathfrak{A}$ also auch für δX.

Die Bedingung von Nr. 5 ist insbesondere erfüllt für die Wallman-Kompaktifizierung $\omega X = \omega_{\mathfrak{F}} X$:

6. *Aus* ωX äqu δX *folgt* $\omega X = \delta X$.

Für die Banaschewski-Kompaktifizierung ϱX — die maximale nulldimensionale Hausdorffsche Kompaktifizierung eines Hausdorffschen nulldimensionalen Raumes X (ind $X = 0$) — gilt $\varrho X = \omega_{\mathfrak{A}} X$, wobei $\mathfrak{A}$ aus allen offen-abgeschlossenen Mengen besteht. Also:

7. *Aus* ϱX äqu δX *folgt* $\varrho X = \delta X$.

X sei jetzt lokal peripher kompakt, d. h., X besitze eine Basis aus offenen Mengen mit kompakter Begrenzung, und Hausdorffsch. Dann gilt für die Freudenthal-Erweiterung φX — die maximale Hausdorffsche Kompaktifizierung mit nulldimensional gelegenem Adjunkt — $\varphi X = \omega_{\mathfrak{A}} X$, wobei $\mathfrak{A}$ aus allen abgeschlossenen Mengen mit kompakter Begrenzung besteht. Daher:

8. *Aus* φX äqu δX *folgt* $\varphi X = \delta X$.

Ist αX die Alexandroffsche Ein-Punkt-Kompaktifizierung eines nicht kompakten Raumes X und αX äqu δX, so ist $|\delta X - X| = 1$, folglich:

9. *Aus* αX äqu δX *folgt* $\alpha X = \delta X$.

Wir betrachten nun die Hewittsche Reellkompaktifizierung vX eines vollständig regulären Raumes X:

10. *Ist* vX äqu δX, *so auch* $vX = \delta X$.

Beweis. φ sei der Homöomorphismus von vX auf δX mit $\varphi(X) = X$. δX ist reellkompakt. $vX = \delta X$ gilt genau dann, wenn für jede abzählbare Familie $\{Z_n : n \in N\}$ von Nullstellenmengen Z_n

$$\overline{\bigcap_{n\in N} Z_n}^{\delta X} = \bigcap_{n\in N} \overline{Z_n}^{\delta X}$$

ist (siehe Gillman and Jerison [3], 8.7.). Aus $\overline{\bigcap_{n\in N} Z_n}^{vX} = \bigcap_{n\in N} \overline{Z_n}^{vX}$ folgt $\overline{\bigcap_{n\in N} \varphi(Z_n)}^{\delta X} = \bigcap_{n\in N} \overline{\varphi(Z_n)}^{\delta X}$. Nun ist aber $\varphi(\mathfrak{Z}) = \mathfrak{Z}$ für $\mathfrak{Z} = \{Z(f) : f \in C(X)\}$, denn $\varphi(Z(f)) = Z(f \circ \varphi^{-1})$ und $Z(f) = \varphi(Z(f \circ \varphi))$ für $f \in C(X)$.

Eine Verallgemeinerung von vX ist die Erweiterung $v_{\mathfrak{m}} X$ von Aquaro, wobei $\mathfrak{m}$ eine transfinite Kardinalzahl ist. $v_{\mathfrak{m}} X$ ist der topologische Raum der Vervollständigung der uniformen Struktur $\mathscr{U}_{\mathfrak{m}}(X)$ von X, die eine Basis aus allen offenen normalen Überdeckungen von X der Mächtigkeit $\leqq \mathfrak{m}$ besitzt (Aquaro [1], [2]). Es ist $vX = v_{\aleph_0} X$. Ein vollständig regulärer Raum X heißt $\mathfrak{m}$-vollständig, wenn $\mathscr{U}_{\mathfrak{m}}(X)$ vollständig ist. Ist δX $\mathfrak{m}$-vollständig, so gilt $\delta X = v_{\mathfrak{m}} X$ genau dann, wenn jede stetige Abbildung von X in einen $\mathfrak{m}$-vollständigen Raum eine stetige Fortsetzung auf δX besitzt.

11. *Gilt* $v_{\mathfrak{m}} X$ äqu δX, *so auch* $v_{\mathfrak{m}} X = \delta X$.

Beweis. φ^* sei der Homöomorphismus von $v_{\mathfrak{m}} X$ auf δX mit $\varphi^*(X) = X$. Es sei $\varphi = \varphi^* | X$. Ist f eine beliebige stetige Abbildung von X in einen $\mathfrak{m}$-vollständigen Raum Y, so ist $f \circ \varphi^{-1}$ stetig auf δX fortsetzbar. Ist nämlich f^* die stetige Fortsetzung von f auf $v_{\mathfrak{m}} X$, so ist $f^* \circ \varphi^{*-1}$ stetig auf δX und $f^* \circ \varphi^{*-1} | X = f \circ \varphi^{-1}$. Wir betrachten nun $f \circ \varphi$. Dann ist $f = (f \circ \varphi) \circ \varphi$ stetig auf δX fortsetzbar.

Ob es nichtextremale Erweiterungen gibt, die die untersuchte Eigenschaft besitzen, bleibt offen.

Literatur

[1] G. Aquaro, Ricovrimenti aperti e strutture uniforme sopra uno spazio topologico, Ann. Math. pura ed appl., ser. IV, **47** (1959), 319—389.
[2] G. Aquaro, Completamenti di spazii uniformi, Ann. Math. pura ed appl., ser. IV, **56** (1961), 87—98.
[3] L. Gillman and M. Jerison, Rings of continuous functions, Princeton 1960.
[4] N. A. Shanin, On special extensions of topological spaces, C. R. (Doklady) Acad. Sci. URSS **38** (1943), 110—113.

A GENERALIZATION OF TOPOLOGICAL SPACES

D. DOIČINOV (Sofia)

Approximately 30 years ago and almost at the same time the theory of uniform spaces and the theory of proximity spaces were established. The first one as it is well known, by A. WEIL, the second — by V. EFREMOVICZ. Both these theories began their development as parts of general topology. Nonetheless each of them was built up independently on its own system of axioms. It was ten years ago that the hungarian mathematician CSÁSZÁR created for a first time a general theory including the theories of the topological, proximity and uniform spaces. Some times later the french mathematician M. HACQUE presented a theory of his own.

In [1] another method leading to such a general theory was proposed — a method, which first of all follows the classical idea of the Hausdorff system of axioms for topological spaces, and secondly preserves the well known analytical concept of uniformity. This method consists in the following:

Let a set X be given and $\mathfrak{M}$ be a family of subsets of X. We consider a set Σ of mappings of $\mathfrak{M}$ into the set $\mathfrak{P}(X)$ of all subsets of X. (The image $U(A)$ for every A from $\mathfrak{M}$ by an arbitrary mapping $U \in \Sigma$ is to be interpreted as a „neighbourhood" of A.) The family Σ satisfies the following conditions:

1. If $U \in \Sigma$ and $A \in \mathfrak{M}$, then $A \subset U(A)$.

2. If $U \in \Sigma$, $V \in \Sigma$ and $A \in \mathfrak{M}$, there exists a $W \in \Sigma$ such that $W(A) \subset \subset U(A) \cap V(A)$.

3. If $U \in \Sigma$ and $A \in \mathfrak{M}$, there exists a $V \in \Sigma$ such that for every $B \in \mathfrak{M}$, $B \subset V(A)$ there is a $W \in \Sigma$, with $W(B) \subset U(A)$.

4. If $\emptyset \in \mathfrak{M}$, there exists $U \in \Sigma$ such that $U(\emptyset) = \emptyset$.

5. If U is a mapping of $\mathfrak{M}$ in $\mathfrak{P}(X)$ and if for every $A \in \mathfrak{M}$ there exists a $V \in \Sigma$ with $V(A) \subset U(A)$, then $U \in \Sigma$.

We call Σ a generalized topology with respect to $\mathfrak{M}$ and X a generalized topological space. A subfamily Σ' of Σ is called a base of Σ if for every $U \in \Sigma$ and for every $A \in \mathfrak{M}$ there exists a $V \in \Sigma'$ with $V(A) \subset U(A)$.

The generalized topologies introduced in a given set X with respect to the same $\mathfrak{M}$ can be compared with each other. We say that Σ_1 is larger than Σ_2, if $\Sigma_1 \supset \Sigma_2$. This permits one to introduce, in the manner of BOURBAKI, the notion of least upper bound of a family of generalized topologies.

If in X_1 (X_2) a generalized topology Σ_1 (Σ_2) with respect to $\mathfrak{M}_1$ ($\mathfrak{M}_2$) is introduced, a mapping f of X_1 into X_2 is called continuous if the following is true:

a) if $A \in \mathfrak{M}_1$, then $f(A) \in \mathfrak{M}_2$;

b) if $V \in \Sigma_2$, then $f^{-1} V f \in \Sigma_1$.

Further, again like in BOURBAKI, the concept of a generalized topology in the product space is introduced.

Different special cases of the concept of generalized topological spaces can be received in two ways — by varying the set $\mathfrak{M}$ or by imposing suplementary conditions on the family Σ. In the case when $\mathfrak{M}$ coincides with the set of one-point subsets of X one receives the classical topological space. The proximity spaces are received if $\mathfrak{M}$ is the set $\mathfrak{P}(X)$ of all subsets of X and Σ satisfies the symmetry condition:

s) If $U \in \Sigma$, $A \in \mathfrak{M}$, $B \in \mathfrak{M}$, and if $U(A) \cap B = \emptyset$, there exists a $V \in \Sigma$ such that $V(B) \cap A = \emptyset$.

Let us note that the mappings whose existence is asserted in axioms 2, 3 and 5 may depend on the choice of some elements of $\mathfrak{M}$. Obviously we shall receive a new concept if we "uniformize" these axioms, requesting that the mappings do not depend on that choice. This leads to the notion of uniformly generalized topological space. A uniformly generalized topology is called symmetric, if it satisfies the uniformized variant of axiom s). In the case when $\mathfrak{M}$ is the set of one-point subsets of X, the notion of symmetric generalized topological space coincides essentially with WEIL's notion of uniform space.

There are many questions arising naturally and concerning the mutual relations between the uniform and nonuniform generalized topologies. Every uniform generalized topology is the base of some (in general nonuniform) generalized topology. Can but every generalized topology be considered as generated in this way? The answer of this question in the general case is now unknown. However we know that the answer is positive if $\mathfrak{M} = \mathfrak{P}(X)$.

References

[1] D. DOIČINOV, On a general theory of topological, proximity and uniform spaces (russ.), Doklady Akad. Nauk SSSR **156** (1964), 21—24.

ON COMPACTIFICATION IN CERTAIN CLASSES OF SPACES

R. Duda (Wrocław)

The original compactification problem was "for a given topological space X find a compactification Y whatever it would be" and in this direction a good deal of interesting results forming together modern Compactification Theory has been obtained. However, as time went on, the words "whatever it would be" became a nuisance and the tendency has appeared to find compactifications with some prescribed properties like, for instance, a compactification Y of X with same dimension, $\dim X = \dim Y$ (see [5], p. 64). The tendency was at first rather weak and appeared in single theorems, but at the present situation has largely changed and the original problem is now more and more often formulated in the form "for a given topological space X and for a given class $\mathfrak{A}$ of topological spaces find (if possible) a compactification Y in the class $\mathfrak{A}$". A fine example of this approach is the lecture given here by Professor Smirnov [8].

The purpose of my communication is to provide two further examples in this direction, one negative and one positive.

I. For a given class τ of topological spaces, a space $X \in \tau$ is called an *absolute retract for* τ (respectively, an *absolute neighbourhood retract for* τ) if, whenever X is imbedded as a closed subset of a space $Z \in \tau$, X is a retract of Z (respectively, X is a retract of some neighbourhood U of X in Z) (see [4]).

Theorem 1. *There exists a metric separable space N such that N is an absolute retract for normal spaces and no compactification N^* of N is an absolute neighbourhood retract for any class τ of Hausdorff spaces enjoying the following property:*

(1) *For every space $X \in \tau$ there exists a locally connected space $Z \in \tau$ such that X is a closed subset of Z.*

From a result of Wojdysławski ([9], p. 186) it follows that the classes of metric and separable metric spaces satisfy (1).

Definition of N is quite simple: it is the union of all segments (in the plane) L_n with ends $(0, 1)$ and $(1/n, 0)$, $N = \bigcup_{n=1}^{\infty} L_n$. Such a space is sometimes called a countable hedge-hog.

Space N is an absolute retract for normal spaces (and so, as metric separable itself, it is also an absolute retract for each class of topological spaces containing the class of metric separable spaces and contained in the class of normal spaces). In fact, it can be shown (see [1]) that N is an absolute retract for metric separable spaces. Hence, being also an absolute G_δ, it must be, by a theorem of HANNER [4], an absolute retract for normal spaces.

Now, it is not very hard to show (see [1] again) that every Hausdorff space Y containing N as a dense subset is not locally connected at any point $p \in Y - N$. Since open subset of a locally connected space is locally connected, and retraction preserves local connectedness, no compactification N^* of N can be an absolute neighbourhood retract for any class τ of Hausdorff spaces enjoying (1).

II. A topological space X is called *ordered* if there exists a linear order in X such that the topology in X is finer than that induced by this order (see [3]).

One of the characteristic features of separable ordered spaces X is the following property (see [3]):

(2) There exists a one-to-one and continuous mapping from X into real line.

This property allows us to construct a good (in a sense) compactification for every metric separable connected ordered space.

A continuum K, i.e. a compact metric connected space, is said to be *irreducible between a and b* if K contains both a und b but no proper subcontinuum of K does. An irreducible between a and b continuum K is of *type λ* if there exists a continuous mapping $\eta: K \to [0, 1]$ such that $\eta(a) = 0$, $\eta(b) = 1$ and that each section $\eta^{-1}(t)$ is a non-dense subcontinuum of K (see [7], § 43).

Theorem 2. *For every metric separable connected ordered space X there exists an irreducible continuum K of type λ and a homeomorphism $h: X \to K$ such that $h(X)$ is a dense subset of K meeting each internal section $\eta^{-1}(t)$, $0 < t < 1$, in precisely one point, and each boundary section $\eta^{-1}(0)$ and $\eta^{-1}(1)$ in one point at most.*

Construction of K is rather complicated and can be found in [2].

Compactification asserted by Theorem 2 seems to be good, because it preserves structure of X given by (2): mapping $\eta | h(X)$ is a one-to-one and continuous mapping from the homeomorph $h(X)$ of X into real line.

It may be perhaps of some interest to point out here some duality. We have proved in Theorem 2 that every metric separable connected ordered space can be imbedded into an irreducible continuum of type λ in a "one point by one section" manner, but the converse is also true. Namely (see [6]), every irreducible continuum of type λ contains a metric separable connected ordered space chosen one point by one section.

References

[1] R. DUDA, On compactification of absolute retracts, Coll. Math. **12** (1964), 1—5.
[2] R. DUDA, On ordered topological spaces, Fund. Math. (in preparation).
[3] S. EILENBERG, Ordered topological spaces, Amer. J. Math. **53** (1941), 39—45.
[4] O. HANNER, Solid space and absolute retracts, Arkiv för Mat. **1** (1952), 375—382.
[5] W. HUREWICZ and H. WALLMAN, Dimension theory, Princeton 1948.
[6] B. KNASTER, Sur les ensembles connexes irréducibles entre deux points, Fund. Math. **19** (1927), 276—297.
[7] C. KURATOWSKI, Topologie II, Warszawa-Wrocław 1952.
[8] JU. M. SMIRNOV, Zusammenhang und bogenweiser Zusammenhang von Kompaktifizierungen und deren Adjunkten, this "Contributions . . .", pp. 211—216.
[9] M. WOJDYSŁAWSKI, Rétractes absolus et hyperespaces des continus, Fund. Math. **32** (1939), 184—192.

ÜBER ERWEITERUNGEN MIT NULLDIMENSIONAL GELEGENEM ADJUNKT

JÜRGEN FLACHSMEYER (Greifswald)

Ein topologischer Raum kann im allgemeinen auf verschiedene Weisen durch Adjunktion neuer Punkte zu einem umfassenden Raum erweitert werden. Die jeweils interessierende Problematik, die auf Erweiterungsbetrachtungen führt, wird oft durch bestimmte natürliche Forderungen von selbst eine gewisse Aussonderung aus der Fülle der Erweiterungsmöglichkeiten vornehmen. Wir befassen uns hier mit Forderungen, die von einigen Autoren im Zusammenhang mit dem Verlangen nach „idealen" (erstrebenswerten) Erweiterungen aufgestellt worden sind.

Unter einer Erweiterung des gegebenen topologischen Raumes X versteht man bekanntlich eine Einbettung $e:X \to Y$ von X in einen topologischen Raum Y, so daß $e:X \to e(X)$ ein Homöomorphismus ist und $e(X)$ in Y dicht liegt. Der dem Raum X bei der Erweiterung $e:X \to Y$ hinzugefügte Raum $Y - e(X)$ heißt das *Adjunkt* der Erweiterung (e, X, Y) (wir schreiben für die Erweiterung abkürzend eX oder ähnlich). Die Begriffe der Gleichheit von Erweiterungen bzw. der Vergleichbarkeit von Erweiterungen werden in dem üblichen Sinne gebraucht.

1. Freudenthalsche Erweiterungen

Im Jahre 1931 hatte H. FREUDENTHAL [10], veranlaßt durch topologisch-gruppentheoretische Untersuchungen, topologische Räume solcherart zu kompakten Hausdorffschen Räumen erweitert, daß dabei das Adjunkt möglichst „dünn" ausfiel, aber dennoch möglichst weitgehend aufgespalten war. Von den Ausgangsräumen wurde hierfür über die separable Metrisierbarkeit hinaus noch lokale Kompaktheit, lokaler Zusammenhang und Zusammenhang verlangt. Geometrisch-anschauliche Vorstellungen führten dabei zu den beiden Forderungen an das Adjunkt, daß es einerseits recht „dünn", aber andererseits doch noch genügend aufgespalten ist. So schreibt wohl unsere Anschauung der offenen Geraden zwei „unendlich ferne" Punkte und einem Strahlenbüschel aus n Strahlen wohl n „unendlich ferne" Punkte zu. Diese durch die Anschauung bevorzugten Abschließungen durch „unendlich ferne" Punkte, wie auch die Abschließung der unendlichen Ebene mittels eines „unendlich fernen" Punktes, intendieren die oben genannten Forderungen an das Adjunkt. Wie wird man nun die Idee von den angestrebten Kompaktifizierungen mathematisch ausdrücken? J. DE GROOT [14] hat das getan durch die Forderungen:

1. Das Adjunkt der gewünschten, der „idealen" Kompaktifizierung soll nulldimensional (im Sinne von ind) sein.

2. Jede andere Kompaktifizierung mit nulldimensionalem Adjunkt ist ein stetiges Bild der gewünschten, „idealen" Kompaktifizierung bei einer Abbildung, die den Ausgangsraum punktweise festläßt. In der nunmehr geläufigen Terminologie gesprochen soll also unter der „idealen" Kompaktifizierung die *größte* mit nulldimensionalem Adjunkt verstanden werden. Nicht jeder Raum besitzt eine ideale Kompaktifizierung in dem vorstehend genannten Sinne.

J. DE GROOT [14] bewies, daß ein separabel metrisierbarer Raum dann und nur dann überhaupt zu einem separabel metrisierbaren Raum mit nulldimensionalem Adjunkt kompaktifiziert werden kann, wenn er lokal peripher kompakt ist. Dieses Theorem ist eine Ausdehnung einer Feststellung von L. ZIPPIN [24], der die separabel metrisierbaren lokal peripher kompakten Räume genau als diejenigen erkannte, die durch Adjunktion von abzählbar vielen Punkten zu einem separabel metrisierbaren Raum kompaktifiziert werden können. Anreregt durch die genannten Untersuchungen von J. DE GROOT und L. ZIPPIN nahm FREUDENTHAL mit einer weiteren Arbeit [11] einen Neuaufbau seiner Endenkompaktifizierungsmethode vor. Von den Ausgangsräumen wurde außer der separablen Metrisierbarkeit nur noch die lokale periphere Kompaktheit gefordert. Für solche Räume, die also Hausdorffsche lokal peripher kompakte Räume mit abzählbarer Basis sind, hat die von FREUDENTHAL konstruierte „Endenkompaktifizierung" φX die folgenden Eigenschaften:

1. Das Adjunkt $\varphi X - X$ ist nulldimensional, ind $(\varphi X - X) = 0$.

2. Die Kompaktifizierung φX ist perfekt, d. h., die Umgebungen der adjungierten Punkte $x \in \varphi X - X$ werden durch das Adjunkt nicht zerlegt in zwei in X offene Mengen, die x beide als Häufungspunkt haben.

Diese Kompaktifizierung φX ist gerade die „ideale" Kompaktifizierung von X (die größte unter denen mit nulldimensionalem Adjunkt). X hat nur in den Fällen eine abzählbare Basis, wenn der Quasikomponenten Raum von X ein kompakter Raum mit abzählbarer Basis ist. Bisher war also festgestellt, daß sich die separabel metrisierbaren lokal peripher kompakten Räume „ideal" kompaktifizieren lassen. Mit der Untersuchung [12] befreite sich FREUDENTHAL auch noch von der Voraussetzung der Existenz einer abzählbaren Basis für den Ausgangsraum. Durch eine irrtümliche Schlußweise glaubte er bewiesen zu haben, daß genau die Hausdorffschen lokal peripher kompakten Räume sich in dem vorher genannten Sinne „ideal" kompaktifizieren lassen. JU. SMIRNOV [23] gab aber einen Raum an, der nicht lokal peripher kompakt ist, bei dem aber die Stone-Čech-Erweiterung ein nulldimensionales Adjunkt hat. Dieser Raum hätte also mit seiner Stone-Čech-Erweiterung eine „ideale" Kompaktifizierung, ohne daß er lokal peripher kompakt wäre. In der Freudenthalschen Arbeit [12] wird der Prozeß der Endenkompaktifizierung gleich allgemeiner in Abhängigkeit von gewissen offenen Basen durchgeführt.

Satz (FREUDENTHAL [12]). *X sei ein Hausdorffscher lokal peripher kompakter Raum und $\mathfrak{B}$ eine Freudenthal-Basis von X, d. h., $\mathfrak{B}$ habe über die Basiseigenschaft hinaus die folgenden Eigenschaften:*

1. *Die Begrenzungen* fr (B) *der Elemente* $B \in \mathfrak{B}$ *sind kompakt;*

2. $B \in \mathfrak{B} \Rightarrow X - \overline{B} \in \mathfrak{B}$;

3. $B_1, B_2 \in \mathfrak{B} \Rightarrow B_1 \cap B_2 \in \mathfrak{B}$ *und* $B_1 \cup B_2 \in \mathfrak{B}$.

Dann hat die mittels $\mathfrak{B}$ nach dem Freudenthalschen Verfahren der Endenkompaktifizierung konstruierte Kompaktifizierung $\varphi_{\mathfrak{B}} X$ ein nulldimensionales Adjunkt.

FREUDENTHAL bewies sogar, daß das Adjunkt $\varphi_{\mathfrak{B}}X - X$ überdies noch nulldimensional gelegen ist in $\varphi_{\mathfrak{B}}X$. Hierbei soll das Adjunkt $eX - X$ einer Erweiterung eX des Raumes X *nulldimensional gelegen* sein in eX, wenn es eine offene Basis des Erweiterungsraumes gibt, deren Basiselemente Begrenzungen haben, die vollständig im Ausgangsraum liegen. Aus der nulldimensionalen Lage des Adjunkts ergibt sich natürlich auch stets die Nulldimensionalität des Adjunkts im Sinne von ind. Der vorhin erwähnte Fehler von FREUDENTHAL besteht einfach darin, daß FREUDENTHAL also die Nulldimensionalität des Adjunkts mit der nulldimensionalen Lage des Adjunkt für gleichwertig hielt.

K. MORITA [16] hat unabhängig von der Freudenthalschen Arbeit [12] ebenfalls die ursprünglichen Freudenthalschen Betrachtungen zur Konstruktion von φX von der Voraussetzung einer abzählbaren Basis befreit. MORITA erkannte in voller Schärfe die Signifikanz der nulldimensionalen Lage für das Adjunkt der Freudenthal-Erweiterung. Die Explikation des Begriffs der idealen Kompaktifizierung wäre also zweckmäßig abzuwandeln in die Form: Unter der „idealen" Kompaktifizierung soll die größte derjenigen mit nulldimensional gelegenem Adjunkt verstanden werden. Die korrekte Antwort auf die Frage nach der Existenz von idealen Kompaktifizierungen ist dann der

Satz (FREUDENTHAL, MORITA). *Ein Hausdorffscher Raum X besitzt genau dann eine Hausdorffsche Kompaktifizierung mit nulldimensional gelegenem Adjunkt, wenn der Raum lokal peripher kompakt ist, d. h., wenn er eine offene Basis besitzt, deren Elemente sämtlich kompakte Begrenzungen haben.*

Ein lokal peripher kompakter Hausdorffscher Raum besitzt unter allen Hausdorffschen Kompaktifizierungen mit nulldimensional gelegenem Adjunkt eine größte (die sogenannte *Freudenthal-Erweiterung* φX).

Während bei FREUDENTHAL die Erweiterung φX aus der maximalen Freudenthal-Basis $\mathfrak{B}_m = \{B \mid B \subset X,\ B$ offen und $\mathrm{Fr}\,(B)$ kompakt$\}$ als Endenerweiterung hervorgeht, hat MORITA φX durch Vervollständigung der mit $\mathfrak{B}_m$ verbundenen uniformen Struktur erhalten (indem man mit TUKEY alle endlichen offenen Überdeckungen mit Elementen aus $\mathfrak{B}_m$ nimmt).

Entsprechend zu dem Vorgehen MORITAS werden bei E. SKLJARENKO [21] alle übrigen Freudenthalschen Erweiterungen $\varphi_{\mathfrak{B}}X$ durch Vervollständigung der mit einer Freudenthal-Basis $\mathfrak{B}$ assoziierten uniformen Struktur (Nachbarschaftsstruktur) erzeugt.

Die folgenden deskriptiven Charakterisierungen der Freudenthalschen Erweiterungen $\varphi_{\mathfrak{B}}X$ finden sich in der Arbeit [8]. Das eine Mal wird die Charakterisierung der $\varphi_{\mathfrak{B}}X$ in der Klasse der Hausdorffschen Kompaktifizierungen und das andere Mal in der Klasse der H-abgeschlossenen Erweiterungen vorgenommen.

Satz ([8], S. 367). *X sei ein Hausdorffscher Raum und $\mathfrak{B}$ eine Freudenthal-Basis von X. Die Freudenthalsche Endenerweiterung $\varphi_{\mathfrak{B}}X$ ist dann eine Hausdorffsche Kompaktifizierung von X* (*mit nulldimensional gelegenem Adjunkt*), *die die folgenden Eigenschaften besitzt:*

1. *Die Fortsetzungen $o(B)$ der Elemente $B \in \mathfrak{B}$ bilden eine offene Basis in $\varphi_{\mathfrak{B}}X$ [$o(B)$ bezeichnet dabei die größte offene Menge in $\varphi_{\mathfrak{B}}X$, deren Spur in X gleich B ist].*

2. *Für je zwei Elemente $B_1, B_2 \in \mathfrak{B}$ mit $B_1 \cup B_2 = X$ gilt*

$$o(B_1 \cup B_2) = o(B_1) \cup o(B_2)\,.$$

$\varphi_{\mathfrak{B}}X$ ist (im wesentlichen) die einzige Hausdorffsche Kompaktifizierung von X mit den Eigenschaften 1 *und* 2.

Satz ([8], S. 366). *X sei ein Hausdorffscher Raum und $\mathfrak{B}$ eine Freudenthal-Basis von X. Die Freudenthalsche Endenerweiterung $\varphi_{\mathfrak{B}}X$ ist dann eine Hausdorffsche Kompaktifizierung von X (mit nulldimensional gelegenem Adjunkt), die die folgenden Eigenschaften besitzt:*

1. *Die Fortsetzungen $o(B)$ der Elemente $B \in \mathfrak{B}$ bilden eine offene Basis von $\varphi_{\mathfrak{B}}X$.*
2. *Für je zwei Elemente $B_1, B_2 \in \mathfrak{B}$ gilt*

$$o(B_1 \cup B_2) = o(B_1) \cup o(B_2).$$

$\varphi_{\mathfrak{B}}X$ ist (im wesentlichen) die einzige H-abgeschlossene Erweiterung von X mit den Eigenschaften 1 *und* 2.

Aus dem letztgenannten Theorem geht hervor, daß die Freudenthal-Erweiterungen (d. h. die Kompaktifizierungen mit nulldimensional gelegenem Adjunkt) eines lokal peripher kompakten Ausgangsraumes sich auch durch den Kompaktifizierungsprozeß von WALLMAN und SHANIN ergeben. Die Wallman-Shanin-Kompaktifizierungen erfreuen sich in jüngster Zeit eines gesteigerten Interesses (vgl. [4], [13], [17], [5]). Es bedarf noch einer klärenden Untersuchung, welche Kompaktifizierungen sich als Wallman-Shanin-Kompaktifizierungen zu gewissen abgeschlossenen Basen des Ausgangsraumes gewinnen lassen. Jedenfalls ergibt der vorstehende Charakterisierungssatz eine Einsicht für Hausdorffsche Kompaktifizierungen mit nulldimensional gelegenem Adjunkt (vgl. auch [17]).

Korollar. *Es sei bX eine Hausdorffsche Kompaktifizierung von X mit nulldimensional gelegenem Adjunkt. bX ist dann die Freudenthal-Erweiterung $\varphi_{\mathfrak{B}}X$ von X bezüglich der offenen Basis $\mathfrak{B}$, die aus allen offenen Mengen $U \subset X$ besteht, deren Fortsetzungen $o(U)$ ganz in X gelegene Begrenzungen haben. Diese Freudenthal-Erweiterung $\varphi_{\mathfrak{B}}X$ stimmt (im wesentlichen) mit der durch die zu $\mathfrak{B}$ duale Basis erzeugten Wallman-Shanin-Erweiterung $\omega_{C\mathfrak{B}}X$ überein.*

Beweis. $\omega_{C\mathfrak{B}}X$ ist als diejenige Hausdorffsche Kompaktifizierung bestimmt, für welche die Abschließungen der $F \in C\mathfrak{B}$ in $\omega_{C\mathfrak{B}}X$ eine abgeschlossene Basis bilden und außerdem für je endlich viele Elemente $F_1, F_2, \ldots, F_n \in C\mathfrak{B}$ die Relation $\overline{F_1 \cap \cdots \cap F_n}^{\omega} = \bar{F}_1^{\omega} \cap \bar{F}_2^{\omega} \cap \cdots \cap \bar{F}_n^{\omega}$ gilt. Beide Eigenschaften folgen sofort aus dem vorstehendem Theorem, da $o(U) = bX - \overline{CU}^{bX}$ bedeutet.

2. Fomin-Shanin-Erweiterungen

Nachdem wir im ersten Teil Kompaktifizierungen mit nulldimensional gelegenem Adjunkt besprochen haben, wollen wir nun zu H-abgeschlossenen Erweiterungen mit nulldimensional gelegenem Adjunkt übergehen. Unsere Untersuchung [8] behandelt die Freudenthalschen Erweiterungen als Sonderfall der H-abgeschlossenen Erweiterungen mit nulldimensional gelegenem Adjunkt, mit den Betrachtungen in [8] wird ein einheitlicher Standpunkt der Freudenthalschen Endentheorie und der Fominschen Endentheorie [9] geschaffen. Den Ausgangspunkt bilden dabei die offenen π-Basen $\mathfrak{B}$ für beliebige Hausdorffsche Räume X. π-Basen für X sollen offene Basen mit den beiden Eigenschaften

1. $U, V \in \mathfrak{B} \Rightarrow U \cap V \in \mathfrak{B}$,

2. $U \in \mathfrak{B} \Rightarrow X - \overline{U} \in \mathfrak{B}$

sein. (Vgl. über π-Basen die Ausführungen in [8], Def. 1. Wir bemerken in Ergänzung zu den dort gemachten historischen Angaben noch, daß additive π-Basen unter der Bezeichnung „symmetrische Basen" bei N. A. Shanin [20] vorkommen.) Mit jeder π-Basis $\mathfrak{B}$ eines Hausdorffschen Ausgangsraumes kann man in natürlicher Weise eine H-abgeschlossene Erweiterung in Verbindung bringen. Darüber gilt der

Satz ([8], S. 356—357). *Es sei X ein Hausdorffscher Raum und $\mathfrak{B}$ eine π-Basis von X. Dann gibt es (im wesentlichen) genau eine durch $\mathfrak{B}$ bestimmte H-abgeschlossene Erweiterung $\sigma_{\mathfrak{B}} X$ von X mit den folgenden Eigenschaften:*

1. *Die Fortsetzungen $o(U)$ der Mengen $U \in \mathfrak{B}$ bilden eine offene Basis in $\sigma_{\mathfrak{B}} X$, d. h., $\sigma_{\mathfrak{B}} X$ ist strikt in bezug auf die Basis $\mathfrak{B}$.*

2. *Die Fortsetzungen $o(U)$ der Mengen $U \in \mathfrak{B}$ haben Begrenzungen, die vollständig in X liegen.*

Insbesondere hat also die Erweiterung $\sigma_{\mathfrak{B}} X$ ein nulldimensional gelegenes Adjunkt. Jede H-abgeschlossene Erweiterung von X mit nulldimensional gelegenem Adjunkt entsteht als eine zu einer geeigneten π-Basis gehörige $\sigma_{\mathfrak{B}} X$-Erweiterung.

Unsere nächste Feststellung soll nun darin bestehen, daß wir die soeben erwähnten H-abgeschlossenen Erweiterungen $\sigma_{\mathfrak{B}} X$ als identisch mit den Fominschen Enden-Erweiterungen und gewissen Shaninschen Erweiterungen erkennen. Die Konstruktion von $\sigma_{\mathfrak{B}} X$ war in [8] mittels einer durch die π-Basis $\mathfrak{B}$ determinierten Boole-Algebra von regulär offenen Mengen vorgenommen worden, während bei Fomin sogenannte Hausdorff-Enden und bei Shanin eine gewisse Modifikation des Wallmanschen Prozesses herangezogen werden.

Satz ([8], S. 362). *Es sei X ein Hausdorffscher Raum und $\mathfrak{B}$ eine π-Basis von X. Dann ist die zu $\mathfrak{B}$ gehörige H-abgeschlossene Erweiterung $\sigma_{\mathfrak{B}} X$ mit nulldimensional gelegenem Adjunkt gleichbedeutend mit der Fominschen Endenerweiterung $F_{\mathfrak{B}} X$ [9] und auch gleichbedeutend mit der zu $\mathfrak{B}$ gehörigen Shaninschen Erweiterung $\chi_{\mathfrak{B}} X$ [19].*

Bemerkung. In [8] hatten wir noch nicht herausgestellt, daß die Erweiterung $\sigma_{\mathfrak{B}} X$ auch mit der Shaninschen Erweiterung $\chi_{\mathfrak{B}} X$ zusammenfällt.[1]) Die zu einer π-Basis $\mathfrak{B}$ gehörige Shanin-Erweiterung $\chi_{\mathfrak{B}} X$ ist eine H-abgeschlossene Erweiterung von X mit den folgenden Eigenschaften ([19], S. 9; [20], S. 113):

1. $\chi_{\mathfrak{B}} X$ ist strikt in bezug auf die Basis $\mathfrak{B}$ (siehe die nachfolgende Definition).

2. Es gilt $o(U \cup V) = o(U) \cup o(V)$ für $U, V \in \mathfrak{B}$.

3. Überdecken die endlich vielen $U_1, U_2, \ldots, U_n$ fast den Raum X, d. h. deren Vereinigung ist in X überall dicht, so überdecken die Fortsetzungen $o(U_1), o(U_2), \ldots, o(U_n)$ das ganze Adjunkt.

Durch diese Eigenschaften ist $\chi_{\mathfrak{B}} X$ charakterisiert. Wir können sofort folgern, daß für jedes $U \in \mathfrak{B}$ $\mathrm{fr}_{\chi_{\mathfrak{B}} X}(o(U)) \subset X$ gilt. Denn U und $V := X - \overline{U}$ überdecken fast

[1]) Die Shaninsche Arbeit [20] lag uns damals nämlich nicht vor.

den Raum X, also gilt $\mathrm{fr}_X(U) = \chi_{\mathfrak{B}} X - o(U \cup V)$, und zum anderen ist

$$\mathrm{fr}_{\chi_{\mathfrak{B}} X}(o(U)) = \chi_{\mathfrak{B}} X - o(U) \cap o(X);$$

wegen $o(U \cup V) = o(U) \cup o(V)$ folgt daraus

$$\mathrm{fr}_{\chi_{\mathfrak{B}} X}(o(U)) = \mathrm{fr}_X(U).$$

$\chi_{\mathfrak{B}} X$ hat damit die für $\sigma_{\mathfrak{B}} X$ charakteristischen Eigenschaften.

Die in [8] bewiesenen Sätze über die Erweiterungen $\sigma_{\mathfrak{B}} X$ stellen damit neue Einsichten über die Fomin-Shanin-Erweiterungen dar. Wir geben nun noch eine Kennzeichnung der Fomin-Shanin-Erweiterungen $\sigma_{\mathfrak{B}} X$, die eine Verschärfung der vorstehend genannten Shaninschen Charakterisierung der $\chi_{\mathfrak{B}} X$ ist.

Wir hatten schon hervorgehoben, daß FREUDENTHAL [11] von der Erweiterung φX (jedenfalls im Fall eines separabel metrisierbaren Ausgangsraumes) bewies, daß das Adjunkt $\varphi X - X$ in keinem seiner Punkte den Raum φX lokal zerlegt. Mit SKLJARENKO [21] hat sich für diese Eigenschaft der Freudenthal-Erweiterung die Bezeichnung *Perfektheit* eingebürgert. SKLJARENKO studierte in [21] an Hausdorffschen Kompaktifizierungen die Perfektheit erstmals etwas ausführlicher. Die Perfektheit stellt eine bemerkenswerte Eigenschaft bei Erweiterungen dar, sie sollte durchaus noch eingehender untersucht werden. RINOW [18] widmete sich den perfekten lokal zusammenhängenden Kompaktifizierungen. SKLJARENKO relativierte in [22] den Perfektheitsbegriff von kompakten Hausdorffschen Erweiterungen, indem er ihn auf gewisse Basen des Ausgangsraumes bezog.

Wir lassen die Voraussetzung einer Hausdorffschen Kompaktifizierung fort.

Definition. Es sei eX eine Erweiterung des topologischen Raumes X und $\mathfrak{B}$ eine offene Basis von X. Die Erweiterung eX soll *in bezug auf die Basis* $\mathfrak{B}$ *perfekt* genannt werden, wenn folgendes gilt:

1. Die Fortsetzungen $o(B)$ oder Basiselemente $B \in \mathfrak{B}$ bilden eine Basis im Erweiterungsraum eX. (Wir sagen hierzu, daß die Erweiterung eX in bezug auf die Basis $\mathfrak{B}$ *strikt* ist; vgl. über strikte Erweiterungen etwa die Ausführungen in [8], S. 354, Fußnote und entsprechender Text.)

2. Für jedes $B \in \mathfrak{B}$ gilt für die Begrenzungen hinsichtlich X und eX

$$\overline{\mathrm{fr}_X(B)}^{eX} = \mathrm{fr}_{eX}(o(B)).$$

Eine Erweiterung soll schlechthin *perfekt* heißen, wenn sie bezüglich der maximalen Basis, bestehend aus allen offenen Mengen, perfekt ist.

Es kann nun der folgende Satz bewiesen werden, der eine Verallgemeinerung des Theorems 1 von SKLJARENKO [21] darstellt. In [21] war der Satz für Hausdorffsche Kompaktifizierungen und für die Perfektheit in bezug auf die größte Basis ausgesprochen worden. In seinem Beweis wurde dort die Erzeugung von kompakten Hausdorffschen Erweiterungen mittels uniformer Strukturen (Nachbarschaftsstrukturen) benutzt. Eine solche Berufung auf Uniformierbarkeit kommt jetzt in der allgemeinen Situation nicht mehr in Frage.

Satz. *Es sei X ein beliebiger topologischer Raum und eX eine Erweiterung dieses Raumes. $\mathfrak{B}$ sei eine offene additive π-Basis*[2]) *von X, d. h., $\mathfrak{B}$ bildet eine offene Basis für*

[2]) Vgl. hierzu die Ausführungen in [8], Def. 1.

X mit den zusätzlichen Eigenschaften:

1. $U, V \in \mathfrak{B} \Rightarrow U \cap V \in \mathfrak{B}$,
2. $U \in \mathfrak{B} \quad \Rightarrow X - \overline{U} \in \mathfrak{B}$,
3. $U, V \in \mathfrak{B} \Rightarrow U \cup V \in \mathfrak{B}$.

Ferner stelle eX eine strikte Erweiterung von X in bezug auf diese Basis dar. Dann sind die folgenden Bedingungen äquivalent:

a) *Die Erweiterung eX ist perfekt bezüglich der Basis $\mathfrak{B}$.*

b) *Für je zwei Elemente $U, V \in \mathfrak{B}$ mit $U \cap V = \emptyset$ gilt $o(U \cup V) = o(U) \cup o(V)$.*

c) *Für kein Element $U \in \mathfrak{B}$ läßt sich ein Adjunktpunkt $x \in eX - X$ finden, der gleichzeitig in $o(U)$ liegt und für den außerdem $x \in \overline{V}^{eX}$, $x \in \overline{W}^{eX}$ gilt, mit irgendwelchen $V, W \in \mathfrak{B}$, wobei $V \cap W = \emptyset$ und $U = V \cup W$. (In keinem Adjunktpunkt werden seine Umgebungen $o(U)$ durch das Adjunkt hinsichtlich der Basis $\mathfrak{B}$ zerlegt.)*

Beweis. a) $\Rightarrow$ b). Aus Monotoniegründen ist $o(U \cup V) \supset o(U) \cup o(V)$. Angenommen, es gibt ein $x \in o(U \cup V)$ mit $x \notin \overline{o(U) \cup o(V)}$. Jedenfalls ist dann $x \in \mathrm{fr}_{eX}(o(U)) \cup \mathrm{fr}_{eX}(o(V))$ und nach a) $x \in \overline{\mathrm{fr}_X(U) \cup \mathrm{fr}_X(V)}^{eX}$. U, V sollen außerdem disjunkt sein, also gilt $\mathrm{fr}_X(U) \cup \mathrm{fr}_X(V) = \mathrm{fr}_X(U \cup V)$. Damit haben wir $x \in \overline{\mathrm{fr}_X(U \cup V)}^{eX} = \mathrm{fr}_{eX}(o(U \cup V))$, was ja $x \in o(U \cup V)$ widerspricht. Demnach muß für $U \cap V = \emptyset$ $o(U \cup V) = o(U) \cup o(V)$ sein.

b) $\Rightarrow$ c). Es sei $U = V \cup W$ mit $V, W \in \mathfrak{B}$ und $V \cap W = \emptyset$. Angenommen, es gibt einen Punkt $x \in eX - X$ mit $x \in o(U)$ und $x \in \overline{V}^{eX} \cap \overline{W}^{eX}$. Wegen b) ist $x \in o(V) \cup o(W)$, etwa $x \in o(V)$. Dann muß $o(V) \cap W \neq \emptyset$, d. h., es muß $V \cap W \neq \emptyset$ sein, was ein Widerspruch ist. Demnach gilt c).

c) $\Rightarrow$ a) Angenommen, es gibt ein $U \in \mathfrak{B}$ mit $\overline{\mathrm{fr}_X(U)}^{eX} \neq \mathrm{fr}_{eX}(o(U))$. Dann existiert ein $x \in \mathrm{fr}_{eX}(o(U))$ mit $x \notin \overline{\mathrm{fr}_X(U)}^{eX}$. Jetzt nutzen wir die Voraussetzung 2 von der π-Basis aus! Es ist danach $V := X - \overline{U} \in \mathfrak{B}$. Wir zeigen, daß $o(U \cup V)$ eine Umgebung von x ist und außerdem $x \in \overline{U}^{eX} \cap \overline{V}^{eX}$ gilt. Das würde aber c) widersprechen, womit a) bewiesen wäre. Wegen $x \notin \overline{\mathrm{fr}_X(U)}^{eX}$ gibt es eine Umgebung W von x mit $W \cap \mathrm{fr}_X(U) = \emptyset$, also gilt $W \cap X \subset U \cap V$ und damit weiter $W \subset o(U \cup V)$, d. h. $x \in o(U \cup V)$. Außerdem ist infolge von $x \in \mathrm{fr}_{eX}(o(U))$ auch $x \in \overline{U}^{eX}$ und $x \notin o(U)$. Es muß dann auch $x \in \overline{V}^{eX}$ sein, denn sonst hätten wir eine Umgebung $W' \subset W$ von x mit $W' \cap V = \emptyset$ und $W' \cap \mathrm{fr}_X(U) = \emptyset$. Für diese Umgebung wäre also $W' \cap X \subset U$. Hieraus ginge im Widerspruch zur Voraussetzung $x \in o(U)$ hervor. Damit ist der Beweis beendet.

Damit haben wir die folgende Kennzeichnung.

Satz. *Es sei X eine Hausdorffscher Raum und $\mathfrak{B}$ eine offene additive π-Basis von X.*[3]) *Dann ist die zu $\mathfrak{B}$ gehörige H-abgeschlossene Erweiterung $\sigma_{\mathfrak{B}} X$ mit nulldimensional gelegenem Adjunkt die einzige H-abgeschlossene Erweiterung von X mit den Eigenschaften:*

1. *Die Erweiterung ist strikt in bezug auf die Basis $\mathfrak{B}$.*
2. *Die Erweiterung ist perfekt in bezug auf die Basis $\mathfrak{B}$.*

---

[3]) Die Additivitätsforderung an die π-Basis $\mathfrak{B}$ bedeutet keine Einschränkung, da jede H-abgeschlossene Erweiterung mit nulldimensional gelegenem Adjunkt durch eine additive π-Basis erzeugt wird.

3. *Jedes nirgends dichte Komplement (in X) einer Menge der offenen Basis $\mathfrak{B}$ ist auch abgeschlossen in bezug auf die Erweiterung.*

Beweis. Es sei HX eine H-abgeschlossene Erweiterung von X mit den 3 genannten Eigenschaften. Wir brauchen nur zu zeigen, daß für jedes $o(U)$ in bezug auf HX gilt:

$$\mathrm{fr}_X(U) = \mathrm{fr}_{HX}(o(U)).$$

Mit $U \in \mathfrak{B}$ ist auch $V := X - \overline{U}$ aus $\mathfrak{B}$. $\mathrm{fr}_X(U)$ ist nirgends dicht und das Komplement von $W = U \cup V$. Also haben wir gemäß der Voraussetzung $\mathrm{fr}_X(U) = HX - o(W)$. Wegen der Perfektheit der Erweiterung in bezug auf $\mathfrak{B}$ ist $o(W) = o(U) \cup o(V)$. Daraus geht $\mathrm{fr}_X(U) = \mathrm{fr}_{HX}(o(U))$ hervor.

3. Zwei von Banaschewski angegebene Erweiterungen

In diesem Abschnitt wollen wir darlegen, daß zwei von Banaschewski konstruierte Erweiterungen sich der Theorie der Erweiterungen mit nulldimensional gelegenem Adjunkt unterordnen.

Satz (Banaschewski [2]). *Es sei X ein Hausdorffscher nulldimensionaler Raum im Sinne von* $\mathrm{ind}\, X = 0$. *X läßt sich dann zu einem kompakten nulldimensionalen Hausdorffschen Raum erweitern. Unter allen nulldimensionalen Hausdorffschen Kompaktifizierungen von X gibt es eine größte ζX. Diese größte nulldimensionale Hausdorffsche Kompaktifizierung von X entsteht aus der Stone-Čech-Erweiterung βX durch Übergang zum Komponentenraum.*

Bei Banaschewski [2] wurde ζX durch Vervollständigung derjenigen präkompakten uniformen Struktur auf X erhalten, die als Basis die endlichen offen-abgeschlossenen Überdeckungen besitzt. Andere Arten der Erzeugung von ζX wären etwa die als Stonescher Darstellungsraum der Boole-Algebra der offen-abgeschlossenen Mengen von X oder die durch ein mit der Basis der offen-abgeschlossenen Mengen verbundenes finites Zerlegungsspektrum (vgl. [6]).

Satz. *Es sei X ein Hausdorffscher nulldimensionaler Raum im Sinne von* $\mathrm{ind}\, X = 0$. *Die größte nulldimensionale Hausdorffsche Kompaktifizierung ζX von X stimmt dann mit der Freudenthal-Erweiterung φX des Raumes X überein (als nulldimensionaler Raum ist ja X selbst lokal peripher kompakt).*

Beweis. Die Bestätigung der Behauptung erfolgt ganz mühelos. Nach Morita [16] ist für einen nulldimensionalen Raum X die Freudenthal-Erweiterung selbst nulldimensional, also gilt $\zeta X \geqq \varphi X$. ζX gehört andererseits zu den Erweiterungen mit nulldimensional gelegenem Adjenkt, also gilt auch $\zeta X \leqq \varphi X$. Auf andere Weise prüft man die Behauptung etwa so: ζX geht durch Vervollständigung der präkompakten uniformen Struktur hervor, die als Basis die endlichen offen-abgeschlossenen Überdeckungen hat. φX wiederum entsteht durch Vervollständigung der präkompakten uniformen Struktur, die als Basis die endlichen offenen peripher kompakten Überdeckungen besitzt. Beide Strukturen stimmen aber überein, da zu jeder Basisüberdeckung der letztgenannten Art eine Verfeinerung der erstgenannten Art existiert (vgl. [7]). Ein weiteres Beweisargument für $\varphi X = \zeta X$ steht mit der Einsicht bereit, daß ζX als Komponentenraum von βX eine perfekte Kompaktifizierung von X ist und φX die kleinste perfekte Kompaktifizierung von X darstellt (vgl. [21]).

Für Hausdorffsche semireguläre Räume X hat BANASCHEWSKI [3] eine im gewissen Sinne maximale semireguläre H-abgeschlossene Erweiterung konstruiert, diese Erweiterung wurde in [3] mit σX bezeichnet.

Satz (BANASCHEWSKI [3]). *Für jeden Hausdorffschen semiregulären Raum X gibt es eine H-abgeschlossene semireguläre Erweiterung σX von X mit der folgenden Eigenschaft: Jeder Filter aus X, der in σX konvergiert, konvergiert auch in jeder anderen semiregulären H-abgeschlossenen Erweiterung von X. Durch diese Eigenschaft ist σX (im wesentlichen) eindeutig bestimmt.*

Wir führen hierzu an den

Satz. *Für jeden Hausdorffschen semiregulären Raum X ist die von* BANASCHEWSKI *konstruierte H-abgeschlossene semireguläre Erweiterung σX mit der größten semiregulären H-abgeschlossenen Erweiterung von X identisch, die ein nulldimensional gelegenes Adjunkt hat.*

Das genannte σX stimmt mit der Fomin-Shanin-Erweiterung von X überein, die zu der aus allen regulär offenen Mengen bestehenden π-Basis gehört.

Man vergleiche hierüber auch die Bemerkung auf S. 380 unserer Arbeit [8].

Literatur

[1] P. S. ALEXANDROFF und W. J. PONOMAREW, Über bikompakte Erweiterungen topologischer Räume (russ.), Doklady Akad. Nauk SSSR **121** (1958), 575—578.

[2] B. BANASCHEWSKI, Über nulldimensionale Räume, Math. Nachr. **13** (1955), 129—140.

[3] B. BANASCHEWSKI, Hausdorffsch-minimale Erweiterungen von Räumen, Archiv Math. **12** (1961), 355—365.

[4] B. BANASCHEWSKI, On Wallman's method of compactification, Math. Nachr. **27** (1963), 105—114.

[5] R. M. BROOKS, On Wallman compactifications, Fund. Math. **60** (1967), 157—173.

[6] J. FLACHSMEYER, Zur Spektralentwicklung topologischer Räume, Math. Annalen **144** (1961), 253—274.

[7] J. FLACHSMEYER, Nulldimensionale Räume, Proc. First Symposium on General Topology, Prague 1961, S. 152—154.

[8] J. FLACHSMEYER, Zur Theorie der H-abgeschlossenen Erweiterungen, Math. Z. **94** (1966), 349—381.

[9] S. FOMIN, Extension of topological spaces, Ann. Math. **44** (1943), 471—480.

[10] H. FREUDENTHAL, Über die Enden topologischer Räume und Gruppen, Math. Z. **33** (1931), 692—713.

[11] H. FREUDENTHAL, Neuaufbau der Endentheorie, Ann. Math. **43** (1942), 261—279.

[12] H. FREUDENTHAL, Kompaktifizierungen und Bikompaktifizierungen, Indagationes Math. **13** (1951), 184—192.

[13] O. FRINK, Compactification and semi-normal spaces, Amer. J. Math. **86** (1964), 602—607.

[14] J. DE GROOT, Topologische Studien, Dissertation, Groningen 1942.

[15] J. R. ISBELL, Uniform spaces, Math. Surveys No. 12, Amer. Math. Soc. 1964.

[16] K. MORITA, On bicompactification of semicompact spaces, Sci. Rep., Tokyo, Bunrika Daigaku, **4** (1952), 222—229.

[17] O. NJÅSTAD, On Wallman-type compactifications, Math. Z. **91** (1967), 267—276.

[18] W. RINOW, Perfekte lokal zusammenhängende Kompaktifizierungen und Primendentheorie, Math. Z. **84** (1964), 294—304.

[19] N. A. SHANIN, On special extensions of topological spaces, Doklady Akad. Nauk SSSR **38** (1943), 6—9.

[20] N. A. SHANIN, On separation in topological spaces, Doklady Akad. Nauk SSSR **38** (1943), 110—113.
[21] E. G. SKLJARENKO, Einige Fragen der Theorie der bikompakten Erweiterungen (russ.), Izv. Nauk SSSR, Ser. Mat., **26** (1952), 427—452.
[22] E. G. SKLJARENKO, Über perfekte bikompakte Erweiterungen (russ.), Doklady Akad. Nauk SSSR **146** (1962), 1031—1034.
[23] JU. M. SMIRNOV, Ein Beispiel eines vollständig regulären Raumes, der ein nulldimensionales Stone-Čech-Adjunkt hat, ohne lokal peripher kompakt zu sein (russ.), Doklady Akad. Nauk SSSR **120** (1958), 1204—1206.
[24] L. ZIPPIN, On semicompact spaces, Amer. J. Math. **57** (1935), 327—341.

ON EXTENSIONS OF HYPERSPACES

J. FLACHSMEYER and H. POPPE (Greifswald)

Let X be a topological space; then by a hyperspace of X we understand as usual a space, whose points are closed subsets of X. Such hyperspaces have been considered by several authors; we mention some few: VIETORIS [12], BORSUK and MAZURKIEWICZ [1], KURATOWSKI [6], KELLEY [5], MICHAEL [8], PONOMAREV [9], IVANOVA [4], ISBELL [3], FLACHSMEYER [2], POPPE [10], [11], MARJANOVIĆ [7].

In our paper we want to have a look to extensions of hyperspaces determined by extensions of the origin space.

Lemma 1. *Let X be an arbitrary topological space with the system $\mathfrak{F}(X)$ of all closed subsets and bX an arbitrary extension of X. We consider a subsystem $\mathfrak{U}(X)$ of $\mathfrak{F}(X)$. Let φ be the (one-to-one) map $F \rightsquigarrow \overline{F}^{bX}$ from $\mathfrak{U}(X)$ into $\mathfrak{F}(bX)$. Then holds:*

1. *If $\mathfrak{U}(X)$ contains the empty set and $\mathfrak{U}(X)$ is closed with respect to finite joins, then the system $\{\langle U\rangle \mid U \in \mathfrak{U}(X)\}$, where $\langle U\rangle = \{F \mid F \in \mathfrak{F}(X)$ and $F \cap U = \emptyset\}$ forms an open base for a topology of $\mathfrak{F}(X)$, which we denote by $\tau_{\mathfrak{U}}$.*[1]
2. *If $U \cap V = \emptyset$ for $U, V \in \mathfrak{U}(X)$ implies $\overline{U}^{bX} \cap \overline{V}^{bX} = \emptyset$, then the map φ^{-1}: $(\varphi(\mathfrak{U}(X)), \tau_{\mathfrak{F}(bX)}) \rightarrow (\mathfrak{U}(X), \tau_{\mathfrak{U}})$ is continuous.*
3. *If $U \in \mathfrak{U}(X)$, $F \in \mathfrak{F}(bX)$ and $\overline{U}^{bX} \cap F = \emptyset$ implies the existence of an element $V \in \mathfrak{U}(X)$ with $F \subset \overline{V}^{bX}$ and $\overline{V}^{bX} \cap \overline{U}^{bX} = \emptyset$ and if the assumption of the statement 2) is fulfilled, then the map φ: $(\mathfrak{U}(X), \tau_{\mathfrak{U}}) \rightarrow (\mathfrak{F}(bX), \tau_{\mathfrak{F}(bX)})$ is continuous.*
4. *For the density of $\varphi(\mathfrak{U}(X))$ in the hyperspace $(\mathfrak{F}(bX), \tau_{\mathfrak{F}(bX)} \vee \tau_l)$*[2] *it is sufficient, that at least one of the following two conditions is fulfilled:*
   a) *bX is a regular space and for each open $G \subset X$, $G \neq \emptyset$, there exists a non-empty $U \in \mathfrak{U}(X)$ with $U \subset G$.*
   b) *bX is a T_1-space and $\mathfrak{U}(X)$ contains all finite sets of X.*

Proof.

1. We have $\langle U\rangle \cap \langle V\rangle = \langle U \cup V\rangle$ and hence by the assumptions the system $\{\langle U\rangle \mid U \in \mathfrak{U}(X)\}$ is not only a subbase, but already a base for $\tau_{\mathfrak{U}}$.

---

[1]) For the case $\mathfrak{U}(X) = \mathfrak{F}(X)$ this topology is well known and is due to A. N. TYCHONOV (see [2]).

[2]) $\tau_{\mathfrak{F}(X)} \vee \tau_l$ is the Vietoris-topology in the sense of MICHAEL [8]; see also [2].

2. φ^{-1} is defined by $\overline{V}^{bX} \rightsquigarrow V$ for $V \in \mathfrak{U}(X)$. For an element $\langle U \rangle$, $U \in \mathfrak{U}(X)$ of the open base of $\tau_{\mathfrak{U}}$ for $\mathfrak{U}(X)$ we have to show the openess of $\{\overline{V}^{bX} \mid V \in \langle U \rangle\}$ in $\varphi(\mathfrak{U}(X))$. $V \in \langle U \rangle$ means $V \in \mathfrak{U}(X)$ and $V \cap U = \emptyset$. From the assumption we obtain $\{\overline{V}^{bX} \mid V \in \langle U \rangle\} = \langle \overline{U}^{bX} \rangle$ (clearly $\langle \overline{U}^{bX} \rangle$ restricted to $\varphi(\mathfrak{U}(X))$).
3. For a $U \in \mathfrak{U}(X)$ and a given neighborhood $\langle F \rangle$, $F \in \mathfrak{F}(bX)$, of $\overline{U}^{bX}$ we must find a neighborhood $\langle V \rangle$, $V \in \mathfrak{U}(X)$, of U, such that $\varphi(\langle V \rangle) \subset \langle F \rangle$. By the assumption exists a $V \in \mathfrak{U}(X)$ with $F \subset \overline{V}^{bX}$ and $\overline{V}^{bX} \cap \overline{U}^{bX} = \emptyset$. This V is the desired one.
4. a) Let $\langle F \rangle \cap \,)G_1(\cap \ldots \cap)G_n($ an open nonempty base element of the topology $\tau_{\mathfrak{F}(bX)} \vee \tau_l$,[3]) where $F \in \mathfrak{F}(bX)$ and $G_1, \ldots, G_n$ open sets in bX. We must find a $U \in \mathfrak{U}(X)$ with $\overline{U}^{bX} \in \langle F \rangle \cap \,)G_1(\cap \ldots \cap)G_n($. Because $\langle F \rangle \cap \,)G_1(\cap \ldots \cap)G_n($ is not empty and the extension space is regular we can choose in each G_i a closed neighborhood V_i, which is disjoint to F. By assumption we find nonempty elements $U_i \in \mathfrak{U}(X)$ such that $U_i \subset \subset V_i \cap X$. Then $U = U_1 \cup \ldots \cup U_n$ is the desired element of $\mathfrak{U}(X)$.

   b) For a proof of b) we choose in $G_i - F$ points x_i of X then $U = \{x_1, \ldots, x_n\}$ is the desired element of $\mathfrak{U}(X)$.

Lemma 2. *Let X be an arbitrary topological space and $\mathfrak{U}(X)$ a subsystem of $\mathfrak{F}(X)$. Let $\mathfrak{U}(X)$ and bX be such that*

a) *the assumptions of the statements* 1), 2), 3), 4a), *or*

b) *the assumptions of the statements* 1), 2), 3), 4b) *of lemma* 1 *are fulfilled.*

Then the map φ: $(\mathfrak{U}(X), \tau_{\mathfrak{U}} \vee \tau_l) \to (\mathfrak{F}(bX), \tau_{\mathfrak{F}(bX)} \vee \tau_l)$ is a topological dense imbedding.

Proof. By lemma 1 we have only to show, that the maps φ and φ^{-1} are also continuous with respect to the topology τ_l in $\mathfrak{U}(X)$ and τ_l in $\mathfrak{F}(bX)$. For this let be G an open nonempty set in X. Then exists an open set H in bX such that $H \cap X = G$. Now for $U \in \mathfrak{U}(X)$, $U \cap G \neq \emptyset$ is equivalent to $\overline{U}^{bX} \cap H \neq \emptyset$. Therefore the subbase elements for the topology τ_l in $\mathfrak{U}(X)$ resp. τ_l in $\mathfrak{F}(bX)$, defined by G resp. H correspond each to another.

With help of our lemmas we now are able to generalize the main theorem of a paper by V. M. IVANOVA [4].

Theorem. *Let X be a T_1-space and $\mathfrak{U}(X)$ a Wallman-Shanin base for the closed subsets of X, containing all one-point sets of X, and bX the corresponding Wallman-Shanin compactification of X. Then by the map φ: U, $U \in \mathfrak{U}(X)$, $\rightsquigarrow \overline{U}^{bX}$ we get a compactification of the hyperspace $(\mathfrak{U}(X), \tau_{\mathfrak{U}} \vee \tau_l)$ with the extension space $(\mathfrak{F}(bX), \tau_{\mathfrak{F}(bX)} \vee \tau_l)$. This compactification is a Wallman-Shanin compactification of $(\mathfrak{U}(X), \tau_{\mathfrak{U}} \vee \tau_l)$ with respect to the Wallman-Shanin base, generated as a lattice of closed sets by sets of the form $\mathfrak{A}(U) = \{V \mid V \in \mathfrak{U}(X), V \subset U\}$ and $\mathfrak{B}(U) = \{V \mid V \in \mathfrak{U}(X), V \cap U \neq \emptyset\}$, when U runs over $\mathfrak{A}(X)$.*

Proof. The Wallman-Shanin compactification bX of the space X with the base $\mathfrak{U}(X)$ is characterized as a T_1-compactification with the following properties:

(1) the closures of the $U \in \mathfrak{U}(X)$ form a closed base of bX,

(2) $\overline{U_1 \cap \ldots \cap U_n}^{bX} = \overline{U}_1^{bX} \cap \ldots \cap \overline{U}_n^{bX}$.

---

[3]) See footnote [2]).

It can be easily seen, that the conditions 1), 2), 3), 4b) of lemma 1 are fulfilled, namely:

1. The Wallman-Shanin base is by definition closed with respect to finite joins and meets.

2. This follows from property (2) of bX.

3. Let be $F \in \mathfrak{F}(bX)$ and $U \in \mathfrak{U}(X)$ with $F \cap \overline{U}^{bX} = \emptyset$; then by property (1) and the compactness of bX there exists a $V \in \mathfrak{U}(X)$ with $F \subset \overline{V}^{bX}$ and $\overline{V}^{bX} \cap \overline{U}^{bX} = \emptyset$.

4. This follows from the assumption that $\mathfrak{U}(X)$ contains all one-point sets.

By lemma 2 and a well-known theorem of Vietoris about the compactness of the topology $\tau_{\mathfrak{F}(bX)} \vee \tau_l$ it follows that $(\mathfrak{F}(bX), \tau_{\mathfrak{F}(bX)} \vee \tau_l)$ is indeed a T_1-compactification of $(\mathfrak{U}(X), \tau_{\mathfrak{U}} \vee \tau_l)$.

For the Vietoris-topology $\tau_{\mathfrak{F}(bX)} \vee \tau_l$ the sets $\mathfrak{A}(F)$ and $\mathfrak{B}(F)$, when F runs over $\mathfrak{F}(bX)$, form a closed subbase, naturally by $\mathfrak{A}(F)$ and $\mathfrak{B}(F)$ we mean the sets $\{W \in \in \mathfrak{F}(bX) \mid W \subset F\}$ and $\{W \in \mathfrak{F}(bX) \mid W \cap F \neq \emptyset\}$: $\mathfrak{F}(bX) - \mathfrak{A}(F) =)\, bX - F($, $\mathfrak{F}(bX) - \mathfrak{B}(F) = \langle F \rangle$. Because $\mathfrak{A}(F) = \bigcap \{\mathfrak{A}(\overline{U}) \mid U \in \mathfrak{U}(X),\ F \subset \overline{U}]$ and $\mathfrak{B}(F) = \bigcap \{\mathfrak{B}(\overline{U}) \mid U \in \mathfrak{U}(X), F \subset \overline{U}\}$ even the sets $A(\overline{U})$, $\mathfrak{B}(\overline{U})$, $U \in \mathfrak{U}(X)$ form a closed subbase of $\tau_{\mathfrak{F}(bX)}) \vee \tau_l$. Now it is enough to proof that $\overline{\varphi(\mathfrak{A}(U_0)) \cap \bigcap_{i=1}^{n} \varphi\ )\mathfrak{B}(U_i))}^{\mathfrak{F}(bX)}$ $= \mathfrak{A}(\overline{U}_0{}^{bX}) \cap \bigcap_{i=1}^{n} \mathfrak{B}(\overline{U}_i{}^{bX}))$: because $\varphi(\mathfrak{A}(U_0)) \subset \mathfrak{A}(\overline{U}_0{}^{bX})$ and $\varphi(\mathfrak{B}(U_i)) \subset \mathfrak{B}(\overline{U}_i{}^{bX})$ the proof reduces to the verification of the inclusion $\mathfrak{A}(\overline{U}_0{}^{bX}) \cap \bigcap_{i=1}^{n} \mathfrak{B}(U_i{}^{bX}) \subset$ $\subset \overline{\varphi(\mathfrak{A}(U_0)) \cap \bigcap_{i=1}^{n} (\varphi \mathfrak{B}(U_i))}^{\mathfrak{F}(bX)}$: let $F_0 \neq \emptyset$ be an element of the left side, this means $F_0 \subset \overline{U}_0{}^{bX}$ and $F_0 \cap \overline{U}_i{}^{bX} \neq \emptyset$ for all i, and let be $\langle H \rangle \ \cap)\ O_1 (\cap \ldots \cap)\ O_m($; $H \in \mathfrak{F}(bX)$, O_j open in bX, an arbitrary neighborhood of F_0. Without loss of generality we may assume that $H \cap O_j = \emptyset$ for all j. We have $F_0 \cap H = \emptyset$, $F_0 \cap O_j \neq \emptyset$ for all j and we must construct a $U \in \mathfrak{U}(X)$ with the following properties:

1. $\overline{U}^{bX} \cap H = \emptyset$,
2. $\overline{U}^{bX} \cap O_j \neq \emptyset$ for all j,
3. $U \subset U_0$,
4. $U \cap U_i \neq \emptyset$ for all i.

From $F_0 \subset \overline{U}_0{}^{bX}$ and $F_0 \cap O_j \neq \emptyset$ we have $O_j \cap \overline{U}_0{}^{bX} \neq \emptyset$ and hence $O_j \cap U_0 \neq \emptyset$ too; we choose elements $x_j \in O_j \cap U_0$. It is $F_0 = \bigcap \{\overline{V}^{bX} \mid V \in \mathfrak{U}(X)$ and $\overline{V} \supset F_0\}$ and $H \cap F_0 = \emptyset$; therefore it exists a $V \in \mathfrak{U}(X)$ with $F_0 \subset \overline{V}^{bX}$ and $\overline{V}^{bX} \cap H = \emptyset$. We put $U = (V \cap U_0) \cup \{x_1, \ldots, x_n\}$. U is the desired element, because $\overline{U}^{bX} = (\overline{V}^{bX} \cap \overline{U}_0{}^{bX}) \cup \{x_1, \ldots, x_n\}$.

References

[1] K. Borsuk et S. Mazurkiewicz, Sur l'hyperespace d'un continu, C. R. Soc. Sci. Varsovie **24** (1931), 149—152.

[2] J. Flachsmeyer, Verschiedene Topologisierungen im Raum der abgeschlossenen Mengen, Math. Nachr. **26** (1963/64), 231—337.

[3] J. R. ISBELL, Supercomplete spaces, Pacific J. Math. **12** (1962), 287—290.
[4] V. M. IVANOVA, Der Raum der abgeschlossenen Teilmengen von bikompakten Erweiterungen (russ.), Mat. Sbornik (N. S.) **50** (1960), 91—100.
[5] J. L. KELLEY, Hyperspace of a continuum, Trans. Amer. Math. Soc. **52** (1942), 23—36.
[6] C. KURATOWSKI, Topologie I, II, Warszawa 1952.
[7] M. MARJANOVIC, Topologies on collections of closed subsets, Publ. Inst. Math. (N. S.) **6** (1966), 125—130.
[8] E. MICHAEL, Topologies on spaces of subsets, Trans. Amer. Math. Soc. **71** (1951), 152—182.
[9] V. I. PONOMAREV, Ein neuer Raum abgeschlossener Mengen und mehrdeutige Abbildungen (russ.), Doklady Akad. Nauk SSSR **118** (1958), 1081—1084.
[10] H. POPPE, Eine Bemerkung über Trennungsaxiome in Räumen von abgeschlossenen Teilmengen topologischer Räume, Archiv Math. **16** (1965), 197—199.
[11] H. POPPE, Einige Bemerkungen über den Raum der abgeschlossenen Mengen, Fund. Mat. **59** (1966), 159—169.
[12] L. VIETORIS, Bereiche zweiter Ordnung, Monatshefte Math. Phys. **33** (1923), 49—62.

ON COMPACTNESS AND PROJECTIONS

ISIDORE FLEISCHER (New York, N.Y./U.S.A.)
and S. P. FRANKLIN (Pittsburgh, Pa./U.S.A.)

0. It is a well known and frequently useful fact that whenever a topological space X is compact, the projection π of $X \times Y$ on any space Y is a closed mapping ([1], p. 227). (The converse, although not so well known is also true [9].) Analogues of this theorem concerning countable compactness, sequential compactness, m-compactness, etc., fairly abound in the literature ([5], [6], [7], [10], etc). In this note, using convergence as our basic concept, we propose to derive improvements and extensions of many of these results, as well as a number of related facts, in a somewhat uniform manner.

Whenever X is countably compact and Y is a sequential space[1], *π is closed*[2]. Following ISIWATA [7], take $\mathfrak{R}$ to be the class of spaces Y such that π is closed for each countably compact X.[3]) As ISIWATA points out, each subspace and each closed continuous image of a space in $\mathfrak{R}$ is again in $\mathfrak{R}$. Hence *every subspace of a sequential space is in* $\mathfrak{R}$. (We are unable to decide whether every space in $\mathfrak{R}$ is a subspace of a sequential space.) As an example of a space not in $\mathfrak{R}$, take a point $p \in \beta \boldsymbol{N} \setminus \boldsymbol{N}$, where $\beta \boldsymbol{N}$ is the Stone-Čech compactification of the natural numbers, and consider $\boldsymbol{N} \cup \{p\}$ as a subspace of $\beta \boldsymbol{N}$. Then $\beta \boldsymbol{N} \setminus \{p\}$ is countably compact, but the projection of $(\beta \boldsymbol{N} \setminus \{p\}) \times (\boldsymbol{N} \cup \{p\})$ on $\boldsymbol{N} \cup \{p\}$ is not closed. Thus $N \cup \{p\}$ does not belong to $\mathfrak{R}$.[4]) It follows immediately that no superset of $\boldsymbol{N} \cup \{p\}$ belongs to $\mathfrak{R}$ and, in particular $\beta \boldsymbol{N} \notin \mathfrak{R}$ (see [7], 2.3).

Letting S_1 be a space consisting of a convergent sequence and its limit, i.e., homeomorphic to the subset $\{0\} \cup \{1/n \mid n \in \boldsymbol{N}\}$ of the real line, the following is a strong converse to the first assertion of the previous paragraph: *if the projection of $X \times S_1$ on S_1 is closed, then X is countably compact.* Let us denote by $\mathfrak{T}$ the class of spaces Y

---

[1]) Call a set *sequentially* open if no sequence outside the set converges to a point of the set. A space is *sequential* if every sequentially open subset is open [2].

[2]) This result improves Lemma 1.1 of [7] and one direction of each of Corollary 1.7 of [5], Corollary 2 of [6], and Theorem 1 of [10].

[3]) Let us note here that our $\mathfrak{R}$ is apparently slightly different from ISIWATA's since he deals only with completely regular spaces. The difference is real, since countably compact subsets of spaces in his $\mathfrak{R}$ are closed ([7], Lemma 1.2) while countably compact subsets of a sequential space are closed iff sequential limits are unique ([3], Prop. 5.4).

[4]) LYNN IMLER points out that this improves an unpublished result of E. MICHAEL which asserts that $\boldsymbol{N} \cup \{p\}$ cannot be embedded in any *Hausdorff* sequential space. Since it is not in $\mathfrak{R}$ our result implies it is not a subspace of *any* sequential space.

such that X is countably compact whenever the projection of $X \times Y$ on Y is closed. Hanai has shown that every space which is not a P-space[5]) belongs to $\mathfrak{T}$ ([5], Theorem 4). It follows immediately that $S_1 \in \mathfrak{T}$. Conversely, *no P-space belongs to* $\mathfrak{T}$, so that $\mathfrak{T}$ is precisely the complement of the class of P-spaces. Also, *no non-discrete P-space belongs to* $\mathfrak{N}$, from which it follows that the *non-discrete spaces in* $\mathfrak{N}$ *also belong to* $\mathfrak{T}$. However, $\boldsymbol{N} \cup \{p\}$, since it is not a *P-space* belongs to $\mathfrak{T}$ but not to $\mathfrak{N}$. Every non-discrete *P-space* belongs to neither $\mathfrak{N}$ nor $\mathfrak{T}$.

Since sequential compactness implies countable compactness and every Fréchet space[6]) is sequential, it follows that whenever X is sequentially compact and Y is a Fréchet space, π is closed. Conversely *if the projection of* $X \times S_1$ *on* S_1 *is closed, then* X *is sequentially compact.*[7]) These results suggest that classes $\mathfrak{N}_s$ and $\mathfrak{T}_s$ be defined bearing the same relation to sequential compactness as $\mathfrak{N}$ and $\mathfrak{T}$ do to countable compactness. Since there are compact spaces which are not sequentially compact (for example $\beta \boldsymbol{N}$), $\mathfrak{T}_s$ is empty. Since sequential compactness implies countable compactness, $\mathfrak{N}_s$ contains $\mathfrak{N}$. We conjecture that the inclusion is proper.

It is easily seen that the corresponding classes, $\mathfrak{N}_c$ and $\mathfrak{T}_c$, for compactness are respectively all spaces and empty. Given Y, let X be the set of ordinals less than the initial ordinal of cardinality $2^{\overline{\overline{X}}}$. X is not compact but the projection of $X \times Y$ on Y is closed.

The unproved assertions of the preceeding paragraphs follow readily from the more general considerations which are sketched out in the next section.

1. X and Y are topological spaces; π is the projection of $X \times Y$ on Y; D and E are classes of nets into X, Y or $X \times Y$, closed under composition with and cancellation of maps between these spaces.

The following are equivalent: (i) For every $S \subseteq X \times Y$, y is a limit of an E-net in $\pi(S)$ only if $\pi^{-1}(Y)$ contains a limit of a D-net in S. (ii) For every (not necessarily continuous) function from Y to X, the range of every convergent E-net in Y contains a D-net converging to the same limit whose image under f converges in X.

Remarks. (i) implies (iii): If S contains all limits of its D-nets, $\pi(S)$ will contain all limits of its E-nets. Conversely, if the adjunction of all D-limits to sets is an idempotent closure operator in $X \times Y$ (for example, if D is closed under iteration in the sense of the construction of [8], p. 69), then (iii) implies (i).

(ii) follows for every Y if every E-net in X has a convergent D-subnet. Conversely, this holds for X if it satisfies (ii) with any class of Y containing for each member of E a point whose neighborhood filter induces on the range of some one-to-one E-net with the same domain exactly the image of the filter of final subsets. If the ranges of these one-to-one nets in the discrete topology (or, more generally, in any for which only the eventually constant D-nets converge) along with their limits actually appear among the Y, then (ii) may be weakened to (iii). (For X T_1, take for S the range of the product E-net; in general, take the union of its point-closures.)

We have use for two special cases: D the class of nets and E the class of sequences; and $D = E$ the class of sequences. We obtain respectively:

For every function from Y to X, every convergent sequence in Y has a subsequence whose image clusters in X iff π sends sequential cluster points onto sequential limits

---

[5]) A *P-space* is one in which every F_σ is closed ([4], p. 62).

[6]) A space is a *Fréchet* space if the closure of each of its subsets may be obtained by taking the limits of the sequences in the subset (see [2]). This is precisely the condition imposed by Isiwata in Lemma 1.1 of [7].

[7]) This strengthens the other direction of Theorem 1 of [10] (see footnote [2])).

iff π sends sets containing their sequential cluster points onto sets containing their sequential limits. If X is countably compact this holds for every Y; conversely if it holds for some Y containing S_1, X is countably compact.

For every function from Y to X, every convergent sequence in Y has a subsequence whose image converges in X iff π sends sequential limits onto sequential limits. If X is sequentially compact this holds for every Y; conversely if it holds for some Y containing S_1, X is sequentially compact; if, moreover, it holds for $Y = S_1$, then X is sequentially compact if π only sends sets containing their sequential limits onto sets containing their sequential limits.[8])

For the remainder of the paper we deal only with $D = E =$ all directed sets with maps. (i) is equivalent to (iii) which says that π is closed; they hold for all Y iff X is compact. We shall, however, want to take X countably compact and inquire about the corresponding Y.

One result follows from what we have shown so far: If π is closed, it preserves closures of countable sets, hence sends sets containing sequential cluster points on sets containing sequential limits. Thus if Y contains S_1, π closed implies X countably compact. The implication already holds if Y only contains a nonclosed F_σ (Hanai [5]); and for no other Y. We shall show this in a somewhat more general setting: If Y contains a non-closed union of $\aleph$ closed sets, then π closed implies that X contains no locally finite collection of $\aleph$ closed sets (else the union of the products of paired closed sets in X and Y under any one-to-one pairing would be a closed set with a non-closed projection); conversely, if every $\aleph$ closed subsets of Y have a closed union, then with X any T_1 space of cardinality at most $\aleph$, π is closed.[9]) Similarly, if Y contains an ascending well-ordered chain of closed subsets, with each set indexed by a limit ordinal the union of those preceding, which is not closed, and if X contains a corresponding descending chain of closed sets with empty intersection, then the obvious union in the product is a closed set whose projection is not closed; in particular, if Y is a nondiscrete P-space and X a suitable transfinite ordinal, π is not closed.

References

[1] J. Dugundji, Topology, Boston 1966.
[2] S. P. Franklin, Spaces in which sequences suffice, Fund. Math. **57** (1965), 107—116.
[3] S. P. Franklin, Spaces in which sequences suffice II, Fund. Math. **61** (1967), 51—56.
[4] L. Gillman and M. Jerison, Rings of Continuous Functions, Princeton 1960.
[5] S. Hanai, Inverse images of closed mappings I, Proc. Japan Acad. **37** (1961), 298—301.
[6] S. Hanai, Inverse images of closed mappings II, Proc. Japan Acad. **37** (1961), 302—304.
[7] T. Isiwata, Normality and perfect mappings, Proc. Japan Acad. **39** (1963), 95—97.
[8] J. L. Kelley, General Topology, Princeton 1955.
[9] S. Mrowka, Compactness and Product Spaces, Coll. Math. **7** (1959), 19—22.
[10] S. B. Nadler, Jr., A note on projections and compactness, Amer. Math. Monthly **73** (1966), 275—276.

---

[8]) One might in the interests of symmetry, wish to consider also π sending sequential cluster points onto sequential cluster points. This leads to a new kind of compactness implied by ordinary and implying countable; and properly as shown by ω_1 and $\beta\boldsymbol{N} \setminus \{p\}$; not implying sequential (else ordinary compactness would) and, we suppose, not implied by it, although we have no counterexample.

[9]) The authors wish to express their thanks to Renababy for the delectable Japanese meal which inspired this observation.

ON SEPARABLE AND NON-SEPARABLE DESCRIPTIVE THEORY

ZDENĚK FROLÍK (Praha)

In separable theory every metrizable "descriptive set" is separable. A survey of a separable theory of analytic and Borel-like sets is given in [1]. Here we want to show how to apply the separable theory described in [1] to a non-separable theory of SOUSLIN, BOREL and distinguishable sets.

In general, if we are given, say, absolute D-sets in a separable theory, we define (in the corresponding non-separable theory) absolute D-sets to be the sets of the form $Y = Z \cap X$ in βY with X an absolute D-set in the separable theory, and Z an absolute G_δ. This requires a separable theory in the class of all uniformizable spaces even if we are only interested in the class of all metrizable spaces. On the other hand, internal characterizations of separable absolute Borel set by means of a certain uniformity complete with respect to the topology of the set go over. Unfortunately, a possibility of application of the elegant separable theory based on multivalued mappings, see [1], is not clear.

There is another way. In separable theory of analytic, Borel-like and distinguishable sets we start with closed (in fact, compact) sets; it is natural to start with open sets in non-separable theory. Both ways are equivalent for metrizable spaces. As concerns the second way, very important is a lemma which describes the sets derived from a given collection of sets by means of countable intersections and unions in terms of the Souslin operation, see [2], Lemma 9, or [3], Lemma 3.

The main difficulties in non-separable theory come from the fact that the role of compactness is indirect and more subtile.

For details see [2] and [3].

References

[1] Z. FROLÍK, Structures in descriptive theory, Proc. Topological Conference in Tempe, Arizona, 1967.

[2] Z. FROLÍK, On absolute Borel and Souslin sets (submitted to Pacific J. Math.).

[3] Z. FROLÍK, A note on $C(P)$ and Baire sets in compact and metrizable spaces, Bull. Acad. Polon. Sci. A **15** (1967), 779–784.

FIXED POINTS OF MAPPINGS OF βM

ZDENĚK FROLÍK (Praha)

The following two Theorems are the main author's results in his paper "On fixed points of maps of βM" (to appear in Bull. Amer. Math. Soc.):

Theorem A. *If M is a discrete space, f is a homeomorphism of βM into itself, and if P_k is the set of all k-periodic points of f, then*

$$P_k = \mathrm{cl}(M \cap P_k).$$

Theorem B. *If X is a Čech-Stone compactification of a discrete space, and if x is a fixed point of a continuous mapping of X into itself then each neighborhood of x contains an f-invariant closed-open neighborhood of x.*

For Čech-Stone compactifications of countable spaces Theorem B has been published in [1] and applied to a simple proof (independent of the continuum hypothesis) of non-homogeneity of $\beta N - N$.

Added in proof. A proof, independent of the continuum hypothesis, of non-homogeneity of $\beta X - X$ for any non-pseudocompact X is given in the author's note "Non-homogeneity of $\beta X - X$" (to appear in Comment. Math. Univ. Carolinae 8, 4).

It should be remarked that Theorem B holds for any extremally disconnected space P, and Theorem A is true for any compact extremally disconnected space (asserting that P_k is both closed and open). Non-homogeneity problems for closed sets in extremally disconnected compact spaces will be discussed elsewhere.

References

[1] Z. FROLÍK, Types of ultrafilters on countable sets, Proc. Second Symposium on General Topology, Prague 1966, pp. 142—143.

EXTREMAL LENGTH AND KURAMOCHI BOUNDARY

TATSUO FUJI'I'E (Kyoto)

1. Preliminary

On a Riemann surface R we consider a family Γ of locally rectifiable curves[1]) c, and a class Φ of non negative covariants ϱ, which satisfy $\iint_R \varrho^2\, dx\, dy \leqq 1$ and for which $\int_c \varrho\, ds$ are defined ($\leqq \infty$) for every curve c of Γ. According to J. JENKINS, we define the extremal length λ_Γ of the family Γ as $\left(\sup_{\varrho \in \Phi} \inf_{c \in \Gamma} \int_c \varrho\, ds\right)^2$, and call each ϱ of Φ admissible for the problem of the extremal length λ_Γ.

Let R be an open Riemann surface and K be a compact disk in R. KURAMOCHI [3] constructed a function $N(z, p)$, named N-Green's function, on $R - K$ as following. Let $\{R_n\}$ be a regular exhaustion of R such that $R_1 \supset K$, and $N_n(z, p)$ be a harmonic function of z in $R_n - K - p$ $(p \in R_n - K)$ which satisfies the following conditions.

(1) $N_n(z, p) + \log |z - p|$ is harmonic in a neighborhood of p.

(2) $N_n(z, p)$ is continuous and equals zero on the boundary ∂K of K.

(3) The normal derivative $\dfrac{\partial N_n(z,p)}{\partial n} = 0$ on ∂R_n.

The sequence $\{N_n(z, p)\}$ converges uniformly on every compact set in $R - K$. $N(z, p)$ is defined as the limit function of $N_n(z, p)$. Using this function, KURAMOCHI compactified R by the method of R. S. MARTIN. That is, a sequence $\{p_i\}$ of points in $R - K$ having no accumulation point in $R - K$, for which the corresponding $\{N(z, p_i)\}$ converges to a harmonic function, is called fundamental. Two fundamental sequences are called equivalent if their corresponding $N(z, p)$'s have the same limit. The class of all fundamental sequences equivalent to a given one determines an ideal boundary point of R. The set of all such ideal boundary points is called Kuramochi boundary and denoted by Δ. We put $R^* = R \cup \Delta$, then R^* is a compact metric space.

Since the function $N(z, p)$ has a finite Dirichlet integral $D(N(z, p))$ over $R - K$ outside a neighborhood V of the pole p of $N(z, p)$, $|\text{grad}\, N(z, p)|/\sqrt{D(N(z, p))}$ is admissible for the problem of extremal length of a family of locally rectifiable curves in $R - K - V$. Let Σ denote a family of curves which start from inner points of R

---

[1]) In this report all curves are assumed to be locally rectifiable.

and tend to the ideal boundary and Σ_0 denote the subfamily of Σ each curve of which does not converge to any point of Kuramochi boundary. From the definition, $N(z, p) = N(p, z)$ for z and p in $R - K$. And along each curve of Σ_0 the function $N(p, z)$ has not a limit. So every curve of Σ_0 has infinite length by the metric $|\mathrm{grad}\, N(p, z)| / \sqrt{D(N(z, p))}$. So we have the following theorem.

Theorem [4], [5], [2]. *The extremal length of Σ_0 is infinite.*

Theory of potentials with the kernel $N(z, p)$ are developed on R^*, and the fine topology is defined on R^* in addition to the original one [1], [3].

2. Kuramochi capacity and extremal length

Kuramochi capacity of a closed set A of R^* is defined as following. Let $\{A_n\}$ be a sequence of neighborhoods of A and $\{R_n\}$ be a regular exhaustion of R. Let ω_{nm} be a continuous superharmonic function in $R_m - K$ such that

(1) $\omega_{nm}(z) = 1$ on $A_n \cap R_m$ and $\omega_{nm}(z) = 0$ on ∂K,

(2) $\omega_{nm}(z)$ is harmonic in $R_m - \bar{A}_n - K$,

(3) $\dfrac{\partial \omega_{nm}(z)}{\partial n} = 0$ on $\partial R_m - \bar{A}_n$ ($\bar{A}_n$ is the closure of A_n in R).

$\{\omega_{nm}\}_m$ converges uniformly on every compact set in $R - \bar{A}_n - K$ and we denote the limit function by $\omega_n(z)$. $\{\omega_n(z)\}$ converges uniformly on every compact set to a harmonic function $\omega_A(z)$ (may be zero) in $R - K$. $\omega_A(z)$ is called an equilibrium potential of A. This is the same as the equilibrium potential constructed by C. CONSTANTINESCU and A. CORNEA [1]. Dirichlet integral $D(\omega_A)$ of $\omega_A(z)$ over $R - K$ is finite and it is called Kuramochi capacity of the set A. Here, we consider the extremal length λ_A of the family of curves which start from points of K and tend to A. Then, we have the following theorem.

Theorem. $1/\lambda_A = D(\omega_A)$.

Remark. If we define the equilibrium potential ω_A' and the extremal length λ_A' with respect to a sequence of fine neighborhoods of A in the same way as ω_A and λ_A, then, we have $\omega_A' = \omega_A$ and $\lambda_A' = \lambda_A$.

3. Analytic mappings

We define the extremal distance between two sets on a metrizable compactification R^* of a Riemann surface R. Let A and B be two sets in R^*, and $\{A_n\}$ and $\{B_n\}$ be the systems of neighborhoods of A and B respectively. We denote by λ_n the extremal length of the family of curves which join $(A_n \cap R)$ and $(B_n \cap R)$. The extremal distance $\lambda(A, B)$ between A and B is defined as $\lambda(A, B) = \lim_n \lambda_n$. If either A or B is void we define the extremal distance infinite.

Now, we consider an analytic mapping φ of a Riemann surface R into a Riemann surface R'. We compactify R' in such a way that the compactification R'^* satisfies the condition that the extremal distance between any two disjoint closed sets in R'^* is positive. And we compactify R in KURAMOCHI's sense, then the compactification R^* also satisfies the above condition.

Here, we suppose that the analytic mapping φ satisfies the following condition: Let A' and B' be arbitrary closed sets in R'. If the extremal distance $\lambda(A', B')$ between A' and B' is positive, then the extremal distance $\lambda(\varphi^{-1}(A'), \varphi^{-1}(B'))$ between $\varphi^{-1}(A')$ and $\varphi^{-1}(B')$ is also positive. Analytic functions in R with finite Dirichlet integrals satisfy this condition as analytic mappings of R into the Riemann sphere R'. For such an analytic mapping φ, we have the following theorem.

Theorem. *φ has fine limits at every point of Δ except a set of vanishing outer capacity.*

Remark. Suppose φ satisfies the following additional condition in a neighborhood of a closed set A' in R'^*. Let $\{A_n'\}$ be a system of neighborhoods of A'. If the extremal distance $\lambda(A', R'^* - A_{n_0}')$ between A' and $R'^* - A_{n_0}'$ is infinite for a certain A_{n_0}', then the extremal distance $\lambda(\varphi^{-1}(A_n'), \varphi^{-1}(R' - A_{n_0}'))$ tends to infinity when A_n' tends to A'.

Under this condition, the set of the boundary Δ, at each point of which φ has fine limits in A', has vanishing inner capacity.

Though this condition is vague, it is clarified by PFLUGER's theorem [6] when R is the unit disk and R' is the Riemann sphere.

References

[1] C. CONSTANTINESCU und A. CORNEA, Ideale Ränder Riemannscher Flächen, Berlin 1963.

[2] T. FUJI'I'E, Extremal length and Kuramochi boundary, J. Math. Kyoto Univ. **4** (1964), 149—159.

[3] Z. KURAMOCHI, Potentials on Riemann surfaces, J. Fac. Sci. Hokkaido Univ., Ser. I, **16** (1962), 1—79.

[4] F. Y. MAEDA, Notes on Green lines and Kuramochi boundary of a Green space, J. Sci. Hiroshima Univ., Ser. A—I Math., **28** (1964), 59—66.

[5] M. OHTSUKA, On limits of BLD functions along curves, J. Sci. Hiroshima Univ., Ser. A—I Math., **28** (1964), 67—70.

[6] A. PFLUGER, Extremallängen und Kapazität, Comment. Math. Helv. **29** (1955), 120—131.

SUPERCOMPACTNESS AND SUPEREXTENSIONS

J. DE GROOT (Amsterdam)

Bases and subbases of all kinds abound in topology. We can also use them to express the seperation axioms as follows.

For the sake of simplicity all our spaces will be T_1 and (sub)base means (sub)base for closed sets, unless stated otherwise.

Definition. Two subsets P_1 and P_2 of a set X are *screened* by the pair A_1, A_2 if

$$A_1 \cup A_2 = X, \quad P_1 \cap A_2 = A_1 \cap P_2 = \emptyset .$$

(Consequently $P_1 \subset A_1$. $P_2 \subset A_2$.)

In general P_1 and P_2 are said to be *screened* by a finite family $\mathfrak{A}$ of subsets of X, if $\mathfrak{A}$ covers X and no element of X meets both P_1 and P_2. Then we have:

(1) A space X is *Hausdorff* iff it is (*sub*)*base Hausdorff* relative to *any* (sub)base $\mathfrak{B}$ of closed sets, i.e. every two points are screened by (a finite subcollection of $\mathfrak{B}$) a pair of elements of $\mathfrak{B}$.

(2) A space is *regular* iff it is (*sub*)*base regular* relative to some suitable (sub)base $\mathfrak{B}$ of closed sets, that is, every $B \in \mathfrak{B}$ and $x \in X$ (with $x \notin B$) are screened by (a finite subcollection) a pair of elements of $\mathfrak{B}$.

(3) X is *completely regular* iff it is (*sub*)*base-regular* and (*sub*)*base-normal* relative to a suitable (sub)base $\mathfrak{B}$.

Base-normality means screening of any two disjoint elements of $\mathfrak{B}$ relative to $\mathfrak{B}$.

(4) X is *normal* iff it is base-normal relative to the base of all closed sets.

See for a proof of (3) DE GROOT and AARTS, Complete regularity as a separation axiom (Canadian J. Math. 1968 or 1969).

In the base-case we can give a very simple proof of (3) by introducing the notion of a *linked system*: A family of subsets of a set X is called linked if every pair of elements of the family meets. Now consider linked systems and then maximal linked systems (m.l.s.) consisting of base elements $\mathfrak{B}$. If the intersection of the elements of an m.l.s. is one point of the space X, it is called fixed. Otherwise it its called free and can be used to "define" a new point. So X is extended to a set X^* and every $B \in \mathfrak{B}$ in a natural way to a $B^* \in \mathfrak{B}^*$. Define $\mathfrak{B}^*$ as a *subbase* for a topology on X^*.

If $\mathfrak{B}$ is base-regular and base-normal it is easy to prove that X^* is compact Hausdorff. The closure X^- of X in X^* is a Hausdorff compactification of X.

X^* is called a *superextension* of X relative to the base $\mathfrak{B}$. If X is a discrete space of 2, 3, or 4 points, X^* is discrete and consists of 2, 4, and 12 points. If X is completely regular and $\mathfrak{B}$ the base of zero sets, $X^- = \beta X$.

Definition. The space T is called *supercompact* (relative to $\mathfrak{S}$), if there exists a subbase of open sets $\mathfrak{S}$ in T, such that every open cover by means of elements of $\mathfrak{S}$ has a subcover by means of two elements.

If $\mathfrak{B}$ is the closed base consisting of the complements of the elements of $\mathfrak{S}$ in T, then every linked system in $\mathfrak{B}$ has a non-empty intersection.

X^* above is supercompact relative to $\mathfrak{B}^*$.

(5) *A supercompact space is compact.*

There exist compact T_1-spaces of a simple nature which are compact but not supercompact (A. VERBEEK). It is unknown whether all compact Hausdorff spaces are supercompact. However,

(6) *Compact polyhedra are supercompact,*

and very probably

(7) *Every compact metric space is supercompact.*

This is proved by considering such a space as an inverse limit of a sequence of polyhedra. To prove (6) we use the fact that a product of supercompact spaces is again supercompact.

This also leads trivially to the result that every completely regular space can be embedded in a supercompact space, namely a hypercube. However, X^* above is also such an embedding of X and this embedding has certain advantages.

Superextension of a space relative to a subbase can be defined in general by defining the m.l.s. as new points and the extended subbase elements as a subbase for the extended space. This extension then is supercompact. Superextensions supply us with a new method to "enlarge" a given space. To my knowledge practically nothing is known of them.

Question. Determine the superextension I^* of a closed interval I relative to the base of all closed subsets. I^* is compact Hausdorff as follows from the methods above. Is I^* a hypercube?

EXTENDED TOPOLOGY: CONTINUITY II

PRESTON C. HAMMER (University Park, Pa./U.S.A.)

Introduction

Continuity has been generalized several times since its introduction into analysis. Two of the more recent generalizations are those on topological spaces and more general neighborhoods spaces. The fundamental lesson to be derived from the topological generalization, in my opinion is that continuity is *not* an intrinsic concept since the same mapping may be continuous in one framework and not in another. What then is the basic meaning of continuity?

My own research into the matter has led me to conclude that continuity and invariance should be considered as dual concepts. A mapping is continuous with respect to whatever properties or relations it leaves invariant. Thus information— or structure-preserving maps are continous whether they preserve limit points, binary operations, distance, measure, dimension, relations among elements, sets or other entities.

I have given a necessary and sufficient condition, for example, for a mapping to preserve connectedness, of a variety of forms, which is expressed in terms of preserving a binary relation among sets [4]. I have shown how algebraic homomorphisms may be embedded in the same structure framework as the homomorphisms of topology [3]. In this paper I extend my work [2] on continuity to embrace arbitrary set-valued set-functions in the place of closures. This is a comparatively narrow view.

Those who may believe there is fundamental merit in the topological definition should consider the following. A constant-valued function is always continuous in topology but it is one of the *worst* mappings to preserve the structure in the domain space. It does not, for example, preserve limit points in any topological spaces of interest. Does generalizing the concept of continuity not weaken the requirements? The answer here will be shown to be the opposite. In general the less stringent the requirement on the space structure, the more rigid are the requirements of continuity.

Terminology

Let M_1, M_2 be two sets with respective null sets N_1 and N_2. Let PX denote always the class of all subsets of a given set X. I first define certain terms with respect to M_1, N_1 which carry over to any pair comprised of a space and its null set.

Let F_1 be the family of all functions f, each mapping PM_1 into itself. In F_1 there is induced, by the set algebra and inclusion relation in PM_1, a corresponding algebra and order relation. For example if $f, g \in F_1$ then $f \cup g$ and $f \cap g$ are defined by $(f \cup g)\, X \equiv (fX) \cup (gX)$, $(f \cap g)\, X \equiv (fX) \cap (gX)$. The order relation $f \subseteqq g$ holds provided $fX \subseteqq gX$ for all $X \subseteqq M_1$. It may be read "f is contained in g". Since the functions in F_1 map PM_1 into itself, F_1 is a composition semigroup, with identity element e_1 where $e_1 X \equiv X$. Composition is indicated by juxtaposition, fg being the function defined by $(fg)X \equiv f(gX)$. Then also $f^2 = ff$ and so on. In F_1 there are three other distinguished functions, the maximum function f_{M_1} (all values equal to M_1), the minimum function f_{N_1} (all values equal to N_1) and the complement function c_1 which maps X into $M_1 \setminus X$.

Consider now a mapping $t\colon M_1 \to M_2$ and allow me to use the same symbol, t, for the induced set-to-set mapping $tX = \{tp : p \in X\}$. Now let $f \in F_1$ and let $g \in F_2$ where F_2 is the family of all functions mapping PM_2 into itself. The mapping t is *(f, g)-continuous at $p \in M_1$* provided $p \in fX$ implies $tp \in g(tX)$.

In case f and g are both Kuratowski closure functions of topological spaces in M_1 and M_2 respectively, then the definition gives the usual continuity of topological spaces. However, I require *no* restrictions on f, g within the framework. Consider now an interpretation. Let f be a logic and read "$p \in fX$" as "X implies p in the logic f", or symbolically "$X \underset{f}{\to} p$". Then t is (f, g)-continuous at p provided t *preserves implication*. From "$X \underset{f}{\to} p$" follows always "$tX \underset{g}{\to} tp$" when t is (f, g)-continuous at p. Only for purposes of particular applications need any restriction be placed on f or g.

Naturally, if t is (f, g)-continuous this property may be expressed by: $tfX \subseteqq gtX$ for all $X \subseteqq M_1$ or, more shortly by: $tf \subseteqq gt$. In the next section I show that composition of continuous functions are continuous and that (f, g)-continuity is indeed, in general, a strong kind of continuity.

Basic theorems in continuity

1. Theorem. *Let M_1, M_2, M_3 be three spaces and let f_i map PM_i into itself for $i = 1$, 2, 3. Let t_1 map M_1 into M_2 and let t_2 map M_2 into M_3. Suppose t_1 is (f_1, f_2)-continuous at $p \in M_1$, and t_2 is (f_2, f_3)-continuous at $t_1 p$. Then $t_2 t_1 : M_1 \to M_3$ is (f_1, f_3)-continuous at p.*

Proof. In view of the assumption suppose $p \in f_1 X$, $X \subseteqq M_1$. Then $t_1 p \in f_2(t_1 X)$ and $t_2(t_1 p) \in f_3 t_2 t_1 X$. Hence $t_2 t_1$ is (f_1, f_3)-continuous at p.::

2. Corollary. *Let f map PM into PM and let t map M into M. Then if t is (f, f)-continuous at $p \in M$, every iterated mapping t^n $(n \geqq 2)$ is also (f, f)-continuous at p.*

This Theorem shows that one of the principle results concerning continuity holds. Observe that the precise language suggests the variety of functions f_i which may occur. Using $\overline{X}$ for the closure of X when there are large numbers of topological closures not isomorphic to each other is not suitable even in topology. In general, if a property is preserved in one transformation and the property is preserved in a following transformation naturally the composition preserves the property. This fact, presented individually in literally thousands of places in the literature in various contexts, should be proved once.

Now let me introduce a concept which is most illuminating in discussing continuity. It is customary to discuss the family of mappings which are continuous with respect to one ordered pair (f, g) from $F_1 \times F_2$. However it is also useful to consider for a given mapping $t : M_1 \to M_2$ the set of all pairs (f, g) such that t is (f, g)-continuous. I now consider global continuity instead of continuity at points.

Definition. Let $C(t) = \{(f, g): tf \subseteqq gt, (f, g) \in F_1 \times F_2\}$. Then $C(t)$ is called the *set of continuities* of t.

The set $C(t)$ is a subset of $F_1 \times F_2$. I will need certain conventions which amount to treating $F_1 \times F_2$ as a Boolean vector lattice. Thus $\bigcup (f_i, g_i) = (\bigcup f_i, \bigcup g_i)$ $(f_1, g_1) \times \times (f_2, g_2) = (f_2 f_2, g_1 g_2)$, and $(f, g)^2 = (f^2, g^2)$ and so on. To each function $f \in F_1$ there exists a unique minimum isotonic function, Σf, which contains f. It is given by $(\Sigma f)X \equiv \bigcup \{fA : A \subseteqq X\}$. There is also a unique maximum isotonic function $\Sigma^* f$, which is contained in f. It is given by $(\Sigma^* f)X \equiv \bigcap \{fA : A \supseteqq X\}$. Then $e_1 \cup \Sigma f$ is the minimum *expansive* (enlarging and isotonic) function containing f and $e_1 \cap \Sigma^* f$ is the maximum *contractive* (shrinking and isotonic) function contained in f. A *closure* function in F_1 is expansive and idempotent. The intersection function of any family of closure functions in a closure function. There exists for $f \in F_1$ a unique minimum closure function f^* which contains f. It can be generated by possibly transfinite iteration of $e_1 \cup \Sigma f$ using unions at limit ordinals. Dually an *interior* function is an idempotent contractive function and there exists a unique maximum interior function f^{**} contained in f, which is obtainable by iterations of $e_1 \cap \Sigma^* f$.

Similar definitions apply, of course, to functions from F_2 and I will use Σg, $\Sigma^* g$, $e_2 \cup \Sigma g$, $e_2 \cap \Sigma^* g$, g^*, g^{**} in similar roles. The point now is to show that if $(f, g) \in \in C(t)$, i.e. if t is (f, g)-continuous then t has many other continuities.

3. Theorem. *Let $t: M_1 \to M_2$ be a fixed arbitrary mapping. Let $C(t)$ be the set of continuities of t. The following statements hold.*

1. *$(e_1, e_2) \in C(t)$ and hence $C(t)$ is not empty.*
2. *If $(f_i, g_i) \in C(t)$ for all values of index i then $\bigcup (f_i, g_i)$ and $\bigcap (f_i, g_i) \in C(t)$.*
3. *If $(f, g) \in C(t)$ then $(\Sigma f, \Sigma g)$ and $(\Sigma^* f, \Sigma^* g) \in C(t)$.*
4. *If $(f, g) \in C(t)$ and g is isotonic then $(f^n, g^n) \in C(t)$ for $n \geqq 2$.*
5. *If $(f, g) \in C(t)$ then (f^*, g^*) and $(f^{**}, g^{**}) \in C(t)$.*

Proof.

1. Since $te_1 = e_2 t = t$, $(e_1, e_2) \in C(t)$.
2. Now $(f_i, g_i) \in C(t)$ is defined by $tf_i \subseteqq g_i t$. Since t is universally additive as applied to subsets of M_1, $t(\bigcup f_i) = \bigcup (tf_i) \subseteqq \bigcup (g_i t) = (\bigcup g_i)\, t$. Hence $(\bigcup f_i, \bigcup g_i) \in C(t)$. Now t is isotonic (but not generally intersective). Hence $t(\bigcap f_i) \subseteqq \bigcap (tf_i) \subseteqq \bigcap (g_i t_i)$ $= (\bigcap g_i)t$ and $(\bigcap f_i, \bigcap g_i) \in C(t)$.
3. Suppose $(f, g) \in C(t)$. Then for $X \subseteqq M_1$

   $t(\Sigma f)X = t \bigcup \{fA : A \subseteqq X\} = \bigcup \{tfA : A \subseteqq X\} \subseteqq \bigcup \{gtA : A \subseteqq X\} = \bigcup \{gY : Y \subseteqq tX\} = \Sigma g(tX)$. Hence t is $\Sigma(f, g)$-continuous. Again $t(\Sigma^* f)X = t \bigcap \{fA : A \supseteqq X\} \subseteqq \bigcap \{tfA : A \supseteqq X\} \subseteqq \bigcap \{gtA : A \supseteqq X\} = \bigcap \{gY : Y \supseteqq tX\} = (\Sigma^* y)\, tX$ and $\Sigma^* (f, g) \in C(t)$.
4. Suppose $(f, g) \in C(t)$ and g is isotonic. Then $tf^2 = tf(f) \subseteqq gt(f)$ since $(f, g) \in C(t)$. But since $tf \subseteqq gt$ and g is isotonic, $g(tf) \subseteqq g^2 t$ and $tf^2 \subseteqq g^2 t$. Hence $(f, g)^2 \equiv (f^2, g^2)$ $\in C(t)$. Suppose $(f^n, g^n) \in C(t)$. Then $tf^{n+1} = tf^n f \subseteqq g^n tf$ and since $tf \subseteqq gt$ and g^n is isotonic if g is isotonic, $g^n tf \subseteqq g^n gt = g^{n+1} t$. Therefore $tf^{n+1} \subseteqq g^{n+1} t$ and $(f^{n+1}, g^{n+1}) \in C(t)$. Hence $(f, g)^n \in C(t)$ for $n \geqq 2$. Note that if g is isotonic and

$(f, g) \in C(t)$ then $(\Sigma f, \Sigma g) \in C(t)$ but $\Sigma g = g$. Hence $(\Sigma f, g) \in C(t)$ holds and $\Sigma f \supseteqq f$ and is isotonic. Therefore not assuming f isotonic is done simply for use in application.

5. Now I use the previous results to establish that if $(f, g) \in C(t)$ then the corresponding closures pair (f^*, g^*) and interior pair (f^{**}, g^{**}) are in $C(t)$. First $\Sigma(f, g) \in \in C(t)$ by part 3. Hence by (1) and (2), $(e_1 \cup \Sigma f, e_2 \cup \Sigma g) \in C(t)$. Now, $f_1 \equiv e_1 \cup \cup \Sigma f$ and $g_1 = e_2 \cup \Sigma g$ are the expansive functions of f and g respectively and they are isotonic. Hence 4 applies to give $(f_1, g_1)^n \in C(t)$ and if $(f_1, g_1)^\omega = \cup (f_1, g_1)^n$ then by (2) $(f_1, g_1)^\omega \in C(t)$. Using simple transfinite induction we find $(f_1, g_1)^\alpha \in C(t)$ for every ordinal α. However for some α, $f_1^\alpha = f^*$ and $g_1^\alpha = g^*$. Hence $(f^*, g^*) \in C(t)$. A dual argument gives $(f^{**}, g^{**}) \in C(t)$.::

Remarks. This Theorem shows that the restriction of (f, g)-continuity tends to be a strong one since it implies "isotonic", "enlarging", "closure" and "interior" continuities as well as composition when f and g are isotonic. The converse is not the case. This a mapping t may be (f^*, g^*)-, $(e_1 \cup f, e_2 \cup g)$-, or $(e_1 \cup \Sigma f, e_1 \cup \Sigma g)$-continuous without being (f, g)-continuous. The continuities of topological spaces are thus seen be to weak. For example, if fX is the set of limit points of X in a topological space in M_1 and gY is also the set of limit points of Y in M_2. Then (f, g)-continuity is a *stronger* condition than (f^*, g^*)-continuity in T_1 topologies.

Example. Let $(M, \cdot)$ be an abelian semigroup and define $f\{p\} = p^2$, $f\{p, q\} = p \cdot q$ when $p \neq q$ and let $fX = N$ for all other sets. Then a mapping $t: M \to M$ is (f, f)-continuous if and only if t is an homorphism. To see this, $tf_1\{p\} \subseteqq ft(p)$ means $t(p^2) \subseteqq (tp)^2$ and hence $t(p^2) = (tp)^2$. Again $tf\{p, q\} \subseteqq f\{tp, tq\} = (tp) \cdot (tq)$ even if $p \neq q$. Hence $t(p \cdot q) \equiv (tp) \cdot (tq)$ and t preserves multiplication. Necessarily, conversely, if t preserves multiplication it is (f, f)-continuous. Now, however, if I should have used $f_1 = e \cup f$, instead of f, then *every* constant mapping t would be (f_1, g_1)-continuous — and thus multiplication would not necessarily be preserved. Note also that the limited set-theoretic framework of this paper prohibits discussing preserving non-commutative operators.

Now from Theorem 3 it is possible to establish several other results. One kind of result concerns the number of continuities a mapping t may have. Another related kind is concerned with *extremal* continuities. I shall say that (f, g) is *no weaker* than (f_1, g_1), $(f_1, g_1) \leqq (f, g)$, provided $f_1 \subseteqq f$ and $g \subseteqq g_1$. If (f, g) is a continuity of a mapping t such that no stronger continuity (f_1, g_1) of t exists then (f, g) is called a *maximal continuity* of t. Suppose we were to restrict the family of continuities of mappings to a particular subset of $F_1 \times F_2$ — e.g. require f, g to be isotonic, expansive, contractive and so on. It is almost trivially true that if $s: M_1 \to M_2$ is a mapping and $C(s) = C(t)$ then $s = t$ in the structure here. However, if the continuities considered are restricted this will not always be the case. A subset R of $F_1 \times F_2$ is said to *distinguish mappings* provided $s, t: M_1 \to M_2$ and $s \neq t$ implies there is $(f, g) \in R \cap C(s)$ such that $(f, g) \notin R \cap C(t)$.

4. Theorem. *Let $t: M_1 \to M_2$ be a given mapping.*

1. *To each $f \in F_1$ there exists uniquely a minimum function $g_0 \in F_2$ such that $(f, g_0) \in C(t)$ and there exists uniquely a maximum function f_1 such that $(f_1, g_0) \in C(t)$. The function g_0 is given by*

$$g_0 Y = \cup \{tfA : tA = Y\} \text{ for } Y \subseteqq tM_1,$$
$$g_0 Y = N_2 \text{ for } Y \nsubseteqq tM_1.$$

The function f_1 *is given by*

$$f_1 X \equiv t^{-1} g_0 t X \text{ for } X \subseteq M_1.$$

Then (f_1, g_0) *is a maximal continuity of* t.

2. *To each* $g \in F_2$ *there exists uniquely a maximum function* f_0 *such that* $(f_0, g) \in C(t)$. *There exists uniquely a minimum function* $g_1 \in F_2$ *such that* $(f_0, g_1) \in C(t)$. *The function* f_0 *and* g_1 *are given by*

$$f_0 = t^{-1} g t,$$
$$g_1 Y = \bigcup \{t f_0 A : tA = Y\} \text{ for } Y \subseteq t M_1,$$
$$g_1 Y = N_2 \text{ for } Y \nsubseteq t M_1.$$

Then (f_0, g_1) *is a maximal continuity of* t.

3. *Let* $R = \{(f, g) : f, g$ are isotonic$\}$. *Then* $R \subseteq F_1 \times F_2$ *distinguishes mappings.*

Proof.

1, 2. If $(f, g_0) \in C(t)$ then $ftX \subseteq g_0 tX$ for each $X \subseteq M_1$. Hence $g_0 tX \supseteq \bigcup \{tfA : tAt = tX\}$ necessarily. Now let $Y = \cdot X$, then $Y \subseteq t M_1$ and hence $g_0 Y = \bigcup \{tfA : tA = Y\}$ is the minimum value to be assigned to g_0 at Y. If $Y \nsubseteq t M_1$ then $g_0 Y = N_2$ is the minimum possible value. Hence g_0 as described is the minimum function in F_2 such that $(f, g_0) \in C(t)$. Now, if $tf_1 \subseteq g_0 t$ then $f_1 = t^{-1} g_0 t$ is the maximum function which satisfies this condition. Note that $tf_1 = g_0 t$ in this case. The proof of part 2 is essentially contained in this one except for the order.

3. Suppose R is the set of all pairs of isotonic functions (f, g) from $F_1 \times F_2$. Let $s: M_1 \to M_2$ be a mapping such that $s \neq t$. Then there exists a point $p \in M_1$ such that $s(p) = q_1 \neq q_2 = t(p)$.
Let $g \in F_2$ be defined as follows. If $p \in s^{-1}(Y \cap t M_1)$ then $gY = \{q_1\}$ otherwise let $gY = N_2$. Let $f = s^{-1} g s$. Now g is isotonic since if $Y_1 \subseteq Y$ then $g Y_1 \subseteq g Y$ and f is hence isotonic. Moreover $sf \subseteq gs$ so $(f, g) \in R \cap C(s)$. Now $p \in f\{p\}$ since $p \in s^{-1} s p$. Hence $q_2 = tp \in tf\{p\}$. But $g\{q_2\} = N_2$ since $p \notin s^{-1}\{q_2\}$. Hence $(f, g) \notin C(t)$. Hence R distinguishes mappings.::

It should be noted that the existence of functions g_0, f_1, f_0, g_1 is readily established from Theorem 3, since, for example $g_0 = \bigcap \{g_i : (f, g_i) \in C(t)\}$ and hence $(f, g_0) \in C(t)$. The representations of these functions directly is here the issue. Several questions now remain unanswered. For example, if f is assumed isotonic is g_0 necessarily isotonic. These questions will be partially disposed of next. Note that the isotonic functions appearing in part 3 provide a very weak kind of continuity since g has only two values and f has but two, $s^{-1} q_1$ and N_1.

5. Theorem. *Let* $t : M_1 \to M_2$. *Let* (f_1, g_0) *be a maximal continuity generated by* f *as in Theorem* 4. *Then if* f *is isotonic* g_0 *is isotonic in* $t M_1$ *and* f_1 *is an isotonic function. If* f *is additive* g_0 *is additive on* $t M_1$. *If* f *is a closure function* g_0, *restricted to* $t M_1$ *is a closure function provided* t *is one-to-one. If* g_0 *is a closure function in* $t M_1$ *then* f_1 *is a closure function.*

Proof. Suppose f is isotonic. Then if $Y \subseteq t M_1$, $g_0 Y = \bigcup \{tfA : tA = Y\} = \bigcup \bigcup \{tfA : tA \subseteq Y\}$ since $fA_1 \supseteq fA$ if $A_1 \supseteq A$ and hence $ft^{-1} Y \supseteq fA$ for all A such that $tA \subseteq Y$. Hence if g_0 is restricted to subsets of $t M_1$, g_0 is isotonic. Now $f_1 =$

$= t^{-1}g_0 t$ is isotonic if g_0 is. Hence the result. Now suppose $f(X \cup Y) \equiv (fX) \cup \cup (fY)$, i.e. f is additive. Then f is in particular isotonic and so is g_0 in tM_1. Consider $Y_1, Y_2 \subseteqq tM_1$. Then

$$g_0(Y_1 \cup Y_2) = \cup \{tfA : tA \subseteqq Y_1 \cup Y_2\} = tft^{-1}(Y_1 \cup Y_2)$$
$$= tf(t^{-1}Y_1 \cup t^{-1}Y_2) = tft^{-1}Y_1 \cup tft^{-1}Y_2 = g_0 Y_1 \cup g_0 Y_2 .$$

Hence g_0 is additive on tM_1. Since $t^{-1}g_0 t = f_1$ and t^{-1}, g_0, t are all additive, f_1 is additive.

Finally, suppose f is a closure function. Then since f is isotonic, if $Y \subseteqq tM_1$, $g_0 Y = = tft^{-1}Y$ and since $fA \supseteqq A$ always $g_0 Y \supseteqq Y$, next if $Y \subseteqq tM_1$, $g_0 Y \subseteqq tM_1$ so $g_0(g_0 Y) = (tft^{-1})(tft^{-1})Y \supseteqq tf^2t^{-1}Y = tft^{-1}Y = g_0 Y$ since $t^{-1}t \supseteqq e_1$. Hence if t is one-to-one then $t^{-1}t = e_1$ and $g_0^2 = g_0$ on tM_1 and g_0 is then a closure function. In any case if g_0 is a closure function then $f_1 = t^{-1}g_0 t = t^{-1}(tft^{-1})t$ is a closure function since $f_1^2 = (t^{-1}g_0 t)(t^{-1}g_0 t) = t^{-1}g_0^2 t = t^{-1}g_0 t$. ::

Remarks. It will be noted that I am "unfair" to intersective and interior functions. The reason is simple. The usual definition of mappings induces universally additive set valued functions t which are not in general intersective. The *dual* theory involves defining mapping from complements of points in M_1 to complements of points in M_2 and in this theory intersective or interior functions would be naturally at home. For example let $Tc_1\{p\} = c_2 t(p)$ for a mapping $t: M_1 \to M_2$, define T. Extend T by defining $TA = \cap \{T\{p\} : p \in c_1 A]$ for $A \subseteqq M_1$. Then if t is (f, g)-continuous $Tc_1 f c_1 X \supseteqq c_2 g c_2 TX$ gives the equivalent dual construct of continuity. Note that $TM_1 = M_2$ and $TN_1 \supseteqq N_2$ with the mapping T. This is one of many reasons to have the null set of a specified space equivalent to the space, not a single unique empty set.

The fact that g_0 need not be a closure in tM_1 in general even when f is a closure does not mean that there is no closure function g in tM_1 such that $(f, g) \in C(t)$. The minimum closure function g_0^* containing g_0 provides on restriction to tM_1 the minimum such closure. It is the case that a strongest continuity in the context I have chosen does not generally imply that g_0 is a closure when f is.

6. Corollary. *If $t: M_1 \to M_2$ is (f, g)-continuous where g is a closure function in M_2, then t is (f^*, g)-continuous where f^* is the closure function of f. In particular $t^{-1}gt = = f_0$ is then a closure and if g is additive so is f_0.*

It is an embarrassing fact of topological spaces that the intersection of two Kuratowski closure function is not, in general a Kuratowski closure function since additivity is not preserved under intersection. In the above Corollary, if I start with $g \in F_2$, a Kuratowski closure, then I have f_0 is a Kuratowski closure but if I start with $f \in F_1$ as a Kuratowski closure and there is no unique choice of a Kuratowski closure h, say, such that $(f, h) \in C(t)$.

In case of isotonic functions it is possible to interpret continuity in terms of generalized neighborhoods. To do this suppose $f \in F_1$ and $g \in F_2$ are isotonic functions. Let $u = c_1 f c_1$ and $v = c_2 g c_2$ be called the respective *dual* functions. Then I shall say a set $A \subseteqq M_1$ is an *f-neighborhood* of p provided $p \in uA$. Likewise if $q \in vB$ for $B \subseteqq M_2$, B is a *g-neighborhood* of q.

7. Theorem. *Let $t: M_1 \to M_2$. Let f, g be isotonic functions in F_1 and F_2 and let u and v be their dual functions. Then the following two statements are equivalent where $q = tp$, $p \in M_1$:*

(1) *t is (f, g)-continuous at p.*

(2) *$q \in vY$ implies $p \in ut^{-1}(Y \cap tM_1)$, i.e. the inverse image of each neighborhood of tp is a neighborhood of p.*

Proof. Suppose first that (1) holds. Then if (2) does not hold there would exist $Y \subseteqq M_2$ such that $q \in vY$ but $p \notin ut^{-1}(Y \cap tM_1)$. In this case, $p \in c_1ut^{-1}(Y \cap tM_1) = fc_1t^{-1}(Y \cup tM_1)$. Since (1) holds then $tp = q \in tfc_1t^{-1}(Y \cap tM_1) \subseteqq \subseteqq gtc_1t^{-1}(Y \cap tM_1)$. But $tc_1t^{-1}(Y \cup tM_1) = c_2Y \cap tM_1$ and hence $q \in g(c_2Y \cap \cap tM_1) \subseteqq gc_2Y$. But $q \in vY = c_2gc_2Y$ and this is a contradiction. Hence (1) implies (2).

Next suppose (2) holds but (1) does not. Then there is a subset X of M_1 such that $p \in fX$ but $tp = q \notin gtX$. Hence $q \in c_2gtX = (c_2gc_2)c_2tX = vc_2tX$. Now with $Y = c_2tX$ $q \in vY$ and hence $p \in ut^{-1}(Y \cap tM_1)$, i.e. $p \notin fc_1t^{-1}(Y \cap tM_1)$. But $t^{-1}(Y \cap tM_1) \subseteqq c_1X$ and hence $X \subseteqq c_1t^{-1}(Y \cap tM_1)$. Hence $p \notin fX$ since f is isotonic. This is a contradiction. Hence (2) implies (1). ::

Note. If $tM_1 = M_2$ (t is onto) then the form of (2) in the above Theorem may be written: If $q \in vY$ then $t^{-1}q \subseteqq u(t^{-1}Y)$; which, intuitively says t^{-1} is (v, u)-continuous if t is (f, g)-continuous.

Applications. In my previous example I showed that a function f with none of the properties of isotonicity, of being expansive, or a closure led to a most reasonable form of continuity. It may be thought that there is a scarcity of applications. On the contrary there are many but, insofar as I know they have not been adequately studied. I therefore mention a few that I have not considered in detail.

1. Let M_1 be endowed with any set of algebraic operations. Let fX be the closure of X with respect to all these operations. Then let M_2 also be endowed with a set of algebraic operations and let gY be the closure of Y with respect to these. Now if $tf \subseteqq gt$ then one cannot, in general say t is an algebraic homomorphism, but he can say, for example, that if Y is a g-closed set in M_2 then $t^{-1}(Y \cap tM_1)$ is an f-closed set in M_1. Here (f,g)-continuity relaxes the more rigid requirement of algebraic homomorphism. It seems likely that such relaxed conditions merit study in detail.

2. Let M_1 and M_2 be linear vector spaces. Let f and g be interpreted as convex (or linear hull) functions. The mappings $t: M_1 \to M_2$ which are (f, g)-continuous are of interest and so are the relativizations.

3. Let M_1 and M_2 be topological spaces and let fX be the set of limit points of Y, and gY the set of limit points of Y. Then $t: M_1 \to M_2$ is (f, g)-continuous if and only if t preserves limit points. These functions, conceivably more important in topology than continuous functions, merit detailed study.

4. Let M_1 and M_2 be topological spaces, and let f and g be the respective interior functions. Then t is (f, g)-continuous if and only if t is an open mapping. These mappings have been intensively studied but not as being a special form of continuity.

5. Let $f = c_1$ and $g = c_2$, the complement functions. Then t is (c_1, c_2)-continuous if and only if t is one-to-one. This is an example of an *antitonic* function continuity. More generally let $f \subseteqq c_1$ and $g \subseteqq c_2$. Then $p \in fX$ implies $p \notin X$. Here (f, g)-continuity may result in preserving limit points of various orders and is generally stronger than corresponding isotonic and closure continuities.

6. Let f, g be contractive functions, i.e., isotonic and $fX \subseteqq X$, $gY \subseteqq Y$ always. Then t is (f, g)-continuous provided the transform of the contraction of X is contained in the contraction of the transform of X. These continuities include, properly, all open mappings. In this case $u = c_1fc_1$, $v = c_2gc_2$ are expansive functions and

if $tM_1 = M_2$ then $t^{-1}v \subseteqq ut^{-1}$ is equivalent to (f, g)-continuity which implies, if t is one-to-one, that t preserves closedness with respect to u and v if it is (f, g)-continuous.

Families of continuous functions

Now I extend the foregoing results in the lattice properties of $C(t)$ to apply to families of transformations. Now suppose T is the set of all mappings from M_1 to M_2. I define a function S from $F_1 \times F_2$ to PT, i.e. $S(f, g) = \{t : t \in T \text{ and } tf \subseteqq gt\}$. Then $S(f, g)$ is the set of all (f, g)-continuous mappings. Note that $C(t)$ defines a mapping from T to $P(F_1 \times F_2)$.

Let these mappings be extended by intersection, i.e. if $T_0 \subseteqq T$ define $C(T_0) = \cap \{C(t) : t \in T_0\}$. The extended C now maps PT into $P(F_1 \times F_2)$. Similarly let $S(D) = \cap \{S(f, g) : (f, g) \in D \subseteqq F_1 \times F_2\}$. Then S maps $P(F_1 \times F_2)$ into PT.

8. Theorem.

1. *Let T_0 be a family of transformations each mapping M_1 into M_2. Let $C(T_0)$ be the set of all continuities of T_0. Then $C(T_0)$ has all the closure properties stated in Theorem 3, and there exist maximal continuities (f_1, g_0) and (f_0, g_1) in $C(T_0)$ induced by $f \in F_1$ and $g \in F_2$ as in Theorem 4.*

2. *The function CS mapping $P(F_1 \times F_2)$ into itself and the function SC mapping PT into itself are both closure functions. If $G \subseteqq F_1 \times F_2$ then $S(G) \times CS(G)$ is a maximal product subset of $PT \times P(F_1 \times F_2)$. If $T_0 \subseteqq T$ then $SC(T_0) \times C(T_0)$ is a maximal product subset of $PT \times P(F_1 \times F_2)$.*

The proof of this Theorem is straightforward. One must not, however, use the representations of g_0, f_1, g_1, f_0 given in Theorem 4. For example in Theorem 8, g_0 and f_1 may be described as follows for $f \in F_1$:

$$g_0 Y = \cup_i \{\cup (t_i f A : t_i A = Y \subseteqq t_i M_1) : t_i \in T_0\},$$

$$g_0 Y = N_2 \text{ if } Y \nsubseteqq t_i M_1 \text{ for any } t_i \in T_0,$$

$$f_1 = \cap \{t_i^{-1} g_0 t_i : t_i \in T_0\}.$$

It is readily seen that if f, for example, is additive then g_0 is additive but if g_0 is additive f_1 may well not be since intersection is used in the representation of f_1.

An interpretation of $SC(T_0)$ may be in order. $C(T_0)$ is the family of all pairs (f, g) such that every $t_i \in T_0$ is (f, g)-continuous. Hence $SC(T_0)$ is the maximum subset of T containing transformations t which have each $(f, g) \in C(T_0)$ as a continuity i.e. such that $C(t) \supseteqq C(T_0)$. Clearly then $CSC(T_0) = C(T_0)$. Two transformations t_1 and t_2 may be called *equivalent* provided $C(t_1) = C(t_2)$. I have shown that if we use $F_1 \times F_2$ then this equivalence is the identity. If we should use the subset of $F_1 \times F_2$ comprised of closure functions pairs for topological spaces, then the equivalence is not the identity.

Extended interpretations of continuity

Heretofore I assumed that the mappings $t : M_1 \to M_2$ were as usual. However, at least two generalizations suggest themselves. One is to directly allow transformations t mapping PM_1 into PM_2 which are not necessarily induced by element-to-element maps. This generalization is useful when t is restricted to additive or isotonic functions in particular. I may then say t is *(f, g)-continuous* provided $tf \subseteqq gt$. For example, suppose M is the plane, considered as a vector space, and $M_1 = M_2 = M$. Let $fX \equiv gX =$ convex hull of X and let $tX = \{(p - q)/2 : p, q \in X\}$ be the *symmetroid* of X. Then t maps PM into itself but it is not induced by an element-to-element map. It is readily verified that $tf = ft$, a significant fact of convexity theory and a special case of continuity.

Consider the case in which t is replaced by a relation $U \subseteqq M_1 \times M_2$. For convenience let us suppose the domain of U is M_1. Then I define $u(p) = \{q : (p, q) \in U\}$ and for $X \subseteqq M_1$ $uX = \bigcup\{u(p) : p \in X\}$. Then u is universally additive and set-valued. The "inverse" function v, associated with u is defined by $v(q) = \{p : (p, q) \in U\}$ and $vY = \bigcup\{v(q) : q \in Y\}$. Then U (or u) may be said to be *(f, g)-continuous* at p provided $p \in fX$ implies $u(p) \subseteqq guX$. Again u is (f, g)-continuous for all p provided $uf \subseteqq gu$. For this kind of continuity there can be a significant portion of the theory saved since u is universally additive. To illustrate suppose M_1 is the n-dimensional vector space comprised of all polynomials of the form $z^n + a_{n-1}z^{n-1} + \cdots + a_0$. Let $u(p)$ be the set of all zeroes of the polynomial $p \in M_1$ where M_2 is then the complex plane. Then $U = \{(p, q) : q \in u(p)\}$. Let fX be the set of limit points of X and let gY be the set of limit points of Y for $X \subseteqq M_1$ and $Y \subseteqq M_2$ in the usual topologies of M_1 and M_2. Then u is (f, g)-continuous, an important fact in the theory and application of polynomials.

Yet another generalization may be mentioned. In this case let M_1, M_2, E_1, E_2 be sets and let mappings s, t, f, g be given where $s : E_1 \to E_2$, $t : M_1 \to M_2$, $f : PM_1 \to PE_1$, $g : PM_2 \to PE_2$. Then the pair (s, t) may be called (f, g)-continuous provided $sf \subseteqq gt$. This gives the following diagram:

$$\begin{array}{ccc} PM_1 & \xrightarrow{\;t\;} & PM_2 \\ {\scriptstyle f}\downarrow & & \downarrow{\scriptstyle g} \\ PE_1 & \xrightarrow[\;s\;]{} & PE_2 \end{array}$$

Thinking of f and g as computing machines, we can interpret points p of M_1 as programs for f, points q of M_2 as programs for g, and E_1 and E_2 as the output sets for f and g respectively. Now t translates programs for f into programs for g and s translates outputs of f into outputs of g. In this case we might say machine g *covers* machine f if (s, t) is (f, g)-continuous. I do not wish to discuss this theory further here bit it is clear that the generalization is not foolish.

Conclusion

For many applications I have shown that continuity based on set-valued set-functions can well have a much broader base than it has had. The restriction to this format does not allow the best discussion of connectedness-preserving maps, for example nor of algebraic homomorphisms. The theory of continuity here presented is rigid, we need *approximate* forms to deal with approximation and modeling problems.

It is necessary to recognize that topological continuity is not intrinsic, there being many non-isomorphic topologies. It is useful to recognize that constant transformations are among the *worst preservers* of structure imaginable and, for many applications should not be considered continuous. Continuity and invariance are dual concepts!

References

[1] M. FRÉCHET, Espaces abstracts, Paris 1928.
[2] P. C. HAMMER, Extended topology: Continuity I, Portugaliae Math. **23** (1964), 79—93.
[3] P. C. HAMMER, Extended topology: The continuity concept, Math. Mag. **36** (1963), 101—105.
[4] P. C. HAMMER, Extended topology: Connected sets and Wallace separations, Portugaliae Math. **22** (1963), 167—187.
[5] P. C. HAMMER and G. C. GASTL, Extended topology: Neighborhoods and convergents, Proc. Copenhagen (1965) Conference on Convexity, Copenhagen 1967.
[6] P. C. HAMMER, Extended topology: Set-valued set-functions, Nieuw Archief voor Wiskunde **10** (1962), 55—77.
[7] A. CSÁSZÁR, Fundaments de la topologie, Budapest 1960.
[8] G. NÖBELING, Analytische Topologie, Berlin 1955.
[9] C. KURATOWSKI, Topology I, Warsaw 1966.
[10] W. J. THRON, Topological structures, New York 1966.
[11] E. ČECH, Topological spaces, New York 1966.

Added in proof: The author acknowledges partial support of the U. S. A. National Science Foundation for this research.

EINIGE EIGENSCHAFTEN DER BOHRSCHEN ERWEITERUNG

S. HARTMAN (Wrocław)

Ist G eine lokal kompakte abelsche (LCA) Gruppe und $\hat{G}_d$ ihre Charaktergruppe mit diskreter Topologie, so heißt die (kompakte) Gruppe $\tilde{G} = (\hat{G}_d)^{\wedge}$ die Bohrsche Kompaktifizierung von G. Eine Menge $E \subset G$ heißt eine $\boldsymbol{I}_0$-Menge, wenn jede auf E definierte beschränkte Funktion eine fastperiodische Erweiterung auf G oder, was dasselbe bedeutet, eine stetige Erweiterung auf $\tilde{G}$ zuläßt. Die $\boldsymbol{I}_0$-Mengen sind dadurch charakterisiert, daß ihre Abschließungen in $\tilde{G}$ („schwache" Abschließungen) topologisch mit dem Čechschen Raum $\beta(N)$ identisch sind.

Man beweist (HARTMAN und RYLL-NARDZEWSKI [1]), daß eine kompakte abelsche Gruppe immer dann den $\beta(N)$-Raum topologisch enthält, wenn ihr topologischer Charakter zumindest gleich continuum ist. Das bezieht sich insbesondere auf die Bohrschen Kompaktifizierungen vieler LCA-Gruppen, wie die der reellen oder der ganzen Zahlen. Um zu beweisen, daß dabei der isolierte Teil von $\beta(N)$ in G selbst und nicht erst in $\tilde{G}$ liegen kann, ist man in dem wichtigsten Fall $G = R$ (die reelle Achse) auf arithmetische Überlegungen angewiesen. Diese gestatten z. B., den Satz zu gewinnen, nach dem jede Hadamardsche Folge in R eine $\boldsymbol{I}_0$-Menge ist (STRZELECKI [5]).

Eine Menge $E \subset G \in$ LCA heißt $\boldsymbol{I}$-Menge, wenn jede auf E definierte und dort gleichmäßig stetige Funktion sich fastperiodisch auf ganz G erweitern läßt. Man beweist folgenden „Verdickungssatz" (HARTMAN und RYLL-NARDZEWSKI [2]): Ist E eine $\boldsymbol{I}_0$-Menge in R, so gibt es ein $\delta > 0$ derart, daß die Vereinigung aller um die Punkte von E geschlagenen Strecken der Länge δ eine $\boldsymbol{I}$-Menge ist. Dieser Satz gilt unter einleuchtender Umformulierung für alle separablen und nach MÉLA [4] sogar für alle metrischen LCA-Gruppen. Aus ihm folgert man leicht, daß die schwache Abschließung einer $\boldsymbol{I}_0$-Menge vom Haarschen Maße Null ist. Nach KAHANE [3] sind diese Abschließungen sogar Helsonsche Mengen, was noch mehr über ihre Spärlichkeit aussagt. Weitere Ergebnisse und offene Probleme schließen sich an.

Literatur

[1] S. HARTMAN and C. RYLL-NARDZEWSKI, Almost periodic extensions of functions, Coll. Math. **12** (1964), 23—39.

[2] S. HARTMAN and C. RYLL-NARDZEWSKI, Almost periodic extensions of functions II, Coll. Math. **15** (1966), 79—86.

[3] J.-P. KAHANE, Sur les ensembles de Ryll-Nardzewski et ensembles de Helson, Coll. Math. **15** (1966), 87–92.
[4] J. F. MÉLA, Sur les ensembles d'interpolation de C. Ryll-Nardzewski et de S. Hartman, Studia Math. **29** (1968), 167–193.
[5] E. STRZELECKI, On a problem of interpolation by periodic and almost periodic functions, Coll. Math. **11** (1963), 91–99.

ON CONSERVATIVE UNIFORM SPACES

JAN HEJCMAN (Praha)

In order to introduce the basic definitions, let us agree on some notation and terminology. A uniformity on a set is a system of some relations (in the sense e.g. of BOURBAKI, KELLEY). If V is a relation, we put $V^1 = V$, $V^n = V \circ V^{n-1}$ and $V^\infty = \bigcup_{n=1}^{\infty} V^n$. The property will always denote some property defined for subsets of uniform spaces.

A uniform space $(S, \mathcal{U})$ is said to be P-conservative, if there exists U in $\mathcal{U}$ such that for each subset X of S having the property P the set $U[X]$ has also the property P.

We are going to characterize P-conservative spaces for some properties P; namely for accessibility (it will be also shortly denoted by A), boundedness (B) and total boundedness (T). If P, R are two properties, we denote by PR the property meaning that both these properties are possessed.

Let us present the definitions of boundedness and accessibility.

A subset X of a uniform space $(S, \mathcal{U})$ is called bounded, if for each U in $\mathcal{U}$ there exists a finite subset K of S and a natural number n such that $X \subset U^n[K]$.

A subset X of a uniform space $(S, \mathcal{U})$ is called accessible, if for each U in $\mathcal{U}$ there exists a point x in S such that $X \subset U^\infty[x]$. A set X which is accessible in the subspace $(X, \mathcal{U}x)$ is said to be chained.

Observe that boundedness and accessibility are relative notions. They depend both on the set and the space. On the other hand, both the properties do not change if the space is replaced by an extension, in which the original space is dense.

Recall that a uniform space $(S, \mathcal{U})$ is said to possess a property P uniformly locally if there exists U in $\mathcal{U}$ such that $U[x]$ has the property P for each x in S.

If P is any property possessed by all one-point sets, then every P-conservative uniform space has the property P uniformly locally. The converse is not true, in general. It holds for accessibility and total boundedness. Concerning boundedness, there is an example of a connected complete metric space which is uniformly locally bounded but is not B-conservative.

Let us introduce some other main results concerning characterizations of A (AB, AT respectively)-conservative spaces.

A uniform space is A-conservative if and only if it is the union of a uniformly discrete family of chained subsets.

A uniform space is AB (resp. AT)-conservative if and only if it is both A-conservative and B (resp. T)-conservative.

Using completions, we obtain this theorem:

A totally bounded uniform space is A-conservative if and only if its completion has a finite number of components.

Detailed proofs of all assertions are contained in my paper in Comment Math. Univ. Carolinae 7 (1966), 411—417.

ON THE CONCEPT OF REFLECTIONS IN GENERAL TOPOLOGY

HORST HERRLICH (Berlin)

According to P. FREYD [7] a full subcategory $\mathfrak{S}$ of a category $\mathfrak{C}$ is called an *(epi)-reflective subcategory of* $\mathfrak{C}$ (or (epi)-reflective in $\mathfrak{C}$), iff for each object X in $\mathfrak{C}$ there exists an object $X_{\mathfrak{S}}$ in $\mathfrak{S}$ and an (epi)-morphism $r_{\mathfrak{S}} : X \to X_{\mathfrak{S}}$ such that for any object S in $\mathfrak{S}$ and any map $f \colon X \to S$ there exists a unique map $\bar{f} : X_{\mathfrak{S}} \to S$ making

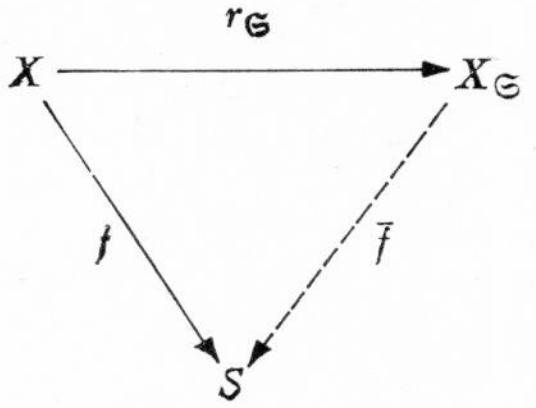

commutative. Examples of reflective subcategories are:

(1) The category of all compact [4], [26] (resp. realcompact [16], zerodimensional compact [2], E-compact [6], [23], $\mathfrak{E}$-compact [12], k-compact [11], m-ultra-compact [30], completely regular [4], T_3- [28]) spaces in the category of all Hausdorff-spaces.
(2) The category of all regular [28] (resp. T_0- [1], T_1-) spaces in the category of all topological spaces.
(3) The category of all complete uniform spaces in the category of all uniform spaces.
(4) The category of all complete metric spaces in the category of all metric spaces.
(5) The category of all complete lattices in the category of all ordered sets (where the maps are the monotone functions preserving greatest lower bounds and least upper bounds).
(6) The category of all idempotent semigroups in the category of all semigroups.
(7) The category of all abelian groups in the category $\mathfrak{G}$ of all groups (moreover each subcategory of $\mathfrak{G}$, which is defined by equations).
(8) The category of all torsion free A-modules in the category of all A-modules.
(9) The category of all semisimple rings in the category of all commutative rings.
(10) The category of all locally convex linear topological spaces in the category of all linear topological spaces.

In this paper we will investigate reflective and epi-reflective subcategories of the category $\mathfrak{T}$ of topological spaces and continuous maps and the category $\mathscr{H}$ of T_2-spaces and continuous maps only. But many results hold in a more general context [15].

In § 1 we develop a general theory of epi-reflections in $\mathfrak{H}$ and $\mathfrak{T}$. In § 2 we construct a pathological reflection in $\mathfrak{H}$ (and $\mathfrak{T}$). This example solves a problem of ISBELL [17] and a problem of KENNISON [20] simultaneously.

For the following reasons epi-reflections seem to be of more interest than reflections in general:

(1) All the examples above are epi-reflections.

(2) There is much known about epi-reflections ([13], [14], [20], [21]) but very little about reflections in general.

(3) For every reflective subcategory $\mathfrak{A}$ of a "suitable" category $\mathfrak{C}$ there exists a subcategory $\mathfrak{B}$ of $\mathfrak{C}$ such that $\mathfrak{A}$ is epi-reflective in $\mathfrak{B}$ and $\mathfrak{B}$ is epi-reflective in $\mathfrak{C}$ (see [21]).

(4) Reflections can be highly pathological even in nice categories (the example of § 2).

§ 1. General theory of epi-reflections in topology

Let $\mathfrak{C}$ be one of the categories $\mathfrak{H}$ and $\mathfrak{T}$, let $\mathfrak{S}$ and $\mathfrak{R}$ be full subcategories of $\mathfrak{C}$ with $\mathfrak{S} \subset \mathfrak{R}$. Throughout the paper we do not distinguish between homeomorphic objects and we assume that all spaces are non-empty.

1.0. Definitions

1.0.1. $\mathfrak{S}$ is called *productive*, iff for each family $\{S_i : i \in I\}$ of objects in $\mathfrak{S}$ the product $\prod_{i \in I} S_i$ is also contained in $\mathfrak{S}$.

1.0.2. Let S be an object of $\mathfrak{S}$, R an object of $\mathfrak{R}$, and $\mathfrak{F} \subset \text{Mor}\,(S, R)$ a family of continuous functions from S into R. The equalizer $D(\mathfrak{F})$ of $\mathfrak{F}$ is the subspace of S, consisting of all points $s \in S$ with the property $f(s) = g(s)$ for all $f \in \mathfrak{F}$, $g \in \mathfrak{F}$.

1.0.3. $\mathfrak{S}$ is called $\mathfrak{R}$-*hereditary* iff $S \in \mathfrak{S}$, $R \in \mathfrak{R}$, and $\mathfrak{F} \subset \text{Mors}\,(S, R)$ implies that $D(\mathfrak{F}) \in \mathfrak{S}$. It is easy to see that $\mathfrak{S}$ is $\mathfrak{T}$-hereditary (resp. $\mathfrak{H}$-hereditary), iff $\mathfrak{S}$ is hereditary (resp. closed-hereditary) in the usual sence.

1.0.4. $\mathfrak{S}$ is called $\mathfrak{R}$-*intersective* iff for each $R \in \mathfrak{R}$ and each family $\{S_i : i \in I\}$ of subspaces of R, which are in $\mathfrak{S}$ the intersection $\bigcap_{i \in I} S_i$ is also in $\mathfrak{S}$.

1.0.5. $\mathfrak{S}$ is called $\mathfrak{R}$-*invertible* iff $S \in \mathfrak{S}$, $R \in \mathfrak{R}$ and $f \in \text{Mor}\,(S, R)$ implies that $f^{-1}[A] \in \mathfrak{S}$ for each subspace A of R, which is in $\mathfrak{S}$.

1.0.6. $\mathfrak{S}$ is called $\mathfrak{R}$-*summable* iff the topological sum $\sum_{i \in I} S_i$ of any family $\{S_i : i \in I\}$ of objects of $\mathfrak{S}$ is in $\mathfrak{S}$ for each index set I, which is (as discrete space) an object of $\mathfrak{R}$.

1.0.7. A space X is called $\mathfrak{S}$-*regular* ($\mathfrak{S}$-*compact*) iff X is homeomorphic to a (closed) subspace of a product of objects in $\mathfrak{S}$.

1.0.8. An *extension of the space X in $\mathfrak{C}$* is a pair (r, rX), where rX is an object of $\mathfrak{C}$ and r an epimorphism $r: X \to rX$ in $\mathfrak{C}$.

1.0.9. An extension (r, rX) of X in $\mathfrak{C}$ is called a *$\mathfrak{S}$-extension of X in $\mathfrak{C}$* iff for each $S \in \mathfrak{S}$ and each map $f: X \to S$ there exists a map $\bar{f}: rX \to S$ such that $\bar{f} \circ r = f$.

1.1. Properties of epi-reflective subcategories of $\mathfrak{C}$

Every reflective subcategorie $\mathfrak{S}$ of $\mathfrak{C}$ is productive and $\mathfrak{S}$-hereditary [22]. Moreover:

1.1.1. Theorem. *Every epi-reflective subcategory $\mathfrak{S}$ of $\mathfrak{C}$ is $\mathfrak{C}$-hereditary.*

Proof. Let S be an object of $\mathfrak{S}$, R an object of $\mathfrak{C}$, $\mathfrak{F} \subset \mathrm{Mor}(S, R)$ a family of maps from S into R, $D = D(\mathfrak{F})$ the equalizer of $\mathfrak{F}$, $j: D \to S$ the inclusion-map, and $r_{\mathfrak{S}}: D \to D_{\mathfrak{S}}$ a reflection.

Then there exists a map $\bar{j}: D_{\mathfrak{S}} \to S$ with $\bar{j} \circ r_{\mathfrak{S}} = j$. Consequently $r_{\mathfrak{S}}$ is a homeomorphism from D into $D_{\mathfrak{S}}$. For arbitrary $f_1 \in \mathfrak{F}$, $f_2 \in \mathfrak{F}$ the mapping $g_i = f_i \circ \bar{j}$ makes the diagram

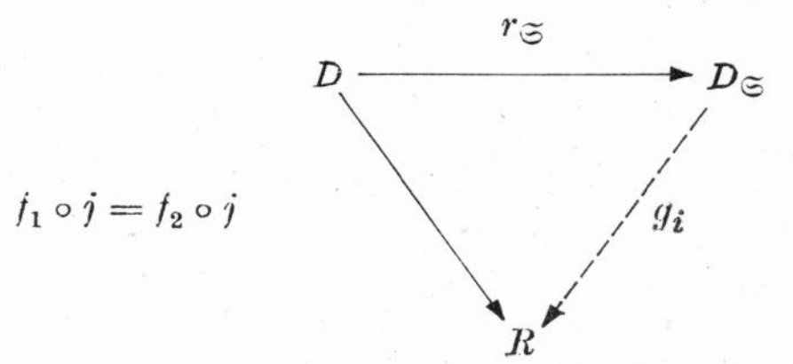

commutative for $i = 1, 2$. Since $r_{\mathfrak{S}}$ is an epi-morphism, it follows that $f_1 \circ \bar{j} = f_2 \circ \bar{j}$. Since this is true for each pair $f_1 \in \mathfrak{F}$, $f_2 \in \mathfrak{F}$ it follows that $\bar{j}\,[D_{\mathfrak{S}}] \subset D$. Each of the mappings $h_1 = 1_{D_{\mathfrak{S}}}$ and $h_2 = r_{\mathfrak{S}} \circ j^{-1} \circ \bar{j}$ makes the diagram

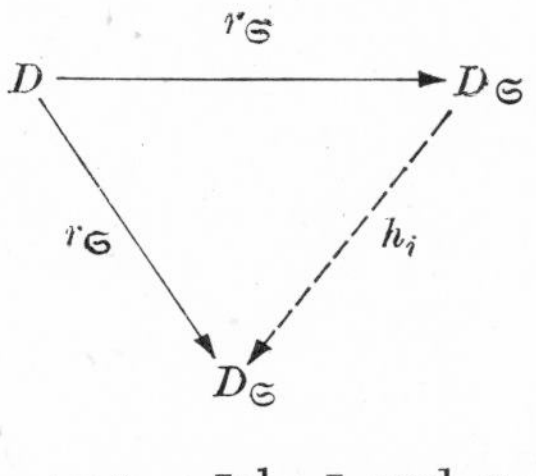

commutative. Consequently, $1_{D_{\mathfrak{S}}} = r_{\mathfrak{S}} \circ \bar{j}^{-1} \circ \bar{j}$ and $r_{\mathfrak{S}}$ maps D onto $D_{\mathfrak{S}}$. Therefore D and $D_{\mathfrak{S}}$ are homeomorphic and D must be in $\mathfrak{S}$.

1.1.2. Theorem. *If $\mathfrak{S}$ and $\mathfrak{R}$ are productive, subcategories of $\mathfrak{C}$, then each of the conditions listed below implies the next one. Moreover* (1) *and* (2) *are equivalent. For $\mathfrak{S} = \mathfrak{R}$ the first four are equivalent.*

(1) *$\mathfrak{S}$ is $\mathfrak{R}$-hereditary,*
(2) *$\mathfrak{S}$ is $\mathfrak{R}$-intersective,*
(3) *$\mathfrak{S}$ is $\mathfrak{R}$-invertible,*
(4) *$\mathfrak{S}$ is $\mathfrak{S}$-hereditary,*
(5) *$\mathfrak{S}$ is $\mathfrak{S}$-summable.*

Proof. (1) $\Rightarrow$ (2): Let R be an object of $\mathfrak{R}$ and $\{S_i: i \in I\}$ a family of subspaces of R, which are objects of $\mathfrak{S}$. Foreach $i \in I$ let $s_i: S_i \to R$ be the inclusion-map and $\Pi_i: \prod_{j \in I} S_j \to S_i$ the i-th projection-map from $\prod_{j \in I} S_j$ onto S_i. Then $\bigcap_{i \in I} S_i$ is homeomorphic to $D(\{s_i \circ \Pi_i: i \in I\})$ and is therefore in $\mathfrak{S}$.

(2) $\Rightarrow$ (3): Let S be an object of $\mathfrak{S}$, R an object of $\mathfrak{R}$, $f: S \to R$ a map, and A a subset of R, which is in $\mathfrak{S}$. $Z = S \times R$ is an object or $\mathfrak{R}$. The subspaces $S_1 = S \times A$ and $S_2 = \{(s, f(s)): s \in S\}$ of Z are objects of $\mathfrak{S}$ and their intersection is homeomorphic to $f^{-1}[A]$.

(3) $\Rightarrow$ (4): Let S and R be objects of $\mathfrak{S}$ and $\mathfrak{F} \subset \mathrm{Mor}(S, R)$ a family of maps from S into R. Let X be the product-space $R^{\mathfrak{F}}$ with the projection-maps $\Pi_f: X \to R$. If D is the diagonal in X, then X and D are objects of $\mathfrak{S}$. If $g: S \to X$ is defined by $\Pi_f \circ g = f$ for each $f \in \mathfrak{F}$, then $D(\mathfrak{F})$ is homeomorphic to $g^{-1}[D]$ and is therefore in $\mathfrak{S}$.

(4) $\Rightarrow$ (5) Let $\{S_i: i \in I\}$ be a family of objects in $\mathfrak{S}$, such that I (with the discrete topology) is also an element of $\mathfrak{S}$. Let $S = \prod_{i \in I} S_i$ be the product of the family $\{S_i: i \in I\}$, $\Pi_i: S \to S_i$ the projection-maps, r a fixed point of S and define for each $i \in I$ a map $f_i: I \times S \to S$ by

$$\Pi_k \circ f_i(j, s) = \begin{cases} \Pi_k(r), & \text{if } i = j \neq k \\ \Pi_k(s) & \text{otherwise.} \end{cases}$$

Then $\sum_{i \in I} X_i$ is homeomorphic to $D(\{f_i: i \in I\})$ and therefore is in $\mathfrak{S}$.

(2) $\Rightarrow$ (1) Let S be an object of $\mathfrak{S}$, R be an object of $\mathfrak{R}$, and $\mathfrak{F} \subset \mathrm{Mor}(S, R)$ a family of maps. $X = S \times R$ is an object of $\mathfrak{R}$ and $A_f = \{(s, f(s)): s \in S\}$ is for each $f \in \mathfrak{F}$ a subset of X, which is homeomorphic to S and therefore is in $\mathfrak{S}$. $D(\mathfrak{F})$ is homeomorphic to $\bigcap_{f \in \mathfrak{F}} A_f$ and therefore is in $\mathfrak{S}$.

Summarizing we can say:

1.1.3. Theorem. *Each reflective subcategory $\mathfrak{S}$ of $\mathfrak{C}$ is productive, $\mathfrak{S}$-hereditary, $\mathfrak{S}$-intersective, $\mathfrak{S}$-invertible, and $\mathfrak{S}$-summable. Each epi-reflective subcategory $\mathfrak{S}$ of $\mathfrak{C}$ is productive, $\mathfrak{C}$-hereditary, $\mathfrak{C}$-intersective, $\mathfrak{C}$-invertible, and $\mathfrak{S}$-summable. Each non-trivial[1]) epi-reflective subcategory of $\mathfrak{T}$ is even $\mathfrak{T}$-summable.*

Proof. It remains to show the last statement. But each non-trivial epi-reflective subcategory $\mathfrak{S}$ of $\mathfrak{T}$ must contain all discrete spaces (even all zerodimensional spaces [12]) and therefore $\mathfrak{T}$-summability follows from $\mathfrak{S}$-summability.

So the properties of reflective and epi-reflective subcategories can be stated in a similar way. But, as mentioned before, the properties of reflections in general are much weaker than those of epi-reflections. In § 2 we will construct a reflective subcategory $\mathfrak{S}$ of $\mathfrak{C}$ which consists only of the powers Y^I of one fixed space Y. So $\mathfrak{S}$-hereditary, $\mathfrak{S}$-intersective, $\mathfrak{S}$-invertible and $\mathfrak{S}$-summable say almost nothing in this case. $\mathfrak{S}$ is neither $\mathfrak{C}$-intersective nor $\mathfrak{C}$-invertible nor $\mathfrak{C}$-hereditary nor $\mathfrak{C}$-summable for $\mathfrak{C} = \mathscr{H}$ or $\mathfrak{C} = \mathscr{T}$. Moreover, and this is essential, the properties listed above characterize epi-reflective subcategories (see 1.2). We know of no satisfactory characterization of reflections in $\mathfrak{C}$.

---

[1]) Non-trivial means that it contains at least one non-indiscrete space.

1.2. Characterization of epi-reflective subcategories of $\mathfrak{C}$

1.2.1. Theorem. *If $\mathfrak{S}$ is a full subcategory of $\mathfrak{C}$, the following conditions,* (1)—(4), *are equivalent. For $\mathfrak{C} = \mathfrak{T}$ they are also equivalent to* (5):

(1) *$\mathfrak{S}$ is epi-reflective in $\mathfrak{C}$,*

(2) *for every $\mathfrak{S}$-regular space X there exists a space $X_{\mathfrak{S}} \in \mathfrak{S}$ and an epimorphism $r_{\mathfrak{S}}$: $X \to X_{\mathfrak{S}}$, which is actually a homeomorphism from X into $X_{\mathfrak{S}}$, such that for each $S \in \mathfrak{S}$ and each map $f: X \to S$ there exists a map $\bar{f}: X_{\mathfrak{S}} \to S$ with $\bar{f} \circ r_{\mathfrak{S}} = f$,*

(3) *$\mathfrak{S}$ is productive and $\mathfrak{C}$-hereditary,*

(4) *$\mathfrak{S}$ is productive and $\mathfrak{C}$-intersective,*

(5) *$\mathfrak{S}$ is productive, $\mathfrak{C}$-invertible, and contains a space consisting only of one point.*

Proof. The equivalence of (1) and (3) was first proved by KENNISON [20]. A more elementary proof of this statement was independently (but later) given by VAN DER SLOT and myself in [13], where we also proved the equivalence of (2) and (3). The remaining equivalences are new. That (3) and (4) are equivalent and imply (5) is already shown in 1.1.2. It remains to show that (5) implies (3) for $\mathfrak{C} = \mathfrak{T}$. Let S be an object of $\mathfrak{S}$ and A be a subset of S. Identifying all points of A one obtains a quotient-space S_A of S. If $f: S \to S_A$ is the corresponding quotient-map, then A is the preimage under f of a single point and therefore is in $\mathfrak{S}$.

1.3. Generation of epi-reflective subcategories

1.3.1. From the characterization-theorem 1.2.1 follows immediately that the intersection of any family of epi-reflective subcategories of $\mathfrak{C}$ is again epi-reflective in $\mathfrak{C}$. Consequently for each subcategory $\mathfrak{S}$ of $\mathfrak{C}$ there exists a smallest epi-reflective subcategory $\mathfrak{C}\mathfrak{S}$ in $\mathfrak{C}$ containing $\mathfrak{S}$. We say that $\mathfrak{S}$ *generates* $\mathfrak{C}\mathfrak{S}$ *in* $\mathfrak{C}$. In case there exists a single space S with $\mathfrak{C}\{S\} = \mathfrak{R}$ we say S *generates* $\mathfrak{R}$ *in* $\mathfrak{C}$ and call $\mathfrak{R}$ *$\mathfrak{C}$-simple.*

1.3.2. It is known [12] that an arbitrary extension $r: X \to rX$ of a space X in $\mathfrak{C}$ is a $\mathfrak{S}$-extension iff it is a $\mathfrak{C}\mathfrak{S}$-extension. Therefore the objects of $\mathfrak{S}$ can serve as "test-objects" for extending functions in spaces of $\mathfrak{C}\mathfrak{S}$. This is of special interest in case $\mathfrak{C}\mathfrak{S}$ is $\mathfrak{C}$-simple. Let us consider the following examples:

(a) The category $\mathfrak{S}$ of compact spaces is $\mathfrak{H}$-simple. The closed unit interval generates $\mathfrak{S}$ in $\mathfrak{H}$.

(b) The category $\mathfrak{S}$ of realcompact spaces is $\mathfrak{H}$-simple. The space of real numbers generates $\mathfrak{S}$ in $\mathfrak{H}$. $\mathfrak{S}$ can be also generated in $\mathfrak{H}$ by each of the following categories[2]) (see [16], [19], [24], [25]):

1. the category of all separable, metrizable spaces,
2. the category of all metrizable spaces,
3. the category of all paracompact spaces,
4. the category of all Lindelöf-T_3-spaces,
5. the category of all completely regular, σ-compact spaces.

(c) The category $\mathfrak{S}$ of completely regular spaces is $\mathfrak{T}$-simple. The closed unit interval (or the space of real numbers) generates $\mathfrak{S}$ in $\mathfrak{T}$.

[2]) Under the assumption that all cardinals are non-measurable.

In view of these three examples the spaces of $\mathfrak{H}\mathfrak{S}$ (resp. $\mathfrak{T}\mathfrak{S}$) are called $\mathfrak{S}$-*compact* (resp. $\mathfrak{S}$-*regular*) [6], [12], [23].

(d) $\mathfrak{T}$ is $\mathfrak{T}$-simple. Each space with three points and three open sets generates $\mathfrak{T}$ in $\mathfrak{T}$.

(e) The category $\mathfrak{S}$ of T_0-spaces is $\mathfrak{T}$-simple. The space X with two points and three open sets generates $\mathfrak{S}$ in $\mathfrak{T}$. X also generates a reflective category $\mathfrak{R}$ in $\mathfrak{T}$, which consists only of those T_0-spaces Y, which enjoy the following property: "If each element of an open filter $\mathfrak{F}$ on Y contains a limit-point of $\mathfrak{F}$, then $\bigcap \mathfrak{F} \neq \emptyset$." In particular, each T_2-space, but no infinite space with cofinite topology, belongs to $\mathfrak{R}$. This pathological reflection gives a negative answer to a problem of KENNISON [20]. A more striking example will be given in § 2.

(f) The category $\mathfrak{S}$ of zerodimensional spaces is $\mathfrak{T}$-simple. The discrete space with two points generates $\mathfrak{S}$ in $\mathfrak{T}$.

(g) The category $\mathfrak{S}$ of indiscrete spaces is $\mathfrak{T}$-simple. The indiscrete space with two points generates $\mathfrak{S}$ in $\mathfrak{T}$.

(h) The category $\mathfrak{S}$ of zerodimensional, compact spaces is $\mathfrak{H}$-simple. The discrete space with two points generates $\mathfrak{S}$ in $\mathfrak{H}$. $\mathfrak{S}$ is the smallest non-trivial, epi-reflective subcategory of $\mathfrak{H}$.

But not all epi-reflective subcategories of $\mathfrak{C}$ are $\mathfrak{C}$-simple. For each T_1-space X exists a T_3-space Y (with more than one point) such that all continuous mappings from Y into X are constant [10]. Consequently, Y cannot be $\{X\}$-regular (see **1.3.3. (a)**). From this it follows:

(i) Neither the category $\mathfrak{S}$ of all T_1-spaces, nor the category $\mathfrak{R}$ of all T_3-spaces, nor any category lying between $\mathfrak{S}$ and $\mathfrak{R}$ can be $\mathfrak{T}$-simple. The category of all T_1-spaces can be generated in $\mathfrak{T}$ by the subcategory of all spaces with cofinite topology [5].

(k) Neither the category $\mathfrak{S}$ of all T_2-spaces, nor the category $\mathfrak{R}$ of all T_3-spaces, nor any category lying between $\mathfrak{S}$ and $\mathfrak{R}$ can be $\mathfrak{H}$-simple. The category of all T_2-closed (resp. T_2-minimal) spaces generates $\mathfrak{H}$ in $\mathfrak{H}$. This follows immediately from the fact that every T_2-space can be embedded as closed subset in a T_2-minimal space (STRECKER and WATTEL [27]).

(l) The category $\mathfrak{S}$ of regular spaces is not $\mathfrak{T}$-simple. (If $\mathfrak{S}$ would be generated in $\mathfrak{T}$ by a space S, then the category of all T_3-spaces would be generated in $\mathfrak{T}$ by the T_0-reflection of S.)

For several interesting epi-reflective categories we do not know whether or not they are simple:

(m) Let Z be the space of entire numbers, Q the space of rational numbers, and I the space of irrational numbers. Each of these three spaces generates in $\mathfrak{H}$ the same category $\mathfrak{S}$. It is neither known whether $\mathfrak{S}$ coincides with the category $\mathfrak{R}$ of all zerodimensional, realcompact spaces nor whether $\mathfrak{R}$ is $\mathfrak{H}$-simple at all.

(n) Let k be an infinite cardinal-number and $\mathfrak{S}_k$ the reflective subcategory of $\mathfrak{H}$ generated by the category of all completely regular spaces, which can be covered by less than k compact subspaces [11]. The categories $\mathfrak{S}_{\aleph_0}$ (consisting of all compact spaces) and $\mathfrak{S}_{\aleph_1}$ (consisting of all realcompact spaces) are $\mathfrak{H}$-simple. It is not known what happens to be for $k > \aleph_1$.

1.3.3. In case $\mathfrak{S}$ is a subcategory of $\mathfrak{H}$ there exist several relations between $\mathfrak{S}$, $\mathfrak{T}\mathfrak{S}$ and $\mathfrak{H}\mathfrak{S}$ [12]:

(a) Since $\mathfrak{T}\mathfrak{S}$ (resp. $\mathfrak{H}\mathfrak{S}$) consists of all subspaces (resp. all closed subspaces) of products of spaces in $\mathfrak{S}$, the following conditions are equivalent for each T_2-space X:

(1) X is $\mathfrak{S}$-regular,

(2) for each closed subset A of X and each point $x \in X - A$ there exists a space $S \in \mathfrak{H}\mathfrak{S}$ and a map $f: X \to S$ with $f(x) \notin \overline{f[A]}$,

(3) X is a subspace of a $\mathfrak{S}$-compact space,

(4) the reflection-map $r_{\mathfrak{H}\mathfrak{S}}: X \to X_{\mathfrak{H}\mathfrak{S}}$ is a homeomorphism from X into $X_{\mathfrak{H}\mathfrak{S}}$.

(b) For each T_2-space X there exists a homeomorphism h from $X_{\mathfrak{H}\mathfrak{S}}$ onto $(X_{\mathfrak{T}\mathfrak{S}})_{\mathfrak{H}\mathfrak{S}}$ such that

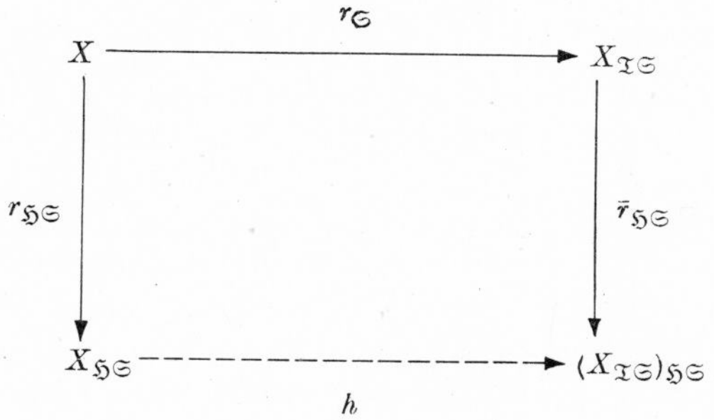

commutes.

1.3.4. We know almost nothing in this connection about reflections in general. It is even not known whether the intersection of two reflective subcategories of $\mathfrak{C}$ is again reflective in $\mathfrak{C}$. Each small subcategory $\mathfrak{S}$ can be embedded in a smallest reflective subcategory of $\mathfrak{C}$ [17] but for general $\mathfrak{S}$ the problem is open.

§ 2. A pathological reflection

The above statements show that there exists a nice theory about epi-reflections, but very little is known about reflections in general. Moreover, the following example shows that reflections can be highly pathological. At the same time this example answers a problem of Kennison [20], whether all reflective subcategories in $\mathfrak{H}$ are already epi-reflective, and a problem of Isbell [17] (see remark 2.7) both in the negative. The example is based essentially on the following theorem of de Groot [9].

2.1. Definition. A Hausdorff-space Y is called *strongly-rigid,* iff the only non-constant, continuous map from Y into itself is the identity.

2.2. Theorem (de Groot). *There exists a connected, locally-connected, strongly-rigid subspace Y of the Euclidean plane with $|Y| = \aleph$.*

2.3. Lemma. *If Y is a strongly-rigid space and n a natural number, then the only non-constant, continuous maps from Y^n into Y are the projections Π_i $(i = 1, 2, \ldots, n)$.*

Proof (by induction). The lemma is true for $n = 1$. Suppose that $n > 1$, that the lemma is true for $n - 1$, and let f be a continuous map from Y^n into Y.

Case 1:

For all $y \in Y$ and all $i = 1, \ldots, n$ f is constant $(= c(y, i))$ on $\Pi_i^{-1}(y)$. From $n > 1$ it follows that there exist $y_0 \in Y$ and $i_0 \in \{1, \ldots, n\}$ with $c(y_0, i_0) \neq y_0$. Therefore f must be constant $(= c(y_0, i_0))$ on $Y_0 = \bigcap_{r \neq i_0} \Pi_i^{-1}(y_0)$, which is homeomorphic to Y. For each $y \in Y$ the sets Y_0 and $\Pi_{i_0}{}^{-1}(y)$ have non-empty intersection. Therefore $c(y, i_0) = c(y_0, i_0)$ for each $y \in Y$ and f must be constant.

Case 2:

There exists $y \in Y$ and $i \in \{1, \ldots, n\}$ such that f is not constant on $Y_1 = \Pi_i^{-1}(y)$. By the induction hypothesis there exist $j \neq i$ with

$$f \mid \Pi_i^{-1}(y) = \Pi_j \mid \Pi_i^{-1}(y). \tag{a}$$

By the induction-hypothesis $f \mid \Pi_j^{-1}(z)$ is constant or a projection for each $z \in Y$. If $z \neq y$ it follows from (a) that there remains only the possibility that f is constant $(= z)$ on $\Pi_j^{-1}(z)$. Consequently:

$$f \mid \Pi_j^{-1}[Y - \{y\}] = \Pi_j \mid \Pi_j^{-1}[Y - \{y\}]. \tag{b}$$

By the induction-hypothesis $f \mid \Pi_i^{-1}(z)$ is constant or a projection for any z. From (b) it follows that there remains only the possibility

$$f \mid \Pi_i^{-1}(z) = \Pi_j \mid \Pi_i^{-1}(z) \text{ for each } z \in Y. \tag{c}$$

This means $f = \Pi_j$.

2.4. Theorem. *If Y is a strongly-rigid space and I an arbitrary index set then the only non-constant, continuous functions from Y^I into Y are the projections Π_i $(i \in I)$.*

Proof. For $u \in Y^I$ denote $\Pi_i(u)$ by u_i. Let f be a continuous function from Y^I into Y, u a fixed point of Y^I, and $Y_J = \{v\colon v \in Y^I,\ v_i \neq u_i \Rightarrow i \in J\}$ for each subset J of I. If f is constant on Y_J for each finite subset J of I, then f is constant on the union of all these Y_J, which is dense in Y^I. Therefore f must be constant. If there exists a finite subset J of I, on which f is not constant, then (according to the lemma) there exists an element $j \in J$ such that

$$f \mid Y_J = \Pi_j \mid Y_J. \tag{a}$$

Let K be a finite subset of I, containing J. According to the lemma $f \mid Y_K$ must be constant or a projection. From (a) it follows that there remains only the possibility $f \mid Y_K = \Pi_j \mid Y_K$. The union of all these Y_K is dense in Y^I. Consequently $f = \Pi_j$.

2.5. Theorem. *If Y is a strongly-rigid space then the full subcategory $\mathfrak{A}$ of $\mathfrak{H}$ the objects of which are the powers*[3]) *Y^I of Y, is reflective in $\mathfrak{H}$.*

Proof. For each Hausdorff space X let $X_{\mathfrak{A}}$ be the space $Y^{\bar{c}(X,Y)}$, where $\bar{c}(X,Y)$ denotes the family of all non-constant, continuous maps from X into Y. Then there

---

[3]) $Y^{\emptyset}$ is supposed to be a one-element space.

exists a unique continuous map $r_{\mathfrak{A}}$ from X into $X_{\mathfrak{A}}$, such that $\Pi_g \circ r_{\mathfrak{A}} = g$ for each $g \in \bar{c}(X, Y)$. (Π_g denotes the corresponding projection from $Y^{\bar{c}(X,Y)}$ onto Y.) It remains to show that $r_{\mathfrak{A}}\colon X \to X_{\mathfrak{A}}$ is a reflection. For any $f \in C(X, Y)$ there exists a $\bar{f} \in C(X_{\mathfrak{A}}, Y)$ with $\bar{f} \circ r_{\mathfrak{A}} = f$ (take $\bar{f} = \Pi_f$, if f is not constant and $\bar{f}$ constant if f is constant). From Theorem 2.4 it follows immediately that $\bar{f}$ is uniquely determined by this property. Consequently, for any index set I, any $g \in C(X, Y^I)$, and any $i \in I$ there exists a unique $\bar{f}_i \in C(X_{\mathfrak{A}}, Y)$ with $\bar{f}_i \circ r_{\mathfrak{A}} = \Pi_i \circ f$. Consequently there exists a unique $\bar{f} \in C(X_{\mathfrak{A}}, Y^I)$ with $\bar{f} \circ r_{\mathfrak{A}} = f$.

2.6. Remark. If X is a Hausdorff-space with exactly two elements, Y the strongly-rigid space of DE GROOT (2.2), and $\mathfrak{A}$ the full subcategory of $\mathfrak{H}$, the objects of which are the powers of Y, then $|X| = 2$ and $|X_{\mathfrak{A}}| = \aleph^{\aleph}$.

2.7. Remark. If X and Y are objects of the category $\mathfrak{U}$ of uniform spaces, $\mathfrak{R}$ (resp. $\mathfrak{A}$) the smallest reflective (resp. epi-reflective) subcategories of $\mathfrak{U}$ containing Y, $r_{\mathfrak{R}}\colon X \to X_{\mathfrak{R}}$ (resp. $r_{\mathfrak{A}}\colon X \to X_{\mathfrak{A}}$) the corresponding reflections (resp. epi-reflections) of X, then (see ISBELL [17], p. 38) the map $U(r_{\mathfrak{A}}, 1)\colon U(X_{\mathfrak{A}}, Y) \to U(X, Y)$ is always an isomorphism. If X and Y are the spaces of 2.6 and $\mathfrak{R}$ is the corresponding reflective subcategory of $\mathfrak{U}$, then the map $U(r_{\mathfrak{R}}, 1)\colon U(X_{\mathfrak{R}}, Y) \to U(X, Y)$ is not an isomorphism. It is even not a homeomorphism. This follows immediately from the fact that each non-constant function f in $U(X_{\mathfrak{R}}, Y)$ is necessarily a projection, which implies $f[X_{\mathfrak{R}}] = Y$, and consequently the set C of all constant functions in $U(X_{\mathfrak{R}}, Y)$ is open in $U(X_{\mathfrak{R}}, Y)$, but the image of C under $U(r_{\mathfrak{R}}, 1)$ is the set of all constant functions in $U(X, Y)$, which is not open (even nowhere dense) in $U(X, Y)$. This gives a negative answer to a problem of ISBELL ([17], p. 38).

Problems

1. According to 1.1.3, reflective subcategories $\mathfrak{S}$ of $\mathfrak{C}$ are productive and $\mathfrak{S}$-hereditary. Do these two properties characterize reflections in $\mathfrak{C}$? If the answer is yes, the next problem would be solved automatically. If the answer is no, there arises the question whether or not there exist other satisfactory characterizations of reflective subcategories of $\mathfrak{C}$.

2. Is the intersection of each family of reflective subcategories of $\mathfrak{C}$ again reflective in $\mathfrak{C}$? Equivalently: Can each subcategory of $\mathfrak{C}$ be embedded in a smallest reflective subcategory of $\mathfrak{C}$?

3. Is the intersection of each finite family of reflective subcategories of $\mathfrak{C}$ again reflective in $\mathfrak{C}$?

4. Are there satisfactory characterizations of $\mathfrak{C}$-simple reflective subcategories of $\mathfrak{C}$? Is the category $\mathfrak{S}$ of zerodimensional realcompact spaces $\mathfrak{H}$-simple? Does a countable discrete space generate $\mathfrak{S}$? Does there exist a cardinal number $k > \aleph_1$, such that the category of all k-compact spaces is $\mathfrak{H}$-simple?

5. The Stone-Čech-compactification [4], [26], the Hewitt-realcompactification [16], the Banaschewski-zerodimensional-compactification [2], the Mrowka-E-compactification [23], the k-compactification [11], and the $\mathfrak{E}$-compactification [12] are embeddings, which can be regarded as epi-reflections in $\mathfrak{H}$. Neither the Katětov-T_2-closed extension [18] of a T_2-space, nor the Banaschewski-T_2-minimal extension

[3] of a semiregular space, nor the Wallman-T_1-compactification of a T_1-space [31] can be regarded as reflection in either $\mathfrak{T}$ or $\mathfrak{H}$. But the Katětov extension can be regarded as epi-reflection in the category of T_2-spaces and continuous semi-open functions [14]. What is the categorial background of all the other extensions? Can they be made into reflections by suitable changes of the underlying category?

References

[1] P. ALEXANDROFF und H. HOPF, Topologie I, Berlin 1935.
[2] B. BANASCHEWSKI, Über nulldimensionale Räume, Math. Nachr. **13** (1955), 129—140.
[3] B. BANASCHEWSKI, Über Hausdorffsch-minimale Erweiterung von Räumen, Archiv Math. **12** (1961), 355—365.
[4] E. ČECH, On bicompact spaces, Ann. Math. **38** (1937), 823—844.
[5] E. ČECH, Topological spaces, Prague 1966.
[6] R. ENGELKING and S. MROWKA, On E-compact spaces, Bull. Acad. Polon. Sci., Ser. Sci. Math. Astr. Phys., **6** (1958), 429—436.
[7] P. FREYD, Abelian categories, New York 1964.
[8] L. GILLMAN and M. JERISON, Rings of continuous functions, Princeton 1960.
[9] J. DE GROOT, Groups represented by homeomorphism groups I, Math. Annalen **138** (1959), 80—102.
[10] H. HERRLICH, Wann sind alle stetigen Abbildungen in Y konstant?, Math. Z. **90** (1965), 152—154.
[11] H. HERRLICH, Fortsetzbarkeit stetiger Abbildungen und Kompaktheitsgrad topologischer Räume, Math. Z. **96** (1967), 64—72.
[12] H. HERRLICH, $\mathfrak{E}$-kompakte Räume, Math. Z. **96** (1967), 228—255.
[13] H. HERRLICH and J. VAN DER SLOT, Properties which are closely related to compactness (to appear).
[14] H. HERRLICH and G. E. STRECKER, H-closed spaces and reflective subcategories (to appear).
[15] H. HERRLICH and G. E. STRECKER, Coreflective subcategories I: Generalities (to appear).
[16] E. HEWITT, Rings of real-valued continuous functions, Trans. Amer. Math. Soc. **64** (1948), 54—99.
[17] J. R. ISBELL, Uniform spaces, Providence 1964.
[18] M. KATĚTOV, Über H-abgeschlossene und bikompakte Räume, Časopis Mat. Fys. **69** (1940), 36—49.
[19] M. KATĚTOV, On real-valued functions in topological spaces, Fund. Math. **38** (1951), 85—91.
[20] J. F. KENNISON, Reflective functors in general topology and elsewhere, Trans. Amer. Math. Soc. **118** (1965), 303—315.
[21] J. F. KENNISON, Full reflective subcategories (to appear).
[22] B. MITCHELL, Theory of categories, New York 1965.
[23] S. MROWKA, A property of Hewitt-extension νX of topological spaces, Bull. Acad. Polon. Sci., Ser. Sci. Math. Astr. Phys., **6** (1958), 95—96.
[24] T. SHIROTA, On spaces with complete structure, Proc. Japan Acad. **27** (1951), 513—516.
[25] T. SHIROTA, A class of topological spaces, Osaka Math. J. **4** (1952), 23—40.
[26] M. H. STONE, Applications of the theory of Boolean rings to general topology, Trans. Amer. Math. Soc. **41** (1937), 375—481.
[27] G. E. STRECKER and E. WATTEL, On semi-regular and minimal Hausdorff embeddings, Indagationes Math. **29** (1967), 234—237.
[28] J. P. THOMAS, Associated regular and T_3-spaces, Notices Amer. Math. Soc. **95** (1967), 71.
[29] J. VAN DER SLOT, Over invariantes van eigenschappen gedefinieerd op klassen topologische ruimten, WN 21 Math. Centrum Amsterdam 1966.
[30] J. VAN DER SLOT, Universal topological properties, ZW 1966—011 Math. Centrum Amsterdam 1966.
[31] H. WALLMAN, Lattices and topological spaces, Ann. Math. **39** (1926), 112—126.

THE EXTENSION OF CONTINUOUS FUNCTORS, EXPONENTIAL FUNCTORS, AND THE ČECH COHOMOLOGY HOPF ALGEBRA OF COMPACT GROUPS

KARL HEINRICH HOFMANN[1] (New Orleans, La./U.S.A.)

While the homotopy groups of a compact abelian group are well known through the work of ANDRÉ [1] and ENOCHS [2], and while it may be considered standard knowledge that the first integral cohomology group of a compact connected abelian group is naturally isomorphic to its character group it is apparently not generally known what the higher cohomology groups look like. The cohomology of any Hopf space (i.e. a compact space with a continuous homotopy associative multiplication with a homotopy identity) is in fact a graded Hopf algebra, so that the more general question arises to compute the Čech cohomology Hopf algebra of a compact abelian group taking all of its algebraic structure into account. Without any appreciable effort it will be possible to generalize our result to compact connected abelian semigroups. Before we formulate the main result, we recall the following facts:

1. Let R be any commutative ring with identity and A an R-module. If with the exterior algebra $\bigwedge A$ over A one defines an R-module morphism $\gamma\colon \bigwedge A \to \bigwedge A \otimes_R \bigwedge A$ by prescribing

$$(a_1 \wedge \ldots \wedge a_n) = \sum (-1)^{e(I,J)} a_{i_1} \wedge \ldots \wedge a_{i_p} \otimes a_{j_1} \wedge \ldots \wedge a_{j_q},$$

where the summation is extended over all disjoint decompositions $\{1, \ldots, n\} = I \cup J$ with $i_1 < \ldots < i_p$ in I and $j_1 < \ldots < j_q$ in J, and $e(I, J) =$ number of pairs (i_s, j_t) with $j_t < i_s$, then one has introduced an associative comultiplication with coidentity which makes $\bigwedge A$ into a graded Hopf algebra over R.

2. Let S be a compact abelian semigroup. Then S has a compact minimal ideal MS which is an abelian group [5].

We now state the main result:

3. Theorem. *If S is a compact connected abelian semigroup with identity, then the character group $(MS)^\wedge$ of its minimal ideal is a discrete torsion free abelian group. Let R be an arbitrary integral domain. Then the graded Čech cohomology Hopf algebra HS of S over R is naturally isomorphic to $R \otimes \bigwedge (MS)^\wedge \cong \bigwedge_R R \otimes (MS)^\wedge$. If G is a compact abelian group, G_0 its identity component, and if $C(G/G_0, A)$ for any ring A denotes the ring of continuous, hence locally constant, functions from G/G_0 into the discrete ring A, then the graded Čech cohomology Hopf algebra over R is naturally iso-*

[1]) This research was supported by National Science Foundation Grant 6219. The author is a fellow of the Alfred P. Sloan Foundation.

morphic to the Hopf algebras

$$R \otimes C(G/G_0, \mathbb{Z}) \otimes \wedge G_0{}^\wedge \cong \wedge_{C(G/G_0,R)} C(G/G_0, R) \otimes G_0{}^\wedge \cong C(G/G_0, \wedge_R R \otimes G_0{}^\wedge).$$

In the context of this theorem the following problems are left: i) Determine the cohomology Hopf algebra of a not necessarily connected compact abelian semigroup. A satisfactory solution to this problem may be difficult due to complications occuring in the structure of non-connected compact semigroups which considerably exceed the ones present in the extension of a compact connected abelian group by a totally disconnected one. ii) Determine the cohomology Hopf algebra for a non-commutative connected compact group. With R as the real or complex field our methods should comparatively easily apply to yield the desired result from the structure of the cohomology Hopf algebra of a Liegroup. Over the integers as coefficients there may be difficulties due to torsion in the cohomology. iii) Determine the singular cohomology Hopf algebra of a connected compact abelian group (over the integers, say). The singular cohomology is definitely different from the Čech cohomology on most compact connected abelian groups. The answer may be in some way related to the first homotopy group, which is $\pi_1(G) \cong \mathrm{Hom}\,(\hat{G}, \mathbb{Z})$. It is noteworthy that this group also is naturally isomorphic to the kernel of the exponential function of G (see [3]).

The methods used in proving the main result are functorial. The basic idea is that the result is known or may be directly computed for torus groups, and that the general result has to follow through limit processes utilizing basic facts about Čech cohomology and the duality of compact groups. The cohomology of a compact connected abelian group over an integral domain R can be shown to be torsion free. Hence by the general Künneth theorem for Čech cohomology $H(X \times Y) \cong HX \otimes HY$ for compact connected abelian groups. Moreover, by the universal coefficient theorem, the cohomology over R is obtained from the integral cohomology by tensoring with R. The functor E from the category of torsion free abelian groups into the category of graded R-modules defined by $ET = H\hat{T}$ satisfies the relation $E(A \oplus A') \cong EA \otimes EA'$. The functor $T \to R \otimes \wedge T$ has the same properties. On the subcategory of finitely generated groups they coincide up to natural equivalence. Moreover they commute with colimits. From these observations we prove that they must be naturally isomorphic on the entire category of torsion free abelian groups. In fact we introduce the concept of convergence on categories in terms of limits and give a meaning to the concept of a dense subcategory and a continuous functor. The functors mentioned above are continuous relative to appropriate structures of convergence, and the full category of all $\mathbb{Z}^n$, $n = 0, 1, \ldots,$ is dense in the category of all torsion free abelian groups. We show that a natural transformation between the restrictions of two continuous functors to a dense subcategory extends uniquely to a natural transformation between the functors. Secondly, motivated by the computation of the cohomology of a compact connected abelian group we investigate quite generally the existence and uniqueness of exponential functors. The main existence theorem, of which (1) above is a special case uses the coadjoint functor theorem by Freyd and produces an exponential functor as the coadjoint of a "logarithmic" functor, i.e. a functor between appropriate categories satisfying $L(X \otimes Y) = LX \oplus LY$. Thus, e.g. the functor from the category of commutative (resp. anticommutative) graded rings with the integers as homogeneous component of degree zero into the category of abelian groups which maps $A_0 + A_1 + A_2 + \ldots$ onto A_1 is logarithmic, and its coadjoint associates with a group G the symmetric (resp. the exterior) algebra over G. Thirdly, we observe, that every exponential functor E on a category with biproducts automatically produces the structure of a Hopf algebra on each EA where by the multiplication is just the image under E of the codiagonal map $A \oplus A \to A$ and the comultiplication the image of the diagonal map $A \to A \oplus A$. The previous considerations are then suitably extended to functors taking values in categories of Hopf algebras with particular emphasis being given to the question to what extend the exponential nature of a functor determines its Hopf structure.

References

[1] M. A. André, L'homotopie des groupes abeliens localement compacts, Comm. Math. Helv. **38** (1963), 1—5.

[2] E. Enochs, Homotopy groups of compact abelian groups, Proc. Amer. Math. Soc. **15** (1964), 878—881.

[3] K. H. Hofmann, Introduction to compact groups I, Tulane Univ. Lecture Notes, Dept. Math. Tulane Univ. 1967.

[4] K. H. Hofmann, Categories with convergence, exponential functors, and the cohomology of compact abelian groups, Math. Z. **104** (1968), 106—140.

[5] K. H. Hofmann and P. S. Mostert, Elements of compact semigroups, Columbus, Ohio, 1966.

[6] S. T. Hu, Cohomology rings of compact connected groups and their homogeneous spaces, Ann. Math. **55** (1952), 391—418.

[7] S. T. Hu, Cohomology theory in topological groups, Mich. Math. J. **1** (1952), 11—59.

[8] V. Poenaru, Sur la cohomologie des cochaînes singulières invariantes sur un groupe topologique compact et connexe, Fund. Math. **50** (1961), 1—12.

EXTENDING C^*-ALGEBRAS BY ADJOINING AN IDENTITY

KARL HEINRICH HOFMANN[1]) (New Orleans, La./U.S.A.)

Even though large parts of our results apply to wider classes of rings we will restrict our attention to C^*-algebras, i.e. complex Banach algebras with an involution satisfying the relation $|x^*x| = |x|^2$ for all elements x. The structure space of a C^*-algebra A is the space Prim A of all primitive ideals in the hull kernel topology. It is always a locally compact T_0-space and is in fact compact if A has an identity. It is rarely Hausdorff. An exception is the commutative case where Prim A for a C^*-algebra A with identity is a compact Hausdorff space; by a famous theorem of Gelfand and Neumark, A is then naturally isomorphic to C (Prim A), the algebra of all complex valued functions on Prim A with the obvious C^*-algebra structure. If A is commutative but does not have an identity, then Prim A is a locally compact but not compact Hausdorff space and A is naturally isomorphic to C_0 (Prim A), the algebra of all complex valued functions on Prim A vanishing at infinity.

Many discussions in the structure theory of C^*-algebras are simpler in the presence of an identity. One tries therefore as often as possible to reduce the case of algebras without identity to the simpler case by adjoining an identity in the standard fashion: On the product $\mathbb{C} \times A$ of complex vector spaces one introduces the multiplication $(r, a)(r', a') = (rr', r \cdot a' + r' \cdot a + aa')$. We will identify A with the ideal $\{0\} \times A$ and $\mathbb{C}$ with the subalgebra $\mathbb{C} \times \{0\}$ and write $\mathbb{C} \dotplus A$ instead of $\mathbb{C} \times A$. It seems feasible to call $\mathbb{C} \dotplus A$ the *standard adjunction of an identitiy*. In the example above $\mathbb{C} \dotplus C_0$ (Prim A) is isomorphic to C (Prim $A \cup \{\infty\}$) where the domain space is the one point compactification of Prim A. Although one has to admit that so one obtains a very natural extension of the given algebra with an identity there are others, e.g. the C^*-algebra of all bounded continuous functions on Prim A which is naturally isomorphic to C (β Prim A), where β Prim A denotes the Stone-Čech compactification of Prim A. It is not at all clear that this considerably larger extension might not have certain advantages over the standard extension.

The consideration of non-standard adjunctions of an identity is almost mandatory in the consideration of certain questions concerning non-commutative C^*-algebras. In their attempts to generalize the Gelfand-Neumark Theorem to non-commutative C^*-algebras, J. DAUNS and the author found it necessary partly to abandon the structure space and to replace it by a space of generally smaller ideals which has a

---

[1]) This research was supported by National Science Foundation Grant 6219. The author is a fellow of the Alfred P. Sloan Foundation.

natural topology, the advantage being that this topology is always completely regular. We therefore call this space of ideals the *complete regularisation space*. A prevalent disadvantage of the standard adjunction is the following: There is no simple relation between the complete regularisation spaces of A and $\mathbb{C} \dot{+} A$; in fact the first one may well be compact Hausdorff whereas the second one is singleton. Thus one arrives naturally at the following problem:

(1) *Find a natural extension $\tilde{A}_1$ of A having an identity such that the complete regularisation space of $\tilde{A}_1$ (which is in this case always the Stone-Čech compactification of* Prim $\tilde{A}_1$) *is an extension of the complete regularisation space of A.*

This is a well motivated question also in view of the fact that for C^*-algebras with identity the complete regularisation space has a simple algebraic description: If b is a primitive ideal of A and A has an identity then the closed ideal m generated by $Z \cap b$, where Z denotes the center of A, is the unique ideal of the complete regularisation space contained in b. A similarly simple algebraic description of the complete regularisation space in the absence of an identity has not been given so far. This leads us to the formulation of the second problem:

(2) *Find an algebraic description of the complete regularisation space and the function which associates with a primitive ideal b the unique ideal of the complete regularisation space contained in b.*

Eventually, one would want to use possible answers to questions (1) and (2) to a more complete solution of the following problem:

(3) *Generalize the theorem of Gelfand and Neumark to non-commutative C^*-algebras as well as possible.*

The basic technique for the solution of problem (3) and the most essential parts of the solution of problem (3) have been given by DAUNS and the author [2]. In using one important part of this work, DIXMIER [4] has proposed an answer to problem (1) by finding the desired extension in the envelopping von Neumann algebra of the given C^*-algebra. Somewhat related questions have been touched by BUSBY in his work about multiplier algebras [5]. The theory discussed in the following is quite different from DIXMIER's approach. It is more algebraic and therefore applicable to other rings, and moreover it yields more detailed information concerning question (1). A complete answer to question (2) is a byproduct, and some significant additional contributions to what has been achieved towards a solution of (3) can be made on the basis of this construction. The full details and the proofs will appear in a joint paper with J. DAUNS [3].

1. Splitting extensions by abelian algebras

Let A be a C^*-algebra and R a commutative C^*-algebra such that A is a left algebra over R. The Banach space product $R \times A$ is given the multiplication $(r, a)\,(r', a') = (rr', r \cdot a' + r' \cdot a + aa')$ and a unique norm making $R \times A$ into a C^*-algebra with involution $(r, a)^* = (r^*, a^*)$. Again we identify A with $\{0\} \times A$ and R with $R \times \{0\}$ and write $\tilde{A} = R \dot{+} A$, so that A is a closed ideal of $\tilde{A}$ and R a closed central subalgebra with $R \cap A = \{0\}$.

Proposition. 1. *Let I be an ideal of $\tilde{A}$. Then $I_0 = R \cap I + A \cap I$ is an ideal of $\tilde{A}$ and $R/(R \cap I) \cong (R + I)/I$ acts on the left of $A/(A \cap I) \cong (A + I)/I$ making the* *latter into a* $R/(R \cap I)$ *left algebra, and* $\tilde{A}/I_0 \cong R/(R \cap I) \dotplus A/(A \cap I)$. *Moreover,* $(A + I_0)/I_0 \cap I/I_0 = \{0\}$.

Either $I = I_0$ *or* $I = \bigcup \{r - r \cdot e + A \cap I : r \in J\}$, *where* e *is some relative identity of* A *modulo* I *and* J *is an ideal of* R *with* $J + A = I + A$. *If* I *is of the second kind and if* $J = R$ *(which is certainly the case if* $R \cap I$ *is maximal), then* $\tilde{A}/I \cong A/(A \cap I)$.

We agree to call an ideal a *box ideal* if it is of the first kind and a *diagonal ideal* if it is of the second. A comparatively straightforward application of proposition 1 leads to

Theorem 1. *An ideal* I *of* $\tilde{A}$ *is primitive exactly if the following two conditions are satisfied:*

(1) $A \cap I$ *is primitive in* A *or* $A \cap I = A$,

(2) $R \cap I$ *is maximal in* R.

The primitive ideal I *is a diagonal ideal if and only if* $A \cap I$ *is a proper modular ideal of* A *and is a box ideal in all other cases.* (Recall that an ideal I is *modular* in A if A/I has an identity.)

Conversely, let $b \in \text{Prim } A$ *and define* $Fb = \{r \in R : r \cdot A \subset b\}$. *Then* $Fb \in \text{Prim } R$. *The unique primitive ideal* $\tilde{b} \in \text{Prim } \tilde{A}$ *with* $A \cap \tilde{b} = b$ *is given by*

$$\tilde{b} = \begin{cases} Fb + b, & \text{if } b \text{ is non-modular in } A \\ \bigcup \{r - r \cdot e + b : r \in R\}, & \text{if } b \text{ is modular in } A \end{cases}$$

where e *is some relative identity of* A *modulo* b. *In both cases* $R \cap \tilde{b} = Fb$. *Moreover all ideals* $p + A$ *with* $p \in \text{Prim } R$ *are primitive (in fact maximal) ideals of* $\tilde{A}$.

Theorem 1 applies particularly to the standard extension $\mathbb{C} \dotplus A$. There the set of all $\tilde{b}$ is in bijective correspondence with Prim A and there is just one additional primitive ideal in $\tilde{A}$, namely A. Thus we may identify Prim $(\mathbb{C} \dotplus A)$ with Prim $A \cup \{A\}$. The hull kernel topology on Prim $A \cup \{A\}$ is described in the following

Proposition 2. *A set* $X \subset \text{Prim } A \cup \{A\}$ *is closed if and only if* $X \cap \text{Prim } A$ *is closed in* Prim A *and if* $\bigcap \{b : b \in X\}$ *is modular in* A.

In the following, Prim $A \cup \{A\}$ will always have this topology.

Theorem 2. *The function* F: Prim $A \to$ Prim R *is continuous. The function* Prim $\tilde{A} \to (\text{Prim } A \cup \{A\}) \times \text{Prim } R$ *which associates with* $\tilde{b}$ *the element* (b, Fb) *and with* $p + A$ *the element* (A, p) *is a homeomorphism from* Prim $\tilde{A}$ *onto graph* $F \cup \{A\} \times \text{Prim } R$. *The function* $b \to (b, Fb)$ *from* Prim A *onto* graph F *is a homeomorphism onto an open subset of this union.*

In all that follows we will always identify Prim $\tilde{A}$ with the subspace graph $F \cup \{A\} \times \text{Prim } R$ of the product space $(\text{Prim } A \cup \{A\}) \times \text{Prim } R$.

Proposition 3. *The set* D *of all* $r - a \in R \dotplus A = \tilde{A}$ *with* $r \cdot x = ax$ *for all* $x \in A$ *is a central ideal of* $\tilde{A}$ *and is, in fact the annihilator of* A *in* $\tilde{A}$. *Every primitive ideal* $\tilde{b}$ *of* $\tilde{A}$ *contains* D. *Denote the algebra* A/D *with* $\tilde{A}_1$. *Then the space* Prim $\tilde{A}_1$ *may be naturally identified with the closed subspace of* Prim $\tilde{A}$ *consisting of all primitive ideals containing* D. *After our identification of* Prim $\tilde{A}$ *with a subspace of* $(\text{Prim } A \cup \{A\}) \times \text{Prim } R$ *we can write*

Prim $A \cong$ graph $F \subset \text{Prim } \tilde{A}_1 \subset \text{Prim } \tilde{A} \subset (\text{Prim } A \cup \{A\}) \times \text{Prim } R$. *Moreover,* Prim $\tilde{A}_1$ *is the closure of graph* F.

The ideal $A_1 = (A + D)/D$ *of the algebra* $\tilde{A}_1$, *is isomorphic to* A *and* $Z_1 = (R + D)/D$ *is the center of* $\tilde{A}_1$. *One has* $\tilde{A}_1 = Z_1 + A_1$ *and* $Z_1 \cap A_1 = (D + Z)/Z$, *where* Z *is the center of* A.

We now define the complete regularisation space of a C^*-algebra. Let A be a C^*-algebra and let f: Prim $A \to \beta$ Prim A be the Stone-Čech compactification. For each $b \in$ Prim A we define the ideal φb of A by $\varphi b = \bigcap \{b' \in \text{Prim}\, A : f(b') = f(b)\}$. The set Cr A of all ideals φb, $b \in$ Prim A is given the topology making the function $\varphi b \to f(b)$ a homeomorphism onto a subspace of β Prim A and is called the *complete regularisation space of* A. The function φ: Prim $A \to$ Cr A is called the *complete regularisation of the structure space.* Note that Cr A is compact Hausdorff whenever Prim A is compact and that φ: Prim $A \to$ Cr A in that case is in fact the Stone-Čech compactification of Prim A.

The following simple pointset topological lemma is used in establishing the subsequent results.

Lemma. *Let* X *be a compact space,* $k: X \to \beta X$ *its Stone-Čech compactification,* Y *a compact Hausdorff space,* $a \in X$, *and* $F: X \setminus \{a\} \to Y$ *a continuous function. Let* $S \subset T$ *be closed subspaces containing* graph F *and contained in* graph $F \cup \{a\} \times Y$. *Then*

(1) $k \times 1_Y : X \times Y \to \beta X \times Y$ *is the Stone-Čech compactification of* $X \times Y$.

(2) *The diagram*

$$\begin{array}{ccccccc} \text{graph } F & \xrightarrow{\subset} & S & \xrightarrow{\subset} & T & \xrightarrow{\subset} & Y \times Y \\ & & \downarrow & & \downarrow & & \downarrow \\ & & \beta S & \longrightarrow & \beta T & \longrightarrow & \beta X \times X \end{array}$$

commutes were the vertical maps are the Stone-Čech compactifications and all horizontal maps are homeomorphisms onto their image.

(3) *If one identifies* βS *and* βT *with subspaces of* $\beta X \times Y$ *under the injections of* (2) *and if* $\bar{a} = k(a)$ *then there is a continuous function* $\bar{F}: \beta X \setminus \{\bar{a}\} \to Y$ *such that*

(a) $\bar{F} k(x) = F(x)$ *for* $x \in X \setminus \{a\}$,

(b) $T =$ graph $\bar{F} \cup \{a\} \times Y$,

(c) graph $\bar{F} \subset S \subset$ graph $\bar{F} \cup \{\bar{a}\} \times Y'$ *where* $Y' = pr_2$ graph F.

Theorem 3. *Let* k: Prim $A \cup \{A\} \to$ Cr $(\mathbb{C} \dot{+} A)$ *be the complete regularisation. Then* $k \times 1_{\text{Prim}\, R}$: (Prim $A \cup \{a\}) \times$ Prim R $\to$ Cr$(\mathbb{C} \dot{+} A) \times$ Prim R *is the Stone-Čech compactification. There is a continuous function* $\tilde{F}$: Cr$(\mathbb{C} \dot{+} A) \setminus \{k(A)\} \to$ Prim R *such that* $\tilde{F} k(b) = F(b)$ *for all* $b \in$ Prim A, *that* graph $\tilde{F} \cup \{k(A)\} \times FB$ *contains a naturally homeomorphic copy of* Cr $\tilde{A}_1$ *which contains* graph $\tilde{F}$, *and that* graph $F \cup \{k(A)\} \times$ Prim R *is naturally homeomorphic to* Cr $\tilde{A}$. *The following diagram commutes*

$$\begin{array}{ccccc} \text{Prim}\, \tilde{A}_1 & \longrightarrow & \text{Prim}\, \tilde{A} & \longrightarrow & (\text{Prim}\, A \cup \{A\}) \times \text{Prim}\, R \\ \tilde{\varphi}_1 \downarrow & & \tilde{\varphi} \downarrow & & \downarrow k \times 1_{\text{Prim}\, R} \\ \text{Cr}\, \tilde{A}_1 & \longrightarrow & \text{Cr}\, \tilde{A} & \longrightarrow & \text{Cr}\, (\mathbb{C} \dot{+} A) \times \text{Prim}\, R \end{array}$$

where $\tilde{\varphi}_1$ and $\tilde{\varphi}$ are the complete regularisations and where all horizontal maps are homeomorphisms onto their images.

For $b \in \mathrm{Prim}\, R$ we have $Fb + \varphi b \subset \tilde{\varphi}\tilde{b}$. Since $D \subset b$, the relation $(Fb + \varphi b)/D \subset \tilde{\varphi}_1\tilde{b}_1$ holds with $\tilde{b}_1 = \tilde{b}/D$. The equality $A \cap \tilde{\varphi}\tilde{b} = \varphi b$ holds if and only if $\varphi b = \varphi b'$ implies $Fb = Fb'$,

Suppose that $\varphi b = A \cap \tilde{\varphi}\tilde{b}$. We say that φb is of type 1 if either it is not modular or else it is modular and contains the center of A. We declare φb to be of type 2 in all other cases. Then

$$\tilde{\varphi}\tilde{b} = \begin{cases} Fb + \varphi b, & \text{if } \varphi b \text{ is of type } 1, \\ \cup \{r - r \cdot e + \varphi b : r \in R\}, & \text{if } \varphi b \text{ is of type } 2, \end{cases}$$

where e is some relative identity of A modulo φb. Correspondingly,

$$\tilde{A}_1/\tilde{\varphi}_1\tilde{b}_1 = \begin{cases} \mathbb{C} \dotplus A/\varphi b, & \text{if } \varphi b \text{ is of type } 1, \\ A/\varphi b, & \text{if } \varphi b \text{ is of type } 2. \end{cases}$$

Finally $\tilde{\varphi}\tilde{b} = Fb + \varphi b$, and $\tilde{A}/\tilde{\varphi}\tilde{b} \cong \mathbb{C} \dotplus A/\varphi b$.

2. The centroid

It became evident towards the end of the last section that in order to find an adjunction of identity which was to be satisfactory for spectral investigations one must find a commutative algebra R with identity acting on A which is large enough so that $\varphi b \neq \varphi b'$ implies $Fb \neq Fb'$. A natural candidate for such an algebra is the centroid of A. The *centroid* of A is the algebra of all vector space endomorphisms r of the vector space endomorphisms of A satisfying $r(aa') = (ra)a' = a(ra')$. All these endomorphisms are automatically continuous. The centroid is a C^*-algebra relative to the operator norm and the involution defined by $r^*a = (ra^*)^*$.

Note that the centroid reduces to the center of A if A has an identity.

In the remainder of this section, A will always denote a C^*-algebra and R its centroid.

Theorem 4.

(a) *If $\varphi b = \varphi b'$ for $b, b' \in \mathrm{Prim}\, A$, then $Fb = Fb'$.*

(b) *$\varphi b = A \cap \tilde{\varphi}\tilde{b}$, and $\varphi b/D = A_1 \cap \tilde{\varphi}_1\tilde{b}_1$.*

(c) $\tilde{A}_1/\tilde{\varphi}_1\tilde{b}_1 \cong \begin{cases} \mathbb{C} \dotplus A/\varphi b, \text{ if } \varphi b \text{ is of type } 1, \\ A/\varphi b, \text{ if } \varphi b \text{ is of type } 2. \end{cases}$

$\tilde{A}/\tilde{\varphi}\tilde{b} = \mathbb{C} \dotplus A/\varphi b.$

(d) Prim $\tilde{A}_1/\tilde{\varphi}_1\tilde{b}_1$ *may be naturally identified with the subspace* Prim $\tilde{A}_1 \cap [(\mathrm{Prim}\, A \cup \cup \{A\}) \times Fb]$ *of* $(\mathrm{Prim}\, \tilde{A} \cup \{A\}) \times \mathrm{Prim}\, R$.

(e) F: Prim $A \to$ Prim R *is the Stone-Čech compactification of* Prim A.

(f) *The inclusion* graph $F \to$ Prim $\tilde{A}_1$ *is the Stone-Čech compactification of* graph F.

(g) *The inclusion $FB \to$* Prim R *is the Stone-Čech compactification of FB.*

(h) Cr A *may be naturally identified with the subspace* graph $\tilde{F} \cup \{k(A)\} \times (FB \setminus Q)$ *and* Cr $\tilde{A}_1$ *with the subspace* graph $\tilde{F} \cup \{k(A)\} \times ((\mathrm{Prim}\, A) \setminus Q)$ *of* $\mathrm{Cr}(\mathbb{C} + A) \times \times \mathrm{Prim}\, R$, *where $Q = \{Fb : \varphi b \text{ is modular}\}$.*

(i) φb = *closed ideal generated by* $(Fb) \cdot A = \bigcap \{b' \in \text{Prim } A : r \cdot A \subset b'$ if and only if $r \cdot A \subset b$ for all $r \in R\}$. *If A has an identity then φb is the closed ideal generated by $Z \cap b$ where Z is the center of A.*

Theorem 4 gives a complete answer to the questions (1) and (2) posed in the introduction. It is helpful to vizualize the situation in a figure:

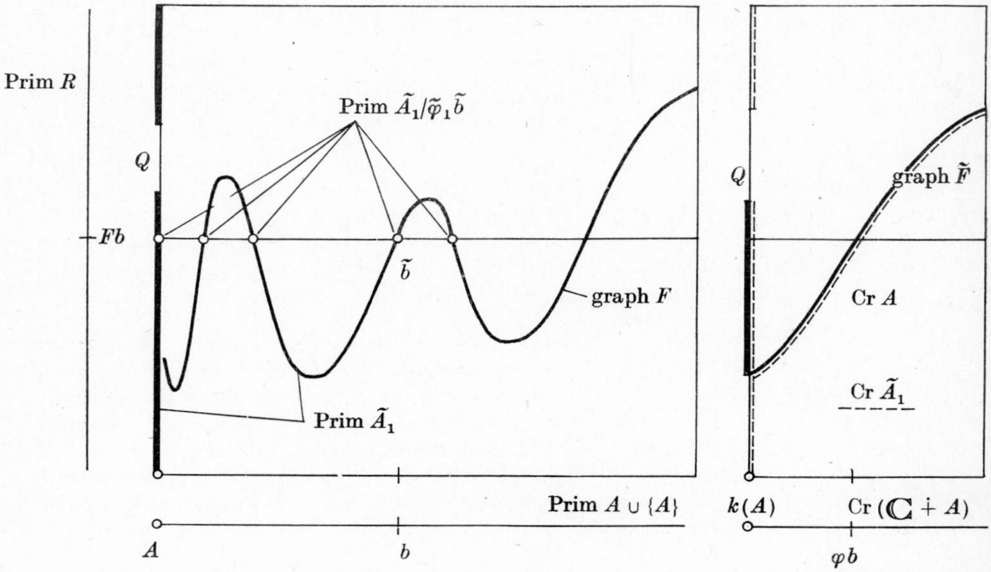

Note that in order to arrive at Prim $\tilde{A}_1$ from Prim $\tilde{A}$ one has to discard exactly those box ideals $p + A$ with $p = Fb$ for which φb is modular and does not contain the center of A.

3. The Gelfand-Neumark theorem for non-commutative C^*-algebras

In the whole section A is a C^*-algebra and R its centroid. Let $E = \bigcup \{\tilde{A}/m : m \in \text{Cr } A\}$ and define $\pi : E \to \text{Cr } A$ by $\pi(a + m) = m$. Let $\tilde{E}_1 = \bigcup \{\tilde{A}_1/m : m \in \text{Cr } \tilde{A}_1\}$ and define $\tilde{\pi}_1 : \tilde{E}_1 \to \text{Cr } \tilde{A}_1$ by $\tilde{\pi}_1(a + m) = m$.

We may and will identify Cr A with a subspace of Cr A_1 according to Theorem 4 (h). Then, for $m \in \text{Cr } A \subset \text{Cr } \tilde{A}_1$ the stalks $\pi^{-1}(m)$ and $\tilde{\pi}^{-1}(m)$ become automatically identified if m is modular, and we may write $\tilde{\pi}_1^{-1}(m) \cong \mathbb{C} \dotplus \pi^{-1}(m)$ if m is not modular. There is a commutating diagram of functions in which all horizontal maps are injective

$$\begin{array}{ccc} E & \xrightarrow{\ \alpha\ } & \tilde{E}_1 \\ {\scriptstyle \pi}\downarrow & & \downarrow{\scriptstyle \tilde{\pi}_1} \\ M & \xrightarrow{\ \subset\ } & \tilde{M}_1 \end{array} \qquad \begin{array}{l} M = \text{Cr } A \\ \tilde{M}_1 = \text{Cr } \tilde{A}_1, \end{array}$$

In earlier investigations by DAUNS and the author the following proposition was established:

Proposition 3. *There are unique coarsets topologies on E and $\tilde{E}_1$ satisfying the following conditions:*

(a) *π and $\tilde{\pi}_1$ are continuous.*

(b) *The functions $\hat{a}: M \to E$ and $\hat{a}_1: \tilde{M}_1 \to \tilde{E}_1$ defined by $\tilde{a}(m) = a + m$ and $\hat{a}_1(m) = a_1 + m$ for $a \in A$ and $a_1 \in \tilde{A}_1$ are continuous.*

(c) *The function $a_1 \to \hat{a}_1: \tilde{A}_1 \to \Gamma(\tilde{\pi}_1)$, where $\Gamma(\tilde{\pi})$ denotes the C^*-algebra of all continuous sections for $\tilde{\pi}_1$ (i.e. functions $\sigma: \tilde{M}_1 \to \tilde{E}_1$ with $\pi\sigma = 1_{\tilde{M}_1}$) is an isomorphism of C^*-algebras.*

In fact, it was also shown that the function $a \to \hat{a}$ from A into the bounded sections for π was an isomorphism of C^*-algebras from A onto the C^*-algebra of all section vanishing at infinity in a certain way which was somewhat technical to describe. The following theorem, however, gives a rather complete insight into the situation by describing in a combined fashion how π and $\tilde{\pi}_1$ should be treated simultaneously. We say that a section σ for π extends to a section $\tilde{\sigma}$ for $\tilde{\pi}_1$ if $\alpha\sigma = \tilde{\sigma}|M$.

Theorem 5. *The algebra A is isomorphic to the C^*-algebra of all continuous sections for π which extend to a section for $\tilde{\pi}_1$ which vanishes outside M, and is therefore isomorphic to the ideal of all sections in $\Gamma(\tilde{\pi}_1)$ which vanish outside M and take their values in $\alpha\pi^{-1}(m)$ for all $m \in M$. The closed ideal of all sections vanishing outside M generally is larger and has as its structure space the open subset interior $\mathrm{pr}_2^{-1} FB$ of $\mathrm{Prim}\, \tilde{A}_1$. It contains an isomorphic copy of the algebra $C_0(M)$ of continuous complex valued functions on M vanishing at infinity whereas $\Gamma(\tilde{\pi}_1)$ itself contains an isomorphic copy of $C(\tilde{M}_1) \cong C(\beta\, \mathrm{Prim}\, A)$ as its center.*

Note that in general there is a whole series of C^*-algebras containing A as an ideal and being contained in $\tilde{A}_1$ as an ideal which have the same complete regularisation space as A. They correspond bijectively to the open subsets of $\mathrm{Prim}\, \tilde{A}_1$ containing graph F and contained in the interior of $\mathrm{pr}_2^{-1} FB$. Theorem 5 gives a fairly complete answer to question (3) of the introduction. It still does not clarify the structure of the stalks, i.e. the structure of the C^*-algebras $A/\varphi b$ for $b \in \mathrm{Prim}\, A$. Some elucidation is brought into this question by Theorem 4 (d). One may, of course, apply the main representation Theorem 5 to $A/\varphi b$ again and repeat this process until cardinality bounds stop continuation, but this may hardly be considered a satisfactory way to collect information about the structure of $A/\varphi b$.

References

[1] R. C. BUSBY, Double centralizers and extensions of C^*-algebras, Trans. Amer. Math. Soc. **132** (1968), 79—99.

[2] J. DAUNS and K. H. HOFMANN, Representation of rings by sections, Memoirs Amer. Math. Soc. **83** (1969).

[3] J. DAUNS and K. H. HOFMANN, Spectral theory of algebras and adjunction of identity, Math. Ann. (1969).

[4] J. DIXMIER, Ideal center of a C^*-algebra, Duke Math. J. **35** (1968), 375—382.

[5] H. LEPTIN, Verallgemeinerte L^1-Algebren und projektive Darstellungen lokal kompakter Gruppen, Inventiones Math. **3** (1967), 257—281; **4** (1967), 68—86.

[6] G. A. REID, A generalisation of W^*-algebras, Pacific J. Math. **15** (1965), 1019—1026.

CATEGORIAL CONNECTIONS BETWEEN GENERALIZED PROXIMITY SPACES AND COMPACTIFICATIONS

MIROSLAV HUŠEK (Praha)

Recently there appeared many generalizations of the Smirnov theorem concerning a relation between proximities and compactifications. But most of them dealt with relations between objects only. In this paper we propose a generalization of the Smirnov theorem including also morphisms (i.e. continuous extensions of proximally continuous mappings).

First, we define a category **Ext** of extensions of topological spaces and investigate its properties. Then we shall construct a basic functor G from a category of generalized proximity spaces into **Ext**. As applications, there are examples of the cases when G is full or at least an embedding. The widest generalization concerns the category of symmetric proximity spaces satisfying the implication $\bar{A}\, p\, \bar{B} \Rightarrow A\, p B$. The functor G defined on this category is a full embedding into a category of compactifications of topological spaces with the property that any proximity space X is a subspace of GX provided with the Wallman proximity.

One obtains further theorems of this type by applying general construction of G to other structures and other extensions.

We shall use the notation from [3] and [4]. By a functor we always mean a covariant faithful functor. A non-void indexed class $\{f_i\}$ is said to be projective if all the f_i have the same domain.

Now we shall introduce the basic definition (the projective form only — the dual one is inductive). Let $F: \mathscr{K} \to \mathscr{C}$ be a functor, $\mathscr{C}'$ a subcategory of $\mathscr{C}$, $\{X_i\}$ an indexed class of objects from $\mathscr{K}$ and let $\{\varphi_i\}$ be a projective indexed class in $\mathscr{C}$ such that $\{FX_i\} = \{\mathrm{E}\varphi_i\}$. We shall denote by $\langle F, \mathscr{C}'\rangle - \varprojlim \langle\{\varphi_i\}, \{X_i\}\rangle$ an object X of $\mathscr{K}$ with the following properties:

> there is an $f_i: X \to X_i$ for each i such that $Ff_i = \varphi_i$; if $\{g_i\}$ is a projective indexed class in $\mathscr{K}$, $g_i: Y \to X_i$, $Fg_i = \varphi_i \circ \varphi$ for each i, where $\varphi \in \mathscr{C}'$, then $Fg = \varphi$ for some $g: Y \to X$.

The object X is said to be *projectively $\langle F, \mathscr{C}'\rangle$-generated by $\langle\{\varphi_i\}, \{X_i\}\rangle$*.

In the case that $\{\varphi_i\} = \{Fh_i\}$, $\{\mathrm{E}h_i\} = \{X_i\}$, $\{h_i\}$ is a projective indexed class, we shall denote X by $\langle F, \mathscr{C}'\rangle - \varprojlim \{h_i\}$. The symbol $\langle F, \mathscr{C}'\rangle - \mathrm{proj}\, \mathscr{K}'$, where $\mathscr{K}'$ is a subcategory of $\mathscr{K}$, designates the class $\mathrm{E}\,\{\langle F, \mathscr{C}'\rangle - \varprojlim \{h_i\} \mid \{h_i\}$ is a projective family ranging in $\mathscr{K}'\}$.

The functor F is called projectively $\langle F, \mathscr{C}'\rangle$-generative if $\langle F, \mathscr{C}'\rangle - \varprojlim \langle\{\varphi_i\}, \{X_i\}\rangle$ exists for any pair of families $\{\varphi_i\}$, $\{X_i\}$ described above. If F is projectively

$\langle F, \mathscr{C}\rangle$-generative, then the $\langle F, \mathscr{C}'\rangle$-generation does not depend on $\mathscr{C}'$ for $\mathscr{C}' \supset \operatorname{obj} \mathscr{C}$ and hence $\mathscr{C}'$ will be omitted in these cases.

Example 1. Denote by **Prox** the following category of generalized proximity spaces. Objects of **Prox** are pairs $\langle P, p\rangle$, where P is a set and p is a relation on $\exp P - (\emptyset)$ satisfying the properties

(i) $A \cup B \subset P$, $A \cap B \neq \emptyset$ implies ApB;

(ii) if $\mathfrak{A}$ and $\mathfrak{B}$ are finite collections of subsets of P, then $\bigcup \mathfrak{A} p \bigcup \mathfrak{B}$ if and only if ApB for some $A \in \mathfrak{A}$, $B \in \mathfrak{B}$;

(iii) if we denote $\bar{A} = \mathrm{E}\,\{a \mid (a)\, pA\}$, then $(a)\, p\bar{A}$ implies $(a)\, pA$.

A morphism in **Prox** from $\langle P, p\rangle$ into $\langle Q, q\rangle$ is a triple $\langle f, \langle P, p\rangle, \langle Q, q\rangle\rangle$ such that ApB implies $f[A] q f[B]$.

The obvious functor from **Prox** into **Top** (see (iii)) is denoted by F_p and the forgetful functor from **Top** into **Ens** is denoted by F_t.

It can be proved by a standard method (see e.g. [3]) that $F_t \circ F_p$ is projectively and inductively $\langle F_t \circ F_p, \textbf{Ens}\rangle$-generative (if a mapping $f\colon \langle P, p\rangle \to \langle Q, q\rangle$ is projectively $F_t \circ F_p$-generating then ApB if and only if $f[A]\; qf[B]$). It is almost evident that F_p is projectively $\langle F_p, \operatorname{obj} \textbf{Top}\rangle$-generative. The following example shows that F_p is not projectively $\langle F_p, \textbf{Top}\rangle$-generative and inductively $\langle F_p, \operatorname{obj} \textbf{Top}\rangle$-generative. Let $\langle P, p\rangle$ be an infinite proximity space such that XpY if and only if either X and Y meet or X is infinite. If g ist a non-constant mapping from P into a discrete topological space $\mathscr{Q}$ with at least one infinite fiber $g^{-1}[y]$, then g is a continuous mapping from $\langle P, p\rangle$ into $\mathscr{Q}$ but is not proximally continuous as a mapping from $\langle P, p\rangle$ into $\langle Q, q\rangle$ for any proximity space $\langle Q, q\rangle$ inducing $\mathscr{Q}$.

Example 2 deals with the category **Ext** of extensions of topological spaces. Objects of **Ext** are triples $\langle \mathscr{P}, f, \mathscr{Q}\rangle$ where $\mathscr{P}$ and $\mathscr{Q}$ are topological spaces and f is a homeomorphism of $\mathscr{P}$ onto a dense subspace of $\mathscr{Q}$. A morphism in **Ext** from $\langle \mathscr{P}, f, \mathscr{Q}\rangle$ into $\langle \mathscr{P}', f', \mathscr{Q}'\rangle$ is a triple $\langle g, \langle \mathscr{P}, f, \mathscr{Q}\rangle, \langle \mathscr{P}', f', \mathscr{Q}'\rangle\rangle$, where g is a continuous mapping from $\mathscr{P}$ into $\mathscr{P}'$ having a continuous extension $\tilde{g}$ on $\mathscr{Q}$ into $\mathscr{Q}'$ (i.e. $\tilde{g} \circ f = f' \circ g$).

We shall denote by F_e the functor $\{\langle g, \langle \mathscr{P}, f, \mathscr{Q}\rangle, \langle \mathscr{P}', f', \mathscr{Q}'\rangle\rangle \to \langle g, \mathscr{P}, \mathscr{P}'\rangle\}\colon \textbf{Ext} \to \textbf{Top}$.

Proposition. *The functor $F_t \circ F_e$ is projectively and inductively $\langle F_t, \circ F_e$, **Ens**$\rangle$-generative. The functor F_e is projectively and inductively $\langle F_e$, **Top**$\rangle$-generative.*

Proof. First, we shall prove the existence of the projective $\langle F_t \circ F_e, \textbf{Ens}\rangle$-generation. Assume that $\{\langle \mathscr{P}_i, f_i, \mathscr{Q}_i\rangle\}$ is a family of extensions and that g_i are mappings from a set P into $\mathscr{P}_i$. Denote by $g\colon P \to \prod \mathscr{Q}_i$ the reduced product of $f_i \circ g_i$, by $\mathscr{Q}$ the disjoint union $P \cup \overline{(g[P]} - g[P])$ with the topology projectively F_t-generated by the mapping $g \cup 1_{\overline{g[P]} - g[P]}\colon \mathscr{Q} \to \prod \mathscr{Q}_i$. If $\mathscr{P}$ is a subspace of $\mathscr{Q}$ with the underlying set P, then $\langle \mathscr{P}, 1_P, \mathscr{Q}\rangle = \langle F_t \circ F_e, \textbf{Ens}\rangle - \underleftarrow{\mathrm{Lim}}\,\langle\{g_i\}, \{\langle \mathscr{P}_i, f_i, \mathscr{Q}_i\rangle\}\rangle$.

If we use this method in the case that all the f_i are the identity mappings of a connected two-point T_0-space $\mathscr{D}$ and that the set of indexes i is equal to $\mathrm{Hom}_{\textbf{Top}}\, \langle \mathscr{P}, \mathscr{D}\rangle$, then we get the existence of an extension $\langle \mathscr{P}, g, g\mathscr{P}\rangle$ such that $\langle h, \langle \mathscr{P}' f', \mathscr{Q}'\rangle, \langle \mathscr{P}, g, g\mathscr{P}\rangle\rangle \in \textbf{Ext}$ for any extension $\langle \mathscr{P}', f', \mathscr{Q}'\rangle$ and any continuous mapping $h\colon \mathscr{P}' \to \mathscr{P}$. The space $g\mathscr{P}$ is compact.

Let $\{\langle \mathscr{P}_i, f_i, \mathscr{Q}_i\rangle\}$ be a family of extensions and g_i be continuous mappings from a topological space $\mathscr{P}$ into $\mathscr{P}_i$. Then $\langle F_e, \textbf{Top}\rangle - \underleftarrow{\mathrm{Lim}}\,\langle\{g_i\}, \{\langle \mathscr{P}_i, f_i, \mathscr{Q}_i\rangle\}\rangle = F_t \circ F_e - \inf\,(\langle \mathscr{P}, g, g\,\mathscr{P}\rangle, F_t \circ F_e - \underleftarrow{\mathrm{Lim}}\,\langle\{F_t g_i\}, \{\langle \mathscr{P}_i, f_i, \mathscr{Q}_i\rangle\}\rangle)$.

One obtains the inductive F_e-generation by means of sum of spaces and of pushout.

Corollary. *The category of compactifications is F_e-projective subcategory of* **Ext** (i.e. an object projectively F_e-generated by mappings ranging in compactifications is a compactification).

Now, we introduce a construction of the basic functor G. Let $\mathscr{K}$ be a full subcategory of **Prox**, $\mathscr{K}'$ be a full subcategory of $\mathscr{K}$, F_K the restriction of F_p to $\mathscr{K}$ and let G' be a full functor from $\langle \mathscr{K}', F_{K'} \rangle$ into $\langle \mathsf{Ext}, F_e \rangle$ (i.e. $F_e \circ G' = F_{K'}$). We shall define a functor G (which is said to be *projectively* $\langle F_K, F_e \rangle$*-generated by* G') from $\langle \mathscr{K}, F_K \rangle$ into $\langle \mathsf{Ext}, F_e \rangle$ in the following way. The image $G\mathscr{P}$ of an object $\mathscr{P}$ from $\mathscr{K}$ is the extension $F_e - \underleftarrow{\mathrm{Lim}} \langle \{F_p f \mid \mathrm{D} f = \mathscr{P}, \mathrm{E} f \in \mathscr{K}'\}, \{G' \mathrm{E} f\} \rangle$, i.e. $G\mathscr{P}$ is the greatest extension of $F_P \mathscr{P}$ such that each proximally continuous mapping from $\mathscr{P}$ into an X from $\mathscr{K}'$ has a continuous extension on $G\mathscr{P}$ into $G'X$. It is easy to extend the mapping to morphisms.

The functor G has many nice properties (see [5] for some further and more general ones):

(1) *If G is one-to-one, then* $\mathscr{K} = \langle F_K, \text{obj } \mathsf{Top} \rangle - \text{proj } \mathscr{K}'$. *The converse holds if* $F_p\, [\mathrm{Hom}_{\mathsf{Prox}} \langle \mathscr{P}, X \rangle] \supset F_e\, [\mathrm{Hom}_{\mathsf{Ext}} \langle G\mathscr{P}, G'X \rangle]$ *for each* $\mathscr{P} \in \text{obj } \mathscr{K}$, $X \in \text{obj } \mathscr{K}'$.

(2) *G is full if and only if* $\mathscr{K} = \langle F_K, \mathsf{Top} \rangle - \text{proj } \mathscr{K}'$ *and* $F_p\, [\mathrm{Hom}_{\mathsf{Prox}} \langle \mathscr{P}, X \rangle] \supset F_e\, [\mathrm{Hom}_{\mathsf{Ext}} \langle G\mathscr{P}, G'X \rangle]$ *for each* $\mathscr{P} \in \text{obj } \mathscr{K}$, $X \in \text{obj } \mathscr{K}'$.

(3) *Assume that* $\mathscr{K} = \langle F_K, \mathsf{Top} \rangle - \text{proj } \mathscr{K}'$. *Then G is full provided that there exists a full functor* $H: \langle \mathscr{K}, F_K \rangle \to \langle \mathsf{Ext}, F_e \rangle$ *extending* G'.

(4) *Suppose that G is full. Then* $G[\mathscr{K}]$ *is a coreflective subcategory of the full subcategory of* **Ext** *generated by* $F_e - \text{proj } G'[\mathscr{K}']$.

(5) *Let G be full,* $\mathscr{K} = F_t \circ F_p - \text{proj } \mathscr{K}'$. *Then for each* $\mathscr{P} \in F_t - \text{proj } F_p[\mathscr{K}']$ *there is an extension* $\langle \mathscr{P}, s, s\mathscr{P} \rangle$ *such that* $\langle g, \langle \mathscr{P}, s, s\mathscr{P} \rangle, \langle \mathscr{P}', f', \mathscr{Q}' \rangle \rangle \in \mathsf{Ext}$ *for any extension* $\langle \mathscr{P}', f', \mathscr{Q}' \rangle \in F_e - \text{proj } G[\mathscr{K}']$ *and for any continuous mapping* $g: \mathscr{P} \to \mathscr{P}'$.

Next, we shall apply the foregoing propositions to special categories $\mathscr{K}$ and $\mathscr{K}'$. Denote by $\mathscr{W}$ the category of Wallman proximity spaces (a generalized proximity space $\langle P, p \rangle$ is called a Wallman space if $A p B$ is equivalent to the fact that the closures of A and B meet).

Proposition. *The category of compact spaces from $\mathscr{W}$ is productive in* **Prox** *and is closed under projective $F_t \circ F_p$-generation by a single mapping onto a closed subspace.*

Proof. Let $\langle P, p \rangle$ be a product in **Prox** of Wallman proximity compact spaces $\langle P_i, p_i \rangle$. We have to prove that $X \cap Y \neq \emptyset$ provided X and Y are closed proximal subsets of $\langle P, p \rangle$. Let $X = \overline{X}$, $Y = \overline{Y}$, $X \cap Y = \emptyset$, $X p Y$. The collection $\mathscr{B} = \mathrm{E}\, \{\prod \{X_i\} \mid X_i$ is a closed subset of $\langle P_i, p_i \rangle$ and all the X_i except one are equal to $P_i\}$ is a closed subbase of $\langle P, p \rangle$. Consequently, there is a family $\{\mathscr{B}_b \mid b \in B\}$ of finite subsets of $\mathscr{B}$ such that $X = \bigcap \{\bigcup \{A \mid A \in \mathscr{B}_b\}\, b \in B\}$. Because of compactness of Y there is a finite subset $B' \subset B$ such that $\bigcap \{\bigcup \mathscr{B}_b \mid b \in B'\} \cap Y = \emptyset$. Therefore we may assume that B is a finite set of natural numbers. Suppose that for each $b \in B$, $b < b'$ there is an $A_b \in \mathscr{B}_b$ such that $(X \cap \bigcap \{A_b \mid b < b'\})\, p\, Y$. Then $\{X \cap A \cap \bigcap \{A_b \mid b < b'\} \mid A \in \mathscr{B}_{b'}\}$ is a finite cover of $X \cap \bigcap \{A_b \mid b < b'\}$ and, hence, $(X \cap \bigcap \{A_b \mid b \leq b'\})\, p\, Y$ for some $A_{b'} \in \mathscr{B}_{b'}$. Thus we have proved by induction the existence of a family $\{A_b \mid b \in B\}$ such that $A_b \in \mathscr{B}$ for each b, $\bigcap \{A_b \mid b \in B\} \subset X$ and $\bigcap \{A_b \mid b \in B\}\, p\, Y$. If we repeat the same for Y, we obtain two closed sets X', Y' with the properties $X' p Y'$, $X' \subset X$, $Y' \subset Y$, $X' = \prod \{\mathrm{pr}_i X'\}$, $Y' = \prod \{\mathrm{pr}_i Y'\}$ and $\mathrm{pr}_i X'$, $\mathrm{pr}_i Y'$ are closed sets in $\langle P_i, p_i \rangle$. It follows that $\mathrm{pr}_i X' \cap \mathrm{pr}_i Y' \neq \emptyset$ for each i and, hence, $X' \cap Y' \neq \emptyset$. This is a contradiction.

Next, we shall prove the second assertion. Let $\langle P, p \rangle = F_t \circ F_p - \underleftarrow{\mathrm{Lim}}(f)$, where $f[P]$ is a closed subspace of a Wallman space $\langle Q, q \rangle$. Then $A p B$ is equivalent to $f[A] q f[B]$, which means that the closures of $f[A]$ and $f[B]$ in $f[P]$ meet. Since the closure $\overline{X}$ of a subset X of $\langle P, p \rangle$ is equal to $f^{-1}[\overline{f[X]}]$, we get that $A p B$ is equivalent to $\overline{A} \cap \overline{B} \neq \emptyset$.

Corollary. *Let $\mathscr{K}'$ be a full subcategory of* Prox, $\mathscr{K} = F_t \circ F_p - \mathrm{proj}\ \mathscr{K}'$. *Assume that each $X \in \mathrm{obj}\ \mathscr{K}'$ is a subspace of the third member of $G'X$ provided with its Wallman proximity and that this member is compact. Then the functor G projectively $\langle F_K, F_e \rangle$-generated by G' is full and each $X \in \mathscr{K}$ is a subspace of the third member of GX provided with its Wallman proximity* (i. e. A, B are proximal in X if and only if their closures in GX meet).

Proof. By the proposition (2) from properties of G, it is sufficient to prove that $F_p[\mathrm{Hom}_{\mathsf{Prox}} \langle X, Y \rangle] \supset F_e[\mathrm{Hom}_{\mathsf{Ext}} \langle GX, GY \rangle]$. Assume that $GX = \langle F_p X, 1, X' \rangle$, $GY = \langle F_p Y, 1, Y' \rangle$. It follows from the preceding proposition that X is a subspace of X' provided with its Wallman proximity. If a continuous mapping g can be continuously extended to a mapping $\tilde{g}$ on X' into Y', then $\tilde{g}$ is proximally continuous for Wallman proximities of X' and Y'. Consequently the restriction g of $\tilde{g}$ is proximally continuous from X into Y.

Example 3. Let $\mathscr{P}_0$ be a proximally discrete two-point space (i.e. only intersecting sets are proximal). Denote by $\mathscr{K}$ the full subcategory of Prox generated by $F_t \circ F_p - \mathrm{proj}\ (\mathscr{P}_0)$, and by $\mathscr{K}'$ the full subcategory of Prox generated by $(\mathscr{P}_0)$. If $G'\mathscr{P}_0 = \langle F_p \mathscr{P}_0, 1, F_p \mathscr{P}_0 \rangle$, then the conditions of the preceding corollary are fulfilled and hence the functor G is a full embedding. The image $G[\mathscr{K}]$ is a representative subcategory of the category $\mathscr{E} = F_t \circ F_p - \mathrm{proj}\ (G'\mathscr{P}_0)$ the objects of which are exactly the uniformizable zero-dimensional compactifications (i.e. the third member of GX is a uniformizable zero-dimensional compact space). Indeed, the functor projectively $\langle F_E, F_K \rangle$-generated by G'^{-1} is full because each proximally continuous mapping from a dense subspace of a uniformizable zero-dimensional compact space provided with its Wallman proximity into $\mathscr{P}_0$ can be continuously extended to the whole space. The compactification $s\mathscr{P}$ from (5) is the Banaschewski compactification from [1].

The spaces $\langle P, p \rangle$ of $\mathscr{K}$ are in a one-to-one relation with additive, multiplicative, and subtractive collections $\mathfrak{A}$ in $\exp P$. If $\langle P, p \rangle$ is an object of $\mathscr{K}$, then $\mathfrak{A} = \mathrm{E}\{A \mid A$ *non* $p(P - A)\}$. Conversely, if $\mathfrak{A}$ is given, then $X p Y$ is equivalent to the fact that each $A \in \mathfrak{A}$ containing X intersects Y. Hence the uniformizable zero-dimensional compactifications of a topological space $\mathscr{P}$ are in a one-to-one relation with additive, multiplicative, and subtractive open bases of $\mathscr{P}$.

Example 4. Let $\mathscr{I}$ be the closed unit intervall with the usual proximity, $\mathscr{K}$ be the full subcategory of Prox generated by $F_t \circ F_p - \mathrm{proj}\ (\mathscr{I})$ (i.e. $\mathscr{K}$ is the category of uniformizable proximities), and let $\mathscr{K}'$ be the full subcategory of Prox generated by $(\mathscr{I})$. Then by the same argument as in the foregoing example, the functor G is a full embedding and $G[\mathscr{K}]$ is isomorphic to the category of uniformizable compactifications (this is the known Smirnov theorem). The compactification $s\mathscr{P}$ from (5) is the Čech-Stone compactification.

Example 5. Let $\mathscr{K}'$ be the full subcategory of Prox generated by the class $\mathrm{E}\{\langle P, p_P \rangle \mid P$ is a set$\}$, where p_P is the Wallman proximity of the coarsest T_1-topology of P. Denote by $\mathscr{K}$ the full subcategory of **Prox** generated by $F_t \circ F_p$ — proj $\mathscr{K}'$. Objects of $\mathscr{K}$ are symmetric proximity spaces satisfying the implication $\bar{A}\, p\, \bar{B} \Rightarrow A\, p\, B$. Let τ be an isotone mapping from Card into Card. If G' is the functor which assigns $\langle F_p \langle P, p\rangle, 1, F_p \langle \tau P, p_{\tau P}\rangle\rangle$ to $\langle P, p_P\rangle$, then the functor G projectively $\langle F_K, F_e\rangle$-generated by G' is a full embedding. If $G\langle P, p\rangle = \langle \mathscr{P}, 1, \mathscr{Q}\rangle$, then $A\,p\,B$ if and only if the closures of A and B in $\mathscr{Q}$ meet. The space $\mathscr{Q}$ is a symmetric compact topological space.

In the remaining part of this example, the mapping τ is the identity. In this case the ideal points of $\mathscr{Q}$ can be characterized in the following way. If $\mathscr{F} = \mathrm{E}\,\{f \mid f \in \mathscr{K}, \mathrm{D}f = \langle P, p\rangle, \mathrm{E}f \in \mathscr{K}', f \text{ is surjective}\}$, then the points of $\mathscr{Q} - \mathscr{P}$ are the families $\{X_f \mid f \in \mathscr{F}\}$ of closed sets in $\mathscr{P}$ such that

(i) $\bigcap \{X_f \mid f \in \mathscr{F}\} = \emptyset$;

(ii) for each $f \in \mathscr{F}$, $X_f = f^{-1}[a]$ for some $a \in \mathrm{E}f$;

(iii) for each finite family $\{a_i\}$, $a_i \in \mathrm{E}f_i$, $a_i \neq f_i[X_{f_i}]$, where $\{f_i\}$ is a finite subfamily of $\mathscr{F}$, the union $\bigcup \{f_i^{-1}[a_i]\}$ is not equal to $\mathscr{P}$.

The closed subbase of $\mathscr{Q}$ is the collection $\mathrm{E}\,[A_a{}^f \mid f \in \mathscr{F}, a \in \mathrm{E}f\}$, where $A_a{}^f = \mathrm{E}\,\{\{X_f \mid f \in \mathscr{F}\} \mid \{X_f\} \in \mathscr{Q} - \mathscr{P}, X_f = f^{-1}[a]\} \cup f^{-1}[a]$.

From this characterization it is possible to derive an internal characterization of objects of $G[\mathscr{K}]$. An extension $\langle \mathscr{P}, f, \mathscr{Q}\rangle$ is an object of $G[\mathscr{K}]$ if and only if there is a family $[\mathscr{X}_\alpha]$ of closed disjoint covers of $\mathscr{Q}$ such that

(i) $\bigcup \{\bigcup \mathscr{X}_\alpha\}$ is a subbase of $\mathscr{Q}$;

(ii) each maximal $\{\mathscr{X}_\alpha\}$-family has a non-void intersection (a family $\{F_\alpha\}$, $F_\alpha \in \mathscr{X}_\alpha$ is a maximal $\{\mathscr{X}_\alpha\}$-family if for each finite family $\{X_\alpha\}$, $X_{\alpha_i} \in \mathscr{X}_{\alpha_i}$, $\bigcup \{X_{\alpha_i}\} = \mathscr{Q}$ there is an index i such that $X_{\alpha_i} = F_{\alpha_i}$);

(iii) let $\mathscr{X}$ be a closed disjoint cover of $\mathscr{P}$ such that any two different members of $\mathscr{X}$ have finite covers $\mathfrak{A}$, $\mathfrak{A}'$ with the property that for each pair $\langle A, A'\rangle \in \mathfrak{A} \times \mathfrak{A}'$ there is $\{\mathscr{X}_\alpha\}$ such that the sets star $(A, \mathscr{X}_\alpha)$, star $(A', \mathscr{X}_\alpha)$ are finite and disjoint. Then $\mathscr{X}$ is a trace in $\mathscr{P}$ of some $\mathscr{X}_\alpha$.

Unfortunately, the functor G is not projective as in the preceding examples. It does not preserve subobjects. Indeed, the image under G of the identity mapping from $\langle P, p_P\rangle$ into $\langle Q, p_Q\rangle$ with card $P <$ card Q is not projectively F_e-generating.

A further "bad" property of G is the fact that the restriction of G to uniformizable proximities does not agree with the Smirnov functor from the example 4. For the proof of this assertion it is sufficient to take the closed unit interval $\mathscr{I}$ with the Wallman proximity as the uniformizable compactification of the set X of rational points in $\mathscr{I}$. Since $\mathscr{I}$ has no countable closed disjoint cover, the identity mapping from X into the set X provided with the coarsest T_1-topology cannot be continuously extended on $\mathscr{I}$. It is easy to prove that the Smirnov compactification of a uniformizable proximity space $\mathscr{P}$ is a uniformizable modification of $G\mathscr{P}$. I do not know if G coincides with the Smirnov functor for some other choice of τ.

In the foregoing examples we have investigated projectively $F_t \circ F_p$-generated categories. Now we turn our attention to projectively F_p-generated categories. Since F_p is not projectively $\langle F_p, \mathsf{Top}\rangle$-generative we cannot expect G to be full. But we may require G to be at least one-to-one.

Proposition. *Let $\mathscr{P}'$ be a topological space, $\langle \mathscr{P}, f, \mathscr{Q}\rangle \in$ **Ext** and let $\mathscr{P}$ have coarser topology than $\mathscr{P}'$. Then there is an extension $\langle \mathscr{P}', f', \mathscr{Q}'\rangle$ such that* $\mathrm{Hom}_{\mathsf{Ext}} \langle\langle \mathscr{P}', f', \mathscr{Q}'\rangle,$

$\langle \mathscr{P}_0, f_0, \mathscr{Q}_0 \rangle\rangle = \mathrm{Hom}_{\mathsf{Ext}} \langle\langle \mathscr{P}, f, \mathscr{Q} \rangle, \langle \mathscr{P}_0, f_0, \mathscr{Q}_0 \rangle\rangle$ for an arbitrary T_1-extension $\langle \mathscr{P}_0, f_0, \mathscr{Q}_0 \rangle$. If $\mathscr{Q}$ is compact then $\mathscr{Q}'$ is compact, too.

Proof uses a method from [2]. Let $\mathscr{Q}'$ be a disjoint union of $\mathscr{P}'$ and of $\mathscr{Q}$. The open sets of $\mathscr{Q}'$ are open sets of $\mathscr{P}'$ and all the unions $X \cup f^{-1}\,[X]$ where X is open in $\mathscr{Q}$. It is clear that if g is a continuous mapping from $\mathscr{Q}'$ into a T_1-space $\mathscr{Q}_0$, then $gx = gfx$ for each $x \in \mathscr{P}'$. The assertion follows.

Corollary. *Let a functor $G: \mathscr{K} \to \mathsf{Ext}$ be projectively $\langle F_K, F_e \rangle$-generated by a functor $G': \mathscr{K}' \to \mathsf{Ext}$. Assume that $\mathscr{K} = \langle F_p, \mathrm{obj}\ \mathsf{Top} \rangle$ — proj $\mathscr{K}'$, that G is full on the subcategory $\langle F_t \circ F_p, \mathsf{Ens} \rangle$ — proj $\mathscr{K}'$ and that objects of $G'[\mathscr{K}']$ are T_1-extensions. Then G is one-to-one.*

Proof. It is sufficient to prove the inclusion $F_p\,[\mathrm{Hom}_{\mathsf{Prox}} \langle \mathscr{P}, X \rangle] \supset F_e\,[\mathrm{Hom}_{\mathsf{Ext}} \langle G\mathscr{P}, GX \rangle]$ for each $\mathscr{P} \in \mathrm{obj}\ \mathscr{K}$, $X \in \mathrm{obj}\ \mathscr{K}'$ and this follows directly from the preceding proposition.

Example 6. Let the situation from the last corollary be given. Briefly, objects of $\mathscr{K}$ are characterized by the characteristic property of objects of $F_t \circ F_p$ — proj $\mathscr{K}'$ required for infinite sets only. E.g., objects $\langle P, p \rangle$ of $\langle F_p, \mathrm{obj}\ \mathsf{Top} \rangle$ — proj $(\mathscr{I})$ are characterized by the property: if X is an infinite subset of P, X *non* pY, then Z *non* pX, $(P - Z)$ *non* pY for some set Z. Since the set of all bounded proximally continuous functions defined on $\mathscr{P}$ is a closed subalgebra of the set of all bounded functions on P, we get one-to-one relation between closed subalgebras of boundes continuous functions on $\mathscr{P}$ containing all the constant mappings and some compactifications of $F_p\mathscr{P}$ (objects of $G[\mathscr{K}]$); see also [2].

References

[1] B. Banaschewski, Über nulldimensionale Räume, Math. Nachr. **13** (1955), 141—150.

[2] H. Bauer und G. Nöbeling, Über die Erweiterung topologischer Räume, Math. Annalen **130** (1955), 20—45.

[3] E. Čech, Topological Spaces, Prague 1966.

[4] M. Hušek, Categorial methods in topology, Proc. Second Symposium on General Topology, Prague 1966; Prague 1967, p. 190—194.

[5] M. Hušek, Construction of special functors and its applications, Comment. Math. Univ. Carolinae 8 (1967), 555—566.

[6] Yu. M. Smirnov, On proximity spaces (russ.), Mat. Sbornik (N. S.) **31** (1952), 543—574.

REGULAR EXTENSIONS OF TOPOLOGICAL SPACES

A. A. Ivanov (Leningrad)

1. Regular extensions. General methods of constructions of regular extensions

Let X' be an extension of a topological space X.

We shall say that two points $x, y \in X'$ are topologically distinguished from within X, if there exists such set $F \subset X$ that we have $x \in \bar{F}^{X'}$, $y \notin \bar{F}^{X'}$ or $x \notin \bar{F}^{X'}$, $y \in \bar{F}^{X'}$.

We shall say that X' is regular extension of the space X if

1. the system $\{\bar{F}^{X'} | F \subset X\}$ is the basis for the closed sets of the space X';
2. any two points $x, y \in X'$, $x \neq y$, $x \in X' \setminus X$ or $y \in X' \setminus X$, are topologically distinguished from within X.

There are two general methods of constructions of regular extensions of topological spaces; one of them uses system of open sets and other uses systems of closed sets.

We shall say that a system γ of non-void closed sets of X is a (closed) cofilter on X if for any closed sets F_1, F_2 we have $F_1 \cup F_2 \in \gamma$ if and only if $F_1 \in \gamma$ or $F_2 \in \gamma$. The system $\gamma(x) = \{F | x \in F\}$ is a cofilter for any point $x \in X$. Let $\gamma(X) = \{\gamma(x) | x \in X\}$.

Let $\tilde{X}$ be some system of cofilters on X such that $\tilde{X} \cap \gamma(X) = \emptyset$. Put $\tilde{F} = \{\gamma | F \in \gamma \in \tilde{X}\}$, F is a closed set in X. As we have $\tilde{F}_1 \cup \tilde{F}_2 = \widetilde{F_1 \cup F_2}$ so we can take the system $\{F \cup \tilde{F} | F \subset X\}$ as a closed basis of the space $X' = X \cup \tilde{X}$. Obviously space X' is regular extension of the space X. We shall say that X' is γ-extension of the space X to be result of the addition of $\tilde{X}$ to X. It is easy to prove that any regular extension X' of a space X is equivalent to γ-extension for corresponding system $\tilde{X}$ of cofilters on X.

Let us consider now an other method of construction of regular extension which is dual to former one.

We shall say that a system ω of non-void open sets of X is a (open) filter on X if for any open sets G_1, G_2 we have $G_1 \cap G_2 \in \omega$ if and only if $G_1 \in \omega$ and $G_2 \in \omega$. The system $\omega(x) = \{G | x \in G\}$ is a filter for any point $x \in X$. Let $\omega(X) = \{\omega(x) | x \in X\}$.

Let $\hat{X}$ be some system of filters on X such that $\hat{X} \cap \omega(X) = \emptyset$. Put $\hat{G} = \{\omega | G \in \omega \in \hat{X}\}$, G is an open set in X. As we have $\hat{G}_1 \cap \hat{G}_2 = \widehat{G_1 \cap G_2}$ so we can take the system $\{G \cup \hat{G} \mid G \subset X\}$ as an open basis of the space $X' = X \cup \hat{X}$. Obviously space X' is regular extension of the space X.

We shall say that X' is ω-extension of the space X to be result of the addition $\hat{X}$ to X. It is easy to prove that any regular extension X' of a space X is equivalent to ω-extension for corresponding system $\hat{X}$ of filters on X.

If γ is a cofilter on X, than $\omega(\gamma) = \{G \mid X \setminus G \notin \gamma\}$ is a filter on X and conversely if ω is a filter on X, then $\gamma(\omega) = \{F \mid X \setminus F \notin \omega\}$ is a cofilter on X. The correspondences $\gamma \to \omega(\gamma)$ and $\omega \to \gamma(\omega)$ are reciprocal and for any $x \in X$ we have $\omega(\gamma(x)) = \omega(x)$, $\gamma(\omega(x)) = \gamma(x)$. From these facts one can deduce that γ-extension $X \cup \tilde{X}$ of the space X is equivalent to ω-extension $X \cup \omega(\tilde{X})$ and ω-extension $X \cup \hat{X}$ of the space X is equivalent to γ-extension $X \cup \gamma(\hat{X})$.

Let X' be now an arbitrary (not necessary regular) extension of a topological space X. Using standard process we can construct regular extension rX' of the space X which corresponds to X'. For that we must remove all topologically indistinguished from within X points of the set $X' \setminus X$ besides may be only one point if such point and any point of X are topologically distinguished from within X. Then on the set which remained, we shall put the structure of a regular extension of the space X. So we get regular extension rX'.

Such process (and its result) we shall call regularisation.

On the other hand, proceeding from a regular extension X' of a space X, we can construct different extensions of X. For that we can add an arbitrary set A_x to every point $x \in X'$, $A_x \cap X' = \emptyset$, $A_x \cap A_y = \emptyset$ for $x \neq y$. Then we shall put topological structure on $X'' = X' \cup \left(\bigcup_{x \in X'} A_x\right)$ induced by φ: $X'' \to X'$, $\varphi(x) = x$ for $x \in X'$, $\varphi(A_x) = x$. At last we can introduce new closed sets adding to any closed set of X'' some subset of $X'' \setminus X$. So we get some extension of the space X. Such process (and its result) we shall call distortion.

It is easy to prove that any extension X' of the space X is a distortion of some regular extension of X. In effect it is a distortion of the regularisation of X'. I will note finally that regular extensions form a principal class of extensions in general theory of extensions. At any rate it is so throughout the present paper.

2. Uniform structures and regular T_1-extensions

Let ϱ be an uniforme structure on topological space X that is some system $\varrho = \{\mathfrak{S}\}$ of open covers $\mathfrak{S}$ of X. I require the following:

1. If $\mathfrak{S}'$ is a refinement of $\mathfrak{S}$ and $\mathfrak{S} \in \varrho$ then $\mathfrak{S}' \in \varrho$;
2. if $\mathfrak{S}, \mathfrak{S}' \in \varrho$ then $\mathfrak{S} \wedge \mathfrak{S}' = \{G \cap G' \mid G \in \mathfrak{S},\ G' \in \mathfrak{S}'\} \in \varrho$.

We shall say that a filter ω is a Cauchy filter relatively ϱ if for any $\mathfrak{S} \in \varrho$ there is such $G \in \mathfrak{S}$ that $G \in \omega$. Let $\hat{X}$ be the set of minimal Cauchy filters relatively ϱ, which distincts from any $\omega(x)$, $x \in X$. Let ϱX be ω-extension of the space X to be result of the addition $\hat{X}$ to X. We shall call it ϱ-extension.

Theorem 1. *Any regular T_1-extension X' of topological space X is equivalent to some ϱ-extension.*

The proof follows at once from consideration of uniforme structure ϱ which consists of covers $\mathfrak{S} = \mathfrak{S}' \wedge X = \{G' \cap X \mid G' \in \mathfrak{S}'\}$ for open covers $\mathfrak{S}'$ of the space X.

This theorem allows to reduce the investigation of regular T_1-extensions to the investigation of uniforme structures.

Let us consider for example a uniforme structure ϱ which consists of such open covers of the space X that in every $\mathfrak{s} \in \varrho$ there are sets $G_1, G_2, \ldots, G_n$ for which $\bigcup_{i=1}^{n} \overline{G}_i = X$ (such covers I call pseudo-finite covers).

Theorem 2. *Let ϱ be an uniforme structure, which consists of pseudo-finite covers of the space X. The extension ϱX of X will be H-closed extension if and only if every maximal filter on X contains a single minimal Cauchy filter relatively ϱ.*

We shall say that a set $A \subset X$ touches a filter ω relatively uniforme structure ϱ if for any $\mathfrak{s} \in \varrho$ there is such a set $U \in \mathfrak{s}$ that $A \cap U \neq \emptyset$ and $U \cap G \neq \emptyset$ for every $G \in \omega$. Let ω be a filter on X and $\mathfrak{s} \in \varrho$. Put $St_{\mathfrak{s}}{}^{\varrho}\omega = \cup G$, for all $G \in \mathfrak{s}$ touching filter ω relatively ϱ.

We shall say that a uniforme structure ϱ is H-structure, if ϱ consists of pseudo-finite covers and if for any maximal filter ω and any cover $\mathfrak{s} \in \varrho$ there is such a cover $\mathfrak{s}' \in \varrho$ that $St_{\mathfrak{s}'}{}^{\varrho}\omega$ is contained in some $G \in \mathfrak{s}$.

Theorem 3. *Let ϱ be a H-structure on a space X, then ϱX is a H-closed extension of X.*

Theorem 4. *Every regular H-closed extension of a space X is equivalent to extension ϱX of X, for some H-structure ϱ on X.*

The proofs of these theorems are in [3]. I will recall here that construction of extensions may be based on cofilters. We shall say that cofilter γ is a Cauchy cofilter relatively ϱ if $C\gamma = \{G \,|\, X \setminus G \in \gamma\} \notin \varrho$. Let a filter ω be a Cauchy filter relatively ϱ then cofilter $\gamma(\omega)$ is a Cauchy cofilter relatively ϱ. Conversely let a cofilter γ be a Cauchy cofilter relatively ϱ then filter $\omega(\gamma)$ is a Cauchy filter relatively ϱ. Besides if γ is a maximal Cauchy cofilter then $\omega(\gamma)$ is a minimal Cauchy filter and if ω is a minimal Cauchy filter then $\gamma(\omega)$ is a maximal Cauchy cofilter relatively ϱ.

It is easy to prove that every ϱ-extension of a space X is equivalent to a γ-extension of X to be result of the addition the set of all maximal Cauchy cofilters relatively ϱ which distincts from any $\gamma(x)$, $x \in X$.

Cofilter's method is expecially useful when ϱ is precompact uniforme structure. In this case any maximal Cauchy filter is simply a maximal σ-contiguity system. I will recall therefore some definitions of contiguity theory (see [1]).

Let a relation σ be such relation for finite system α of closed sets of the topological space X that

1. if any $F \in \alpha$ contains some $F' \in \alpha'$ and we have $\sigma(\alpha')$ then we have $\sigma(\alpha)$;

2. if we have $\sigma(\alpha \vee \alpha')$ then we have $\sigma(\alpha)$ or $\sigma(\alpha')$, $\alpha \vee \alpha' = \{F \cup F' \,|\, F \in \alpha,\ F' \in \alpha'\}$.

We shall say that such relation σ is a contiguity relation.

We shall say that a finite system α of closed sets of the topological space X is a σ-contiguity system if we have $\sigma(\alpha)$, and we shall say that an arbitrary system of closed sets of X is a σ-contiguity system if its any finite subsystem is σ-contiguity system.

Let ϱ be some uniforme structure on X (not necessary precompact). Relation σ is a contiguity relation if we have $\sigma(\alpha)$ if and only if $C\alpha \notin \varrho$. We shall say that such relation σ is conforming to ϱ.

Every ϱ-extension of a space X for precompact uniforme structure ϱ on X is equivalent to a γ-extension of X to be result of the addition the set of all maximal

σ-contiguity system distinct from any $\gamma(x)$, $x \in X$, σ being contiguity relation which is conforming to ϱ. Such γ-extension we shall call σ-extension σX of X.

3. Contiguity relations and regular extensions

We shall say that some extension X' of a topological space X is conforming to contiguity relation σ on X if for any finite system $F_1, F_2, \ldots, F_n$ of closed sets of X such that $\bigcap_{i=1}^{n} \bar{F}_i^{X'} \neq \emptyset$ we have $\sigma(F_1, F_2, \ldots, F_n)$.

Let $\tilde{\sigma} X$ be γ-extension of a space X (σ is an arbitrary contiguity relation on X) to be result of the addition the set $\tilde{X}_\sigma$ of all cofilters being σ-contiguity systems distinct from any $\gamma(x)$, $x \in X$.

Theorem 5. *Any regular extension of a space X, being conforming to some contiguity relation σ on X, is equivalent to some extension $X' \subset \tilde{\sigma} X$.*

This theorem allows to consider not all regular extensions of a space X but only subspaces X' of space $\tilde{\sigma} X$, $X \subset X' \subset \tilde{\sigma} X$. Thus one can get some results (see [4]).

Theorem 6. *The set of all H-closed regular extensions of a space X being conforming to contiguity relation σ on X is the set of all maximal subspace $X' \in T_2$ of $\tilde{\sigma} X$ containing the space X.*

Theorem 7. *Any regular extension $X' \in T_2$ of a space X being conforming to contiguity relation σ on X is contained in some H-closed, regular extension being conforming to σ.*

Put $\sigma \leqq \sigma'$ if for any finite system α of closed sets of X $\sigma'(\alpha)$ is implying $\sigma(\alpha)$. We shall say that a closed set $F \subset X$ is H_X-closed if it is closed in any extension $X' \in T_2$ of X. Let σ_H denotes a contiguity relation on X for which we have $\sigma_H(F_1, F_2, \ldots, F_n)$ if and only if $\bigcap_{i=1}^{n} F_i \neq \emptyset$ or all $F_1, F_2, \ldots, F_n$ are not H_X-closed. Diversity of H-closed regular extensions may be demonstrated in the following way.

Theorem 8. *If $\sigma_H \leqq \sigma$, $\sigma \neq \sigma_H$ then there is some regular extension $X' \in T_2$ being no conforming to σ.*

It is easy to see that any extension $X' \in T_2$ is contained in $\tilde{\sigma}_H X$. Therefore further decrease of contiguity relation will give us nothing new.

We shall say that an extension X' of a topological space X is a σ-combinatorial extension (here σ is some contiguity relation on X) if $\bigcap_{i=1}^{n} \bar{F}_i^{X'} \neq \emptyset$ if and only if we have $\sigma(F_1, F_2, \ldots, F_n)$.

Let us notice now that a set of all extensions of a space X which are conforming to some contiguity relation σ on X is the same one as a set of all subspaces of $\tilde{\sigma} X$ which containe a space X. Each of these extensions is a σ'-combinatorial extension for some contiguity relation $\sigma' \geqq \sigma$. As any contiguity relation is no more than contiguity relation σ_0 according to intersections then if X' is an extension of a space X being conforming to σ_0 then X' is a σ_0-combinatorial extension of X. On the other hand any extension of a space X is conforming to minimal contiguity relation on X and any extension $X' \in T_2$ is conforming to contiguity relation σ_H.

The notion of a σ-combinatorial extension is the natural generalization of the notion of combinatorial extension (see [4]). This notion allows us to give some classification of extensions. In this connexion one can formulate following question. Let us take some contiguity relation σ on given topological space X whether exists σ-combinatorial extension of X? I don't know full answer on this question and can inform only some particular results.

Theorem 9. *Any metric space of countable weight has σ_H-combinatorial H-closed extension.*

The proof see in [4].

If a space X is a locally compact space so one-point compactification is a σ_H-combinatorial H-closed extension but in otherwise σ_H-combinatorial H-closed extensions are more complicate and there are spaces without of σ_H-combinatorial H-closed extensions. On the other hand there are spaces, for example metric spaces of countable weight, which have σ_H-combinatorial H-closed extensions but in general have no some σ-combinatorial H-closed extensions. Let us note at last that for some principal (see [1]) contiguity relations σ there are not σ-combinatorial H-closed extensions and for some no principal contiguity relations σ there are σ-combinatorial H-closed extension. Thus the question about existing σ-combinatorial H-closed extensions is rather complicate.

4. Some compact extensions

Contiguity relations are in my opinion the most natural basis of the theory of compact extensions especially in the class T_1. It is easy to prove that any regular compact extension of a space X is equivalent such X' that $X \subset \sigma X \subset X' \subset \tilde{\sigma} X$ and if $X' \in T_1$ so $X' = \sigma X$. Later on we shall limit oneself by consideration of extensions in T_1 and consequently by consideration of σX for different σ on X.

The Wallman compactification ωX was defined for any topological space as σ-extension for following contiguity relation σ:

We have $\sigma(F_1, F_2, \ldots, F_n)$ if and only if $\bigcap_{i=1}^{n} F_i \neq \emptyset$ (contiguity relation according to intersection).

The Čech-compactification βX can be defined for any topological space as σ-extension for following contiguity relation σ:

We have $\sigma(F_1, F_2, \ldots, F_n)$ if and only if for any continuous functions $f_1, f_2, \ldots, f_n$ equal zero on $F_1, F_2, \ldots, F_n$ accordingly and for any $\varepsilon > 0$ there exists a point $x \in X$ such that $|f_i(x)| < \varepsilon$.

The Freudenthal-compactification FX can be defined as σ-extension for following contiguity relation σ:

σ is a principal contiguity relation and we have no $\sigma(F_1, F_2)$ if and only if $F_1 \cap F_2 = \emptyset$ and exists such compact set $A \subset X$ that no one component of connectness of the set $X \setminus A$ contains points of the sets F_1, F_2 at the same time.

The compactification of a space X according to some open basis $\mathfrak{B}$ can be defined as σ-extension for following contiguity relation σ:

We have $\sigma(F_1, F_2, \ldots, F_n)$ if and only if for any elements $G_1, G_2, \ldots, G_n$ of $\mathfrak{B}$ such that $F_i \subset G_i$ $(i = 1, 2, \ldots, n)$ we have $\bigcap_{i=1}^{n} G_i \neq \emptyset$.

Let $\mathfrak{A}$ be a system of sets of a topological space X (not necessary open or close) closed relatively finite intersections and unions, and $\sigma_{\mathfrak{A}}$ is the contiguity relation for which we have $\sigma_{\mathfrak{A}}(F_1, F_2, \ldots, F_n)$ if and only if $\bigcap_{i=1}^{n} A_i \neq \emptyset$ for any $A_i \in \mathfrak{A}$, $F_i \subset A_i$.

The compactification $\sigma_{\mathfrak{A}} X$ is natural generalization of extension according to open basis.

Let $\mathfrak{B}$ be any cofilter in X and $\sigma_{\mathfrak{B}}$ is contiguity relation for which we have no $\sigma_{\mathfrak{B}}(F_1, F_2, \ldots, F_n)$ if and only if $\bigcap_{i=1}^{n} F_i = \emptyset$ and there is $F_i \notin \mathfrak{B}$. The compactification $\sigma_{\mathfrak{B}} X$ is natural generalization one-point-Alexandroff-compactification for locally compacte space.

In the class of all compactifications of a space X we can distinguish the class of homogeneous compactifications. A compactification σX of a space X we shall call homogeneous if any topological mapping of X on X may be extended to topological mapping of σX on σX. A compactification σX will be homogeneous if and only if σ is invariant relatively any topological mapping of X on X. From here follows that Wallman's, Čech's and Freudenthal's compactifications are homogenous compactifications.

Any extension σX of a space X can be associated the homogeneous extension $\sigma' X$, σ' being minimal invariant relatively all topological mappings of X on X contiguity relation greater than contiguity relation σ. In general σX is not natural continuous image of $\sigma' X$. I do not know if exists natural continuous mapping of $\sigma' X$ on σX for $\sigma X \in T_2$. It is interesting full description of all homogeneous compact extensions of a space X, if only in the class T_2. In the simple case of countable discrete space answer is trivial, but in the common case this problem is rather complicate. Its decision nead of full description of all relations Φ noncompact subsets of X for which we have Φ for $F = \bigcup_{i=1}^{n} F_i$ if and only if we have Φ for some F_i $(i = 1, 2, \ldots, n)$.

References

[1] V. M. Ivanova and A. A. Ivanov, Contiguity spaces and bicompact extensions (russ.), Izv. Akad. Nauk SSSR, Ser. Mat., **23** (1959), 613–634.

[2] A. A. Ivanov, Contiguity relations on topological spaces (russ.), Doklady Akad. Nauk SSSR **128** (1959), 33–36.

[3] A. A. Ivanov, Regular extensions of topological spaces (russ.), Izv. Akad. Nauk BSSR, Ser. Fiz. Mat., **1** (1966), 28–35.

[4] V. M. Ivanova and A. A. Ivanov, Contiguity relations and H-closed extensions (russ.), Proc. Second Symposium on General Topology, Prague 1966.

ON THE CHARACTER OF POINTS IN $\beta N_{\mathfrak{m}}$

I. JUHÁSZ (Budapest)

I. Let $N_{\mathfrak{m}}$ be the discrete topological space of power $\mathfrak{m}$ and $\beta N_{\mathfrak{m}}$ its Stone-Čech compactification. B. POSPÍŠIL proved in [1] that there exist $\exp\exp \mathfrak{m} = |\beta N_{\mathfrak{m}}|$ points in $\beta N_{\mathfrak{m}} \setminus N_{\mathfrak{m}}$ having the character $\exp \mathfrak{m}$.

We present here two topological theorems both implying Pospišil's result immediately:

Theorem 1. *Let* $f\colon R \to \mathop{\times}\limits_{\alpha\in A} R_\alpha$ *be a continuous and closed mapping of* R *onto a product, where each factor* R_α *is a* T_1*-space. Assume* $y \in \mathop{\times}\limits_{\alpha\in A} R_\alpha$ *and* $f^{-1}(y)$ *is compact. Then there exists a point* $x \in f^{-1}(y)$ *for which*

$$\chi(x, R) \geqq |A|.$$

($\chi(x, R)$ denotes the character of x in R.)

Theorem 2. *Let* $f\colon R \to R'$ *be a perfect mapping of the regular space* R *onto* R', *where* R' *is a compact Hausdorff space all regular closed subsets of which are* G_δ*'s. Then there exists a closed subset* $F \subset R$ *with* $f(F) = R'$ *and*

$$\chi(x, R) \geqq \chi(x, F) \geqq \chi(f(x), R')$$

for all $x \in F$.

Applying a continuous surjective mapping

$$f\colon \beta N_{\mathfrak{m}} \to D^{\exp \mathfrak{m}},$$

where D is the two-point discrete space, both of our theorems yield POSPÍŠIL's theorem as an immediate consequence.

POSPISIL's theorem can be reformulated as follows: there exist ($\exp\exp \mathfrak{m}$) ultrafilters in a set of power $\mathfrak{m}$, which cannot be generated by less than $\exp \mathfrak{m}$ of their elements. Recently A. HAJNAL gave a very elegant set-theoretical proof of this purely set-theoretical fact.

II. Using the following theorem we obtain a partial improvement of POSPÍŠIL's result.

Theorem 3. *Let* R *be Hausdorff and assume that every disjoint family of open subsets of* R *is of a cardinality* $\leqq \mathfrak{m}$. *Let* $q \geqq \mathfrak{m}$ *and* H_q *be the set of points in* R *with a character* $\leqq q$. *Then*

$$|H_q| \leqq \exp q\,.$$

Corollary. *For almost every* $x \in \beta N_{\mathfrak{m}}$ *we have*

$$\exp \chi(x, \beta N_{\mathfrak{m}}) = \exp \exp \mathfrak{m},$$

i.e.

$$|\{x\colon \exp \chi(x, \beta N_{\mathfrak{m}}) < \exp \exp \mathfrak{m}\}| < |\beta N_{\mathfrak{m}}|\,.$$

This result is in contrast to the easily provable fact that for every $\mathfrak{m}$ the set of points in $\beta N_{\mathfrak{m}}$ with a small character — precisely with a character $\leqq \exp \aleph_0$ — contains a dense open set.

Finally assuming the generalized continuum hypothesis and using set-theoretical methods, we are able to describe the exact cardinality of the set of points with a certain character, in all the possible cases.

Theorem 4. *Assume the generalized continuum hypothesis. Then every point of* $\beta N_{\mathfrak{m}} \setminus N_{\mathfrak{m}}$ *has a character of form* $\exp q$ *where* $\aleph_0 \leqq q \leqq \mathfrak{m}$. *Let* M_q *be the set of points with the character* $\exp q$. *Then*

$$|M_q| = \exp \exp q \cdot \mathfrak{m}^q\,.$$

All these results can be found in [2] with complete proofs.

References

[1] B. POSPÍŠIL, On bicompact spaces, Publ. Fac. Sci. Univ. Masaryk No. 270 (1939).
[2] I. JUHÁSZ, On a theorem of B. Pospišil (russ.), Comment. Math. Univ. Carolinae 8 (1967), 1.

SEQUENTIAL ENVELOPES AND COMPLETENESS

V. Koutník (Praha)

In this note we shall consider the sequential envelopes of convergence spaces and their relation to the notion of completeness of $\mathscr{U}\mathscr{L}$-spaces. The sequential envelope of a sequentially regular convergence space was introduced by J. Novák in [4] and [5]. A. Goetz defined the notion of a $\mathscr{U}\mathscr{L}$-space in [1] and [2]. The completion of $\mathscr{U}\mathscr{L}^{\square}$-spaces was studied by V. Z. Poljakov in [6] who used the theory of proximity spaces.

Let $(L, \mathfrak{L}, \lambda)$ be a convergence space and consider the set L of all $\mathscr{U}\mathscr{L}^*$-structures in L compatible with the convergence $\mathfrak{L}^*$. This set contains the least element $\mathbf{l}_0^*$ and the largest element $\mathbf{l}_I^*$. It is shown in [2] that if the space $(L, \mathfrak{L}, \lambda)$ is countably compact, then card $\mathsf{L} = 1$. More precisely we have the following.

Theorem 1. *Let* $(L, \mathfrak{L}, \lambda)$ *be a convergence space and let* L *be the set of all* $\mathscr{U}\mathscr{L}^*$-*structures compatible with* $\mathfrak{L}^*$. *Then*

card $\mathsf{L} = 1$ *iff* $(L, \mathfrak{L}, \lambda)$ *is countably compact,*

card $\mathsf{L} \geqq \aleph_1$ *otherwise.*

There are therefore generally many $\mathscr{U}\mathscr{L}^*$-structures compatible with a given convergence $\mathfrak{L}^*$. Let us consider the question of completeness of these $\mathscr{U}\mathscr{L}^*$-spaces. The following statement holds:

Theorem 2. *The* $\mathscr{U}\mathscr{L}^*$-*space* $(L, \mathbf{l}_0^*)$ *is complete for all spaces* $(L, \mathfrak{L}, \lambda)$. *The* $\mathscr{U}\mathscr{L}^*$-*space* $(L, \mathbf{l}_I^*)$ *is complete iff the space* $(L, \mathfrak{L}, \lambda)$ *is countably compact, i.e. iff* $\mathbf{l}_I^* = \mathbf{l}_0^*$.

This theorem shows that $\mathbf{l}_0^*$ and $\mathbf{l}_I^*$ are extreme cases when completeness is concerned. Let us turn to a more suitable $\mathscr{U}\mathscr{L}^*$-structure.

Let $(L, \mathfrak{L}, \lambda)$ be a convergence space and denote $\mathfrak{F}(L)$ the family of all functions on L to $\langle 0, 1\rangle$ which are continuous on $(L, \mathfrak{L}, \lambda)$. Define $\{x_n\}\ \mathbf{l}\ \{y_n\}$ if for each function $f \in \mathfrak{F}(L)$ and for each subsequence $\{n_i\}$ of $\{n\}$ there is a subsequence $\{n_{i_j}\}$ of $\{n_i\}$ such that $\lim f(x_{n_{i_j}}) = \lim f(y_{n_{i_j}})$ in the sense that both limits exist and are equal. Assume that the family $\mathfrak{F}(L)$ has the following property (P): for each $x \neq y$ there is $f \in \mathfrak{F}(L)$ such that $f(x) \neq f(y)$. Then $(L, \mathbf{l})$ is a $\mathscr{U}\mathscr{L}^*$-space generated by the family $\mathfrak{F}(L)$ [2].

Theorem 3. *Let* $(L, \mathfrak{L}, \lambda)$ *be a convergence space and suppose that the family* $\mathfrak{F}(L)$ *has the property (P). Let* $(L, \mathbf{l})$ *be the* $\mathcal{U}\mathcal{L}^*$*-space generated by* $\mathfrak{F}(L)$. *Then*

1) $\mathbf{l}$ *preserves the convergence* $\mathfrak{L}$, *i.e.* $(\{x_n\}, x) \in \mathfrak{L} \Rightarrow \{x_n\}\, \mathbf{l}\, \{x\}$.

2) $\mathbf{l}$ *is compatible with* $\mathfrak{L}^*$ *iff the space* $(L, \mathfrak{L}, \lambda)$ *is sequentially regular.*

In [3] the sequential envelope of a sequentially regular space is obtained directly by successive adjoining of "ideal points" to the given space. The following definitions are used:

A sequence $\{x_n\}$ is called a *remarkable* sequence in $(L, \mathfrak{L}, \lambda)$ if the sequence $\{f(x_n)\}$ converges for all $f \in \mathfrak{F}(L)$.

A sequentially regular convergence space $(L, \mathfrak{L}, \lambda)$ is called $\mathcal{L}$*-complete* if all remarkable sequences in L are $\mathfrak{L}^*$-convergent.

Lemma 1. *Let* $(L, \mathfrak{L}, \lambda)$ *be a sequentially regular space and let* $(L, \mathbf{l})$ *be the* $\mathcal{U}\mathcal{L}^*$*-space generated by* $\mathfrak{F}(L)$. *A sequence* $\{x_n\}$ *is a remarkable sequence in* $(L, \mathfrak{L}, \lambda)$ *iff it is a Cauchy sequence in* $(L, \mathbf{l})$.

Therefore we have the following

Theorem 4. *A sequentially regular space* $(L, \mathfrak{L}, \lambda)$ *is* $\mathcal{L}$*-complete iff the* $\mathcal{U}\mathcal{L}^*$*-space* $(L, \mathbf{l})$ *generated by* $\mathfrak{F}(L)$ *is complete.*

It is easy to see that two remarkable sequences $\{x_n\}$ and $\{y_n\}$ in $(L, \mathfrak{L}, \lambda)$ are equivalent ([3]) iff $\{x_n\}\, \mathbf{l}\, \{y_n\}$. Hence we have

Theorem 5. *Let* $(L', \mathfrak{L}', \lambda')$ *be the sequential envelope of a sequentially regular space* $(L, \mathfrak{L}, \lambda)$ *and let* $(L', \mathbf{l}')$ *and* $(L, \mathbf{l})$ *be the* $\mathcal{U}\mathcal{L}^*$*-spaces generated by* $\mathfrak{F}(L')$ *and* $\mathfrak{F}(L)$ *respectively. Then*

1) $(L', \mathbf{l}')$ *is a complete space,*

2) $(L, \mathbf{l})$ *is a subspace of* $(L', \mathbf{l}')$,

3) $L' = L$ *iff* $(L, \mathbf{l})$ *is complete.*

We can therefore consider $(L', \mathbf{l}')$ as a completion of $(L, \mathbf{l})$. The sequential envelopes can be characterized as those sequentially regular spaces $(L, \mathfrak{L}, \lambda)$ for which the $\mathcal{U}\mathcal{L}^*$-spaces generated by the family $\mathfrak{F}(L)$ are complete.

Example. Let $(\mathsf{M}, \mathfrak{M}, \mu)$ be a convergence system of sets. Define the uniform continuity of functions on M as follows: a function f is uniformly continuous on M if $\lim |f(A_n) - f(B_n)| = 0$ whenever $\lim A_n \triangle B_n = \emptyset$, where $\triangle$ denotes the symmetric difference of sets. For example all probability measures are uniformly continuous functions. Denote $\mathfrak{F}_u(\mathsf{M})$ the family of all uniformly continuous functions on M.

Let $\{A_n\}\, \mathbf{m}\, \{B_n\}$ whenever $\lim A_n \triangle B_n = \emptyset$. Then $(\mathsf{M}, \mathbf{m})$ is a space which is generated by the family $\mathfrak{F}_u(\mathsf{M})$. It follows from Theorem 5 that the problem of constructing a $\mathfrak{F}_u$-sequential envelope of M is equivalent to the problem of completing the $\mathcal{U}\mathcal{L}^*$-space $(\mathsf{M}, \mathbf{m})$.

References

[1] A. Goetz, A notion of uniformity for $\mathscr{L}$-spaces of Fréchet, Proc. First Symposium on General Topology, Prague 1961; Prague 1962, p. 177—178.
[2] A. Goetz, A notion of uniformity for $\mathscr{L}$-spaces of Fréchet, Coll. Math. **9** (1962), 223—231.
[3] V. Koutník, On sequentially regular convergence spaces, Czechoslovak Math. J. **17** (1967), 232—247.
[4] J. Novák, On the sequential envelope, Proc. First Symposium on General Topology, Prague 1961; Prague 1962, p. 292—294.
[5] J. Novák, On convergence spaces and their sequential envelopes, Czechoslovak Math. J. **15** (1965), 74—100.
[6] В. З. Поляков, О равномерных пространствах сходимости, Coll. Math. **13** (1965), 167—179.

COMPLETIONS BASED ON PROXIMITY AND BOUNDEDNESS[1])

SOLOMON LEADER (New Brunswick, N.J./U.S.A.)

Which topological spaces Y can be reconstructed from an arbitrary dense subspace X if all we know about X is which pairs of its subsets are "close" (i.e. have intersecting closures in Y) and which of its subsets are "bounded" (i.e. have compact closures in Y)? We shall show here how such a reconstruction is possible if

(I) $\left\{\begin{array}{l}Y \text{ is a regular hausdorff space in which a point in the closure of a set } E\\ \text{must lie in some compact set which is the closure of a subset of } E.\end{array}\right.$

The latter condition in (I) is not severely restrictive since it will hold in any hausdorff space which is either locally compact or topologized by sequential convergence.

We begin with a set X, a proximity relation "A is close to B" between certain subsets of X, and a class of "bounded" subsets of X subject to the following axioms:

(1) A close to B implies B close to A.
(2) A close to B implies $B \neq \emptyset$.
(3) A meets B implies A close to B.
(4) A close to B and B contained in C imply A close to C.
(5) A close to $B \cup C$ implies A close to B or to C.
(6) $[x]$ close to $[y]$ implies $x = y$.
(7) Given A bounded and any B such that for all E either A is close to E or B is close to $X - E$, then A is close to B.
(8) If A is close to B then A is close to some bounded subset of B.
(9) If for every filter $\mathscr{F}$ in X to which A belongs there exists some bounded set B close to every member of $\mathscr{F}$, then A is bounded.
(10) Let $\mathscr{H}$ be a filter in X with some bounded member and $\mathbb{F}$ a set of ultrafilters in X with each member of $\mathscr{F}$ having some bounded member. Let E be close to every member of $\mathscr{H}$ for every set E which belongs to every member of $\mathbb{F}$. Then the latter condition holds for some subset $\mathbb{K}$ of $\mathbb{F}$ such that if $\mathscr{L}$ is any filter in X with each member of $\mathscr{L}$ close to every member of some member of $\mathbb{K}$ and if A is any member of $\mathscr{H}$, there exists a bounded subset of A which is close to every member of $\mathscr{L}$.

Spaces X with such a proximity-boundedness structure form a category under mappings which preserve proximity and boundedness: A close to B implies fA

[1]) Work in progress under NSF GP-7539.

close to fB, A bounded implies fA bounded. Defining the closure of B to be the set of all points in X which are close to B, we induce a regular hausdorff topology in X. We call X complete if every closed bounded subset is compact.

If in a topological space Y we call A close to B whenever their closures intersect and call A bounded whenever its closure is compact, then (1)—(10) hold if and only if (I) holds. Such spaces Y are precisely the complete spaces in our theory. If X is a dense subset of a complete space Y then X, with the proximity relation and boundedness in Y restricted to subsets of X, satisfies (1)—(10). The converse is the

Completion Theorem. *If a set X is endowed with a proximity-boundedness structure satisfying* (1)—(10) *then X is a dense subspace of a unique complete space $\overline{X}$. Mappings which preserve proximity and boundedness are just restrictions of continuous mappings between the completions.*

Our proof of the Completion Theorem uses the technique introduced in [1]. A cluster $\boldsymbol{c}$ is defined to be any class of subsets of X such that:

(a) A, B in $\boldsymbol{c}$ implies A close to B.

(b) A close to every member of $\boldsymbol{c}$ implies A belongs to $\boldsymbol{c}$.

(c) $A \cup B$ in $\boldsymbol{c}$ implies A or B is in $\boldsymbol{c}$.

(d) $\boldsymbol{c}$ has some bounded member.

Each point x in X determines a cluster $\boldsymbol{x}$ consisting of all subsets of X which are close to $[x]$. In this way X is imbedded in the set $\overline{X}$ of all clusters. We define the closure of a set P of clusters as follows: A cluster $\boldsymbol{c}$ belongs to $\overline{P}$ if every subset of X which belongs to every member of P also belongs to $\boldsymbol{c}$. Under the resulting topology $\overline{X}$ satisfies (I) and is the required completion of X.

For X a metric space one can define A close to B whenever A and B respectively contain a pair of equivalent cauchy sequences, and take boundedness to be total boundedness. Then (1)—(10) hold and $\overline{X}$ is just the metric completion of X.

If with our axiom system X itself is bounded then X is just a proximity space and $\overline{X}$ is the Smirnov compactification [3] [1].

If (7) is strengthened by restricting the hypothesis to all *bounded* E then X is a local proximity space and $\overline{X}$ is the local compactification [2].

References

[1] S. Leader, On clusters in proximity spaces, Fund. Math. **47** (1959), 205—213.

[2] S. Leader, Local proximity spaces, Math. Annalen **169** (1967), 274—281.

[3] Yu. M. Smirnov, On proximity spaces (russ.), Mat. Sbornik (N. S.) **31** (1952), 543—574.

DIMENSIONAL PROPERTIES OF COMPACTIFICATIONS

A. LELEK (Warszawa)

The existence of the natural quasi-order $\leq$ in the collection of compactifications of a given space allows us to specify problems which involve finding compactifications with some prescribed properties. For instance, given a compactification cX of a space X we might raise a problem as to whether cX follows a compactification whose dimension is not much higher than the dimension of X. In other words, we are interested in estimating the least upper bound of the dimension of $c'X$ where $c'X \leq cX$. Actually the problem seems to be completely settled only in the case of complete separable metric spaces which possesse some types of infinite dimension.

Recall that a space X is said to be *weakly infinite-dimensional* or *Smirnov-weakly infinite-dimensional* provided, for each infinite sequence

$$(A_1, B_1),\ (A_2, B_2),\ \ldots$$

of pairs of closed subsets of X such that $A_i \cap B_i = \emptyset\ (i = 1, 2, \ldots)$, there exists an infinite sequence $C_1, C_2, \ldots$ of closed subsets of X such that C_i cuts X between A_i and B_i $(i = 1, 2, \ldots)$ and

$$\bigcap_{i=1}^{\infty} C_i = \emptyset \qquad \text{or} \qquad \bigcap_{i=1}^{n} C_i = \emptyset,$$

respectively. Here the integer n can depend on the choice of sequence of pairs (A_i, B_i). The space X is said to be *countable-dimensional* or *strongly countable-dimensional* provided X is a countable union of sets which are 0-dimensional or closed finite-dimensional, respectively.

In the present report we restrict ourselves to separable metric spaces and metrizable compactifications. It is known [1] that if a G_δ-space X is weakly infinite-dimensional or countable-dimensional, then each compactification of X follows a compactification which is weakly infinite-dimensional or countable-dimensional, respectively. Moreover, this is not true for F_σ-spaces because it can be shown [4] that an increasing countable union of cubes admits no weakly infinite-dimensional compactification; the latter space is not Smirnov-weakly infinite-dimensional.

Question 1. Does each compactification of a Smirnov-weakly infinite-dimensional space follow a Smirnov-weakly infinite-dimensional compactification?

It is known [4] that each Smirnov-weakly infinite-dimensional space admits a Smirnov-weakly infinite-dimensional compactification.

Question 2. Does each compactification of a strongly countable-dimensional G_δ-space follow a strongly countable-dimensional compactification?

It is known [3] that each strongly countable-dimensional G_δ-space admits a strongly countable-dimensional compactification.

Now, given a finite-dimensional space X and its compactification cX let us denote

$$r(cX) = \min\{\dim c'X - \dim X \mid c'X \leqq cX\}.$$

There are trivial examples of G_δ-spaces, as well as of F_σ-spaces, and their compactifications cX such that $r(cX) = 1$. It is known [2] that there exists a G_δ-space X and a compactification cX such that $r(cX) = 2$.

Question 3. Does there exist, for each integer $n \geqq 3$, a space X and its compactification cX such that $r(cX) = n$?

Question 4. Does there exist a finite-dimensional F_σ-space X and its compactification cX such that $r(cX) \geqq 2$?

References

[1] A. Lelek, On the dimension of remainders in compact extensions (russ.), Doklady Akad. Nauk SSSR **160** (1965), 534—537.

[2] A. Lelek Some problems in metric topology, Louisiana State University (Lecture Notes), Baton Rouge 1966.

[3] A. W. Schurle, Compactification of strongly countable dimensional spaces, Bull. Amer. Math. Soc. **73** (1967), 909—912.

[4] E. G. Skljarenko, On dimensional properties of infinite-dimensional spaces (russ.), Izv. Akad. Nauk SSSR, Ser. Mat., **23** (1959), 197—212.

FUNCTION SPACES AND THE ALEKSANDROV-URYSOHN CONJECTURE[1])

PAUL R. MEYER (New York, N.Y./U.S.A.)

In 1923 ALEKSANDROV and URYSOHN [1] asked whether every first countable compact (Hausdorff) space has cardinality $\leq c$, the cardinality of the continuum. Their still unanswered question can be given an equivalent formulation in terms of a generalized Lindelöf condition on LORCH's ι-topology. (The ι-topology is the weak topology induced by the Baire functions; see § 1.) Although almost nothing seems to be known about the circumstances under which the ι-topology satisfies the generalized Lindelöf condition, the ordinary Lindelöf property for the ι-topology has been studied in detail, and there is reason to hope that some of these results can be generalized. In this paper the reformulation of the problem is given and conditions under which the ι-topology has the ordinary Lindelöf property are summarized. The complete paper is to appear in Annali di Mat.

The conjecture that this question can be answered affirmatively is called "the Aleksandrov-Urysohn conjecture" in the literature, and we follow this nomenclature. However, the present writer has not seen such an explicit conjecture on their part. In their 1923 paper [1] and more recently (1929 and 1960) they state it only as an open question.

1. Background

Let R^X denote the algebra of all real-valued functions on a set X, with the algebra operations defined pointwise, and let $(R^X)^*$ be the subalgebra of all bounded functions. If τ is one of several topologies on X, the subalgebra of all (resp. all bounded) τ-continuous functions is denoted by C_τ (C_τ^*).

The algebra of Baire functions on the compact space (X, β) is defined as the smallest class of bounded functions containing C_β and closed under the operation of taking pointwise limits of sequences. (Compact spaces are assumed to be Hausdorff.) Basic material on Baire functions can be found in LORCH [4]; we summarize briefly some results from [4], § 5, that will be needed here. The weak topology on X generated by the Baire functions is called the ι-topology. Thus the Baire functions form a (possibly proper) subalgebra of C_ι^*. The zero sets of C_β form a basis for the ι-open sets.

---

1) The author gratefully acknowledges the support of the National Science Foundation, Grand GP 6411.

The ι-topology is of course larger than the β-topology and is a P-space topology (as defined in [3]).

On R^X (or on a subset of R^X) let p denote the usual pointwise topology. We are interested in the extent to which p can be described by means of its convergent sequences. For this problem the following definitions from [2] are useful. Topological spaces whose Kuratowski closure operator can be obtained by iteration of the sequential closure operator are called *sequential spaces*. Sequential spaces in which the Kuratowski closure operator coincides with the sequential closure operator are called *Fréchet spaces*. In [6] this approach is extended to $\mathfrak{m}$-*sequential spaces* and $\mathfrak{m}$-*Fréchet spaces* by using $\mathfrak{m}$-nets instead of sequences in the above definitions. (For an infinite cardinal number $\mathfrak{m}$, an $\mathfrak{m}$-net is a net for which the cardinality of the directed set is $\leq \mathfrak{m}$.) For recent work involving pointwise convergent $\mathfrak{m}$-nets of real-valued functions see [9] and [11].

2. The reformulation of the Aleksandrov-Urysohn conjecture

Definition. A topological space is said to be $\mathfrak{m}$-*Lindelöf* (where $\mathfrak{m}$ is an infinite cardinal number) if every open covering of the space has a subcovering of cardinality $\leq \mathfrak{m}$.

Theorem. *The Aleksandrov-Urysohn conjecture is equivalent to the following statement*:

If (X, β) *is a first countable compact space then* (X, ι) *is* $\mathfrak{c}$-*Lindelöf*.

3. When is the ι-topology $\aleph_0$-Lindelöf?

There are many conditions which are equivalent to the $\aleph_0$-Lindelöf property for the ι-topology. In addition to those given here, there are 16 equivalent conditions in [8] and more in [7]. For another approach to the question of when the p-sequential closure operator is idempotent, see [10], p. 312.

It should be noted that under the equivalent conditions in the following theorem, (C_β, p) need not be first countable and (X, ι) need not be discrete. For example, let X be the set of all ordinals $\leq$ the first uncountable ordinal and let β be the order topology.

Theorem. *If* (X, β) *is compact, then the following conditions are equivalent*:

a) (X, ι) *is* $\aleph_0$-*Lindelöf*.

b) (X, β) *is dispersed*.

c) (X, β) *does not contain a generalized Cantor set* (as defined in [5], p. 37).

d) (C_ι^*, p) *is sequential*.

e) (C_ι^*, p) *is Fréchet*.

f) (S, p) *is sequential, where S is any subalgebra and sublattice of* C_β *which distinguishes points and contains the constants*.

g) (S, p) *is Fréchet, where S is as in* f).

h) *Every uniformly closed subalgebra of* C_β *which contains the constants has Baire order* ≤ 1 (*i.e., its sequential closure in* C_ι^* *is sequentially closed*).

References

[1] P. Alexandroff et P. Urysohn, Sur les espaces topologiques compacts, Bull. Acad. Polon. Sci. (A) 1923 (1924), 5—8.

[2] S. P. Franklin, Spaces in which sequences suffice, Fund. Math. **57** (1965), 107—115.

[3] L. Gillman and M. Jerison, Rings of continuous functions, New York 1960.

[4] E. R. Lorch, Compactification, Baire functions, and Daniell integration, Acta Sci. Math. Szeged **24** (1963), 204—218.

[5] P. R. Meyer, The Baire order problem for compact spaces, Duke Math. J. **33** (1966), 33—39.

[6] P. R. Meyer, Sequential space methods in general topological spaces, Notices Amer. Math. Soc. **14** (1967), 664.

[7] H. E. Lacey and P. D. Morris, Continuous linear operators on spaces of continuous functions, Proc. Amer. Math. Soc. **17** (1966), 848—853.

[8] A. Pelczyński and Z. Semadeni, Spaces of continuous functions (III) (Spaces $C(\Omega)$ for Ω without perfect subsets), Studia Math. **18** (1959), 211—222.

[9] H. Poppe, Eine Charakterisierung $\mathfrak{m}$-quasikompakter Räume, Math. Nachr. **29** (1965), 247—253.

[10] V. Sediva-Trnkova, Non-F-spaces, Proc. First Symposium on General Topology, Prague 1961.

[11] P. R. Strauss, Topologies and Borel structures associated with Banach algebras of functions, Thesis, Columbia University 1965.

H-CLOSED SPACES AND PROJECTIVENESS

J. Mioduszewski (Katowice)
and L. Rudolf (Wrocław)

The theory of projective topological spaces and resolutions, initiated by Gleason [1], is in the case of categories consisting of compact (Hausdorff) spaces and their (continuous) mappings well known. The following result of Henriksen and Jerison [2] may be regarded as a final one in this theory: let $\alpha^X : \alpha X \to X$ be the projective resolution of a space X, let P be a projective space and let $f: P \to X$ be a mapping; the diagram

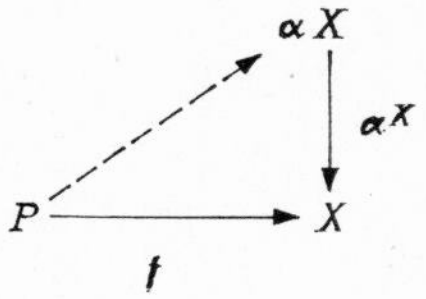

may be completed by a mapping $P \to \alpha X$; mapping $P \to \alpha X$ is uniquely determined by f if and only if for each regularly open subset U of X there is $\mathrm{Int}\, f^{-1}(\overline{U}) \subset \overline{f^{-1}(U)}$. Call mappings like f *H.-J.-mappings*. Let us see that in categories consisting of compact spaces and their H.-J.-mappings the theory of projective (= extremally disconnected) spaces is, in a satisfactory manner, dual to that of Čech-Stone extensions of completely regular spaces.

The aim of the communication is to examine the analogous situation when we pass from compact spaces to more general H-closed spaces. We shall sketch here some partial results including counterexamples. The communication consists of three parts, the two first of which have an auxiliary character. It is a part of a paper which will be published later.

1. Maximal H-closed spaces

Let X be a space. A space X' having the same as X underlying set is called an *expansion* of X if the topology of X' contains that of X (the space X is called a *contraction* of X'). Also the mapping $X' \to X$, being the identity on underlying set, is called an expansion (contraction). An expansion $X' \to X$ will be called *regularly open*, shortly *r.o. expansion*, if the families of regularly open subsets of X and of X' are the same.

A space X is said to be *r.o. maximal* if it admits no r.o. expansion $X' \to X$ except the topological identity. It is easy to prove that

1.1. A space X is r.o. maximal if and only if each dense subset of X is open.

So r.o. maximal spaces coincide with spaces considered by Hewitt [3]. By the Kuratowski-Zorn lemma it is easy to get that

1.2. Each space X admits, not necessarily unique, r.o. expansion to an r.o. maximal space.

Let us note that if in the expansion $X' \to X$ the space X' is H-closed then the expansion is r.o. On the other hand, if $X' \to X$ is an r.o. expansion and X is H-closed then X' is so. Thus, by 1.2.,

1.3. For each H-closed space X there exists, not necessarily unique, maximal H-closed topology on the underlying set of X, containing the topology of X.

Call the spaces mentioned above the *maximal H-closed spaces*.

Note that r.o. expansions preserve in both directions the extremal disconnectedness of the space.

Call a mapping $f\colon X \to Y$ *expansionfree* if the topology of Y is generated by r.o. subsets of Y and by subsets $f^{-1}(U)$, where U are open in X. An expansion is expansionfree if and only if it is a topological identity.

Call a H-closed space *compact-like* if it admits a contraction (in fact an r.o. contraction) to a compact space. E.g. each extremally disconnected space is compact-like.

2. Resolutions of spaces

Let X be a Hausdorff space. A mapping $p\colon\ Y \xrightarrow{\text{onto}} X$ will be called an *r.o. resolution* of X if for each r.o. subset V of Y there is $\overline{p(Y - V)} \neq X$ if $V \neq \emptyset$. If Y is H-closed then $p(Y - V)$ is closed and the condition reduces to $p(Y - V) \neq X$ for non empty r.o. subsets V of Y. Let us see that the irreducible mappings onto X, in the sense e.g. considered in the paper [4] of Iliadis, are r.o. resolutions of X.

The notion of resolution of a space is, in a satisfactory manner, dual to that of dense embedding of a space. If a space X is given then non isomorphic r.o. resolutions of X form a *set* which is partially ordered by composition of mappings.

We shall consider *e.d.r.o. resolution*, i.e. such an r.o. resolutions $p\colon\ Y \to X$, where Y is extremally disconnected.

2.1. For each space X there exixts a maximal e.d.r.o. resolution of X, determined by X up to an isomorphism.

Denote the above resolution by $\alpha^X\colon \alpha X \to X$. It differs from the absolute of X constructed in Iliadis paper [4] only in topology.

Let us restrict considerations to H.-J.-mappings observing that each r.o. resolution is H.-J. Let us note two facts:

2.2. In categories (sufficiently complete) consisting of H.-J.-mappings r.o. resolutions are monomorphisms.

2.3. If the composition $Z \to Y \to X$ is a H.-J.-mapping and $Y \to X$ is an r.o. resolution then $Z \to Y$ is a H.-J.-mapping.

These facts are used in the proof of the following characterization of maximal e.d.r.o. resolutions:

2.4. For each space X the maximal e.d.r.o. resolution $\alpha^X : \alpha X \to X$ is determined up to an isomorphism as an e.d.r.o. resolution $E \to X$ such that for each e.d. space E' and each H.-J.-mapping $E' \to X$ there exists unique H.-J.-mapping filling up the diagram

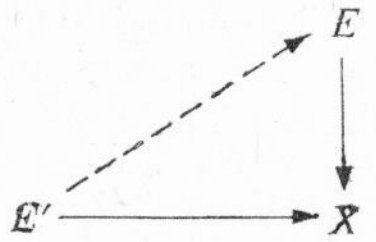

Let us note that if X is H-closed or compact then αX is so. An analogous implication for non compact minimal Hausdorff spaces is not true.

3. Projectiveness

We relativize the notion of projective object of a category as follows: if C is a category and A is a class of morphisms of C then an object P of C is called *A-projective* if for each morphism $g: Y \to X$ of A and ach morphism $f: P \to X$ of C there exists a morphism $h: P \to Y$ such that $g \cdot h = f$.

We shall consider categories C consisting of H-closed spaces. The first observation: if A is the class of all onto mappings of C then even extremally disconnected r.o. maximal spaces fail to be A-projective (for example the space which is an r.o. maximal expansion of the maximal e.d.r.o. resolution of the closed interval). In order to exclude the triviality (= discreteness) of projective spaces we shall assume that A consists only of all expansionfree onto mappings of C.

Then using GLEASON's results of [1] we get

3.1. If C is a (sufficiently complete) category consisting of compact-like spaces and A is the class of all expansionfree onto mappings of C then the class of all A-projective spaces of C coincides with extremally disconnected spaces of C.

An example shows that the result fails to be true for H-closed spaces in general.

A satisfactory result may be obtained if we restrict the considerations to H.-J.-mappings and if we generalize projectiveness as follows: a space is said to be *weakly A-projective* if the mapping completting the diagram from the definition of A-projective object is *weakly continuous*, i.e. it is a mapping $g: P \to Y$ such that for each $p \in P$ and each open neighbourhood U of p there exists V, an open neighbourhood of $g(p)$, such that $g(\overline{U}) \subset \overline{V}$. Weakly continuous mappings are called by some authors θ-continuous (see [4]).

Using the results of the preceeding section concerning maximal e.d.r.o. resolutions we get

3.2. If C is a (sufficiently complete) category consisting of H-closed spaces and H.-J.-mappings, and A is the class of all expansionfree irreducible mappings of C, then the class of all weakly A-projective spaces of C coincides with extremally disconnected spaces of C; maximal extremally disconnected spaces are A-projective.

An example shows that "weakly A-projective" does not be replaced by "A-projective". Also the restriction to expansionfree mappings is in both theorems essential.

References

[1] A. M. GLEASON, Projective topological spaces, Illinois J. Math. **2** (1958), 482—489.
[2] M. HENRIKSEN and M. JERISON, Minimal projective extensions of compact spaces, Duke Math. J. **32** (1965), 291—295.
[3] E. HEWITT, A problem of set theoretic topology, Duke Math. J. **10** (1943), 309—333.
[4] С. Илиадис, Абсолюты хаусдорфовых пространств, Doklady Akad. Nauk SSSR **149** (1963), 22—25.

SOME ASPECTS OF EXTENSION THEORY IN GENERAL TOPOLOGY

JUN-ITI NAGATA[1]) (Pittsburgh, Pa./U.S.A.)

In this lecture it is attempted to pick up some topics concerning comparatively new results in the field of general topology which seem to the speaker interesting. Thus no complete or systematic survey of extension theory is intended here.

1. Construction of compactifications from some other compactifications

The structures of interesting compactifications like Stone-Čech compactification βX and Wallman compactification ωX are never simple even if X is a simple space. But in some cases βX for example can be constructed from the Stone-Čech compactifications of simpler spaces. For example, I. GLICKSBERG [6] proved that $\beta(\prod_\alpha X_\alpha) = \prod_\alpha (\beta X_\alpha)$ *if and only if* $\prod_\alpha X_\alpha$ *is pseudo-compact, where we assume* $\prod_{\alpha \neq \alpha_0} X_\alpha$ *is infinite for every* α_0 *and each* X_α *is completely regular.*

Pursueing an analogy we can pose the following question: Let $\{X_\alpha, \pi^\alpha_\beta \mid \alpha, \beta \in A, \alpha > \beta\}$ be an inverse system of completely regular spaces $X_\alpha, \alpha \in A$; then each $\pi^\alpha_\beta | X_\alpha \to X_\beta$ can be extended to a continuous mapping $\beta\pi^\alpha_\beta | \beta X_\alpha \to \beta X_\beta$. Thus $\{\beta X_\alpha, \beta\pi^\alpha_\beta | \alpha, \beta \in A, \alpha > \beta\}$ is an inverse system of compact Hausdorff spaces. We can easily see that $\varprojlim \{\beta X_\alpha, \beta\pi^\alpha_\beta\}$ is a Hausdorff compactification of $\varprojlim \{X_\alpha, \pi^\alpha_\beta\}$ if each π^α_β is an onto mapping. Then what is the condition in order that $\beta \varprojlim \{X_\alpha, \pi^\alpha_\beta\} = \lim \{\beta X_\alpha, \beta\pi^\alpha_\beta\}$? Since the problem depends not only on the property of X_α but also on that of π^α_β, it might not be so easy to find a complete answer in the general case. To consider some conditions in special cases, let us assume A is the directed set of all natural numbers and each π^α_β is an onto mapping. Furthermore, put $X_\infty = \varprojlim \{X_\alpha, \pi^\alpha_\beta\}$. Then, for examples, the following two are sufficient conditions:

1. *Each* X_α *is* 1-*st countable and normal, and* X_∞ *is countably compact.*

2. *Each* π^α_β *is an open mapping, each* X_α *is normal and* X_∞ *is pseudo-compact.*

As for a necessary condition, if $(\pi^\alpha_\beta)^{-1}(x)$ contains at least two points for any $\alpha, \beta \in A$ and for any $x \in X_\beta$, then $\beta X_\infty = \varprojlim \{\beta X_\alpha, \beta\pi^\alpha_\beta\}$ (where $X_\infty = \varprojlim \{X_\alpha, \pi^\alpha_\beta\}$ as before) implies that

3. X_∞ *is pseudo-compact.*

---

[1]) The author acknowledges the support of NSF Grant No. 5674.

Connecting the conditions 2 and 3 we know the pseudo-compactness of X_∞ is a necessary and sufficient condition under a special circumstance. We can give a little more general condition in this aspect. For each natural number n we define a subset Y_n of X_∞ by $Y_n = \{x \mid x \in X_\infty,$ and there is $x' \in X_\infty$ such that $x' \neq x$, $x_\alpha' = x_\alpha$ for some $\alpha \geqq n\}$, where x_α denotes the α-coordinate of x.

Then, under the assumption that each π_β^α is open and each X_α is normal, we have the following proposition:

$\beta \varprojlim \{X_\alpha, \pi_\beta^\alpha\} = \varprojlim \{\beta X_\alpha, \beta\pi_\beta^\alpha\}$ if and only if for any continuous (real-valued) function f on $X_\infty = \varprojlim \{X_\alpha, \pi_\beta^\alpha\}$ and for any sequence $\{y_n\}$ with $y_n \in Y_n$ $(n = 1, 2, \ldots)$ f is bounded on $\{y_n\}$.

Since in 1961 at the First Prague Topological Symposium P. S. ALEXANDROFF [1] posed the question to represent spaces as images (or inverse images) of nice spaces under nice continuous mappings, many interesting results have been obtained in this area. The following problem should be concerned on this background. Let $f \mid X \to Y$ be a continuous mapping satisfying some property P; then does the continuous extension $\beta f \mid \beta X \to \beta Y$ also satisfy P? This problem becomes trivial in some cases like that P is 'closed', 'perfect' etc. But in the other cases like that P is 'open', 'finite-to-one', 'n-dimensional', 'monotone' etc. the question will deserve a consideration. As for open mappings A. ARHANGELSKI and A. TAIMANOV [2] proved that

Let f be an open closed continuous mapping of X onto Y. If X and Y are normal spaces, then βf is also an open (and naturally closed) mapping.

T. ISHIWATA [7] generalized this result as follows:

Let f be a continuous open WZ-mapping of X onto Y (both completely regular). Then βf is also an open mapping, where f is called a WZ-mapping if $\overline{f^{-1}(y)}^{\beta X} = (\beta f)^{-1}(y)$ for every $y \in Y$.

It is easy to see that every closed mapping is WZ and also that if f is a continuous monotone WZ-mapping of X onto Y, then βf is also monotone. As for monotone mappings we can show more generally that

Let f be a continuous mapping of X onto Y (both completely regular). Then βf is monotone if and only if there is no closed subset K of Y such that $f^{-1}(K) = F \cup G$ for some completely separated closed sets F, G in X satisfying $\overline{f(F)} \cap \overline{f(G)} \cap \operatorname{Int}(K) \neq \emptyset$ where closed sets F, G in X are called completely separated if there are disjoint complete closed sets (= the zero sets of continuous functions) F', G' satisfying $F' \supset F$, $G' \supset G$.

It will be needless to say that some of the problems in this section will be interesting for some other compactifications and extensions than βX, though we have dealt with βX as a representative of interesting extensions.

2. General methods of extension

There are many attempts to establish a general method of extension, e.g. N. A. SHANIN [16], S. FOMIN [5], G. NÖBELING and H. BAUER [14], J. FLACHSMEYER [4], to name a few of them. FLACHSMEYER's recent result seems especially interesting as it reconstructed Stone-Čech compactification and Wallman compactification by use of the method of inverse limit spaces, which might be applicable to obtain some other extensions, too. But, now, let us give a quick view at a newer result by S. MITANI [10] who obtained a generalized completion which includes the usual completion of a uniform space as well as Alexandroff's one point compactification as special cases.

Let X be a given topological space. Then the point of his method is to axiomatically define the collection M of the Cauchy filters in X without considering a system of uniform coverings of X. Here we shall give his definitions and result in a modified form. Let M be a collection of open filters (= filters consisting of open sets) of X satisfying

i) $\mathfrak{F} \in M$ and $\mathfrak{G} \supset \mathfrak{F}$ imply $\mathfrak{G} \in M$;

ii) the open filter $\mathfrak{N}(x)$ of all open neighborhoods of x belongs to M for each $x \in X$.

Then each member of M is called a *Cauchy filter*. If every Cauchy filter of X converges, then (X, M) is called *complete*. Let M^* be the collection of the Cauchy filters of X^*. Then (X^*, M^*) is called a *completion* of (X, M) if

1) X is a subspace of X^*;

2) (X^*, M^*) is complete;

3) for every open set U of X there corresponds an open set U^* of X^* such that $U^* \cap X = U$ and such that $\{U^* \mid U \text{ is open in } X\}$ is a basis of X^*;

4) $\mathfrak{F} \in M^*$ implies $\{A \cap X \mid A \in \mathfrak{F}\} \in M$, and $\mathfrak{F} \in M$ implies $\mathfrak{F}^* \in M^*$, where $\mathfrak{F}^*$ is the open filter of X^* generated by $\mathfrak{F}$;

5) if $x \notin U^*$ for an open set U of X and a point x of X^*, then there is $\mathfrak{F} \in M$ which satisfies $\mathfrak{F} \to x$ in X^* and $U \notin \mathfrak{F}$;

6) each $\mathfrak{F} \in M$ converges to only one point in X^* and for each $x \in X^* - X$, there is at least one $\mathfrak{F} \in M$ which converges to x.

Let $\mathfrak{F}$ be a Cauchy filter of X, i.e. $\mathfrak{F} \in M$, then we put $[\mathfrak{F}] = \cap \{\mathfrak{G} \mid \mathfrak{G} \subset \mathfrak{F}, \mathfrak{G} \in M\}$. Now, the following is the main result of MITANI:

(X, M) *has its completion if and only if it satisfies that for any non-converging Cauchy filter* $\mathfrak{F}$ *of* X, $[\mathfrak{F}]$ *is also a non-converging Cauchy filter of* X. *The completion* (X^*, M^*) *is uniquely determined by* (X, M).

It might be possible to modify MITANI's theory to include more different types of extensions.

3. Dimension and extensions

It is well-known that many extensions have the same dimension with the original space as far as it is finite-dimensional. For examples, $\dim X = \dim CX$ for every metric space X and its completion CX (and accordingly $\operatorname{Ind} X = \operatorname{Ind} CX$). $\dim X = \dim \omega X$ for every T_1-space X, $\dim X = \dim \beta X$ for every completely regular space X, and $\operatorname{Ind} X = \operatorname{Ind} \beta X$ for every normal space X. (As for definitions in dimension theory, see J. NAGATA [13].) Thus it is no wonder that more efforts have been concentrated on extensions of infinite-dimensional spaces in these years. Among the remarkable results in this connection are K. NAGAMI and J. H. ROBERTS [12], E. SKLYARENKO [17], A. LELEK [8], A. W. SCHURLE [15]. For example, A. W. SCHURLE proved quite recently that every strongly countable-dimensional, absolute G_δ, separable metric space has a strongly countable-dimensional metric compactification though, as shown by SKLYARENKO, it is not true without the condition of absolute G_δ. (As for more details in this area, see A. LELEK [9].) So far most investigations are restricted to metric spaces, so we can look for more results for non-metrizable spaces in future.

On the other hand, recently some interesting investigations have been done on dimension of adjunct in compactification. YU. SMIRNOV [18] characterized dim ($\beta X - X$) in case that X is normal. J. DE GROOT and T. NISHIURA [3] also did an extensive investigation in this area dealing with the long unsolved problem:

cmp $X \leqq n$ for a separable metric space X if and only if there is a (metric) compactification $\tilde{X}$ of X for which dim $(\tilde{X} - X) \leqq n$, where cmp $X \leqq n$ is inductively defined in a similar way as ind $X \leqq n$ is defined, but starting with the definition that cmp $X = -1$ for every compact X.

In this connection it is remarkable that J. M. AARTS has recently solved a similar problem but replacing compactness in the problem of DE GROOT with completeness. Define Icd X of a metric space X as follows:

i) Icd $X = -1$ if X is complete;

ii) if for any disjoint closed sets F, G of X, there is an open set U such that

$$F \subset U \subset X - G, \quad \text{Icd Bdr } U \leqq n - 1,$$

then Icd $X \leqq n$.

Then AARTS' result is that

Icd $X \leqq n$ *if and only if* X *has a completion* Y *such that* Ind $(Y - X) \leqq n$.

While DE GROOT's problem still remains open, we can pose some modified problems which might be easier and help us to work on the original problem. For example σ-cmp $X \leqq n$ for a separable metric space X if and only if there is a σ-compact metric space Y such that X is dense in Y and dim $(Y - X) \leqq n$ if we define σ-cmp $X \leqq n$ by

i) σ-cmp $X = -1$ if X is σ-compact;

ii) if for any point x of X and its open neighborhood U there is an open neighborhood V of x such that $V \subset U$ and σ-cmp Bdr $V \leqq n - 1$, then σ-cmp $X \leqq n$?

Finally, it should be noted that in these years compactifications (especially βX) have greatly increased their importance by virtue of H. TAMANO [19], K. MORITA [11] and other mathematicians in the field of applications to characterize various properties of topological spaces and to study normality of product spaces. However, the detail will not be touched here hoping that H. TAMANO [20] will talk on the recent developments in this interesting area of extension theory.

References

[1] P. S. ALEXANDROFF, On some results concerning topological spaces and their continuous mappings, Proc. First Symposium on General Topology, Prague 1961; Prague 1962, p. 41—54.

[2] А. В. Архангельский и А. Тайманов, Об одной теореме В. Пономарева, Doklady Akad. Nauk SSSR **135** (1960), 247—248.

[3] J. DE GROOT and T. NISHIURA, Inductive compactness as a generalization of semicompactness, Fund. Math. **58** (1966), 201—218.

[4] J. FLACHSMEYER, Zur Spektralentwicklung topologischer Räume, Math. Annalen **144** (1961), 253—274.

[5] S. FOMIN, Extensions of topological spaces, Ann. Math. **44** (1943), 471—480.

[6] I. GLICKSBERG, Stone-Čech compactifications of products, Trans. Amer. Math. Soc. **90** (1959), 369—382.

[7] T. ISHIWATA, Mappings and spaces, Pacific J. Math. **20** (1967), 455—480.

[8] A. Lelek, On dimension of remainders in compact extensions (russ.), Doklady Akad. Nauk SSSR **160** (1965), 534—537.
[9] A. Lelek, Dimensional properties of compactifications, this „Contributions", p. 147—148.
[10] S. Mitani, A generalization of the Cauchy filter and the completion, Proc. Japan Acad. **42** (1966), 463—466.
[11] K. Morita, Paracompactness and product spaces, Fund. Math. **50** (1962), 223—236.
[12] K. Nagami and J. H. Roberts, A note on countable-dimensional metric spaces, Proc. Japan Acad. **41** (1965), 155—158.
[13] J. Nagata, Modern dimension theory, Amsterdam-Groningen 1965.
[14] G. Nöbeling und H. Bauer, Über die Erweiterungen topologischer Räume, Math. Annalen **130** (1955), 20—45.
[15] A. W. Schurle, Compactification of strongly countable-dimensional spaces (to appear).
[16] N. A. Shanin, On special extensions of topological spaces; On separation in topological spaces; On the theory of bicompact extensions of topological spaces, Doklady Akad. Nauk SSSR **38** (1943), 6—9; 110—113; 154—156.
[17] Е. Г. Скляренко, О размерностных свойствах бесконечномерных пространств, Izv. Akad. Nauk SSSR **23** (1959), 197—212.
[18] Yu. Smirnov, Über die Dimension der Adjunkten bei Kompaktifizierungen, Monatsberichte Deutsche Akad. Wiss. Berlin **7** (1965), 230—232.
[19] H. Tamano, Normality and product spaces, Proc. Second Symposium on General Topology, Prague 1966; Prague 1967, p. 349—352.
[20] H. Tamano, The role of compactifications in the theory of Tychonoff spaces, this „Contributions", p. 219—220.

EXTENSION OF CONTINUOUS FUNCTIONS IN βD

S. NEGREPONTIS[1]) (Montreal/Can.)

1. Let D be a discrete set of infinite cardinality m, βD its Stone-Čech compactification, and K the set of all elements of $\beta D - D$ that are not in the closure of any subset of D having cardinality less than m. Results on the C^*-embedding of the open subsets of K are given here, in the spirit of the beautiful results obtained earlier by FINE and GILLMAN [1] for $m = \aleph_0$ (in which case $K = \beta N - N$). In our exposition we will mostly follow the notation of [1], [2].

We state for reference, without proof, some known or simple facts and two definitions.

1.1. K is a compact space of cardinality exp exp (m).

1.2. Every open-and-closed set in K is of the form $A' = \mathrm{Cl}_{\beta D} A \cap K$ for some subset A of D (having cardinality m).

1.3. For sets A, B in D, $A' = B'$ iff the symmetric difference of A and B has cardinality less than m.

1.4. For sets A, B in D, $(A \cap B)' = A' \cap B'$.

1.5. The cardinal $\overline{m}$ is defined to be the least among the cardinals k, such that a discrete set of cardinality $\overline{m}$ can be expressed as the union of k sets of cardinality less than m. We shall call m *regular* if $m = \overline{m}$. It can be shown that $\overline{m}$ is always a regular cardinal, and thus for every m we have the relations $\aleph_0 \leqq \overline{\overline{m}} = \overline{m} \leqq m$.

1.6. Definition. For an open set G in K we let $n(G)$ be the least among the cardinals n, for which G can be expressed as the union of n open-and-closed subsets of K. Sometimes $n(G)$ will be called the *type* of G.

We denote by N the set of positive integers.

2. *The case of* $n(G) < \overline{m}$.

2.1. Theorem. *If G is an open set in K, such that $n(G) < \overline{m}$, then the closure $\overline{G}$ of G in K is open.*

Proof. Let $n(G) = n$. Thus G can be expressed as the union of sets of the form A_i', $i \in I$, where A_i is a subset of D of cardinality m, and the index set I has cardinal-

[1]) Research supported by N. R. C. (Canada) under Grant A-4035. The results of this paper have appeared in Proc. Nederl. Akad. Wet., Ser. A, 71 (1968), 393—400.

ity $n < \overline{m}$. We set $A = \bigcup_{i \in I} A_i$, and $H = A'$. Thus H is open-and-closed, and the closure of G is contained in H. Suppose that $\overline{G} \neq H$. Let P be an open-and-closed, non-empty set in K, say $P = E'$, such that $P \cap G = \emptyset$, $P \subset H$. Clearly we may assume that $E \subset A$. Since $n < \overline{m}$, there is $i \in I$ such that $A_i \cap E$ has cardinality m. Hence $(A_i \cap E)' = A_i' \cap E'$ is non-empty and contained in G; thus $P \cap G \neq \emptyset$.

2.2. Corollary. *Let G be open in K, $n(G) < \overline{m}$, and H any open set of K disjoint from G; then $\overline{G} \cap \overline{H} = \emptyset$. As a consequence, any open set of K of type less than $\overline{m}$ is C^*-embedded in K.*

Proof. The first statement follows immediately from 2.1. To prove that G is C^*-embedded in K, we use Urysohn's extension theorem (see e.g. [2], 1.17). Let A and B be two closed sets in G, completely separated by a continuous function in G. We can find cozero-sets of G, A_1 and B_1, such that $A_2 \supset A$, $B_1 \supset B$, and $A_1 \cap B_1 = \emptyset$. Let $G = \bigcup_{i \in I} C_i$, where each C_i is open-and-closed, and I has cardinality $n < \overline{m}$. For each $i \in I$, the set $A_1 \cap C_i$ is a cozero-set of C_i, and hence equal to a countable union of open-and-closed sets of K; thus A_1 is the union of $n \cdot \aleph_0 = n$ open-and-closed sets of K. By the first statement of this corollary, $\overline{A}_1 \cap \overline{B}_1 = \emptyset$. Thus A_1 and B_1 are completely separated in K.

3. *The case of $n(G) = \overline{m}$.* If $m = \aleph_0$, and thus $\overline{m} = \aleph_0$, then this case corresponds to a cozero-set G which is not open-and-closed. Two results are known concerning such sets: First, G is C^*-embedded in $\beta N - N$; this can be easily seen using the fact that $N \cup G$ is a σ-compact space (and thus normal) of which G is a closed subset. Secondly, $\overline{G}$ is never open in $\beta N - N$. This fact is proved in [2], 6W, for example. We will now obtain the corresponding statements for the space K for any cardinal m. The argument required to show that G is C^*-embedded in K will by necessity be more involved, since no simple criterion exists for the normality of $D \cup G$. In fact it is not known to the author whether $D \cup G$ is normal. The situation with the second statement (involving the closure of G) is more complicated, and the results describing it appear in 3.2., 3.4.

3.1. Theorem. *If G is the union of m open-and-closed sets in K, then G is C^*-embedded in K.*

Proof. Let Σ be the least ordinal of cardinality $\overline{m}$, and set $G = \bigcup \{A_\lambda' : \lambda < \Sigma\}$. We set $C_\lambda = \bigcup_{\beta \leq \lambda} A_\beta'$ for all $\lambda < \Sigma$, so that $G = \bigcup_{\lambda < \Sigma} C_\lambda$ and $C_\lambda \subset C_\beta$ for all $\lambda < \beta$. Further C_λ is the union of less than $\overline{m}$ open-and-closed sets of K, and by 2.1., $\overline{C}_\lambda$ is open-and-closed, with C_λ C^*-embedded in $\overline{C}_\lambda$. We set $H = \bigcup_{\lambda < \Sigma} \overline{C}_\lambda$, and prove that G is C^*-embedded in H. Notice that G is dense in H. Let $f \in C^*(G)$, and define $f_\lambda = f \mid C_\lambda$ for all $\lambda < \Sigma$. There is a (unique) continuous extension $\bar{f}_\lambda$ of f_λ over $\overline{C}_\lambda$. We define $\bar{f} = \bigcup_{\lambda < \Sigma} \bar{f}_\lambda$. It is clear that $\bar{f}$ will be continuous if it is well-defined. To prove the latter let $p \in \overline{C}_\lambda \cap \overline{C}_\beta$, and let us assume that $\lambda < \beta$. Then $C_\lambda \subset C_\beta$, $\overline{C}_\lambda \subset \overline{C}_\beta$, and clearly $\bar{f}_\beta \mid \overline{C}_\lambda = \bar{f}_\lambda$.

Let now $\overline{C}_\lambda = A_\lambda'$ for subsets A_λ of D. We define $B_\lambda = \bigcup_{\beta \leq \lambda} A_\beta$ for all $\lambda < \Sigma$. Clearly then $B_\lambda' = A_\lambda' = \overline{C}_\lambda$, and $B_\lambda \subset B_\beta$ for $\lambda < \beta$. Let $A = \bigcup_{\lambda < \Sigma} A_\lambda$. We want to extend $\bar{f}$ to a continuous, bounded real-valued function on $A \cup H$. For simplicity of notation, let $\bar{f}$ be denoted also by f. Let $f_\lambda = f \mid \bar{C}_\lambda$. We proceed by transfinite induction. Notice that $B_1 \cup \bar{C}_1$ is easily seen to be a paracompact (and thus normal) space, with $\bar{C}_1$ a closed subset of it. We let $\bar{f}_1 \in C^*(B_1 \cup \bar{C}_1)$ be any continuous and bounded extension of f_1. Suppose that we have defined extensions $\bar{f}_\beta$ for all $\beta < \lambda$, such that $\bar{f}_\beta \in C^*(B_\beta \cup \bar{C}_\beta)$ and $\bar{f}_\beta \mid B_\gamma \cup \bar{C}_\gamma = \bar{f}_\gamma$ for all $\gamma < \beta < \lambda$. Notice that the last statement makes sense since $\bar{C}_\beta \cup B_\beta \supset \bar{C}_\gamma \cup B_\gamma$. We want to define $\bar{f}_\lambda$ on $B_\lambda \cup \bar{C}_\lambda$. There is an obvious mapping f_λ^* already defined on $(\bigcup_{\beta<\lambda} B_\beta \cup \bar{C}_\beta) \cup \bar{C}_\lambda$. Set $B_\lambda^* = \bigcup_{\beta<\lambda} B_\beta$, and notice that $B_\beta{}' = B_\beta \cup \bar{C}_\beta$; the set of all ordinals β less than λ has cardinality less than $\bar{m}$, and the proof of theorem 2.1. clearly implies that $(B_\lambda^*)' = \overline{\bigcup_{\beta<\lambda} C_\beta} \cup B_\lambda^*$. The inductive assumption implies that $f_\lambda^* \mid (B_\lambda^*)'$ is continuous, and of course $f_\lambda^* \mid \bar{C}_\lambda$ is continuous. Thus, f_λ^* will be continuous, if it is well-defined. But f_λ^* is obviously well-defined since $(B_\lambda^*)' \cap \bar{C}_\lambda \subset \bar{C}_\lambda \subset H$. We employ now the paracompactness of $B_\lambda \cup \bar{C}_\lambda$, and the fact that $\bar{C}_\lambda$ is a closed subset of it, to extend f_λ^* to $\bar{f}_\lambda \in C^*(B_\lambda \cup \bar{C}_\lambda)$. Clearly, $\bar{f}_\lambda \mid B_\beta \cup \bar{C}_\beta = \bar{f}_\beta$ for all $\beta < \lambda$. We now define $\bar{f} = \bigcup_{\lambda<\Sigma} \bar{f}_\lambda$, which obviously is a continuous bounded function on $A \cup H$. But $\mathrm{Cl}_{\beta D} A = \beta A$, and $A \subset A \cup H \subset \beta A$, so that $A \cup H$ is in fact C^*-embedded in βA; since βA is open-and-closed in βD, $A \cup H$ is C^*-embedded in βD. It is now clear that G is C^*-embedded in K.

We now determine the cases for which an open set G, with $n(G) = \bar{m}$, has an open closure in K. Recall that such sets do not exist if $m = \aleph_0$.

3.2. Theorem. *Let G be an open set of K of type $\bar{m}$; then the closure $\bar{G}$ is open iff G contains densely an open set of type less than $\bar{m}$.*

Proof. The converse implication follows from 2.1. For the non-trivial implication we notice that we may express G as the union of open sets of type less than $\bar{m}$, say G_λ, $\lambda < \Sigma$, such that $G_\lambda \subset G_\beta$ for all $\lambda < \beta < \Sigma$, and such that $\bigcup_{\beta<\lambda} G_\beta$ is not dense in G_λ for all $\lambda < \Sigma$. Such a construction can be carried out inductively starting with a family of open-and-closed sets of cardinality $\bar{m}$ whose union is G, and making use of the fact that no open set of type less than $\bar{m}$ is dense in G. (Σ denotes as before the least ordinal of cardinality $\bar{m}$.) Let $H = \bigcup_{\lambda<\Sigma} G_\lambda$, then $G \subset H \subset \bar{G}$, and H is open in K. We actually prove that $\bar{H} = \bar{G}$ is not open. Let $\bar{G}_\lambda = A_\lambda{}'$ for subsets A_λ of D, and let A be any subset of D such that $A' \supset H$. Notice that for all $\lambda < \Sigma$, the set $A \cap A_\lambda - \bigcup_{\beta<\lambda} A_\beta$ has cardinality m; for suppose that it has cardinality less than m. Then $\emptyset = (A \cap A_\lambda - \bigcup_{\beta<\lambda} A_\beta)' = (A \cap A_\lambda)' - (\bigcup_{\beta<\lambda} A_\beta)' = A_\lambda{}' - (\overline{\bigcup_{\beta<\lambda} A_\beta{}'}) = G_\lambda - \overline{\bigcup_{\beta<\lambda} G_\beta}$, contradicting our construction of the sets G_λ. Let now Ω be the least ordinal of cardinality m, and let $\{\delta_\lambda : \lambda < \Sigma\}$ be an increasing set of ordinals less than Ω, forming a cofinal set in the set of all ordinals less than Ω. For each $\lambda < \Sigma$ we choose a subset B_λ of $A \cap A_\lambda - \bigcup_{\beta<\lambda} A_\beta$ of cardinality equal to the cardinality of δ_λ, and define $B = \bigcup_{\lambda<\Sigma} B_\lambda$. Clearly B has cardinality m. Let $C = A - B$. Now $A_\lambda - C$ is a set of cardinality less than m, and hence $A_\lambda{}' \subset C'$ for all $\lambda < \Sigma$; thus $H \subset C'$. On the other hand $A - C = B$ has cardinality m and hence $C' \neq A'$. It follows that G is not open.

It is almost obvious that for all cardinals n, $\aleph_0 \leq n \leq m$, there are open sets G, such that $n(G) = n$, and which contain densely no open set of smaller type. E.g. let $\{A_i : i \in I\}$ be a family of subsets of D, each of cardinality m, pairwise disjoint, and with index set I having cardinality n; and set $G = \bigcup_{i \in I} A_i'$. In particular we may take $n = \overline{m}$. The following is an immediate corollary of 3.2. and the succeeding remark.

3.3. Corollary. *For all (infinite cardinals) m, K is not extremally disconnected.*

On the other hand it is not obvious for which m, sets of type $\overline{m}$ with open closure exist. We prove below that this is the case iff $\overline{m} > \aleph_0$.

3.4. Theorem. *If $\overline{m} = \aleph_0$, then every open set in K of type $\overline{m}$ has closure that is not open. If $\overline{m} > \aleph_0$ and $\aleph_0 \leqq n \leqq m$ (in particular we may take $n = \overline{m}$), then there is an open set G in K of type n, such that G contains densely a cozero-set of K. In fact G in addition is dense in K.*

Proof. The first statement follows by 3.2. We now assume that $\overline{m} > \aleph_0$. If m is a measurable cardinal, then K meets the non-empty set $vD - D$. It is easy to prove that vD does not contain K, and thus we may choose $p \in K - vD$. We next modify the proof in [1], 5.3., to prove the existence in K of a proper dense cozero-set. Indeed, there is $f \in C(\beta D)$ such that $f(p) = 0$, and $f(d) > 0$ for all $d \in D$. Let C be the cozero-set of f/K, and we are to prove that C is a proper dense subset of K. Clearly $p \notin C$. Let A' be a non-empty open-and-closed subset of K, let $D_n = \{d \in D \colon f(d) > n^{-1}\}$; thus $A = \bigcup_n (D_n \cap A)$. Since A has cardinality m and $\overline{m} > \aleph_0$, it follows that for some n, $D_n \cap A$ has cardinality m. Thus $\emptyset \neq (D_n \cap A)' \subset A' \cap C$, i.e. C is dense in K. Clearly $\beta C = K$. It is easy to see that C can be expressed as the pairwise disjoint union of an infinite sequence of open-and-closed subsets of K, i.e. C is homeomorphic to $K \times N$. We let π be the canonical mapping from $\beta(K \times N)$ onto $K \times \beta N$, and π^* the induced mapping of $K - C$ onto $K \times (\beta N - N)$. Let now $\{A_i \colon i \in I\}$ be a family of subsets of D, each of cardinality m, pairwise disjoint, with the index set I having cardinality n. We set $V = \bigcup_{i \in I} A_i'$. Let q be any fixed element of $\beta N - N$, and set $H_i = \pi^{*-1}(A_i' \times (q))$, $H = \bigcup_{i \in I} H_i$. For every $i \in I$, there is C_i open-and-closed in K, such that $C_i \cap (K - C) = H_i$. We finally set $G = C \cup \bigcup_{i \in I} C_i$. Since $C \subset G \subset K$, G contains densely the cozero-set C. It is clear that $n(G) = n$, since the sets C_i are open-and-closed and pairwise disjoint in the compact space $K - C$.

3.5. Corollary. *The following statements are equivalent:*

(i) $\overline{m} = \aleph_0$.

(ii) *K is not basically disconnected.*

(iii) *The closure of every non-closed cozero-set of K is not open.*

(iv) *Every zero-set of K is the closure of its interior.*

(v) *K has no proper dense cozero-set.*

The proof of this corollary is essentially contained in the previous results. Notice that there are arbitrarily high cardinal numbers satisfying $\overline{m} = \aleph_0$.

4. *Some facts on $n(G) > \overline{m}$.* We note here some elementary facts concerning open sets G in K of type larger than $\overline{m}$. One fact is the existence of such sets; this follows from a result on almost disjoint families of sets, due to SIERPINSKI. We denote by

$\overline{m}^+$ the successor of $\overline{m}$ in the usual well-ordering of the cardinals. For sets G, open in K and of type not exceeding $\overline{m}^+$ the C^*-embedding of certain open subsets of G is shown. This result, which will be needed in the next section, is a generalization of [1], theorem 4.1.

4.1. Theorem ([3], p. 448). *There is a family $\mathscr{A}$ of subsets of D such that* card $\mathscr{A} > m$, card $(F_1 \cap F_2) < m$ *for all* F_1, F_2 *in* $\mathscr{A}$, *and* card $F = m$ *for all* $F \in \mathscr{A}$.

An elegant proof of this theorem has been communicated to the author by W. W. Comfort: Use [2], 12.8, to get a family E of mappings from D into D, such that card $E > m$, and such that any two members of E agree only on a set of cardinality less than m, and let $\mathscr{A}$ be the family of graphs of all mappings in E.

4.2. Corollary. *There are open sets G in K of type larger than m, that contain densely no open set of type $\leqq m$.*

Indeed the set $G = \cup \{F' : F \in \mathscr{A}\}$, where $\mathscr{A}$ is as in 4.1, clearly satisfies the requirements.

4.3. Remark. There is another way of finding open sets of type larger than m. In fact for any $p \in K$, the set $K - (p)$ has type larger than m. This can be seen by first noting, as in [2], 4 G. 2, that p has no basis for the filter of its neighborhoods having cardinal $\leqq m$, and next using a familiar compactness argument to verify that in fact p cannot be the intersection of at most m open-and-closed subsets of K, i.e. $K - (p)$ has type larger than m. However, the two constructions (4.2 and 4.3) differ in one important aspect. As it has been noted, the set G constructed via Sierpinski's theorem does not contain densely any open subset of type $\leqq m$; but the set $K - (p)$, in case $\overline{m} > \aleph_0$, and barring some exceptions for measurable cardinals, always contains densely a cozero-set of K, as it has been noted in 3.4.

4.4. Theorem. *Let G be an open set of K, $G = \bigcup_{i \in I} C_i$, where C_i is open-and-closed for all $i \in I$, and I has cardinality not exceeding $\overline{m}^+$, and let H be an open subset of G such that $H \cap C_i$ is of type not exceeding $\overline{m}$ for all $i \in I$. Then H is C^*-embedded in G.*

Proof. The only case that does not follow trivially from the theorems we have already proved is that of I having cardinality $\overline{m}^+$. For simplicity of notation let us assume that I is the smallest ordinal of cardinality $\overline{m}^+$, and that the indices i form the set of all ordinals less than I. Let $G_i = \bigcup_{j \leqq i} C_j$. Let $f \in C^*(H)$, and set $f_i = f \mid H \cap G_i$. Suppose that f_j has been extended to a function $\bar{f}_j \in C^*(G_j)$ for all $j < i$, in such a way that $\bar{f}_j$ is an extension of $\bar{f}_k$ for all $k < j < i$. Clearly then there is a function f_i^* defined on $G_i^* = \bigcup_{j<i} G_j \cup (H \cap G_i)$, continuous and bounded, and an extension of all the $\bar{f}_j$, $j < i$, and of f_i. The set G_i^* is the union of $\leqq \overline{m}$ open-and-closed sets in K, since $H \cap G_i = \bigcup_{j \leqq i} (H \cap C_j)$; and hence, by 3.2., G_i^* is C^*-embedded in K, and in particular in G_i; we let $\bar{f}_i$ be a continuous and bounded extension of f_i^* over G_i. Finally $\bar{f} = \bigcup_{i<I} \bar{f}_i$ provides a continuous extension of f over G.

5. *The condition $\langle p, G \rangle$*. We define in this section the condition $\langle p, G \rangle$ and prove two elementary facts concerning it. We reserve for the next section the proof of the deeper theorem on the non-C^*-embedding of open sets of type larger than m for

regular cardinals m. The outlook of the present two sections is remarkably similar to the treatment of FINE and GILLMAN [1] of the case $m = \aleph_0$.

5.1. Definition. Let G be an open subset of K and p an element of $\overline{G} - G$. We say that *the condition $\langle p, G\rangle$ is satisfied* if there is a neighborhood V of p, and an open set H of K, $H \subset G$, H of type not exceeding $\overline{m}$, such that $(G \cap V) - H$ has empty interior.

5.2. Proposition. *If G is an open set in K, such that $\langle p, G\rangle$ holds for all $p \in \overline{G} - G$, then G contains densely an open set of K, of type not exceeding $\overline{m}$.*

Proof. By $\langle p, G\rangle$, we get an open neighborhood $V(p)$ of p, and an open set $H(p)$, such that $n(H(p)) \leqq \overline{m}$, $H(p) \subset G$, and such that $(G \cap V(p)) - H(p)$ has empty interior for all $p \in \overline{G} - G$. Since $\overline{G} - G$ is compact there is a finite cover $\{V_1, \ldots, V_n\}$ of $\overline{G} - G$, chosen among the $V(p)$, whose corresponding open sets are, say, $\{H_1, \ldots, H_n\}$. The set $A = \overline{G} - (V_1 \cup \ldots \cup V_n)$ is compact and disjoint from $\overline{G} - G$. Let C be a cozero-set in K, contained in $\overline{G}$, containing A, and disjoint from $\overline{G} - G$, and set $H = H_1 \cup \ldots \cup H_n \cup C$. It is clear that H is an open subset of G, of type not exceeding $\overline{m}$, and dense in G.

5.3. Proposition. *Let G be open in K, $p \in \overline{G} - G$, and suppose that $\langle p, G\rangle$ holds. Then G is C^*-embedded in $G \cup (p)$.*

Proof. Let V and H be as in definition 5.1. Let $f \in C^*(G)$, and we consider $f \mid H$. Since, by 3.2., H is C^*-embedded in K, we can extend $f \mid H$ to a (unique) function $g \in C^*(H \cup (p))$. We define $\bar{f}$ on $G \cup (p)$ by $\bar{f} = f$ on G, and $\bar{f}(p) = g(p)$. Then $\bar{f}$ is continuous, since $\bar{f} \mid G$ and $\bar{f} \mid V \cap (G \cup (p))$ are continuous.

6. *The case $n(G) > m$ for regular m.* For our final results we will have to restrict attention to regular cardinals. It will not be surprising that we also have to assume a segment of the generalized continuum hypothesis.

6.1. Theorem. *Let $\overline{m} = m$ and assume $m^+ = \exp(m)$. Let G be an open set in K of type larger than m. Then, either G contains densely an open set of type not exceeding m, or else G is not C^*-embedded in K. In the latter case, there is a two-valued continuous function in $C^*(G)$ that cannot be continuously extended, and* card $(\beta G) \geqq \exp\exp(m^+)$.

Proof. If G contains densely an open set of type not exceeding m, then G is C^*-embedded in K, by 3.2. Suppose that G contains no such set. By 5.2., there is $p \in \overline{G} -$ $- G$, such that the condition $\langle p, G\rangle$ fails. Let I be the smallest ordinal of cardinality m^+, and let $G = \bigcup_{i<I} C_i$, where C_i is open-and-closed in K. Let $G_i = \bigcup_{j\leqq i} C_j$. Further let $\{V_i : i \in I\}$ be a basis of open-and-closed neighborhoods for p. Assuming $m^+ = \exp(m)$, the cardinality of a basis of neighborhoods for p is given in [2], 4 G. 2, and is consistent with our notation. We suppose that for all $j < i$ $(< I)$, we have defined open sets A_j, B_j, such that $n(A_j) \leqq m$, $n(B_j) \leqq m$. Since $\langle p, G\rangle$ fails, there are disjoint, non-empty open sets A_i, B_i of type not exceeding m, contained in $G \cap V_i - \bigcup_{j<i} (A_j \cup B_j \cup G_j)$. Define $A = \bigcup_{i<I} A_i$, $B = \bigcup_{i<I} B_i$, and $E = A \cup B$. By the construction, for every $i < I$, $E \cap G_i$ is the open set $\bigcup_{j<i} (A_j \cup B_j) \cap G_i$, clearly of type $\leqq m$. By 4.4., E is C^*-embedded in G. But A and B are complementary open sets in E, each of which

meets every neighborhood of p. Hence E is not C^*-embedded in $E \cup (p)$. It follows that G is not C^*-embedded in $G \cup (p)$. Further there is a two-valued continuous function of $C^*(E)$, which can be extended to a two-valued function of $C^*(G)$, but cannot be extended continuously over $G \cup (p)$. This can be seen by an argument similar to [1], 4.1 (b), that will not be repeated here. To obtain the lower estimate of card (βG) we note that G contains a closed C^*-embedded copy of a discrete space of cardinality m^+.

It is to be noted that by arguments similar to those in 3.4. and 4.2., we can prove that both cases of theorem 6.1. actually occur.

6.2. Corollary. *Let* $\overline{m} = m$ *and assume* $m^+ = \exp(m)$. *Let* G *be an open set in* K *and* $p \in \bar{G} - G$. *Then* G *is* C^**embedded in* $G \cup (p)$ *iff* $\langle p, G\rangle$ *holds.*

6.3. Corollary. *Let* $\overline{m} = m$ *and assume* $m^+ = \exp(m)$. *An open set* G *of* K *is* C^**-embedded in* K *iff* G *contains densely an open set of type not exceeding* m.

References

[1] N. J. Fine and L. Gillman, Extension of continuous functions in βN, Bull. Amer. Math. Soc. **66** (1960), 376–381.
[2] L. Gillman and M. Jerison, Rings of continuous functions, Princeton 1960.
[3] W. Sierpiński, Cardinal and ordinal numbers, Warszawa 1958.

EXTENSION THEORY OF CONVERGENCE STRUCTURES AND ITS APPLICATION TO PROBABILITY THEORY

J. NOVÁK (Praha)

Let (L, λ) be a convergence space (abbr. c.space), λ being a convergence closure defined by closures of sets $A \subset L$

$$\lambda A = \{x = \lim x_n; \ \bigcup x_n \subset A\}.$$

Define

$$\lambda^0 A = A, \quad \lambda^\xi A = \bigcup_{\eta<\xi} \lambda\lambda^\eta A,$$

ξ denoting any ordinal. A real valued function f on L is sequentially (abbr. s.) continuous if $x \in L$ and $\lim x_n = x$ implies $\lim f(x_n) = f(x)$. Denote $\mathscr{F}(L)$ the class of all s.continuous functions on L. Let $\mathscr{F}_0(L) \subset \mathscr{F}(L)$. The c. space L is $\mathscr{F}_0$ sequentially regular if for each $x \in L$ the following property is fulfilled:

If $x \in L$ and $\{x_n\}$ is a sequence no subsequence of which converges to x then there is $f \in \mathscr{F}_0(L)$ such that $\{f(x_n)\}$ does not converge to $f(x)$.

A c.space (S, σ) is an $\mathscr{F}_0$ sequential envelope of an $\mathscr{F}_0$ s.regular space (L, λ) if

1. L is a subspace S and $\lambda^{\omega_1} L = S$.

2. Each $f \in \mathscr{F}_0(L)$ can be continuously extended to a function $\bar{f} \in \mathscr{F}(S)$ and S is $\overline{\mathscr{F}}_0(S)$ sequentially regular, $\mathscr{F}_0(S)$ being the class of all $\bar{f} \in \mathscr{F}(S)$ such that $\bar{f} \mid L \in \mathscr{F}_0(L)$.

3. There is no c.space (T, τ) containing S as a proper subspace fulfilling 1. and 2. with regard to L and T.

The $\mathscr{F}$ s.regularity of c.spaces corresponds to the complete regularity of topological spaces and $\mathscr{F}$ s.envelope is an analogous notion to the Čech-Stone compactification. Each $\mathscr{F}_0$ s.regular space has an $\mathscr{F}_0$ s.envelope and two $\mathscr{F}_0$ s.envelopes of the same c.space are homeomorphic to each other.

Let X be a point set and 2^X the system of all subsets of X. Then $(2^X, \lambda)$ is a c.space, its convergence being defined in the usual way: $\text{Lim}\, A_n = A$ whenever $\text{Lim inf}\, A_n = \text{Lim sup}\, A_n = A$.

Let $\mathbb{A}$ be a set algebra on X (i.e. $X \in \mathbb{A}$). Denote $\mathscr{F}(\mathbb{A})$ the class of all sequentially continuous set functions on $\mathbb{A}$ and $\mathscr{P}(\mathbb{A})$ the class of all probability measures on $\mathbb{A}$. Then $\mathscr{P}(\mathbb{A}) \subset \mathscr{F}(\mathbb{A})$ and $(\mathbb{A}, \lambda)$ is both an $\mathscr{F}$ and $\mathscr{P}$ sequentially regular space.

Consequently there exist $\mathscr{F}$ and $\mathscr{P}$ sequential envelopes of $\mathbb{A}$. The following theorem holds:

Theorem. *Let $\mathbb{A}$ be an algebra of sets on X. Then the sigma algebra $\mathbb{S}(\mathbb{A})$ generated by $\mathbb{A}$ is a $\mathscr{P}$ sequential envelope of $\mathbb{A}$.*

Example. Let X be an infinite point set and $\mathbb{F}$ a set algebra consisting of all subsets $F \subset X$ such that F or $X - F$ is finite. Then $\mathbb{F}$ itself is an $\mathscr{F}$ sequential en velope of $\mathbb{F}$. V. Koutník has constructed a ring of sets $\mathbb{R}$ such that its $\mathscr{F}$ sequen tial envelope differs from $\mathbb{R}$.

The question arises as follows: Is it possible to define probability functions on convergence algebras which are not Boolean algebras? The answer is positive. This will be shown by constructing algebra like this:

Let X be a non empty point set and $\mathbb{A}$ an algebra of sets on X. Let $p > 2$ be a prime number. Denote $\dot{\mathbb{A}}$ $(\dot{2}^X)$ the collection of all elements

$$[E_1, E_2, \ldots, E_{p-1}]$$

where E_i, $i = 1, 2, \ldots, p - 1$, are disjoint subsets belonging to $\mathbb{A}$ (to 2^X) as elements. Define

$$[E_i] + [F_i] = [(E_i - \bigcup_1^{p-1} F_j) \cup (F_i - \bigcup_1^{p-1} E_j) \cup \bigcup_{m+n \equiv i(p)} E_m \cap F_n,$$

$$[E_i] \cdot [F_i] = [\bigcup_{m \cdot n \equiv i(p)} E_m \cap E_n],$$

$$\lim_n [E_i^n] = [\operatorname{Lim}_n E_i^n].$$

Then $\dot{\mathbb{A}}$ $(\dot{2}^X)$ is a convergence algebra which fails to be Boolean. Now, let P be any probalibity measure on $\mathbb{A}$. Put

$$\dot{P}([E_i]) = \sum_1^{p-1} P(E_i)^{\cdot}.$$

The function $\dot{P}$ has the basic properties of probability measures: $\dot{P}$ is non negative, additive and sequentially continuous on $\dot{\mathbb{A}}$ and such that $P(e) = 1$, e being the unit of $\dot{\mathbb{A}}$. The function $\dot{P}$ can be continuously extended onto the smallest convergence algebra in $\dot{2}^X$ containing $\dot{\mathbb{A}}$ which is closed in $\dot{2}^X$.

ON SOME PROXIMITY PROPERTIES DETERMINED ONLY BY THE TOPOLOGY OF THE COMPACTIFICATION

V. Z. Poljakov (Moskau)

It is well known (the result of Yu. M. Smirnov [9]) that every property of a proximity space P can be described, principally, with help of its (unique) compactification, i.e. equicontinuous injection $i: P \subset \overline{P}$ into a compact Hausdorff space $\overline{P}$ such that $[\mathrm{Im}\, i] = \overline{P}$. But it is not possible in many cases to characterise effectively some concrete properties of the proximity space used only the compact space $\overline{P}$: it is not clear, for example, what properties distinguish the compactifications of a Tychonoff space which proximities are complete, or exact (i.e. are equipped by the finest uniformity [6]), or precompact, etc. By the other hand there are some proximily properties which may be characterised by the topology of $\overline{P}$: such property is, for instance, "the small proximily dimension" δd [11] (becouse $\delta d P = \dim \overline{P}$); if the topology of P is special enough it may be occure that some supplementary properties of P can be known with help the space $\overline{P}$: for instance, non-homeomorphic compactifications of a discrete space induce on it non-equimorphic proximities. Having counted this it is interesting to establish which properties of the proximity spaces (or of the spaces with the certain types of the topologies) are determined by the topologies of their compactifications. We will show in this article that if the topology of the proximity space satisfies the first countable axiom then many its "natural" properties are such. In common case the situation is not so nice: the example of two proximity spaces having the homeomorphic topologies and compactifications will be presented such that one of these spaces will be precompact and the other one will not be exact. But we can show some conditions for the compactification $\overline{P}$ which equip exactness of the proximity space P.

Theorem 1. *Let P be any proximity space and $\overline{P}$ be its Smirnov compactification. Suppose there exists a metric space M which Smirnov compactification is homeomorphic with $\overline{P}$. Then the proximity space P is exact.*

Lemma 1. *Let $\mathfrak{z} = \{z_n\}$ be a sequence of points of a proximity space P such any two its infinite subsequences such. Then the sequence $\mathfrak{z}$ is fundamental (i.e. it has a unique limit in the completion cP).*

Proof. Consider the filter $\mathscr{F}$ of the subsets of P with the base $\{\{z_j \mid j > i\} \mid i \in N\}$ and demonstrate that it is a Cauchy filter. For this let $\mathfrak{U}$ be any uniform covering and $\mathfrak{V}$ its uniform star refinement. We state that there exists a number i such, for any $j > i$, $z_j \in \mathrm{St}(z_i, \mathfrak{V})$ holds hence $\{z_j \mid j > i\} \subset U \in \mathfrak{U}$. Suppose not. Then there is, for any i, some $j_i > i$ such $z_{j_i} \notin \mathrm{St}(z_i, \mathfrak{V})$. It is proved in [8] (lemma 1, necessity) that if there are two infinite sequences $\{x_k\}$, $\{y_k\} \subset P$ such $x_k \notin \mathrm{St}(y_k, \mathfrak{V})$ for any k and some uniform covering $\mathfrak{U}$, then these sequences have far infinite subsequences.

Lemma 2. *Every equicontinuous mapping $f: P \to M$ into a complete metric space can be extended on some G_δ-extention of P (which may be assumed as a subset of the compactification $\overline{P}$).*

Proof. Let $f: P \to M$ be equicontinuous. Denote $\mathfrak{D}_n = \{O_{1/n}\, z \mid z \in M\}$ ("the exact $\frac{1}{n}$-covering of M") and let $\mathfrak{M}_n = f^{-1}\, \mathfrak{D}_n$. Futher let the symbol $O\langle A\rangle$, for any $A \subset P$, means the union of all open sets $G \subset \overline{P}$ such $G \cap P = A$. Consider now the neighborhoods $O_n = \bigcup \{O\langle A\rangle \mid A \in \mathfrak{M}_n\}$ in $\overline{P}$ of P and let $Q = \bigcap_{n=1}^{\infty} O_n$. The set Q is desirable G_δ-extension of P.

The extension $\tilde{f}: Q \to M$ is defined in the points $x \in Q \setminus P$ by the following way: For any integer n there is $z_n \in M$ such $q \in [f^{-1}\, O_{1/n} z]$. This points z_n exist: naturally, $q \in O\langle O_{1/n} z_n\rangle$, for some $z_n \in P$, and $O\langle O_{1/n} z_n\rangle \subset [O_{1/n} z_n]_{\overline{P}}$. Denote $\mathfrak{z} = \{z_n\}$ and let $\mathfrak{x}$ and $\mathfrak{y}$ be any two infinite subsequences of $\mathfrak{z}$. The sets $\mathfrak{x}$ and $\mathfrak{y}$ touch. Suppose not. Then there is a positive ε such $O_\varepsilon\, \mathfrak{x}\, \bar{\delta}\, O_\varepsilon\, \mathfrak{y}$ hence $f^{-1} O_\varepsilon\, \mathfrak{x}\, \bar{\delta}\, f^{-1} O_\varepsilon\, \mathfrak{y}$. But $[f^{-1} O_\varepsilon\, \mathfrak{x}] \cap \cap [f^{-1} O_\varepsilon\, \mathfrak{y}] \ni q$. This is a contradiction. Using the lemma 1 we state the sequence $\mathfrak{z}$ is fundamental hence it has a unique limit z. Let by definition $\tilde{f}q = z$. It is not diffecult to prove that the mapping $\tilde{f}$ is continuous hence equicontinuous too.

Corollary. *There is, for any non-exact proximity space P, a non-exact G_δ-extension Q, $P \subset Q \subset \overline{P}$.*

Proof. There are (see [7], Th. 4) two equicontinuous mappings $f: P \to A$ and $g: P \to B$ into metric spaces such the "vector-mapping" $(f, g): P \to A \times B$ is not equicontinuous. There exist the extensions $F: Q_1 \to cA$ and $G: Q_2 \to cB$ such the sets Q_1 and Q_2 are G_δ. Hence the both mappings f and g can be extended on the G_δ-set $Q = Q_1 \cap Q_2$. The mapping $(F \mid Q, G \mid Q)$ can not be equicontinuous becouse its shrinking $(F \mid Q, G \mid Q) \mid P = (f, g)$ is not equicontinuous.

Proof of Theorem 1. Let a space M be metric and $\overline{P} \approx \overline{M}$. We will assume $\overline{P} = \overline{M}$. Suppose P is not exact. Then there exists a non-exact space Q which is dense in $\overline{P}$ and is of G_δ-type.

Consider the intersection $Q \cap cM$. This set is an intersection of two G_δ-sets hence it is dense in $\overline{P}$. But this space is metrizable hence exact. This is a contradiction because if a proximity space has an exact dense subspace it is exact too (see [7], Th. 4, cor. 2).

Corollary 1. *A compact space X is metrizable iff $X \times X$ has a dense equimetrizable subset.*

Proof. Let $M \subset X \times X$ be such subset. Using [6], Th. 3, we are able to state that its projection $\pi M \subset X$ is equimetrizable too. We will show that all dense subsets of X are precompact. If not F had been a non-precompact and dense subset of X then its squire $F \cdot F$ be non-exact ([7], Th. 4) and dense in $X \times X$. This is a contradiction for the precide theorem.

Therefore πM is precompact hence $X = c\pi M$. The completion of a metric proximity space is metrizable too (see [10]).

Corollary 2. *A non-metrizable compactification of any metric proximity space can be open mapped onto the cartesian product of no its inverse images.*

Proof. Let A be a metrizable proximity space and let $X = \bar{A}$ be not metrizable. Hence A is not precompact. Suppose Y and Z are compact spaces and the mappings $g: Y \to X$ and $h: Z \to X$ are continuous. Consider the proximity spaces $B = g^{-1}A$ and $C = h^{-1}A$ (their compactifications are Y and Z). Since the shrink mappings $g \mid B \to A$ and $h \mid C \to A$ are equicontinuous the spaces B and C are not precompact. This implies that the proximity space $B \cdot C$ is not exact (see [7], Th. 7, cor. 1) but is dense in the product $Y \times Z$.

Now let $f: X \to Y \times Z$ be an open continuous mapping onto $Y \times Z$. Consider any desirable dense subspace $D \subset Y \times Z$ and set $E = f^{-1}D$. The proximity space E is dense in X hence exact. The shrink mapping $f \mid E \to D$ is equicontinuous and equi-open hence D is exact too (see [6], def. 1 and 4, Th. 7). Therefore any dense subspace of $Y \times Z$ is exact. We have been led to a contradiction.

The condition of the theorem 1 is not, of course, necessary, more, the necessary and sufficient conditions are not possible.

Example. *There exist two proximity spaces P and Q with homeomorphic topologies and compactifications such P is precompact and Q is not exact.*

Let E be the real line and T be its Smirnov compactification. Consider a space $E \times N + T \times N$ (the symbol "$+$" means that the sets are not intersect, N is a countable discrete set) and assume that its adjoint consists from two points which are corresponded to the first and second sets. Let P be the squire of this space. The proximity space P is precompact.

The subspace $E \times N + (E + T \times N)$ of the space $E \times N + T \times N$ (with the induced proximity) is not precompact. Let Q be its squire assumed as a subspace of P. Q is homeomorphic with P and dense in it hence $\bar{P} = \bar{Q}$. However the proximity space Q is not exact.

If the topology of a learning proximity is simple enough the situation is better:

Theorem 2. *Let the topology $\tilde{P}$ of a proximity space P satisfy the first countable axiom. Then the following properties of $\bar{P}$ are determined by the compact space $\bar{P}$:*

a) *equimetrizability,* a') *equimetrizability of the exaction $P!$*[1]);

b) *exactness*;

c) *precompactness*;

d) *the large and the small wages* (*i.e. the minima of the cardinalities of the bases of all its uniform coverings and finite uniform coverings*);

e) *the dimensions* Δd *and* $\delta\,\mathrm{Ind}$ (see [2], [3] and [4]);

f) *locally finess* ([1]), *locally finess of the exaction $P!$*

Corollary. *If the topological spaces $\tilde{P}$ and $\bar{P}$ are known we can establish the proximity space P is or is not metrizable.*

Proof. Let P and Q be any two proximity spaces such $\bar{P} \approx \bar{Q}$. We shall assume that $\bar{P} = \bar{Q} = X$. Consider the set L of all points of X which have a countable base of neighborhoods; our assumptions imply that $P \cup Q \subset L$. Let cP and cQ be the

---

[1]) This property is useful for studying of the spectra of the proximity spaces (see [5]).

completions of the spaces P and Q. We are going to show that $cP \supset L$. Naturally let $x \in L$ and $\{O_i\}$ be a base of neighborhoods of x. Pick $x_i \in O_i \cap P$. Using the lemma 1 we can state the sequence $\{x_i\}$ is fundamental in P hence there is $\lim x_i = x' \in cP$. Supposing $x \neq x'$ we have immediately been led to a contradiction.

Therefore we have

$$cP \cap cQ \supset L \supset P \cup Q$$

hence $cP = cQ = cL$. Consequently we may establish the following

Theorem 2′. *Let the property* $\mathfrak{P}$ *of proximity spaces satisfy the condition*

$$\mathfrak{P}(P) \Leftrightarrow \mathfrak{P}(cP).$$

Then, if the topology of a proximity space P satisfies the first countable axiom, the property $\mathfrak{P}$ *is determined only by the topological space* $\overline{P}$.

This condition is satisfied for exactness ([5], Th. 4, and [10], Th. 9, cor.) and for precompactness by the definition. The desirable result on the dimension δ Ind was proved by J. R. Isbell ([3], [4]); the analogical proposition on the dimension Δd and the both "proximity wages" are obvious because the uniform coverings of a proximity space and of its completion are in one-to-one correspondance. Since metrizability is the conjunction $P = P!$ and $\mathrm{Wg}\, P \leqq \aleph_0$ this is true for it too. For metrizability of the exaction: Let $(cP)!$ be metrizable. The shrinking of this space on P is metrizable too. This proximity is finer than P and coarser than $P!$ hence it is equal with $P!$. Conversely if $P!$ is metrizable it may be shown that $c(P!) = (cP)!$.

Locally finess belongs to the considering class too. This property was firstly introduced by S. Ginsburg and J. R. Isbell in [1] as a property of the uniform spaces. Meaning our problematics it is necessary for us to consider the analogical property namely for the proximity spaces. The Ginsburg-Isbell definition may be translated for them without some changing but the existence of the operator λ is proved by the special way. This occures becouse it is not generally possible to extend a uniform covering from a proximity subspace on the whole space.

Lemma 3. *Let a uniform covering can be extended from a set A in a proximity space P on some uniform neighborhood* $O \Supset A$. *Then the covering can be extended on whole P.*

Proof. Let us suppose that the uniform covering $\mathfrak{U}$ of the proximity subspace $O \subset P$ extends the uniform covering of A. A desirable extension on P is $\mathfrak{V} = \mathfrak{U} \cup \cup \{P \setminus A\}$.

Naturally let $\mathfrak{U}_1$ be a uniform star refinement of $\mathfrak{U}$. We may assume $S_1 = \mathrm{St}(A, \mathfrak{U}) \Subset O$. Then there is a uniform star refinement $\mathfrak{U}_2$ of $\mathfrak{U}_1$ such $S_2 = \mathrm{St}(S_1, \mathfrak{U}_2) \Subset O$. Inductively let $\mathfrak{U}_{i+1} \ll \mathfrak{U}_i$ and $S_{i+1} = \mathrm{St}(S_i, \mathfrak{U}_{i+1}) \Subset O$. Set $\mathfrak{V}_i = \mathfrak{U}_i \cup \{P \setminus S_{i-1}\}$. $M \Subset \mathrm{St}(M, \mathfrak{V}_i)$ and $\mathfrak{V}_{i+1} \ll \mathfrak{V}_i$ hold for any subset $M \subset P$ and integer i.

Lemma 4. *A locally fine proximity space is exact.*

Proof. Let $\mathfrak{U}$ and $\mathfrak{V}$ be uniform coverings. The intersection $\mathfrak{U}\,(\cap)\,\mathfrak{V}$ is uniformly locally uniform relatively $\mathfrak{U}$ (and relatively $\mathfrak{V}$) hence is a uniform covering.

Now we define λP as a maximum of the following transfinite sequence:

$$P_0 = P;\ P_{\alpha+1} = \text{Близ}\,(\lambda P_\alpha\,!^{\times});\ P_{\lim \alpha} = \sup P_\alpha.$$

(There $Q^{\times}$ is the finest uniformity of Q and Близ X is the proximity of the uniformity X.)

It is clear if Q is finer then P and locally fine it is finer than λP. We will demonstrate that λP is locally fine.

Suppose a covering $\mathfrak{A}$ is locally uniform relatively a covering $\mathfrak{U}$ and let the second one be uniform in λP. There is a uniform covering $\mathfrak{B}$ such, for every $V \in \mathfrak{B}$, there exists some $U \in \mathfrak{U}$ such $V \Subset U$. All coverings $\mathfrak{A} \mid U$ are uniform in the spaces $U \subset P$ hence all coverings $\mathfrak{A} \mid V$ can be extended on whole λP. Since the space λP is obviously exact we may consider the uniform space $(\lambda P)^{\times}$. This uniform space is locally fine and $\mathfrak{A}$ is locally uniform relatively the uniform covering $\mathfrak{B}$ (the covering $\mathfrak{A}$ is not, generally, locally uniform relatively $\mathfrak{U}$ in the uniform space!). Therefore $\mathfrak{A}$ is uniform in $(\lambda P)^{\times}$ hence in λP.

Lemma 5. *Let cP and $\overline{P}$ be correspondely the completion and the compactification of the proximity space P. Consicer any point $y \in \overline{P} \setminus P$. The system $\mathfrak{A} = \{\overline{P} \setminus O \mid y \in \operatorname{Int} O\}$ (O is any subset of $\overline{P}$) is a uniform covering of P iff $y \notin cP$.*

Proof. If $y \in cP$ the covering $\mathfrak{A}$ can not be extended on cP as a uniform covering hence $\mathfrak{A}$ is not uniform.

Suppose $y \notin cP$. The ultrafilter $\{P \cap O \mid y \in \operatorname{Int} O\}$ does not converge in cP hence is not a Cauchy filter.

Let $\mathfrak{B}$ be the second uniform star refinement of $\mathfrak{U}$ hence for any $V \in \mathfrak{B}$ there is some $U \in \mathfrak{U}$ such $V \Cup U$and consequently $y \notin [V]_{\overline{P}}$. But $W \subset P \setminus (\overline{P} \setminus [W])$ hence $\mathfrak{B} < \mathfrak{A}$.

Lemma 6. *If $G \Subset H \subset P$ then $[G]_{cP} \subset cH$.*

Proof. Consider $y \in [G]$ (all closures are in cP) and assume, conversely to the statement of the lemma, $y \notin cH$. Let $\mathscr{B}$ be a base of the neighborhoods of y in cP. The covering $\mathfrak{B} = \{H \setminus O | O \in \mathscr{B}\}$ is uniform, hence $\mathfrak{D} = \mathfrak{B} \cup \{P \setminus F\}$, for any $F \Subset H$, is a uniform covering of P. Assume yet F is canonically open in P and $F \Supset G$. Now $\operatorname{Int} [F] \Supset [G] \in y$, hence there is $O \in \mathscr{B}$ such $O \subset \operatorname{Int} [F]$. Therefore $\mathfrak{D}$ is a refinement of the covering $\mathfrak{C} = \{P \setminus O \mid O \in \mathscr{B}\}$. Consequently $\mathfrak{C}$ is uniform and, used the preside lemma, $y \notin cP$.

Lemma 7. *The system of all completions of the elements of any covering of a proximity space forms a uniform covering of its completion.*

Proof. Let $\mathfrak{U}$ be a uniform covering of P and let $\mathfrak{W}$ be the second uniform star refinement of $\mathfrak{U}$. The covering $\mathfrak{H} = \{[W]_{cP} \mid W \in \mathfrak{W}\}$ is uniform in cP (see [10], Th. 2).

Consider now the system $\mathfrak{Y} = \{cU \mid U \in \mathfrak{U}\}$. There is, for any $W \in \mathfrak{W}$, $U \in \mathfrak{U}$ such $W \Subset U$. Hence $[W] \Subset cU$ and therefore $\mathfrak{H} < \mathfrak{Y}$.

Theorem 3. *The completion of a proximity space is locally fine iff the proximity space is locally fine.*

Proof. Firstly, if P is locally fine and P is dense in Q then Q is locally fine too. Suppose not. Since $Q \neq \lambda Q$ the induced proximities are distinct on P. One of them is P and the second one is between P and λP. But $P = \lambda P$.

Conversely, suppose cP is locally fine and let $\mathfrak{A}$ which covers P be uniform relatively a uniform covering $\mathfrak{B}$ of P. Denote $\mathfrak{W} = \{cV \mid V \in \mathfrak{B}\}$.

Since all $\mathfrak{A} \mid V$ are uniform coverings of the proximity spaces $V \subset P$ they may be extended as uniform coverings $\mathfrak{B}_V$ on the completions cV. The union $\mathfrak{B} = \bigcup \{\mathfrak{B}_V \mid V \in \mathfrak{B}\}$ is uniform relatively $\mathfrak{W}$ hence is a uniform covering. It is clear that $\mathfrak{B} \mid P < \mathfrak{A}$.

References

[1] S. GINSBURG and J. R. ISBELL, Some operators on uniform spaces, Trans. Amer. Math. Soc. **93** (1959), 145—168.

[2] J. R. ISBELL, On finite dimensional uniform spaces, Pacific J. Math. **9** (1959), 107—121.

[3] Д. Р. Исбелл, Об индуктивной размерности пространств близости, Доклады АН СССР **134** (1960), 36—38.

[4] J. R. ISBELL, On finite dimensional uniform spaces II, Pacific J. Math. **12** (1962), 291—302.

[5] В. З. Поляков, Правильность, произведение и спектры пространств близости, Доклады АН СССР **154** (1964), 51—54.

[6] В. З. Поляков, Открытые отображения пространств близости, Доклады АН СССР **155** (1964), 1014—1017.

[7] В. З. Поляков, Правильность и произведение пространств близости, Матем. сборник **67** (1965), 428—439.

[8] В. З. Поляков, О равномерных пространствах сходимости, Coll. Math. **13** (1965), 167—179.

[9] Ю. М. Смирнов, О пространствах близости, Матем. собрник **31** (1952), 543—574.

[10] Ю. М. Смирнов, О полноте пространств близости, Труды Моск. Матем. общества **3** (1954), 271—306.

[11] Ю. М. Смирнов, О размерности пространств близости, Матем. сборник **38** (1956), 283—302.

ALGEBRAIC EXTENSIONS OF TOPOLOGICAL SPACES[1])

VLASTIMIL PTÁK (Praha)

The usefulness of topological extensions of topological spaces is well established; in the present lecture we intend to describe another type of extension, algebraic as well as topological, which has already proved its worth in Functional Analysis.

An extension is obtained by adding to the original space a certain set of new points which we propose to call ideal points and by extending the original structure to the larger set. The density of the original space in the extension may then be expressed as a statement about approximation of ideal points by means of points of the space we started with. We propose now to perform first an algebraic extension by adjoining formal linear combinations of points and then proceed to construct a topological extension.

Let us start with a topological space T and consider a topological extension εT. If $L(T)$ is the set of all formal linear combinations of points of T to which the topological structure has been extended in a suitable way, we take $\varepsilon L(T)$. This may be of advantage even for the study of εT. Indeed, εT is now a subset of $\varepsilon L(T)$ so that an ideal point in εT may now be considered as a limit of points of $L(T)$ instead of T only. In other words, since we have a larger set to choose from, there is a better chance of getting a good approximation. To see that, let us consider an example. Take T to be a countable set in the discrete topology. If t_n are the points of T, consider a limit point t_0 of the sequence t_n in βT. Now, given a positive ε and a finite set $F \subset C(T)$, there exists, in T, a point t which approximates t_0; for each $x \in F$, $|x(t) - x(t_0)| < \varepsilon$. A similar approximation statement is no more possible if we replace the finite set F by an infinite one. Nevertheless, it may remain true even for infinite F if the approximating point is taken from the larger set $L(T)$. Consider, as an example, the set H consisting of all functions $x \in C(T)$ for which $\sum |x(t_n)| \leqq 1$. Clearly $x(t_0) = 0$ for each $x \in H$. Since H contains also the unit functions e_n (defined by $e_n(t_n) = 1$, $e_n(t_j) = 0$ for $j \neq n$) there is no point $t \in T$ which satisfies $|x(t) - x(t_0)| < 1$ for all $x \in H$. Nevertheless, if n is large enough, the point $u = \frac{1}{n}(t_1 + \dots + t_n)$ fulfills

$$| x(u) - x(t_0) | < \varepsilon$$

for all $x \in H$.

---

[1]) A survey lecture presented at the invitation of the organizing committee.

This situation may be compared with and is, indeed, related to the well known behaviour of Fourier series. Denote by B the space of all 2π-periodic continuous functions on the real line S with the norm $|x| = \max |x(s)|$, $s \in S$. If $t \in B$, denote by t_n the sequence of Fourier sums for t. It is a well known fact that the t_n do not converge to t in general. The Fejér theorem shows, however, that we do get good approximation (i.e. uniform convergence), if we replace the t_n by their Cesàro sums $\frac{1}{n}(t_1 + \ldots + t_n)$.

Another instance where approximation of ideal points by elements of $L(T)$ may be useful is the following.

Let T be a completely regular topological space and let x_n be a sequence of continuous functions on T such that $|x_n| \leq 1$ and $x_n(t) \to 0$ for each $t \in T$. Is the same true for the points of βT as well?

Denote by S the set of all elements of the sequence x_n and take an ideal point $t_0 \in \beta T$. We ask now whether $x_n(t_0) \to 0$ as well. There is an obvious sufficient condition, the existence, for each $\varepsilon > 0$, of a point $t \in T$ such that $|x(t) - x(t_0)| < \varepsilon$ for all $x \in S$; this approximation of t_0 by a $t \in T$ uniformly with respect to the infinite set S, however, is too strong. Such a point t will exist, in general, for finite sets S only. If we admit approximations taken from the larger set $L(T)$ however, there is a less exacting condition which gives the same result. Suppose we know that, for each $\varepsilon > 0$, there exists a convex combination $\lambda_1 t_1 + \ldots + \lambda_n t_n$ of points in T which approximates t_0 uniformly with respect to S. Then it is easy to show that $x_n(t_0) \to 0$ as well. The precise formulation of this condition is as follows.

For each $\varepsilon > 0$ there exist a natural number n, points $t_1, \ldots, t_n \in T$ and nonnegative numbers $\lambda_1, \ldots, \lambda_n$ with $\sum \lambda_i = 1$ such that

$$|\sum \lambda_i x(t_i) - x(t_0)| < \varepsilon$$

for each $x \in S$.

If we agree to consider the sum $\sum \lambda_i x(t_i)$ as the value of x at the point $\sum \lambda_i t_i \in L(T)$, we have thus

$$|x(\sum \lambda_i t_i) - x(t_0)| < \varepsilon$$

for all $x \in S$.

Indeed, the only result thus far in the theory of these extensions has the form of a statement about the existence of a convex mean which approximates an ideal point uniformly with respect to a given set of continuous functions.

To get to the starting point of these investigations we have to go back a few years. In 1954 the present author obtained the following result [4]:

Theorem 1. *Let T be a pseudocompact completely regular topological space. Let Y be the space dual to $C(\beta T)$. Let us denote by $L(T)$ the subspace of Y consisting of all linear combinations $\lambda_1 t_1 + \ldots + \lambda_n t_n$ where $t_i \in T$. The weak topology of $C(T)$ corresponding to the space $L(T)$ will be called the point topology of $C(T)$. Let $B \subset C(T)$ be symmetrical convex and compact in the point topology. Then B is compact in the weak topology corresponding to the space Y.*

As we shall see later, this theorem is nothing more than the dual form of the statement that the completion of $L(T)$ in a certain uniformity coincides with $C(\beta T)'$. Thinking about problems of this type one is immediately struck by the different rôle played by the functions and by the points; it is exactly this disparity which prevents us from using the powerful tool of duality theory to its full extent. Whereas it is perfectly natural to perform all kinds of algebraic operations on functions in a natural way the possibility of doing the same with points has not been systematically exploited.

The main idea of our further investigations consists, accordingly, in treating both functions and points exactly the same way thus establishing full symmetry in the role of functions and points. If S is a system of functions on a set T we propose to consider the value of s at the point t as a function of two variables $f(s, t)$ on the cartesian product $S \times T$. In this manner the points $t \in T$ themselves may be considered as functions on the set S and the possibility of considering linear combinations of points becomes perfectly natural.

In order to investigate the approximation of ideal points by means of convex combinations of actual points the present author established, in 1959, a combinatorial lemma which essentially describes the degree of approximation of a nonnegative measure by means of convex combinations of points; this lemma seems to contain everything essential; the majority of the results on weak compactness follow from it just by pure logic. Using the lemma, the proofs are straightforward and do not require further ideas.

We propose now to state the combinatorial lemma and give an example of its applications. The lemma describes conditions for the existence of certain convex means. For the exact formulation it will be useful to introduce some notation.

Let S be a nonvoid set. Denote by $P(S)$ the set of all real functions λ defined on S and fulfilling the following conditions:

1⁰. $\lambda(s) \geqq 0$ for all $s \in S$;

2⁰. the set $N(\lambda)$ of all $s \in S$ for which $\lambda(s) > 0$ is finite;

3⁰. $\sum_{s \in S} \lambda(s) = 1$.

If $A \subset S$ we denote by $\lambda(A)$ the sum $\sum_{s \in A} \lambda(s)$. Further, suppose we are given a certain family $\mathscr{W}$ of subsets of S. For $H \subset S$ and $\varepsilon > 0$ we denote by $M(H, \mathscr{W}, \varepsilon)$ the set of all $\lambda \in P(S)$ such that $N(\lambda) \subset H$ and $\lambda(W) < \varepsilon$ for each $W \in \mathscr{W}$. Our task consists in finding conditions for $M(H, \mathscr{W}, \varepsilon)$ to be nonempty. It is possible to give an intuitive interpretation of this problem as follows: We are supposed to divide a unit mass into a finite number of points contained in H in such a way that the mass of each set of the family $\mathscr{W}$ does not exceed ε. It is obvious that the condition for the existence will have a combinatorial character. An especially simple formulation is possible if we consider indexed families. Assume, accordingly, that the system $\mathscr{W}$ consists of sets $W(a)$ where a runs over an index set A. Such a family may be visualized as a subset B of $S \times A$ in the obvious manner: we take $[s, a] \in B$ if and only if $s \in W(a)$. The system $\mathscr{W}$ appears thus as the system of sections of B parallel to S. We shall use the following notation: if $s \in A$, we take $B(a)$ to be the set of all s for which $[s, a] \in B$ (so that $B(a) = W(a)$) and, similarly, for $s \in S$, $B(s)$ will be the set of those $a \in A$ for which $[s, a] \in B$. Using this notation we may formulate the combinatorial lemma as follows

Theorem 2. *The following two statements are equivalent*:

1⁰. *There exists an infinite* $H \subset S$ *and an* $\varepsilon > 0$ *such that* $M(H, \mathscr{W}, \varepsilon)$ *is void*;

2⁰. *there exists a sequence of distinct elements* $s_i \in S$ *such that the intersection* $B(s_1) \cap \cap \ldots \cap B(s_n)$ *is nonvoid for each* n.

The implication $2^0 \to 1^0$ is obvious. Indeed, if 2^0 is satisfied, take for H the set consisting of the elements of the sequence s_i so that H is infinite and choose an ε with $0 < \varepsilon < 1$. To show that $M(H, \mathscr{W}, \varepsilon)$ is void, take a $\lambda \in M(H, \mathscr{W}, \varepsilon)$. Since $N(\lambda)$ is finite and contained in H, there is a natural number n such that $N(\lambda) \subset \subset \{s_1, \ldots, s_n\}$. According to condition 2^0, there exists an $a \subset B(s_1) \cap \ldots \cap B(s_n)$ so that $\{s_1, \ldots, s_n\} \subset B(a)$. We have thus $N(\lambda) \subset B(a) \in \mathscr{W}$. It follows that $1 = = \lambda(S) = \lambda(N(\lambda)) \leqq \lambda(B(a)) < \varepsilon < 1$ which is a contradiction.

The nontrivial point of the equivalence of course consists in showing that there exists a $\lambda \in M(H, \mathscr{W}, \varepsilon)$ for each infinite H and each $\varepsilon > 0$ provided the set B does not contain an infinite triangle. Indeed, condition 2^0 may be given the following geometrical interpretation: "there exists a sequence of distinct elements $s_i \in S$ and a sequence $a_n \in A$ (not necessarily distinct) such that B contains all pairs $[s_i, a_n]$ for $i \leqq n$". Such a set may well be called a triangle. The proof of this implication $1^0 \to 2^0$ is the only point in the whole theory which requires a certain effort. Once the combinatorial result is established, the rest is straightforward. The proof may be found in the 1959 paper [5] and is reproduced in [3] and [6].

To explain how the theorem on convex means is used we intend to apply it, as an illustration, to the proof of a classical and well known theorem.

At this point our concern is not the result itself; we choose a particularly simple theorem to explain the method of convex means; the proof represents a typical application of the lemma on convex means and puts into evidence the idea underlying all further applications.

Theorem 3. *Let T be compact Hausdorff, $x_n \in C(T)$ and $|x_n| \leqq 1$. Suppose that $\lim x_n(t) = 0$ for each $t \in T$. Let $\varepsilon > 0$ be given. Then there exist nonnegative numbers $\lambda_1, \ldots, \lambda_p$ with $\sum_1^p \lambda_i = 1$ such that $\left| \sum_1^p \lambda_i x_i \right| < \varepsilon$.*

This theorem, although formulated in the simplest topological terms, does not seem to admit a simple proof. The easiest way of proving this seems to be the following. We show first that x_n converges to zero weakly in $C(T)$ and then apply the Hahn-Banach theorem according to which weak convergence implies norm convergence of suitable convex means. To establish weak convergence, we use the Riesz theorem on the representation of linear functionals on $C(T)$ as integrals and the Lebesgue dominated convergence theorem according to which equiboundedness and pointwise convergence implies convergence of integrals. Although simple, this proof is by no means an elementary one. Let us present now a proof based on the combinatorial lemma .We emphasize once more that, for the proof of this theorem, the combinatorial lemma has a methodological significance only; nevertheless, the proof enables us to present, on a simple example, the basic idea underlying the proofs of all further results.

In conformity with our basic principle we shall replace the sequence $x_n(t)$ by a function of two variables, the index n and the point $t \in T$. Denote by S the set of all natural numbers and define a function f on $S \times T$ by the formula

$$f(s, t) = x_s(t).$$

Let $\varepsilon > 0$ be fixed. Consider the set $B \subset S \times T$ consisting of those $[s, t]$ for which $|f(s, t)| \geqq \varepsilon$. Notice the intuitive meaning of B. It is obtained by cutting off the "surface" given by the function $|f(s, t)|$ at the height ε. The system of all sections $B(t)$, $t \in T$ will be denoted by $\mathscr{W}$. Let us show now that the problem of constructing a convex combination of the given functions which is uniformly small will be solved if we find some $\lambda \in M(S, \mathscr{W}, \varepsilon)$. Indeed, we intend to show that for such λ, the function $\sum_s \lambda(s) x_s$ shall not exceed 2ε in absolute value on the whole of T. To see that take an arbitrary $t \in T$; to estimate the sum $\sum_{s \in S} \lambda(s) x_s(t)$ we split it into two parts (notice that this splitting depends on t)

$$\left| \sum_{s \in S} \lambda(s) x_s(t) \right| \leqq \sum_{s \in B(t)} \lambda(s) |x_s(t)| + \sum_{s \in S - B(t)} \lambda(s) \; |x_s(t)|.$$

In the first sum we use the estimate $|x_s(t)| \leqq 1$ and $\sum_{S \in B(t)} \lambda(s) < \varepsilon$ since $B(t) \in \mathscr{W}$ and $\lambda \in M(S, \mathscr{W}, \varepsilon)$. In the second sum, $s \in S - B(t)$ so that $|x_s(t)| < \varepsilon$; at the same time the sum of all $\lambda(s)$ does not exceed one. Both summands being $\leqq \varepsilon$, the function $x = \sum \lambda(s) x_s$ satisfies $|x| \leqq 2\varepsilon$. Accordingly, it remains to show that there exists a $\lambda \in M(S, \mathscr{W}, \varepsilon)$. Suppose, on the contrary, that $M(S, \mathscr{W}, \varepsilon)$ is void. By the existence theorem, there exists a subsequence R of natural numbers $s_1 < < s_2 < s_3 < \ldots$ such that $B(s_1) \cap \ldots \cap B(s_n)$ is nonvoid for each n. Now $B(s)$ is, by definition, the set of all $t \in T$ for which $|x_s(t)| \geqq \varepsilon$ so that $B(s)$ is closed in T. The space T being compact there exists a point t_0 which belongs to all $B(r)$, $r \in R$. Hence $|x_r(t_0)| \geqq \varepsilon$ for infinitely many r which is a contradiction with $\lim x_s(t_0) = 0$. The proof is complete.

The proofs of the deeper results to follow, although technically more complicated, are based essentially on the same idea. Also, we observe that the assumptions of the preceeding theorem have not been used to the full extent; indeed, since we are dealing with a sequence of closed sets $B(s)$ of a special nature, pseudocompactness of T would have been sufficient. This observation establishes a direct link to Theorem 1. Before proceeding further let us state another result which connects the method of convex means with one of the fundamental problems of analysis, the question of inverting the order of two limit operations. Indeed, the method of convex means has been devised to deal with some aspects of this fundamental problem. We propose now to discuss the simplest case of a double sequence. Later, in the main theorem we shall establish a connection between the behaviour of double sequence and the general case of functions of two variables.

First some terminology. Let a_{pq} be a double sequence and suppose that $\lim_q a_{pq} = = a_{p0}$ exists for each p. We shall say that the convergence is *almost uniform with respect to* p if, for each $\varepsilon > 0$ and each infinite set R of indices q, there exists a finite $K \subset R$ such that

$$\min_{k \in K} |a_{pk} - a_{p0}| < \varepsilon \qquad \text{for each } p.$$

We shall say that the convergence is *uniform in the mean with respect to* p if, for each $\varepsilon > 0$ and each infinite set R of indices q, there exists a finite $K \subset R$ and nonnegative λ_k such that $\sum_{k \in K} \lambda_k = 1$ and

$$\left| \sum_{k \in K} \lambda_k a_{pk} - a_{p0} \right| < \varepsilon \text{ for each } p.$$

It will be convenient to call a double sequence a_{pq} *convergent* if $\lim_q a_{pq} = a_{p0}$ exists for each p and $\lim_q a_{pq} = a_{0q}$ exists for each q. Now we are able to state

Theorem 4. *Let a_{pq} be a bounded convergent double sequence. Then the following statements are equivalent:*

1^0. *The convergence* $\lim_p a_{pq} = a_{p0}$ *is almost uniform with respect to* p;

2^0. *the convergence* $\lim_p a_{pq} = a_{0q}$ *is almost uniform with respect to* q;

3^0. *both limits* $\lim_p a_{p0}$ *and* $\lim_q a_{0q}$ *exist and are equal to each other;*

4^0. *the convergence* $\lim_q a_{pq} = a_{p0}$ *is uniform in the mean with respect to* p;

5^0. *the convergence* $\lim_p a_{pq} = a_{0q}$ *is uniform in the mean with respect to* q.

The proof of the equivalence of the first three statements is quite elementary; the rest requires integration theory. It is highly instructive to follow a proof of the equivalence based on the combinatorial lemma. Not only does it eliminate integration theory but also it is highly intuitive. A combinatorial treatment of convergence properties of double sequences may be found in [6].

It will be convenient to call the convergence *almost uniform* if one (and hence all) of the conditions of Theorem 4 is satisfied.

To return to our original programme, to study systems of functions as a function of two variables, consider, again, a family S of function on a set T and the function $f(s, t)$ generated by it. Assume now that the set T is a topological space and that the functions $s \in S$ are continuous. Further, the space S is to be equipped with a topology as well, such as the topology of pointwise convergence or some finer topology. Then $f(s, t)$ becomes a separately continuous function on $S \times T$. We shall investigate bounded separately continuous functions on $S \times T$ only. We shall try to add to the domain of definition of f linear combinations of functions and points.

The most direct way to the study of convex combinations of points is the well known imbedding of a topological space in the adjoint of the space of all bounded continuous functions. If T is a completely regular topological space, we denote by $C_\beta(T)$ the Banach space of all bounded continuous functions on T and by $C_\beta(T)'$ its adjoint taken in the topology $\sigma(C_\beta(T)', C_\beta(T))$. It is possible to assign, in a natural manner, to every point $t \in T$ a certain functional $E(t) \in C_\beta(T)'$ such that the value of $E(t)$ at the point $x \in C_\beta(T)$ equals the value $x(t)$. The mapping E is one-to-one and homeomorphic so that we may identify T with the subset $E(T)$ of $C_\beta(T)'$. From now on we take T to be simply a subset of $C_\beta(T)'$. In this manner our topological space is imbedded in a locally convex space where algebraic operations are meaningful. This applies to the product $S \times T$ as well so that $S \times T \subset \subset C_\beta(S') \times C_\beta(T)'$ and the study of convex combinations of functions and points is possible if we treat f as a bilinear form on the linear extensions of S and T. The connection with tensor products is obvious. Of course we shall be interested to know under what conditions the functions f will retain its continuity properties in the process of extension. More precisely, we ask the following question: Let f be a bounded separately continuous function on $S \times T$. Under what conditions does there exist a separately continuous bilinear form on $C_\beta(S)' \times C_\beta(T)'$ which extends f? In 1963, this question was discussed by the author in [7]. The main theorem of the extension theory may be formulated in the following manner.

Theorem 5. *Let S and T be two completely regular topological spaces and let f be a bounded separately continuous function on $S \times T$. Then the following statements are equivalent:*

1⁰. *There exists a separately continuous bilinear form on* $C_\beta(S)' \times C_\beta(T)'$ *which extends* f;

2⁰. *given two sequences* $s_i \in S$ *and* $t_j \in T$ *such that both* $\lim_i \lim_j f(s_i, t_j)$ *and* $\lim_j \lim_i f(s_i, t_j)$ *exist then they have to be equal*;

3⁰. *every convergent double sequence of the form* $f(s_i, t_j)$ *is almost uniformly convergent.*

First of all, it is obvious that the existence of an extension implies condition 2⁰. The equivalence of 2⁰ and 3⁰ is easily established by means of theorem 4. Clearly the essential part of theorem 5 consists in proving that the double limit condition implies the existence of an extension.

An interesting feature of this result is the fact that it enables us to conclude the continuity of a function in a topology which has an uncountable character from purely sequential assumptions.

The proof is based exclusively on the combinatorial result 2 and the basic idea — although technically more complicated — is essentially identical with the proof of theorem 3 about pointwise convergent sequences of continuous functions. Roughly speaking the proof consists in showing that invertibility of the simplest limit operations implies a sort of Fubini theorem about the invertibility of two integrations. Indeed, if $p \in C_\beta(S)'$ and $q \in C_\beta(T)'$, we may apply to $f(s, t)$ as a function of s the functional p (integrate with respect to s). We obtain thus a certain function of t which we denote by $f(p, t)$; the Lebesgue dominated convergence theorem would yield sequential continuity of this function. Under our hypothesis of invertibility of limits we may apply the combinatorial method to show that $f(p, t)$ is actually continuous. Similarly, we construct $f(s, q)$ and prove its continuity in s. Now we may apply q to the function $f(p, \circ)$; we obtain a certain number $\langle f(p, \circ), q\rangle$. Another application of the combinatorial method shows that the same result is obtained upon doing this in the inverse order, $\langle f(\circ, q), p\rangle$. The common value of these two double integrals is then the value of our extension B at the point $[p, q]$. We have thus

$$B(p, q) = \langle f(p, \circ), q\rangle = \langle f(\circ, q), p\rangle .$$

Since $f(p, \circ) \in C_\beta(T)$, it follows from the first expression for $B(p, q)$ that B is a continuous function of q on $C_\beta(T)'$. Continuity in p follows similarly from the second expression.

The significance of the fact that it is possible to extend $f(s, t)$ may not be obvious at first glance; to explain that, let us consider again a separately continuous function $f(s, t)$ which stems from a certain family S of functions on a space T. Take a $q \in C_\beta(T)'$ and construct $f(s, q)$, the result of applying the functional q to the function $f(s, \circ)$ or, which is the same, to the function $s(\circ)$. To say that q behaves as a continuous linear functional on S is the same as to say that $f(s, q)$ is continuous on S, in other words that $f(s, t)$ may be extended to a larger domain $S \times T^*$ such that $q \in T^*$ and stays continuous in the first variable.

To give another example, consider βS. Since every $t \in T$ is a bounded continuous function on S, for each $p \in \beta S$ the value $f(p, t)$ has a meaning. To say that the "ideal function" p is continuous on T is the same as saying that f may be extended to $(S \cup \{p\}) \times T$ and stay continuous in the second variable.

The extension theorem admits a whole series of equivalent formulations, some of which are not without interest; these may be found in [8]. As an illustration, let us state an immediate consequence of the extension theorem, a result which includes as special cases both the theorem of Eberlein and the theorem of Krein.

Theorem 6. *Let E be a Banach space and $A \subset E$ a bounded set which satisfies the following condition: given two sequences $a_i \in A$ and $x_j' \in U^0$ (the unit cell of the adjoint space) such that $\lim_i \lim_j \langle a_i, x_j' \rangle$ and $\lim_j \lim_i \langle a_i, x_j' \rangle$ both exist then they are equal. Then A^{00} is compact in the weak topology of E.*

It is easy to see that the condition is satisfied if A is countably compact in the weak topology. The set A^{00} is thus compact. Since the weak closure of A is contained in A^{00}, the set A is relatively weakly compact and this is Eberlein's theorem. Since A^{00} is convex, we have Krein's theorem as well.

Let us explain now how this result follows from the extension theorem. We take for S the set A in the topology $\sigma(E, E')$ and for T the set U^0 in the topology $\sigma(E', E)$; the function f will be the scalar product in the duality of E and E'. The hypotheses of the extension theorem being satisfied, there exists a bilinear extension B of f to $V \times U^0$ where V is the unit cell of $C_\beta(S)'$. Given $v \in V$, we use first continuity in the second variable. The value $B(v, \circ)$ behaves as a linear and weakly continuous form on U^0 and, accordingly, may be identified with a certain element $P(v)$ of E. We have thus a clearly linear mapping P of V into E such that

$$B(v, x') = \langle P(v), x' \rangle$$

for all $x' \in U^0$. Now we use continuity in the first variable; clearly this means that P is weakly continuous. Since B is an extension of f, the mapping P is a retract, $P(a) = a$ for $a \in A$. We have thus a weakly continuous linear mapping P of V into E. Since V is weakly compact and absolutely convex, the set $P(V)$ is an absolutely convex and weakly compact subset of E. Since $A \subset P(V)$, the theorem is established.

The reader will have observed that the results reported about thus far are motivated exclusively by the applications in functional analysis. These alone, we think, should be sufficient evidence in favour of algebraic extensions of topological spaces. Indeed, the applications seem to indicate that a systematic study of algebraic extensions from the topological point of view could be of interest. This has been done, in 1962, by M. Katětov [1] and, in 1964, by D. A. Rajkov [9].

Whereas, in our investigations, we have given a direct construction to deal with a specific problem, for the topological study, the categorical method is more appropriate. Let us describe first a natural notion, discussed by Rajkov, that of the free locally convex space of a given completely regular space T. It is defined as a locally convex space E and a homeomorphic imbedding ω of T into E with the following properties: given a continuous mapping g of T into a locally convex space F there exists a continuous linear mapping G of E into F such that $g = G \circ \omega$:

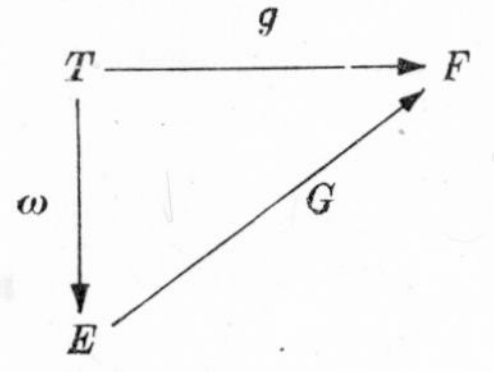

Now a locally convex space induces, on the subset $\omega(T)$, not only a topology but also a uniformity; this makes it possible to study uniform spaces as well. It suffices to require ω to be uniformly homeomorphic and g to be uniformly continuous. It is not difficult to give a direct description of these extensions. The answer is as follows. The set E consists of all formal linear combinations of the points $t \in T$, the topology is that of uniform convergence on a class $\mathscr{C}$ of function sets of a certain type. In both cases, these function sets have to be pointwise bounded. In the case of a uniform space, the sets $H \in \mathscr{C}$ are to be uniformly equicontinuous; in the case of a completely regular space this reduces to the requirement of equicontinuity. At any rate, we have a uniform space (T, u), the set $L(T)$ and a locally convex topology v on $L(T)$ such that the dual space $(L(T), v)'$ coincides with the space $C_u(T)$ of all uniformly continuous functions on T. It is a well known fact from functional analysis that there is a whole range of locally convex topologies w on $L(T)$ for which the dual space is exactly $C_u(T)$. Given such a topology w, the following question presents itself: to describe the completion of $(L(T), w)$. This is KATĚTOV's main concern. To give an example of results of this type, let us recall one of KATĚTOV's first results:

Theorem 7. *Let T be compact Hausdorff and let m be the finest locally convex topology on $E(T)$ such that $(E(T), m)' = C(T)$. Then the completion of $(E(T), m)$ coincides with $C(T)'$.*

Proofs of this statement have been given by KATĚTOV and his students; it is easy to see, however, that results of much earlier date yield even a stronger result if duality theory is used. We use this opportunity to bring another argument in favour of duality methods. A result, obtained independently by A. GROTHENDIECK and the author, states that the completion $E^\wedge$ of a locally convex space E consists of those linear forms on E' which are continuous on equicontinuous sets of E' in the weak topology $\sigma(E', E)$. It follows from Tichonov's theorem that the equicontinuous sets of E' are compact in the topology $\sigma(E', E)$. Further, it follows from the characterization of the completion stated above that they are also compact in the finer topology $\sigma(E', E^\wedge)$. In fact, roughly speaking, the completion might also be characterized as the set of those linear forms on E' which may be added to E without disturbing the weak topology $\sigma(E', E)$ on equicontinuous sets in E'. Let us recall now theorem 1 and show that theorem 7 and even a stronger result is an immediate consequence. Indeed, the assumption of compactness may be replaced by that of pseudocompactness. Let us sketch briefly how this may be done.

We use first the characterization of the elements of the completion to dualize the statement of the theorem.

We consider the Banach space $C(\beta T)$ and its dual $Y = C(\beta T)'$. Since T is pseudocompact, $C(T)$ coincides, as a set, with $C(\beta T)$. Now $L(T)$ is a subspace of Y. We note first that there exists, on Y, a locally convex topology w such that (Y, w) is complete and the restriction of w to $L(T)$ is coarser than m. (It suffices to take as w the topology of uniform convergence on compact subsets of $C(\beta T)$.) It follows that the completion of $(L(T), m)$ will be contained in Y. Of course the nontrivial part of the theorem consists in proving that the completion of $(L(T), m)$ will be the whole of Y. According to what has been said above, this will be done if we show that each equicontinuous subset of $(L(T), m)'$ is also compact in the weak topology $\sigma(C(\beta T), Y)$. Indeed, take the equicontinuous subsets of $(L(T), m)'$. By the Tichonov theorem, they are automatically compact in the weak topology $\sigma(C(\beta T), L(T))$. If we show that they remain compact even in the finer topology $\sigma(C(\beta T), Y)$ we have shown that Y is contained in the completion and hence $(L(T), m)^\wedge = Y$. But this is exactly the statement of Theorem 1.

Other completion theorems may be dealt with in a similar manner. We use first the characterization of the elements of the completion to dualize the statement of the theorem and reduce it to a statement about weak compactness. This, in its turn, may be disposed of using the extension theorem or the extension theorem may be applied directly.

To sum up, we hope we have shown that the methods of duality theory may be applied with some advantage to the study of completions. The dual object to a uniform space being a linear space (the space of all uniformly continuous functions), it becomes natural to extend the uniform space to a linear space as well. A further systematic study of linear extensions of topological and uniform spaces especially in connection with tensor products seems to be of some interest. Also, it would be interesting to have some more information about the inductive topology of the cartesian product $S \times T$, i.e. the topology which yields as continuous functions exactly the set of all separately continuous functions.

References

[1] M. Katětov, On a category of spaces, Proc. First Symposium on General Topology, Prague 1961; Prague 1962.

[2] M. Katětov, On certain projectively generated continuity structures, Celebrazioni archimedee del secolo XX, Simposio di topologia 1964, p. 47—50.

[3] G. Köthe, Topologische lineare Räume, Berlin 1960.

[4] V. Pták, Weak compactness in convex topological vector spaces, Czechoslovak Math. J. **79** (1954), 175—186.

[5] V. Pták, A combinatorial lemma on systems of inequalities and its application to analysis, Czechoslovak Math. J. **84** (1959), 629—630.

[6] V. Pták, A combinatorial lemma on the existence of convex means and its application to weak compactness, Amer. Math. Soc., Proc. Symposia Pure Math. **7** (1963), 437—450.

[7] V. Pták, An extension theorem for separately continuous functions and its application to functional analysis, Comment. Math. Univ. Carolinae **4** (1963), 109—116.

[8] V. Pták, An extension theorem for separately continuous functions and its application to functional analysis, Czechoslovak Math. J. **89** (1964), 562—581.

[9] Д. А. Райков, Свободные локально выпуклые пространства равномерных пространств, Матем. сборник **63** (1964), 582—590.

DIE FREUDENTHALSCHE TRENNUNGSRELATION UND BERÜHRUNGSSTRUKTUREN

W. Rinow (Greifswald)

H. Freudenthal [1], [2] benutzt zur Konstruktion seiner Primendenkompaktifizierung eine Trennungsrelation zwischen Teilmengen eines topologischen Raumes. Die Negation dieser Relation ist eine Art von Berührungsrelation. Es erhebt sich die Frage, unter welchen Bedingungen diese Relation eine Berührungsrelation im Sinne Efremowitschs ist. In der vorliegenden Note wird hierfür eine notwendige und hinreichende Bedingung formuliert und ein Zusammenhang aufgezeigt zu der von E. G. Skljarenko [5] eingeführten minimalen perfekten Kompaktifizierung eines topologischen Raumes.

1. A, B, C seien Teilmengen eines topologischen Raumes R. A heißt zwischen B und C zusammenhängend, wenn jede relativ $A \cup B \cup C$ offene und abgeschlossene Teilmenge, die B enthält, mit C Punkte gemein hat. Ein Filter Φ auf R heißt zwischen B und C zusammenhängend, wenn jedes Element von Φ zwischen B und C zusammenhängt. Ein Filter Φ auf R heißt abgeschlossen, wenn er eine Basis aus abgeschlossenen Mengen besitzt.

Die Freudenthalsche Trennungsrelation wird wie folgt definiert: Zwei offene Teilmengen G, H von R heißen entfernt, $G \curlywedge H$, wenn $\overline{G} \cap \overline{H} = \emptyset$ ist und kein abgeschlossener, zwischen G und H zusammenhängender Filter existiert, dessen Adhärenz verschwindet.

Über das Verhältnis zur ursprünglichen Freudenthalschen Definition vgl. [3]. Für beliebige Teilmengen A, B von R definiere man: A, B heißen entfernt, $A \curlywedge B$, wenn in R offene Mengen G, H existieren, für die $A \subseteq G$, $B \subseteq H$ und $G \curlywedge H$ gelten. Diese Trennungsrelation hat folgende Eigenschaften (vgl. [4]):

1.1. a) Aus $A \curlywedge B$ folgt $\overline{A} \cap \overline{B} = 0$.

b) Aus $A \curlywedge B$, $C \subseteq A$ und $D \subseteq B$ folgt $C \curlywedge D$.

c) Aus $A \curlywedge B$ und $A \curlywedge C$ folgt $A \curlywedge B \cup C$.

d) Aus $A \curlywedge B$ folgt $B \curlywedge A$.

e) $\emptyset \curlywedge R$.

Die Bedingungen a) bis e) besagen, daß die Relation $A \curlywedge R - B$ eine symmetrisch topogene Ordnung im Sinne von Császár ist. Die zugehörige Berührungsrelation $A \overline{\curlywedge} B$ ($A \curlywedge B$ gilt nicht) ist jedoch im allgemeinen keine Berührungsrelation im

Sinne Efremowitschs. Sie ist es jedoch genau dann, wenn folgende Bedingung erfüllt ist:

f) Ist $A \curlywedge B$, so existieren Teilmengen C und D, so daß $C \cup D = R$ und $A \curlywedge D$, $B \curlywedge C$ gilt.

Nach Definition der Freudenthalschen Trennungsrelation ist diese Bedingung mit der folgenden äquivalent:

1.2. Die zur Freudenthalschen Trennungsrelation gehörige Berührungsrelation ist genau dann eine Nachbarschaftsstruktur, wenn gilt:

f′) Ist für zwei offene Teilmengen G, H von R $G \curlywedge H$, so existieren offene Teilmengen U, V von R mit $U \cup V = R$, $G \curlywedge V$, $H \curlywedge U$.

Die der Berührungsrelation $\overline{\curlywedge}$ unterliegende Topologie sei $\mathfrak{T}^{\curlywedge}$, und die Topologie von R sei $\mathfrak{T}$. Es ist $A \in \mathfrak{T}^{\curlywedge}$ genau dann, wenn aus $x \in A$ stets folgt $x \curlywedge R - A$. Aus der Definition von $\curlywedge$ ergibt sich unmittelbar, daß $\mathfrak{T}$ feiner ist als $\mathfrak{T}^{\curlywedge}$: $\mathfrak{T}^{\curlywedge} \subseteqq \mathfrak{T}$.

1.3. Die Relation $\overline{\curlywedge}$ ist genau dann mit $\mathfrak{T}$ verträglich, $\mathfrak{T}^{\curlywedge} = \mathfrak{T}$, wenn gilt:

g) Zu jedem $x \in R$ und jeder offenen Umgebung U von R gibt es offene Mengen G, H mit $x \in G$, $R - U \subseteqq H$ und $G \curlywedge H$ (d. h. $x \curlywedge R - U$).

1.4. $\overline{\curlywedge}$ ist genau dann eine mit $\mathfrak{T}$ verträgliche Berührungsrelation im Sinne Efremowitschs, wenn die Bedingungen f′) und g) erfüllt sind.

2. R' sei eine Erweiterung von R. $O_{R'}(G)$ bezeichne für eine in R offene Menge G die Vereinigung aller in R' offenen Mengen G' mit $G' \cap R = G$.

Bilden die Mengen $O_{R'}(G)$, wobei G die offenen Mengen von R durchläuft, eine Basis für R' und gilt $O_{R'}(G \cup H) = O_{R'}(G) \cup O_{R'}(H)$ für je zwei in R offene und disjunkte Mengen G, H, so heißt R' nach E. G. Skljarenko [5] eine perfekte Erweiterung von R.

2.1. R sei ein vollständig regulärer Raum und R' eine perfekte T_2-Kompaktifizierung von R. Dann gilt: Aus $G \curlywedge H$ folgt $\overline{G}^{R'} \cap \overline{H}^{R'} = \emptyset$.

Beweis. Es sei $\overline{G}^{R'} \cap \overline{H}^{R'} \neq \emptyset$ und $\overline{G} \cap \overline{H} = \emptyset$. Für ein $x' \in \overline{G}^{R'} \cap \overline{H}^{R}$ sei Φ' der Umgebungsfilter von x' und Φ seine Spur in R. Da Φ' abgeschlossen ist, ist Φ ein in R abgeschlossener Filter, und wegen $\overline{G} \cap \overline{H} = \emptyset$ ist die Adhärenz von Φ in R leer. Angenommen, Φ sei nicht zwischen G und H zusammenhängend. Dann existiert zunächst eine Menge $W \in \Phi$, die nicht zwischen G und H zusammenhängt. Da jede Teilmenge einer nicht zwischen G und H zusammenhängenden Menge nicht zwischen G und H zusammenhängt, darf man W als in R offen annehmen. Es existieren relativ zu $G \cup W \cup H$ offene und abgeschlossene Mengen A, B mit $A \cup B = G \cup W \cup H$, $G \subseteqq A$, $H \subseteqq B$ und $A \cap B = \emptyset$. Man setze $U = A \cap W$, $V = B \cap W$. Dann gilt $W = U \cup V$, $U \cap V = \emptyset$, und U, V sind in R offen. Wegen der Perfektheit von R' gilt $x' \in O_{R'}(W) = O_{R'}(U) \cup O_{R'}(V)$, also $x' \in O_{R'}(V)$, oder $x' \in O_{R'}(U)$. Hieraus folgt, daß U oder V sowohl mit G als auch mit H Punkte gemein hat. Es ist aber $U \cap H = \emptyset$ und $V \cap G = \emptyset$.

2.2. R sei ein vollständig regulärer Raum; βR bezeichne die Čech-Stonesche Kompaktifizierung von R; G und H seien in R offene Mengen mit $\overline{G}^{\beta R} \cap \overline{H}^{\beta R} = \emptyset$

und Φ ein zwischen G und H zusammenhängender abgeschlossener Filter in R, dessen Adhärenz in R verschwindet. Dann ist die Adhärenz $D' = \bigcap_{X \in \Phi} \overline{X}^{\beta R}$ von Φ in βR eine zusammenhängende kompakte Teilmenge von $\beta R - R$, und es ist $D' \cap \overline{G}^{\beta R} \neq \emptyset$, $D' \cap \overline{H}^{\beta R} \neq \emptyset$.

Dieser Hilfssatz entspricht dem Satz 1.2 in [4]. Der dort angegebene Beweis kann wörtlich übernommen werden, wenn man $R' = R$ setzt und berücksichtigt, daß der Filter Φ in der dortigen Sprechweise ein β-Filter ist.

2.3. R sei ein vollständig regulärer Raum und R' eine T_2-Kompaktifizierung von R mit punktiformem Adjunkt. Dann gilt:

Aus $\overline{G}^{R'} \cap \overline{H}^{R'} = \emptyset$ *folgt* $G \curlywedge H$.

Beweis. Es sei $G \overline{\curlywedge} H$. Ist dann $\overline{G} \cap \overline{H} \neq \emptyset$, so ist auch $\overline{G}^{R'} \cap \overline{H}^{R'} \neq \emptyset$. Es sei also $\overline{G} \cap \overline{H} = \emptyset$ und Φ ein abgeschlossener zwischen G und H zusammenhängender Filter in R, dessen Adhärenz in R verschwindet. Nach 2.2 ist $D' = \bigcap_{X \in \Phi} \overline{X}^{\beta R}$ eine zusammenhängende kompakte Teilmenge von $\beta R - R$. Die Identität von R läßt sich zu einer stetigen Abbildung f von βR auf R' erweitern. $f(D')$ ist eine zusammenhängende kompakte Teilmenge von $R' - R$, besteht also, weil $R' - R$ als punktiform vorausgesetzt ist, aus einem einzigen Punkt x'. Ist $O_{R'}(U)$ eine Umgebung von x' in R', so hat U wegen $D' \cap \overline{G}^{\beta R} \neq \emptyset$ und $D' \cap \overline{H}^{\beta R} \neq \emptyset$ sowohl Punkte mit G als auch mit H gemein. Mithin ist $x' \in \overline{G}^{R'} \cap \overline{H}^{R'}$.

2.4. R sei ein vollständig regulärer Raum. Dann sind folgende Aussagen äquivalent:

a) $\overline{\curlywedge}$ ist eine mit der Topologie von R verträgliche Berührungsrelation.

b) R besitzt eine T_2-Kompaktifizierung mit punktiformem Adjunkt.

c) R besitzt eine kleinste perfekte T_2-Kompaktifizierung.

Ist a) erfüllt, so ist die zur Berührungsrelation $\overline{\curlywedge}$ gehörige T_2-Kompaktifizierung die zugleich kleinste perfekte und größte punktiforme T_2-Kompaktifizierung von R.

Beweis. Es sei a) erfüllt. Dann ist die zu $\overline{\curlywedge}$ gehörige T_2-Kompaktifizierung von R nach 2.1 kleiner als jede perfekte T_2-Kompaktifizierung R' von R. Denn ist δ die R' erzeugende Berührungsrelation, so gilt $G \overline{\delta} H$ genau dann, wenn $\overline{G}^{R'} \cap \overline{H}^{R'} = \emptyset$ ist. Nun hat E. G. Skljarenko [5] folgendes bewiesen: Existiert eine T_2-Kompaktifizierung von R, die kleiner ist als alle perfekten T_2-Kompaktifizierungen von R, so existiert eine kleinste perfekte Kompaktifizierung. Aus a) folgt also c). — E. G. Skljarenko [5] hat ferner die Äquivalenz von b) und c) bewiesen und daß die kleinste perfekte T_2-Kompaktifizierung von R zugleich die größte T_2-Kompaktifizierung mit punktiformem Adjunkt ist. Nach 2.1 und 2.3 ist mithin $\overline{\curlywedge}$ eine Berührungsrelation im Sinne Efremowitschs, und es gilt auch der Zusatz von 2.4.

2.5. R sei ein lokal peripherkompakter T_2-Raum. Dann ist $\overline{\curlywedge}$ eine Berührungsrelation im Sinne Efremowitschs, und $\curlywedge R$ ist die Freudenthalsche Endenkompaktifizierung. Es gilt $A \curlywedge B$ genau dann, wenn peripherkompakte offene Mengen G, H existieren mit $A \subseteq G$, $B \subseteq H$ und $\overline{G} \cap \overline{H} = \emptyset$.

Beweis. Ist R lokal peripherkompakt, so ist nach Skljarenko die Freudenthalsche Endenkompaktifizierung die kleinste perfekte T_2-Kompaktifizierung und zugleich die größte T_2-Kompaktifizierung mit punktiformem Adjunkt. Hieraus ergibt sich der erste Teil der Behauptung als Folge von 2.4. — Für einen lokal peripherikompakten Raum R ist die Menge aller peripherkompakten offenen Mengen von R

eine vollständige π-kompakte Basis im Sinne Skljarenkos [5]. Definiert man mit Skljarenko: $A < B$ genau dann, wenn eine peripherkompakte offene Menge G existiert, so daß $\bar{A} \subseteqq G$ und $\bar{G} \subseteqq \operatorname{Int}(B)$, so ist $A < R - B$ diejenige Berührungsrelation im Sinne Efremowitschs, deren zugehörige Kompaktifizierung gerade die Freudenthalsche Endenkompaktifizierung ist. Hieraus folgt der zweite Teil der Behauptung.

Literatur

[1] H. Freudenthal, Enden und Primenden, Fund. Math. **39** (1952), 189—210.

[2] H. Freudenthal, Bündige Räume, Fund. Math. **48** (1960), 307—312.

[3] W. Rinow, Zur Theorie der Primenden, Math. Nachr. **29** (1965), 367—373.

[4] W. Rinow, Perfekte lokal zusammenhängende Kompaktifizierungen und Primendentheorie, Math. Z. **84** (1964), 294—304.

[5] E. G. Skljarenko, Über perfekte bikompakte Erweiterungen (russ.), Doklady Akad. Nauk SSSR **146** (1962), 1031—1034.

[6] E. G. Skljarenko, Einige Fragen aus der Theorie der bikompakten Erweiterungen (russ.), Izv. Akad. Nauk SSSR **26** (1962), 427—452.

CATEGORICAL APPROACH TO EXTENSION PROBLEMS

Z. Semadeni (Warszawa)

Many topological extension problems can be formulated in the language of the theory of categories. We may classify them as follows:

Type A: Unique factorizations.

Type B: Non-unique existence problems.

Type C: Essential extensions and quotient maps.

According to the Eilenberg-MacLane program, whenever we define a class of mathematical objects, we should try to describe the induced construction of maps as to obtain a functor. The problems of Type A lead to functors in a natural way; the constructions of Types B and C are usually non-functorial.

We may distinguish four groups of problems of Type A.

Type A_1. Let $\mathfrak{B}$ be a subcategory of $\mathfrak{A}$, and let $\mathfrak{B}^0$ and $\mathfrak{A}^0$ be the corresponding classes of objects. Suppose that for each A in $\mathfrak{A}^0$ we have an object $\Phi(A)$ in $\mathfrak{B}^0$ together with an $\mathfrak{A}$-morphism $\tau: A \to \Phi(A)$ such that for every $\mathfrak{A}$-morphism $\varphi: A \to B$ with B in $\mathfrak{B}^0$ there exists a unique $\mathfrak{B}$-morphism $\psi: \Phi(A) \to B$ such that $\psi\tau = \varphi$. If $\alpha: A \to A'$ is any $\mathfrak{A}$-morphism, let $\Phi(\alpha)$ be the unique $\mathfrak{B}$-morphism such that

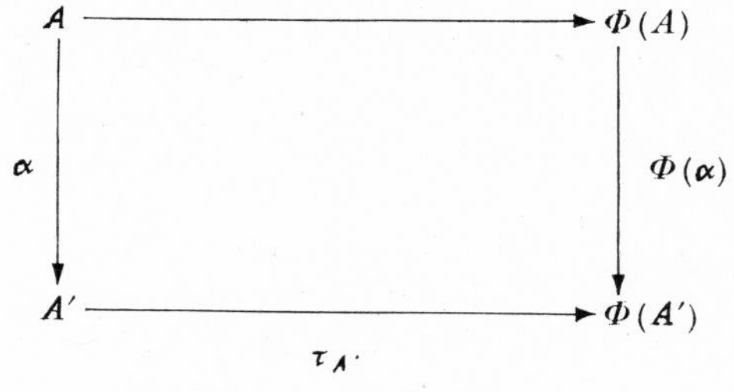

is commutative. Then $\Phi: \mathfrak{A} \to \mathfrak{B}$ is a covariant functor (called a *reflector*; see Freyd [2], Kennison [5]). A typical example is the *Stone-Čech functor* β: **Top** $\to$ **Comp**, where **Top** denotes the category of topological spaces (no separation axioms assumed) and continuous maps and **Comp** is the full subcategory of compact (Hausdorff) spaces. There are many functors of this type: the *component functor* from **Comp** to the category **Comp**$_0$ of compact 0-dimensional spaces ($\Phi(A)$ is the space of components), the completion of a uniform space, the Bohr compactification.

Type A$_2$. Instead of the embedding functor from $\mathfrak{B}$ into $\mathfrak{A}$ we are given a forgetful functor $\square: \mathfrak{B} \to \mathfrak{A}$ (a functor "forgeting" some structures imposed on objects of $\mathfrak{B}$ or some properties of them) and we suppose that for each A in $\mathfrak{A}^0$ there is an $\mathfrak{A}$-morphism $\tau_A: A \to \square(\Phi(A))$ with a similar unique-factorization property. Examples: free objects of various kinds, e.g., the free compact spaces βS generated by (discrete) sets S yield a covariant functor **Ens** $\to$ **Comp**; the *simplex functor* $\mathscr{S}$ from **Comp** to the category **Compconv** of compact convex sets and continuous affine maps (SEMADENI [10]). Another example follows.

If X is a topological space, $\mathscr{C}(X)$ is the space of all bounded scalar-valued continuous functions on X (the scalar field is either $\boldsymbol{R}$ or $\boldsymbol{C}$). If $\varphi: X \to Y$ is a continuous map, $\mathscr{C}(\varphi): \mathscr{C}(Y) \to \mathscr{C}(X)$ is the induced linear operator defined as $\mathscr{C}\varphi . g = g \circ \varphi$ for g in $\mathscr{C}(Y)$. **Ban**$_1$ denotes the category of Banach spaces and linear contractions (i.e., linear operators of norm ≤ 1). It is clear that $\mathscr{C}$: **Top** $\to$ **Ban**$_1$ is a contravariant functor. **Bcf** denotes the image of $\mathscr{C}$ in **Ban**$_1$; thus, a **Bcf**-object is a space $\mathscr{C}(X)$ and a **Bcf**-morphism is an operator $\mathscr{C}(\varphi)$.

Let F be a Banach space and let $\bigcirc^* F$ denote the unit ball in the conjugate space F^* provided with the *weak topology. If $\alpha: F \to G$ is a **Ban**$_1$-morphism, $\bigcirc^* \alpha$ will denote the restriction of the conjugate map $\alpha^*: G^* \to F^*$ to the set $\bigcirc^* G$. It is clear that $\bigcirc^*$: **Ban**$_1$ $\to$ **Comp** is also a contravariant functor. The composition

$$\mathbf{Ban}_1 \xrightarrow{\ \bigcirc^*\ } \mathbf{Comp} \xrightarrow{\ \mathscr{C}\ } \mathbf{Bcf}$$

is called the *Banach-Mazur functor*; it is covariant. If F is a Banach space, $\varkappa_F: F \to \mathscr{C}(\bigcirc^* F)$ will denote the canonical injection $\varkappa_F f . \xi = \xi(f)$ for ξ in $\bigcirc^* F$. By a well-known theorem of Banach and Mazur, $\varkappa_F$ is a linear isometry.

Theorem. *For any compact space Y and any linear contraction $\beta: F \to \mathscr{C}(Y)$ there exists a unique continuous map $\varphi: Y \to \bigcirc^* F$ such that*

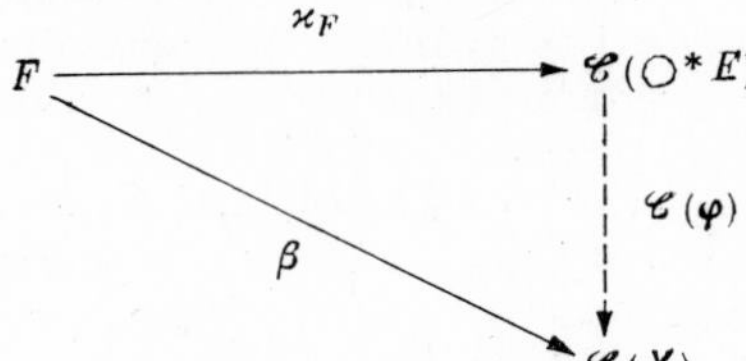

is commutative.

Type A$_3$. *Inputs* (or left roots) and *outputs* (or right roots) of diagrams. This includes products, equalizers, inverse limits, pullbacks, etc., and the dual notions of coproducts (sums), coequalizers, inductive limits, and pushouts. A category $\mathfrak{A}$ is *complete* [*cocomplete*] iff every diagram (i.e., covariant functor from a small category to $\mathfrak{A}$) has an input [output]; it is enough if $\mathfrak{A}$ has all products and equalizers [all coproducts and coequalizers]. See FREYD [2] and MITCHELL [7] for more details.

It is well known that the categories **Top**, **Comp**, and **Comp**$_0$ are complete and cocomplete.

Problem. *Classify all categories of topological spaces which are both complete and cocomplete.*

Type A_4. Adjoint functors in the sense of D. KAN [4] (see MACLANE,[6], FREYD [2], MITCHELL [7]). This notion includes the three preceding types A_1, A_2 A_3.

The systematic use of various notions of the types described above essentially simplifies certain proofs. There are many theorems concerning problems of types A_1, A_2, A_3, and A_4; the topologists ought to be aware whether a theorem is a consequence of a general theorem on categories and functors or is a specific property of the spaces in question. Furthermore, a proof involving diagrams and arrows may appear to be ismpler than a traditional proof using neighborhoods, nets, etc.

Top$_\square$ [**Comp**$_\square$] will denote the category of topological [compact] spaces with base points and base-point-preserving continuous maps. **Top**$_{\mathscr{P},\subset}$ [**Comp**$_{\mathscr{F},\subset}$] will denote the following category: an object means a pair (X, A), where X is a topological [compact] space and A is a [closed] subset of X; a morphism from (X, A) to (Y, B) is a continuous map $\varphi: X \to Y$ such that $\varphi(A) \subset B$. Together with **Top** and **Comp**, these categories give rise to twenty canonical covariant functors.

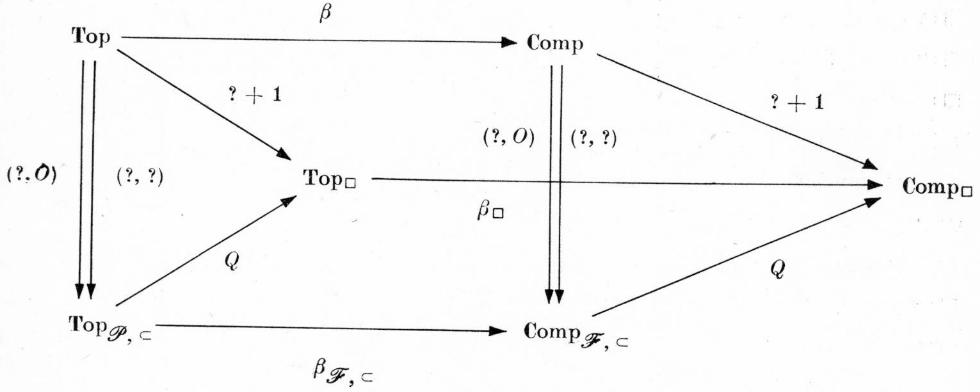

Only eleven of those functors are drawn in the diagram (the other nine functors are forgetful functors in the opposite directions). We shall describe their object transformations. $\beta_\square$ assigns to each pair (X, x_0), where $x_0 \in X$, the pair $(\beta X, y_0)$, where y_0 is the image of x_0, while $\beta_{\mathscr{F},\subset}$ assigns to each pair (X, A) the pair $(\beta X, B)$ where B is the closure of the image of A in βX. The quotation mark ? is the symbol of a variable; ? + 1 assigns to each space X the space $X + 1$, the new isolated point being the base point; (?, O) assigns (X, O) to X, where O is the empty set; (?, ?) assigns (X, X) to X. Finally, Q assigns to each pair (X, A), where $A \neq O$, the quotient space obtained by pinching A to a base point and assigns $X + 1$ to each pair (X, O).

It can easily be shown that all those six categories are complete and cocomplete. The tabulation below shows some preservation properties of those functors.

The sign + means that the functor listed in the row preserves the property listed in the column; the sign — means that it does not. The 6 columns and 20 functors yield 120 questions; there are 92 answers + and 28 answers —. The functors β, $\beta_\square$, $\beta_{\mathscr{F},\subset}$ and the six functors ? + 1, (?, O), Q are left adjoints of the corresponding forgetful functors; the functors

$$(?, ?): \mathbf{Top} \to \mathbf{Top}_{\mathscr{P},\subset} \quad \text{and} \quad (?, ?): \mathbf{Comp} \to \mathbf{Comp}_{\mathscr{F},\subset}$$

are right adjoints of the corresponding forgetful functors. Thus, one half of all answers in the above tabulation follows from the general theorem: *the right adjoints*

	Product	Equalizer	Inverse limit	Co-product	Co-equalizer	Inductive limit
$\square$: **Comp** $\to$ **Top**	+	+	+	−	−	−
$\square$: $\mathbf{Comp}_\square \to \mathbf{Top}_\square$	+	+	+	−	−	−
$\square$: $\mathbf{Comp}_{\mathscr{F},\subset} \to \mathbf{Top}_{\mathscr{P},\subset}$	+	+	+	−	−	−
β: **Top** $\to$ **Comp**	−	−	−	+	+	+
$\beta_\square$: $\mathbf{Top}_\square \to \mathbf{Comp}_\square$	−	−	−	+	+	+
$\beta_{\mathscr{F},\subset}$: $\mathbf{Top}_{\mathscr{P},\subset} \to \mathbf{Comp}_{\mathscr{F},\subset}$	−	−	−	+	+	+
$\square$: $\mathbf{Top}_\square \to \mathbf{Top}_{\mathscr{P},\subset}$	+	+	+	−	+	+
$\square$: $\mathbf{Comp}_\square \to \mathbf{Comp}_{\mathscr{F},\subset}$	+	+	+	−	+	+
$\square$: $\mathbf{Top}_\square \to \mathbf{Top}$	+	+	+	−	+	+
$\square$: $\mathbf{Comp}_\square \to \mathbf{Comp}$	+	+	+	−	+	+
$? + 1$: $\mathbf{Top} \to \mathbf{Top}_\square$	−	+	+	+	+	+
$? + 1$: $\mathbf{Comp} \to \mathbf{Comp}_\square$	−	+	+	+	+	+
Q: $\mathbf{Top}_{\mathscr{P},\subset} \to \mathbf{Top}_\square$	−	−	−	+	+	+
Q: $\mathbf{Comp}_{\mathscr{F},\subset} \to \mathbf{Comp}_\square$	−	+	+	+	+	+
$\square$: $\mathbf{Top}_{\mathscr{P},\subset} \to \mathbf{Top}$	+	+	+	+	+	+
$\square$: $\mathbf{Comp}_{\mathscr{F},\subset} \to \mathbf{Comp}$	+	+	+	+	+	+
$(?, O)$: $\mathbf{Top} \to \mathbf{Top}_{\mathscr{P},\subset}$	+	+	+	+	+	+
$(?, O)$: $\mathbf{Comp} \to \mathbf{Comp}_{\mathscr{F},\subset}$	+	+	+	+	+	+
$(?, ?)$: $\mathbf{Top} \to \mathbf{Top}_{\mathscr{P},\subset}$	+	+	+	+	+	+
$(?, ?)$: $\mathbf{Comp} \to \mathbf{Comp}_{\mathscr{F},\subset}$	+	+	+	+	+	+

preserve all inputs and the left adjoints preserve all outputs (FREYD [2], p. 81). The other half can also be verified (note that if $O \neq A_t \subset X_t$, then the canonical bijection

$$Q(\lim^{\leftarrow} X_t) \to \lim^{\leftarrow} Q(X_t)$$

need not be a homeomorphism).

A contravariant functor $\Phi\colon \mathfrak{A} \to \mathfrak{B}$ will be called *continuous* iff the following condition is satisfied: if $(A_\infty, (\pi_t)_{t\in T})$ is an $\mathfrak{A}$-inverse limit of an inverse family $((A_t)_{t\in T}, (\pi_t^s)_{t\leqq s})$ in $\mathfrak{A}$, then $(\Phi A_\infty, (\Phi\pi_t)_{t\in T})$ is a $\mathfrak{B}$-inductive limit of the inductive family $((\Phi A_t)_{t\in T}, (\Phi\pi_t^s)_{t\leqq s})$.

Theorem. *The functor* $\mathscr{C}$: **Comp** $\to \mathbf{Ban}_1$ *is continuous.*

It is easy to show that the functor $\mathscr{C}$: **Top** $\to \mathbf{Ban}_1$ is not continuous. E.g., let $X_1 \leftarrow X_2 \leftarrow \ldots$ be an inverse family in **Top** and let X_∞ be empty. Then $\beta X_1 \leftarrow$

$\leftarrow \beta X_2 \leftarrow \ldots$ is also an inverse family with nonempty inverse limit Y. The space $\mathscr{C}(Y)$ yields a $\mathbf{Ban}_1$-inductive limit of $\mathscr{C}(X_1) \to \mathscr{C}(X_2) \to \ldots$ and contains nonzero functions. Therefore $\mathscr{C}(Y)$ is not $\mathbf{Ban}_1$-isomorphic to $\mathscr{C}(X_\infty) = \mathscr{C}(O) = \{0\}$.

Type B. Given certain objects and morphisms, we are looking for a morphism satisfying certain prescribed conditions. For instance, some extension and lifting problems may be formulated as follows: can the diagram

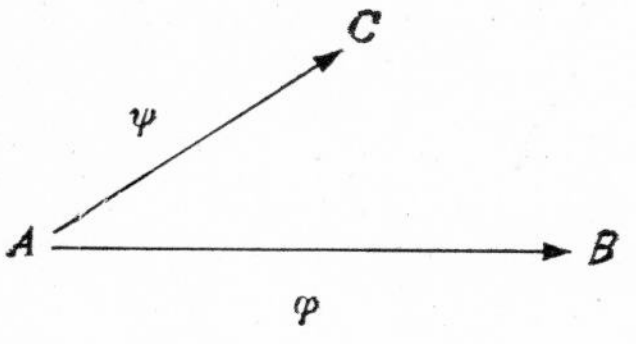

or

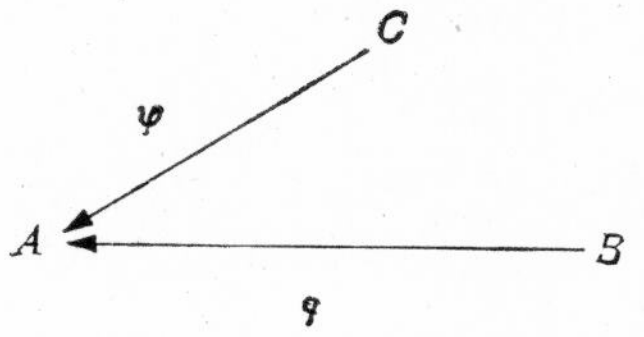

be extended to a commutative triangle? (If A is a subset of a topological space B and $\varphi: A \to B$ is the embedding, then any $\vartheta: B \to C$ satisfying $\vartheta\varphi = \psi$ is an extension of φ.) The questions: "Is A homeomorphic to a subset of B?", "Is A a continuous image of B?" are other instances of such non-unique existence problems. We shall not discuss this topic here (some information on it can be found in SEMADENI [9]).

Type C. The essential extensions and quotient objects are two notions whose definitions may be put as follows: given a class $\mathfrak{M}$ of morphisms, we consider the class

$$\{\alpha\text{: for every morphism } \beta, \text{ if } \beta\alpha \text{ is defined and } \beta\alpha \in \mathfrak{M}, \text{ then } \beta \in \mathfrak{M}\}.$$

We begin with quotient morphisms. Let $\mathfrak{A}$ be a concrete category. A *quotient morphism* is a morphism $\pi: A \to B$ satisfying the following conditions: (i) π is a surjection, (ii) if C is any object and $\beta: B \to C$ is any map such that $\beta\pi$ is a morphism, then β is a morphism. The following proposition illustrates the advantage of diagrammatic proofs of certain topological theorems.

Proposition. *Let $\mathfrak{B}$ be a full subcategory of $\mathfrak{A}$, let $\pi: B \to A$ be an $\mathfrak{A}$-quotient morphism, let $\tau: A \to \Phi(A)$ have the Type* A_1 *property described above and let τ be a surjection. Then $\tau\pi: B \to \Phi(A)$ is $\mathfrak{B}$-quotient.*

The proof is straightforward. If we apply this proposition in the case where $\mathfrak{A} = \mathbf{Top}$ and $\mathfrak{B} = \mathbf{Comp}$, we get

Corollary. Let $\sim$ be any equivalence relation on a compact space X and let $X/\sim$ be the quotient space (with the quotient topology). Then $X/\sim$ is quasi-compact, the canonical map $\tau: X/\sim \to \beta(X/\sim)$ is a surjection, and the composition of τ with the canonical surjection $\pi: X \to X/\sim$ is a $\mathbf{Comp}$-quotient morphism, i.e., $\tau\pi$ is determined by a semicontinuous decomposition of X

Let us now suppose that $\mathfrak{A}$ is a category and $\mathfrak{S}$ is a subcategory of $\mathfrak{A}$ such that each isomorphism belongs to $\mathfrak{S}$ and each morphism in $\mathfrak{S}$ is monic. A typical example is the class of all homeomorphic injections in $\mathbf{Top}$. An *$\mathfrak{S}$-essential extension* or an *$\mathfrak{S}$-envelope* of an object A is any $\sigma: A \to B$ in $\mathfrak{S}$ satisfying the following condition: if $\beta: B \to C$ is any morphism such that $\beta\sigma \in \mathfrak{S}$, then $\beta \in \mathfrak{S}$. The dual notion is an $\mathfrak{S}$-coenvelope, where $\mathfrak{S}$ is a subcategory of epimorphisms. An *envelope* [*coenvelope*] of A is an $\mathfrak{S}_0$-envelope [$\mathfrak{S}_0$-coenvelope] where $\mathfrak{S}_0$ is the class of all monomorphisms [epimorphisms].

It is easy to verify that a **Comp**-morphism $\pi: X \to Y$ is a coenvelope if and only if π is an irreducible surjection (this means that the conditions $F = \bar{F} \subset X$ and $\pi(F) = Y$ imply $F = X$).

Proposition. *Let* $\pi: X \to Y$ *be a* **Comp**-*morphism. Then* $\mathscr{C}(\pi): \mathscr{C}(Y) \to \mathscr{C}(X)$ *is an* $\mathfrak{S}$-*envelope in* $\mathbf{Ban}_1$, *where* $\mathfrak{S}$ *is the class of all linear isometrical injections, if and only if* π *is a coenvelope in* **Comp**.

Proposition. *For every Banach space* B *there exists a closed subset* X *of* $\bigcirc^* B$ *such that the canonical injection* $B \to \mathscr{C}(X)$ *is an* $\mathfrak{S}$-*envelope.*

If we combine the two above propositions with some well-known theorems of NACHBIN [8] and GLEASON [3], we get the following theorem of H. B. COHEN [1]: *every Banach space has a* $\mathbf{Ban}_1$-*injective envelope.*

Proofs and details will appear in the forthcoming book "Banach spaces of continuous functions".

Added in proof. Dr. A. WIWEGER has pointed out that the functor (?,?): $\mathbf{Top} \to \mathbf{Top}_{\mathscr{P},\subset}$ has not only a left adjoint $\square: \mathbf{Top}_{\mathscr{P},\subset} \to \mathbf{Top}$, where $\square\,(X,A) = X$ and $\square\,\varphi = \varphi$, but also has a right adjoint $\square': \mathbf{Top}_{\mathscr{P},\subset} \to \mathbf{Top}$ defined as follows: $\square'(X, A) = A$, $\square'\,(\varphi)\ \varphi/A$. The same remark applies to the categories $\mathbf{Comp}_{\mathscr{F},\subset}$ and **Comp**.

The theorem announced on p. 196 has been proved in the author's paper "Inverse limits of compact spaces and direct limits of spaces of continuous functions", Studia Math. **31** (1968), 373–382, in the following more general form: The functor $\mathscr{C}_0: \mathbf{Comp}_{\mathscr{F},\subset} \to \mathbf{Ban}_1$ is continuous, where $\mathscr{C}_0(X, A) = \{f \in C(X): f/A = O\}$.

In this paper, a product in a category means a product of a nonempty set of objects. Dr. A. BIALYNICKI-BIRULA has pointed out that the functors $(?, O)$ do not preserve the terminal objects ([6], p. 42), which may be regarded as products of the empty set of objects.

References

[1] H. B. COHEN, Injective envelopes of Banach spaces, Bull. Amer. Math. Soc. **70** (1964), 723–726.

[2] P. FREYD, Abelian categories, New York 1964.

[3] A. M. GLEASON, Projective topological spaces, Illinois J. Math. 2 (1958), 482–489.

[4] D. M. KAN, Adjoint functors, Trans. Amer. Math. Soc. 87 (1958), 294–329.

[5] J. F. KENNISON, Reflective functors in general topology and elsewhere, Trans. Amer. Math. Soc. **118** (1965), 303–315.

[6] S. MACLANE, Categorical algebra, Bull. Amer. Math. Soc. **71** (1965), 40–106.

[7] B. MITCHELL, Theory of categories, New York and London 1965.

[8] L. NACHBIN, A theorem of the Hahn-Banach type for linear transformations, Trans. Amer. Math. Soc. **68** (1950), 28–46.

[9] Z. SEMADENI, Projectivity, injectivity and duality, Rozprawy Matematyczne **35** (1963), 1–47.

[10] Z. SEMADENI, Categorical methods in convexity, Proc. Conference on Convexity, Copenhagen 1965; Copenhagen 1967, p. 281–307.

FRONTIÈRES ASSOCIÉES A DES CONES CONVEXES DE FONCTIONS S.C.I.

D. SIBONY (Paris)

Ceci est une partie d'un travail fait en commun avec G. MOKOBODZKI (cf. [7]) en vue des applications à une théorie globale du potentiel généralisant la théorie de HUNT.
Ω est un espace localement compact dénombrable à l'infini.

Définition 0. Soit g une fonction numérique, $g \geqq 0$ sur Ω. $o(g)$ est alors l'espace des fonctions f réelles sur Ω telles que: pour tout $\varepsilon > 0$ il existe K compact $\subset \Omega$ tel que

$$(x \in \complement K) \Rightarrow (|f(x)| \leqq \varepsilon g(x)).$$

Si C est un ensemble de fontions positives sur Ω on pose

$$o(C) = \bigcup_{g \in C} o(g).$$

Définition 1. Soit C un cône convexe de fonctions numériques s. c. i. sur Ω.
1^0. On appelle *point-frontière de* Ω relatif à C, tout $x \in \Omega$ tel que si $\mu \in \mathfrak{M}^+(\Omega)$,

$$\int |v| \, d\mu < +\infty \quad \text{et} \quad \int v \, d\mu \leqq v(x), \quad \forall v \in C,$$

alors $\mu = \varepsilon_x$.
2^0. On appelle *frontière fine* de Ω relative à C, ou frontière de Choquet, l'ensemble des points-frontière de Ω relatifs à C. On notera cet ensemble $\delta(C)$.
L'étude des frontières fines dans le cas où Ω est compact a été abondamment traitée, et a permis de dégager des conditions suffisantes simples pour que la frontière fine ait la propriété:

$$(v \in C \text{ et } v(x) \geqq 0, \quad \forall x \in \delta(C)) \Rightarrow (v(x) \geqq 0, \quad \forall x \in \Omega).$$

Nous nous proposons d'étendre ces résultats au cas où Ω est localement compact et où le cône convexe C est adapté en un certain sens.
Soit C un cône convexe de fonctions numériques, on notera par C^+ l'ensemble des fonctions positives de C, et par inf (C, o) l'ensemble $\{\inf(f, o)\}_{f \in C}$.
On a alors le résultat suivant:

Proposition 2. *Soit C un cône convexe de fonctions numériques s. c. i. sur Ω. On suppose que C^+ est linéairement séparant, que*

$$\inf(C, o) \subset o(C^+) \quad \textit{et} \quad C \neq C^+.$$

Dans ces conditions, $\delta(C)$ est non vide et

$$(v \in C, v(x) \geqq 0, \quad \forall\, x \in \delta(C)) \Rightarrow (v(x) \geqq 0, \quad \forall\, x \in \Omega).$$

Avant de démontrer cette proposition, rappelons quelques définitions extraites de MOKOBODZKI [7] (cf. aussi BAUER [2]).

(a) Un fermé $F \subset \Omega$ est dit *stable* si, pour tout $x \in F$, et toute mesure $\mu \geqq 0$ sur Ω telle que

$$\int v\, d\mu \leqq v(x), \quad \forall\, v \in C,$$

a mesure μ est portée par F.

Toute intersection de fermés stables est un fermé stable, et tout compact stable contient un compact stable minimal.

(b) Si on désigne par Ω^+ l'ensemble $\Omega^+ = \bigcap_{v \in C} \{v \geqq 0\}$, un point de $x \in \complement\, \Omega^+$ est point-frontière si, et seulement si, $\{x\}$ est un compact stable minimal.

Lemme 3. *Pour tout $v \in C$, $v \notin C^+$, il existe un compact stable $K \subset \{v < 0\}$.*

Démonstration. Soit $x_0 \in \Omega$ tel que $v(x_0) < 0$. Il existe une suite

$$(v_n) \subset C^+,$$

telle que $\sup v_n(x) > 0$, $\forall\, x \in \Omega$, et

$$\sum^n v_n(x_0) < +\infty.$$

La fonction $w = \sum v_n$ peut prendre éventuellement la valeur $+\infty$, de plus on peut supposer que inf $(v, o) \in o(w)$.

Posons alors

$$\lambda = \{\sup \alpha, \alpha > 0, \ -\alpha v \leqq w\}.$$

Il est facile de voir, en posant $u = w + \lambda v$, que l'ensemble $u^{-1}(0) = \{w = -\lambda v\}$ est non vide, et que c'est un compact stable. Enfin,

$$u^{-1}(0) \subset \{v < 0\}.$$

On démontrerait de la même manière le lemme suivant.

Lemme 4. *Soient F un fermé stable de Ω, $v \in C$, tels que $\{v < 0\} \cap F \neq \emptyset$. Il existe alors un compact stable $K \subset \{v < 0\} \cap F$.*

La proposition va alors résulter du lemme suivant.

Lemme 5. *Tout compact stable minimal K, $K \not\subset \Omega^+$, est réduit à un point (donc identifiable à un point-frontière).*

Démonstration. Soient $x \in K$, $v \in C$, tels que $v(x) < 0$. S'il existait $x_1 \in K$, $x_1 \neq x$, on pourrait trouver $w \in C$ tel que $v(x) + w(x) < 0$ et $v(x_1) + w(x_1) \geqq 0$ (C est linéairement séparant), on conclut alors à l'aide du lemme précédent.

Remarque 1. Soit C un cône convexe de fonctions numériques s. c. i. La frontiere $\delta(C)$ ne change pas si on adjoint au cône C, l'ensemble des fonctions s. c. i. $v \geqq 0$

telles que

$$\int v\,d\mu \leqq v(x),$$

$\forall\, \mu \geqq 0$ sur Ω, $x \in \Omega$ tels que

$$\int s\,d\mu \leqq s(x), \quad \forall\, s \in C.$$

Remarque 2. Si on sature, par enveloppe inférieure finie, le cône convexe C, on obtient un cône C' tel que $\delta(C) = \delta(C')$, et si $\inf(C, o) \subset o(C^+)$, on a encore

$$\inf(C', o) \subset o(C'^+).$$

Soit C un cône convexe de fonctions s.c.i. sur Ω, tel que $\mathscr{C}_K(\Omega) \subset o(C^+)$. Pour toute $\varphi \in \mathscr{C}_K(\Omega)$, on pose

$$\hat{\varphi} = \inf_{\substack{f \in C \\ f \geqq \varphi}} f.$$

On a la caractérisation suivante de $\delta(C)$:

Proposition 6. *Pour qu'un point $x \in \delta(C)$, il faut et il suffit que, pour toute $\varphi \in \mathscr{C}_K(\Omega)$, on ait*

$$\varphi(x) = \hat{\varphi}(x).$$

Démonstration.

1°. Supposons $\varphi(x) = \hat{\varphi}(x)$ pour toute $\varphi \in \mathscr{C}_K(\Omega)$, et soit μ une mesure $\geqq 0$ telle que

$$\int s\,d\mu \leqq s(x), \quad \forall\, s \in C.$$

On aurait alors, pour $s \in C$, $s \geqq \varphi$, $\varphi \in \mathscr{C}_K(\Omega)$,

$$\int \varphi\,d\mu \leqq \int s\,d\mu \leqq s(x).$$

Par suite,

$$\int \varphi\,d\mu \leqq \varphi(x), \quad \forall\, \varphi \in \mathscr{C}_K(\Omega),$$

d'où $\mu = \varepsilon_x$.

2°. On suppose toujours que $\inf(C, o) \subset o(C^+)$.

Pour toute mesure $\mu \geqq 0$, finie sur $o(C^+) \cap \mathscr{C}(\Omega)$, et toute $v \in C$, on a

$$\int v\,d\mu = \{\sup \int \varphi\,d\mu;\quad \varphi \leqq v;\quad \varphi \in o(C^+) \cap \mathscr{C}(\Omega)\}.$$

Soit alors $x \in \delta(C)$. Sur $o(C^+) \cap \mathscr{C}(\Omega)$, l'application $p: \varphi \to \hat{\varphi}(x)$ est sous-linéaire, croissante. Pour toute mesure μ sur Ω, $\mu \leqq p$, on remarque que μ est $\geqq 0$, et que $\int s\,d\mu \leqq s(x)$, $\forall\, s \in C$. On a supposé $x \in \delta(C)$, par suite $\mu = \varepsilon_x$, ce qui montre que p est linéaire, et puisque l'on a $\varepsilon_x \leqq p$,

$$p(\varphi) = \varphi(x) = \hat{\varphi}(x), \quad \forall\, \varphi \in o(C^+) \cap \mathscr{C}(\Omega).$$

Proposition 7. *Soit C un cône convexe de fonctions numériques s. c. i. satisfaisant aux conditions de la proposition 2. Alors $\overline{\delta(C)}$ est le plus petit fermé F ayant les deux* *propriétés suivantes équivalentes:*

1°. $(v \in C;\ v(x) \geqq 0,\ \forall\, x \in F) \Rightarrow (v(x) \geqq 0, \forall\, x \in \Omega)$.

2°. *Pour tout* $x \in \Omega$, *il existe une mesure* $\mu \geqq 0$ *sur* Ω *portée par* F *telle que*

$$\int v\, d\mu \leqq v(x), \quad \forall\, v \in C.$$

Démonstration. On voit immédiatement que $2^0 \Rightarrow 1^0$, et que $\delta(C) \subset F$, d'apres la proposition 2, par suite $\overline{\delta(C)} \subset F$.

Montrons que $1^0 \Rightarrow 2^0$. Soit $x_0 \in \Omega$. Sur F, considérons l'espace vectoriel $H = o(C^+) \cap \mathscr{C}(F)$, c'est un expace adapté (i.e. $H \subset o(H)$), et, pour toute mesure $\mu \geqq 0$ sur F et tout $v \in C$, on a

$$\int v\, d\mu = \sup_{\substack{\varphi \leqq v \\ \varphi \in H}} \int \varphi\, d\mu.$$

Sur H, considérons la forme sous-linéaire finie p,

$$\varphi \to p(\varphi) = \inf_{\substack{v \in C \\ v \geqq \varphi}} v(x_0).$$

Soit T une forme linéaire sur H, $T \leqq p$. Il existe alors une mesure $\mu \geqq 0$ sur F telle que

$$\int \varphi\, d\mu = (T, \varphi) \leqq p(\varphi).$$

Par suite,

$$\int v\, d\mu \leqq v(x_0), \quad \forall\, v \in C.$$

Proposition 8. *Soit* C *un cône convexe de fonctions numériques s. c. i. sur* Ω, *tel que* C^+ *soit linéairement séparant. On suppose qu'il existe un compact* $K \subset \Omega$ *tel que*

$$(v \in C,\ v(x) \geqq 0,\ \forall\, x \in K) \Rightarrow (v \geqq 0).$$

Si $C \neq C^+$, *alors* $\delta(C) \neq \emptyset$ *et* $\delta(C) \subset K$, *de plus*

$$(v \in C;\ v(x) \geqq 0,\ \forall\, x \in \delta(C)) \Rightarrow (v \geqq 0).$$

Démonstration.

1°. En appliquant la proposition précédente à un compact $K' \supset K$ et au cône C_K' des restrictions de C à K', on voit que $\delta(C_{K'}) = \delta(C_K)$ et que, pour toute mesure $\mu \geqq 0$ sur Ω, à support compact, il existe une mesure $\nu \geqq 0$, à support dans K, telle que

$$\int v\, d\nu \leqq \int v\, d\mu, \quad \forall\, v \in C.$$

Toute $\mu \in \mathfrak{M}^+(\Omega)$ s'écrivant $\mu = \sum \mu_\alpha$, où les mesures $\mu_\alpha \in \mathfrak{M}^+(\Omega)$ sont à support compact, on a la même propriété pour les mesures $\mu \in \mathfrak{M}^+(\Omega)$ telles que

$$\int v\, d\mu < +\infty, \quad \forall\, v \in C.$$

2°. Montrons que $\delta(C_K) = \delta(C)$. On a évidemment $\delta(C) \subset \delta(C_K)$.

Soit $x \in \delta(C_K)$. Supposons qu'il existe $\mu \in \mathfrak{M}^+(\Omega)$, $\mu \neq \varepsilon_x$, telle que $\int v\, d\mu \leqq v(x)$, $\forall\, v \in C$.

Soit K' compact, $K' \cap K = \emptyset$, $\mu(K') > 0$. Il existe alors deux mesures $\geqq 0$, ν_1 et ν_2, portées par K, telles que

$$\int v \, d\nu_1 \leqq \int v \, d\mu|_{K'}, \quad \forall v \in C,$$
$$\int v \, d\nu_2 \leqq \int v \, d\mu|_{\complement K'}.$$

Par suite.

$$\int v \, d(\nu_1 + \nu_2) \leqq v(x), \quad \forall v \in C,$$

et $\nu = \nu_1 + \nu_2 = \varepsilon_x$, puisque $x \in \delta(C_K)$.

Soit $f \in \mathscr{C}(K \cup K')$ definie par

$$f(K) = 0, \quad f(K') = 1.$$

Comme $x \in \delta(C_{K \cup K'})$, pour tout $\varepsilon > 0$, il existe $v \in C$ tel que $v \geqq f$ et

$$v(x) \leqq \varepsilon + f(x) = \varepsilon;$$

par suite, il existe $v_0 \in C$ tel que

$$\int v_0 \, d\nu_1 < \int v_0 \, d\mu|_{K'}.$$

On aurait donc

$$\int v_0 \, d\nu < \int v_0 \, d\mu \leqq v_0(x),$$

ce qui est contradictoire, puisqu'on doit avoir

$$\int v_0 \, d\nu = v_0(x).$$

On a donc bien $\delta(C) = \delta(C_K)$, et la proposition s'ensuit immédiatement.

Remarque. On peut améliorer la proposition précédente en réplaçant le compact K par un fermé F tel que

$$\inf(C, o)_F \subset o(C_F).$$

Lemme 9. *Soit C un cône convexe de fonctions s. c. i. sur Ω tel que $\mathscr{C}_K \subset o(C^+)$. Soient ω un ouvert relativement compact, (φ_n) une suite d'éléments de $\mathscr{C}_K(\Omega)$, à support dans ω, convergeant uniformément sur Ω vers $\varphi \in \mathscr{C}_K(\Omega)$.*

Alors,

$$\hat{\varphi} = \lim \hat{\varphi}_n.$$

Démonstration. L'application $\varphi \to \hat{\varphi}$ est croissante sous-additive.

Soit $\varphi_0 \in \mathscr{C}_K^+(\Omega)$, $0 \leqq \varphi_0 \leqq 1$, $\varphi_0(x) = 1$, $\forall x \in \overline{\omega}$, et soit $v_0 \in C^+$, $v_0 \geqq \varphi_0$.

De $\|\varphi_n - \varphi\| \leqq \varepsilon$, on déduit

$$\varphi_n \leqq \varepsilon\varphi_0 + \varphi \quad \text{et} \quad \varphi \leqq \varphi_n + \varepsilon\varphi_0,$$

d'où

$$\hat{\varphi} \leqq \hat{\varphi}_n + \varepsilon\hat{\varphi}_0 \leqq \hat{\varphi}_n + \varepsilon v_0;$$

de même

$$\hat{\varphi}_n \leqq \hat{\varphi} + \varepsilon v_0,$$

ce qui donne

$$|\hat{\varphi} - \hat{\varphi}_n| < \varepsilon v_0.$$

Proposition 10. *On suppose que Ω est à base dénombrable. Soit $C \subset \mathscr{C}(\Omega)$ un cône convexe, linéairement séparant,*

$$\inf(C, o) \subset o(C), \quad \mathscr{C}_K(\Omega) \subset o(C).$$

Dans ces conditions, $\delta(C)$ est un G_δ.

Démonstration. L'espace Ω étant séparable, il existe une suite $(\varphi_n) \subset \mathscr{C}_K(\Omega)$ telle que, pour tout $\varphi \in \mathscr{C}_K(\Omega)$, et tout voisinage ω du support de φ, il existe une suite (φ_{n_p}) extraite, dont les éléments sont à support dans ω, suite qui converge uniformément vers φ.

En vertu de la proposition 6 et du lemme précédent,

$$\delta(C) = \bigcap_n \{\hat{\varphi}_n = \varphi_n\},$$

et, pout tout n, $\hat{\varphi}_n$ est s. c. s., donc $\{\hat{\varphi}_n = \varphi_n\}$ est un G_δ.

Citons encore sans demonstration le corollaire suivant.

Corollaire 11. *Pour toute mesure $\mu \geqq 0$ sur Ω telle que*

$$\int v \, d\mu < +\infty, \quad \forall v \in C^+,$$

il existe une mesure $\nu \geqq 0$ portée par $\delta(C)$ telle que

$$\int v \, d\nu \leqq \int v \, d\mu, \quad \forall v \in C.$$

Nous avons donc montré que la théorie du balayage, définie sur un espace compact par un cône convexe de fonctions, s'étend sans difficulté au cas non compact, en imposant aux cônes convexes considérés d'être adaptés.

Bien d'autres considérations, comme celles portant sur le «bord» et les ensembles «bordants», ou sur l'existence de noyau-diffusion associé à deux mesures μ et ν balayées l'une de l'autre, etc., peuvent être traitées dans ce nouveau cadre. Le lecteur pourra trouver, dans Meyer [5], un exposé détaillé de ces questions pour le cas compact.

Le problème des frontières associées aux espaces vectoriels adaptés était déjà aborda, dans Choquet [3], en connexion avec la représentation intégrale.

Applications. *Notions de support relatif, de support fin relatif.*

Soit C un cône convexe de fonctions numériques s.c.i., $\geqq 0$ sur Ω, linéairement séparant.

Définition 12.

1°. Pour toute fonction numérique s.c.s. $\varphi \geqq 0$, semi continue supérieurement, $\varphi \in o(C)$, on appelle *support fin de φ*, relatif à C, noté $\delta(\varphi)$, la frontière fine du cône convexe $(C - R^+\varphi)$.

2°. Lorsque la relation suivante est vérifiée pour φ, s.c.s., $\geqq 0$,

$$\big(v \in C;\ v(x) \geqq \varphi(x), \ \forall x \in \delta(\varphi)\big) \Rightarrow (v \geqq \varphi),$$

on appellera *support fermé de* φ, relatif à C, l'ensemble

$$\operatorname{Supp} \varphi = \overline{\delta(\varphi)}.$$

Proposition 13. *Soit* φ, s.c.s., $\geqq 0$; *si* $\varphi \in o(C)$, $\varphi \neq 0$, *alors* $\delta(\varphi) \neq \emptyset$, *et* $\overline{\delta(\varphi)}$ *est le plus petit fermé* $F \subset \Omega$ *ayant la propriété*

$$(v \in C;\ v(x) \geqq \varphi(x),\ \forall\, x \in F) \Rightarrow (v \geqq \varphi).$$

Démonstration. Il suffit de transcrire la proposition 7.

Proposition 14. *Soit* φ, *s. c. s.*, $\geqq 0$. *S'il existe un compact* $K \subset \Omega$, *tel que*

$$(v \in C;\ v(x) \geqq \varphi(x),\ \forall\, x \in K) \Rightarrow (v \geqq \varphi),$$

et si $\varphi \neq 0$, *alors* $\delta(\varphi) \neq 0$ *et* $\delta(\varphi) \subset K$.

De plus,

$$(v \in C; v(x) \geqq \varphi(x),\ \forall\, x \in \delta(\varphi)) \Rightarrow (v \geqq \varphi).$$

Démonstration. On transcrit cette fois la proposition 8.

Proposition 15. *Soit* C_2 *un cône convexe de fonctions s. c. i.* $\geqq 0$ *sur* Ω, *linéairement séparant, et soit* C_1 *un sous-cône convexe de* C_2,

$$C_1 \subset C_2 \cap \mathscr{C}^+(\Omega).$$

Pour tous $\varphi_1, \varphi_2 \in C_1$, *on a*

$$\delta(\varphi_1 + \varphi_2) \supset \delta(\varphi_1) \cup \delta(\varphi_2),$$
$$\delta(\lambda\varphi_1) = \delta(\varphi_1).$$

Démonstration. Soient $x \in \delta(\varphi_1)$, et $\mu \in \mathfrak{M}^+(\Omega)$ telle que

$$\int v\, d\mu \leqq v(x),\quad \forall\, v \in C_2,$$

et

$$\int (\varphi_1 + \varphi_2)\, d\mu = (\varphi_1 + \varphi_2)(x).$$

On en déduit

$$\int \varphi_1\, d\mu = \varphi_1(x),$$

et comme $x \in \delta(\varphi_1)$, $\mu = \varepsilon_x$, ce qui montre que $x \in \delta(\varphi_1 + \varphi_2)$.

Bibliographie

[1] R. Arens, Representation of moments by integrals, Illinois J. Math. **7** (1963), 609—614.

[2] H. Bauer, Silovscher Rand und Dirichletsches Problem, Ann. Inst. Fourier **11** (1961), 89 bis 136.

[3] G. Choquet, Le problème des moments, Séminaire Choquet: Initiation à l'Analyse, 1re année, 1962, n^0 4.

[4] A. Grothendieck, Espaces vectoriels topologiques, 3a ediçao, Sao Paulo 1964 (multigr.).

[5] P.-A. Meyer, Probabilités et potentiel, Act. Sci. et Ind. No. 1318, Paris 1966 (Publ. Inst. Math. Univ. Strasbourg No. 14).

[6] G. Mokobodzki, Balayage défini par un cône convexe de fonctions numériques sur un espace compact, C. R. Acad. Sci. Paris **254** (1962), 803—805.

[7] G. Mokobodzki et D. Sibony, Cônes de fonctions continues, C. R. Acad. Sci. Paris **264** (1967), 15—18.

[8] I. Namioka, Partially ordered linear topological vector spaces, Memoirs Amer. Math. Soc. 24 (1957).

[9] D. Sibony, Sur les transformations conservant l'harmonicité, C. R. Acad. Sci. Paris **262** (1966), 748—751.

ORDERED SET OF CLASSES OF COMPACTIFICATIONS

Ladislav Skula (Brno)

n this report I shall mean by a topological space a space R fulfilling following axioms: $\overline{\emptyset} = \emptyset$; $X \subseteqq \overline{X}$ for each $X \subseteqq R$; $\overline{X \cup Y} = \overline{X} \cup \overline{Y}$ for each $X, Y \subseteqq R$ and any two distinct points have disjoint neighbourhoods.

In his book [1], Čech calls this space a *separated closure space*. We can get the axioms of this space from axioms for Hausdorff space by omitting the axiom $\overline{\overline{X}} = \overline{X}$.

Let R be a topological space, $\mathfrak{a}$ be a proper filter on R and x be an element of R. We shall say that x is a *cluster point* of $\mathfrak{a}$ in R if x belongs to $\bigcap \overline{A}\ (A \in \mathfrak{a})$. R is said to be *compact* if every proper filter on R has a cluster point in R.

A system $\mathscr{S}$ of sets of a space R is called a *cover* (*interior cover*) of a set $M \subseteqq R$ if there exists to any $p \in M$, $X \in \mathscr{S}$ such that $p \in X$ (X is a neighbourhood of p).

These notions (cluster point of a filter, compact space, cover and interior cover) are introduced in [1]. Here the following assertion 1 is introduced, too.

1. *A space is compact iff each interior cover contains a finite cover.*

Let R be a topological space. A set $Q \subseteqq R$ is called *relatively compact in the space R* if any interior cover of a space R contains a finite cover of the set Q.

The notion of a relatively compact set in topological spaces without axiom $\overline{\overline{X}} = \overline{X}$ is introduced in [2].

The space R is called a *compactification* (*relative compactification*) of the space Q if Q is a dense subspace of R and R is compact (Q is relatively compact in R).

If P_1 and P_2 are compactifications (relative compactifications) of a topological space Q, let us put $P_1 \leqq P_2$ if there exists a mapping f of P_2 into P_1 such that $f(x) = x$ for $x \in Q$ with the following property: $z \in P_2$ and V is a neighbourhood of $f(z)$, then a neighbourhood U of the point z exists such that $U \cap Q \subseteqq V$.

For completely regular compactifications P_1, P_2 of a completely regular space Q, we usually define $P_1 \leqq P_2$ iff there exists a continuous mapping f of P_2 into P_1 such that $f(x) = x$ for $x \in Q$. This definition of the relation $\leqq$ is equivalent to the former definition of the relation $\leqq$ but for completely regular compactifications of a completely regular space.

The following assertions are introduced without proofs. Those will be published in a paper in Czechoslovak Mathematical Journal.

2. *The relation* $\leqq$ *is a quasiordering.*

Let us put $P_1 \sim P_2$ for compactifications (relative compactifications) P_1, P_2 of a topological space Q, if $P_1 \leqq P_2$ and $P_2 \leqq P_1$. The relation $\sim$ is an equivalence and the relation $\leqq$ for classes of this equivalence is an ordering. Let us denote by $K(Q)$ $(R(Q))$ the set of all classes of this equivalence ordered by means of the relation $\leqq$.

3. *For a space* Q *it holds* $K(G) \cong R(Q)$.

Let us denote for a space $Q: l(Q) = \text{card}\,\{\mathfrak{a} \mid \mathfrak{a}$ is an ultrafilter on Q which has not a cluster point in $Q\}$. Then it holds:

4. *The ordered sets* $K(Q)$ *and* $R(Q)$ *are modular (distributive) lattices iff* $l(Q) \leqq 3$ $(l(Q) \leqq 2)$.

I know some families of spaces when $K(Q)$ and $R(Q)$ are lattices, but I do not know necessary and sufficient conditions for a topological space Q when $K(Q)$ and $R(Q)$ are lattices.

Let Q be a topological space embedded into a topological space P. Let f be a continuous mapping of Q into a space R. The mapping F of the space P into R is a *χ-extension of the mapping f on P* if F has the following properties:

1) $F(x) = f(x)$ for $x \in Q$,

2) for $z \in P$ and for a neighbourhood V of the point $F(z)$ there exists a neighbourhood U of the point z such that $F(U - Q) \subseteqq \overline{V \cap f(Q)}$ and $F(U \cap Q) = f(U \cap \cap Q) \subseteqq V \cap f(Q)$.

A space P is called an *$\mathfrak{h}$-compactification of a space Q* if P is a compactification of the space Q and if to any continuous mapping of the space Q into some compact space there exists a χ-extension on P.

5. *For any space* Q *there exists an* $\mathfrak{h}$*-compactification. If* P_1, P_2 *are* $\mathfrak{h}$*-compactifications of a space* Q*, then there exists a homeomorphismus* h *of the space* P_2 *on the space* P_1 *such that for* $x \in Q$ *we have* $h(x) = x$.

According to this assertion $\mathfrak{h}$-compactification of a space Q is "in the essential" one-to-one defined and we are going to denote it by $\mathfrak{h}(Q)$.

6. *Let* Q *be a space and* $\mathfrak{h} \in K(Q)$ $(R(Q))$ *such that* $\mathfrak{h}(Q) \in \mathfrak{h}$*. Then* $\mathfrak{h}$ *is the greatest element in the ordered set* $K(Q)$ $(R(Q))$.

7. *To any continuous mapping* f *of a space* Q *into a space* R *in which the set* $f(Q)$ *is relatively compact, there exists a* χ*-extension on the space* $\mathfrak{h}(Q)$.

We shall call a topological space R a *D-space* if it is a Hausdorff space and if for any dense set H in R, the set $R - H$ is relatively compact in R.

In case, Q is a completely regular space, then it holds $\mathfrak{h}(Q) \geqq \beta(Q)$. The following theorem gives necessary and sufficient conditions when $\mathfrak{h}(Q) = \beta(Q)$.

8. *Let* Q *be a topological space. Then the following statements are equivalent:*

(A) $\mathfrak{h}(Q)$ *is a Hausdorff space,*

(B) Q *is a completely regular space and* $\mathfrak{h}(Q) = \beta(Q)$,

(C) Q *is a D-space.*

References

[1] E. ČECH, Topological spaces, Prague 1966.

[2] E. ČECH, Topologické prostory, Praha 1959.

A GENERAL REALCOMPACTIFICATION METHOD

J. VAN DER SLOT (Amsterdam)

It is well-known (see [4]) that if X is a completely regular space, then there exists a (unique) Hausdorff compactification βX of X with the following properties: 1) the closures in βX of the zerosets of X form a base for the closed sets of βX, 2) every two disjoint zerosets of X have disjoint closures in βX. In the literature βX is called the Čech-Stone compactification of X.

Definition. Two subsets A and B of a topological space are *screened* by a finite collection of subsets $\mathfrak{E}$, iff no member of $\mathfrak{E}$ intersects both A and B. A subbase $\mathfrak{S}$ for the closed sets of a space X satisfies the condition of *subbase-regularity* if each point p and member $S \in \mathfrak{S}$ not containing p are screened by a finite cover of X consisting of members of $\mathfrak{S}$. $\mathfrak{S}$ satisfies the condition of *subbase-normality* iff each two disjoint members of $\mathfrak{S}$ are screened by a finite cover of X consisting of members of $\mathfrak{S}$.

If X is a completely regular space then the family of all zerosets is a closed (sub)-base of X which satisfies the conditions of subbase-regularity and subbase-normality.

The following generalization of the Čech-Stone compactification has been proved in [1] and [3] (see also [2]).

Theorem. *Let X be a T_1-space and $\mathfrak{S}$ a closed subbase for X, which satisfies the conditions of subbase-regularity and subbase-normality. Then there exists a Hausdorff compactification $\beta_{\mathfrak{S}} X$ of X with the following properties.*

1⁰. *The closures in $\beta_{\mathfrak{S}} X$ of the members of $\mathfrak{S}$ form a closed subbase for $\beta_{\mathfrak{S}} X$ which satisfies the conditions of subbase-regularity and subbase-normality.*

2⁰. *Every two disjoint members of $\mathfrak{S}$ have disjoint closures in $\beta_{\mathfrak{S}} X$.*

It is natural to ask whether or not the Hewitt realcompactification vX of a completely regular space X can be generalized in a similar way. The purpose of this note is, to show, that this is indeed the case.

Recall that a space is *realcompact* provided that every maximal centered family of zerosets with the countable intersection property, has nonempty intersection. Every completely regular space X has a completely regular realcompactification vX such that 1. the closures in vX of the zerosets of X form a base for the closed sets of vX; 2. if a countable family of zerosets of X has empty intersection then their closures in vX have empty intersection in vX. vX is called the *Hewitt realcompactification* of X (see [4]).

Definition. A subbase $\mathfrak{S}$ for the closed sets of a space X satisfies the *countability condition*, iff each countable cover of X by members of $\{X \setminus S \mid S \in \mathfrak{S}\}$ has a countable refinement of members of $\mathfrak{S}$.

Theorem. *Let be X a T_1-space and $\mathfrak{S}$ a closed subbase for X, which satisfies the subbase-regularity, subbase-normality and countability conditions. Then there exists a completely regular realcompactification $v_{\mathfrak{S}} X$ of X with the following properties:*

1^0. *The closures in $v_{\mathfrak{S}} X$ of the members of $\mathfrak{S}$ form a closed subbase for $v_{\mathfrak{S}} X$ which satisfies the subbase—regularity, subbase-normality and countability conditions. Each maximal centered system of this collection satisfying c.i.p. (countable intersection property) has non empty intersection in $v_{\mathfrak{S}} X$.*

2^0. *If $\{S_i \mid i = 1, 2, \ldots\}$ is a countable subcollection of $\mathfrak{S}$ with empty intersection, then their closures in $v_{\mathfrak{S}} X$ have empty intersection in $v_{\mathfrak{S}} X$.*

Furthermore we have $v_{\mathfrak{S}} X = X$ if and only if each maximal centered family of members of $\mathfrak{S}$ satisfying c.i.p. has non empty intersection in X.

Theorem. *Let X and Y be spaces, and $\mathfrak{S}$ and $\mathfrak{T}$ closed subbases for X and Y respectively, which satisfy the subbase-regularity, subbase-normality and countability conditions. If f is a (continuous) map of X into Y such that $f^{-1}(T) \in \mathfrak{S}$ for each $T \in \mathfrak{T}$, then there exists a continuous extension of f which carries $v_{\mathfrak{S}} X$ into $v_{\mathfrak{T}} Y$.*

References

[1] J. M. AARTS, Dimension and Deficiency in General Topology, Thesis, Amsterdam 1966.
[2] O. FRINK, Compactifications and seminormal spaces, Amer. J. Math. **86** (1964), 602—607.
[3] J. DE GROOT and J. M. AARTS, Complete regularity as a separation axiom (issued for publication).
[4] L. GILLMAN and M. JERISON, Rings of continuous functions, Princeton 1960.

ZUSAMMENHANG UND BOGENWEISER ZUSAMMENHANG VON KOMPAKTIFIZIERUNGEN UND DEREN ADJUNKTEN

Ju. M. Smirnow (Moskau)

Für eine umfangreiche Raumklasse $\mathcal{H}$[1]) von vollständig regulären Räumen, unter denen insbesondere alle Räume mit abzählbarer Basis vorkommen, werden wir notwendige und hinreichende Bedingungen dafür angeben, daß jeder Raum $X \in \mathcal{H}$ eine zusammenhängende oder lokal zusammenhängende Kompaktifizierung hat (Theorem 8 und 9). Außerdem werden wir bestätigen, daß jeder Raum X der Klasse $\mathcal{H}$ eine Kompaktifizierung cX mit zusammenhängendem, lokal zusammenhängendem sowie bogenweise zusammenhängendem Adjunkt $cX - X$ besitzt (Theorem 4). Die genannten Aussagen sind alle recht eng miteinander verknüpft. In allen Fällen kann man überdies noch von der zu konstruierenden Kompaktifizierung verlangen, daß sie dasselbe Gewicht wie X hat und die Dimension $\dim cX$ nicht größer als $1 + \dim X$ ist.[2]) Sämtliche mitgeteilten Resultate sind, wie uns scheint, interessant und sogar für Räume mit abzählbarer Basis neu. Das Theorem 4 kann man noch erheblich verschärfen, wenn man den Begriff des bogenweisen Zusammenhanges in der folgenden Weise modifiziert.

A. Mit I^n bezeichnen wir einen n-dimensionalen Kubus, d. h. das Tychonoffsche Produkt von n abgeschlossenen Intervallen $[\![a_i, b_i]\!]$, $n = 1, 2, \ldots, \infty$. Mit $\check{I}^n$ bezeichnen wir das ,,Innere"[3]) dieses Kubus, d. h. das n-fache Tychonoffsche Produkt der offenen Intervalle $[\![a_i, b_i]\!] - \{a_i, b_i\}$.

Definition 1. Die eineindeutigen stetigen Bilder $\check{f}\check{I}^n$ des ,,Inneren" des Kubus $\check{I}^n$ nennen wir *Kraken der Ordnung n*.

Definition 2. Kompaktifizierungen bK^n des Kraken K^n werden *Fortsetzungen des Kraken* genannt, wenn die eineindeutige stetige Abbildung $\check{f}\colon \check{I}^n \to K^n$ eine stetige Fortsetzung $f\colon I^n \to bK^n$ zuläßt.[4])

---

[1]) Vgl. zur genauen Erklärung von $\mathcal{H}$ die Definition 7.

[2]) Die Dimension ist hier im Sinne der Überdeckungsdimension gemeint. Der Summand 1 kann bei nulldimensionalem Ausgangsraum schon nicht mehr entbehrt werden.

[3]) Das ,,Innere" des Hilbertschen Kubus I^∞ ist allerdings nicht offen in I^∞, es ist auch nicht bei Homöomorphien invariant.

[4]) Die angegebenen Definitionen sind für die Ordnung $n = 1$ nicht sehr belangreich, obwohl sie nicht sinnlos werden. Es gibt überhaupt nur fünf topologisch verschiedene Fortsetzungen des Kraken K^1, das sind die Strecke, die Kreislinie, die ,,Ziffern" 8 und 9 sowie der ,,Kneifer" (d. h. zwei durch einen Steg verbundene Kreislinien).

Lemma 1. *Es sei* $2 \leqq i \leqq n \leqq \infty$. *Jeder n-dimensionale Kubus* I^n *ist eine Fortsetzung eines Kraken* K^i *der Ordnung i, wobei* $K^i \subset \check{I}^n$ *gilt.*

Lemma 2. *Es sei* $2 \leqq i \leqq n \leqq \infty$. *Jede Fortsetzung* bK^n *eines Kraken* K^n *der Ordnung n ist auch eine Fortsetzung eines in* K^n *liegenden Kraken* K^i *der Ordnung i.*

Theorem 1. *Zu jedem Raum X der Klasse* $\mathscr{H}$ *gibt es eine Kompaktifizierung* cX, *deren Adjunkt* $cX - X$ *eine Basis von (in* $cX - X$*) offenen Mengen U besitzt, so daß* $cX - X$ *selbst zu dieser Basis gehört und die abgeschlossene Hülle* $\overline{U}^{cX}$ *für jedes U der Basis Fortsetzung eines in* $\overline{U}^{(cX-X)}$ *liegenden Kraken von unendlicher Ordnung ist. Insbesondere ist also* $\overline{cX - X}^{cX}$ *selbst die Fortsetzung eines Kraken* K^∞.

Bemerkung 1. Von der Kompaktifizierung cX kann man verlangen, daß sie dasselbe Gewicht wie X hat.

Bemerkung 2. Anstelle von Kraken unendlicher Ordnung kann man in dem Theorem auch Kraken der Ordnung n $(n > 1)$ verlangen. (Bei $n = 1$ müßte man die Definition des Kraken der Ordnung 1 ändern.)

Bemerkung 3. Bei Betrachtungen mit der Krakenordnung n kann von cX gefordert werden, daß $\dim cX \leqq 1 + n + \dim X$ gilt.

Bemerkung 4. Alle zu Beginn des Artikels genannten Resultate sind einfache Folgerungen aus unserem Theorem 1, mit Ausnahme des Satzes über die Dimension der gesuchten Kompaktifizierung cX für nulldimensionale Räume X.

Definition 3. Die Erweiterung cX des Raumes X nennen wir *I^n-zusammenhängend innerhalb X*, wenn je zwei Punkte x und y aus cX einer topologischen Zelle hI^n angehören mit $hI^n - \{x, y\} \subset X$.

Definition 4. Die Erweiterung cX des Raumes X nennen wir *lokal-I^n-zusammenhängend innerhalb X*, wenn eine solche offene Basis von X existiert, daß für alle Elemente U dieser Basis die abgeschlossenen Hüllen $\overline{U}^{cX}$ innerhalb $\overline{U}^X$ I^n-zusammenhängend sind.

Bemerkung 5. In den vorstehenden Definitionen kann man überdies von den Punkten x, y voraussetzen, daß sie „Randpunkte" der Zelle hI^n sind, d. h. nicht zu $h\check{I}^n$ gehören.

Lemma 3. *Jede Fortsetzung* bX^n *eines Kraken* K^n *ist für* $n = 2, 3, \ldots, \infty$ *I^n-zusammenhängend innerhalb* K^n.

Theorem 2. *Zu jedem Raum X der Klasse* $\mathscr{H}$ *gibt es eine Kompaktifizierung* cX, *so daß* $\overline{cX - X}^{cX}$ *innerhalb des Adjunkts* $cX - X$ *lokal-I^n-zusammenhängend ist.*

Definition 3'. Der Raum X heißt *I^n-zusammenhängend*, wenn er innerhalb X I^n-zusammenhängend ist.

Definition 4'. Der Raum X heißt *lokal-I^n-zusammenhängend*, wenn er innerhalb X lokal-I^n-zusammenhängend ist.

Theorem 3. *Zu jedem Raum X der Klasse* $\mathscr{H}$ *gibt es eine Kompaktifizierung* cX, *deren Adjunkt* $cX - X$ *lokal-I^∞-zusammenhängend sowie I^∞-zusammenhängend ist. Daraus folgt dann also für das Adjunkt* $cX - X$ *der bogenweise Zusammenhang im großen wie im kleinen.*

Definition 5. Der Raum X heißt *zusammenhängend in der Dimension* n ($n = 1, 2, \ldots, \infty$), wenn er bei $n < \infty$ durch keine höchstens $(n - 2)$-dimensionale und bei $n = \infty$ durch keine höchstens schwach-unendlich-dimensionale[5]) abgeschlossene Menge zerlegt wird.

Definition 6. Der Raum X heißt *lokal zusammenhängend in der Dimension* n, wenn er eine offene Basis hat, deren Elemente im Sinne der vorherigen Definition zusammenhängend in der Dimension n sind.

Lemma 4. *Jeder lokal-I^n-zusammenhängende Raum ist auch in der Dimension* n ($n = 1, 2, \ldots, \infty$) *lokal zusammenhängend.*

Theorem 4. *Zu jedem Raum der Klasse* $\mathscr{H}$ *gibt es eine Kompaktifizierung* cX, *deren Adjunkt* $cX - X$ *zusammenhängend in der Dimension* ∞ *und auch lokal zusammenhängend in der Dimension* ∞ *ist.*

Bemerkung. In den Theoremen 2, 3, 4 kann man zusätzlich von der Kompaktifizierung cX noch erreichen, daß ihr Gewicht gleich dem Gewicht des Ausgangsraumes ist. Außerdem kann man, wenn man anstelle der geforderten Eigenschaft für $n = \infty$ nur $n < \infty$ verlangt, erreichen, daß $\dim cX \leqq 1 + \max\{n, \dim X\}$ ist.

Definition 7. Einen vollständig regulären Raum X zählen wir genau dann *zur Klasse* $\mathscr{H}$, wenn er eine Kompaktifizierung cX besitzt, so daß dabei $\overline{cX - X}^{cX}$ metrisierbar ist und in $cX - X$ eine dichte Menge D existiert, wovon jeder Punkt $x \in D$ eine abzählbare Umgebungsbasis bzgl. cX hat.[6])

B. Jeder Raum mit abzählbarer Basis gehört zur Klasse $\mathscr{H}$.

Bemerkung 6. Nicht jeder lokal kompakte Raum gehört zur Klasse $\mathscr{H}$; dennoch hat jeder lokal kompakte Raum natürlich in seiner Alexandroff-Kompaktifizierung eine Kompaktifizierung mit zusammenhängendem und lokal-zusammenhängendem Adjunkt.

Beispielsweise liegt der Raum T_Ω aller transfiniten Zahlen, die kleiner als Ω sind, nicht in der Klasse $\mathscr{H}$; T_Ω läßt sich nur einpunktig kompaktifizieren.

C. Wenn der Raum X eine Kompaktifizierung cX hat, für deren Adjunkt die Abschließung $\overline{cX - X}^{cX}$ die Fortsetzung eines Kraken ist, so ist $\overline{cX - X}^{cX}$ metrisierbar.

Bemerkung 7. Die zweite Bedingung in der Definition 7 ist wesentlich. Man kann nämlich leicht zwei zusammenhängende im Čechschen Sinne [1] vollständige (d. h. absolute G_δ-) Räume konstruieren, wobei beide eine Kompaktifizierung mit metrisierbarer Abschließung ihres Adjunkts besitzen, aber der erste Raum keine Kompaktifizierung mit zusammenhängendem Adjunkt und der zweite keine Kompaktifizierung mit lokal zusammenhängendem Adjunkt besitzt.

---

[5]) Der Raum X heißt schwach-unendlich-dimensional [2], wenn für jede abzählbare Familie von abgeschlossenen Mengenpaaren A_i, B_i disjunkte Umgebungen OA_i und OB_i existieren mit $\bigcap_i (X - OA_i - OB_i) = \emptyset$. Bekanntlich ist der Hilbertsche Kubus I^∞ in der Dimension ∞ zusammenhängend.

[6]) Die Räume der Klasse $\mathscr{H}$ kann man auch mittels des Begriffs einer Struktur von fortsetzbaren Säumen [3] charakterisieren.

Die erste Bedingung der Definition 7 ist gleichfalls wesentlich in dem folgenden Sinne: Es gibt einen perfekt normalen Raum, der keine Kompaktifizierung mit zusammenhängendem Adjunkt besitzt, obwohl er aber Kompaktifizierungen aufweist, deren Adjunkt in allen ihren Punkten eine abzählbare Basis hat.

Der Beweis des Theorems 1 greift auf die folgenden drei Sätze zurück. Dazu führen wir an die

Definition 8. Wir sagen, daß der Raum Y *mit n-dimensionalen topologischen Zellen ausgefüllt ist* ($n = 0, 1, \ldots, \infty$), wenn eine Familie von zueinander paarweise fremden n-dimensionalen Zellen in Y existiert, so daß jede nicht leere offene Menge des Raumes Y eine dieser Zellen enthält.

Theorem 5. *Es sei $n = 1, 2, \ldots, \infty$. Gibt es zu dem Raum X eine Kompaktifizierung aX, deren Adjunkt $aX - X$ eine abzählbare dichte Menge enthält, so daß die Kompaktifizierung aX in jedem dieser Punkte der dichten Adjunktmenge eine abzählbare Basis besitzt, so läßt sich auch eine Kompaktifizierung $bX \geqq aX$ mit den folgenden Eigenschaften finden:*

1. $\dim bX \leqq \max\{n, \dim aX\}$.
2. *Für das Gewicht der Kompaktifizierung gilt $w(bX) = w(aX)$ und $w(\overline{bX - X}^{bX}) = w(\overline{aX - X}^{aX})$.*
3. *Das Adjunkt $bX - X$ ist mit n-dimensionalen Zellen ausgefüllt.*

Theorem 6. *Ist die Kompaktifizierung bY des Raumes Y mit n-dimensionalen Zellen ausgefüllt ($n = 2, 3, \ldots, \infty$), so existieren ein Raum X und eine Kompaktifizierung cX von X mit den folgenden Eigenschaften:*

1. *bY läßt sich durch eine Abbildung f stetig auf cX abbilden, wobei $Y = f^{-1}(X)$ und die Abbildung auf dem Adjunkt $bY - Y$ sogar eineindeutig ist.*
2. $\dim cX \leqq 1 + \dim bY$.
3. *Die Kompaktifizierung cX besitzt die im Theorem 1 genannten Eigenschaften hinsichtlich der Kraken der Ordnung n.*

Theorem 7. *Hat der Raum X eine Kompaktifizierung bX, deren Adjunkt $bX - X$ mit n-dimensionalen Zellen ausgefüllt ist ($n = 2, 3, \ldots, \infty$), und läßt sich die Abschließung $\overline{bX - X}^{bX}$ metrisieren, so gibt es zu X eine Kompaktifizierung cX mit den folgenden Eigenschaften:*

1. $cX \leqq bX$.
2. $\dim cX \leqq 1 + \dim bX$.
3. *cX besitzt die im Theorem 1 genannten Eigenschaften hinsichtlich der Kraken der Ordnung n.*

Wir führen nun noch die Theoreme über zusammenhängende und lokal zusammenhängende Kompaktifizierungen an.

Definition 9. Den Raum X nennen wir *kompakt-zusammenhängend*, wenn er keine eigentliche offen-abgeschlossene kompakte Menge enthält.

D. Jeder zusammenhängende Raum ist kompakt-zusammenhängend. Jeder kompakt-zusammenhängende kompakte Raum ist auch zusammenhängend.

E. Jede offene Menge eines Hausdorffschen kompakt zusammenhängenden Raumes ist auch kompakt-zusammenhängend.

F. Hat ein kompakt zusammenhängender Raum X eine Kompaktifizierung cX mit zusammenhängendem Adjunkt $cX - X$, so ist cX zusammenhängend.

Theorem 8. *Zu jedem Raum aus der Klasse $\mathscr{H}$ gibt es genau dann eine zusammenhängende Kompaktifizierung, wenn er kompakt-zusammenhängend ist.*

Bemerkung 8. Man kann hier ähnlich zu der Bemerkung 7 und 7′ Beispiele von Räumen dafür angeben, daß die Bedingungen der Definition 7 für die Gültigkeit des Theorems wesentlich sind.

Bemerkung 9. Für die Konstruktion der gesuchten Kompaktifizierung sind zwei Schritte und deren Konsequenzen wesentlich. Es sei zum Beispiel aS das Produkt der Strecke I mit der Folge $\{o\} \cup \left\{\frac{1}{n} \mid n \in N\right\}$ und $S = aS - \left\{\left(p, \frac{1}{n}\right) \mid n \in N\right\}$, wobei p einen Endpunkt der Strecke bezeichnet. Dann ist der Raum S kompakt-zusammenhängend, er hat demzufolge eine zusammenhängende Kompaktifizierung. Ist jedoch $cS \geqq bS \leqq aS$, so kann cS (und auch bS) nicht zusammenhängend sein. Also ist auch das Adjunkt $cS - S$ nicht zusammenhängend.

Theorem 9. *Der Raum X aus der Klasse $\mathscr{H}$ besitzt genau dann eine lokal zusammenhängende Kompaktifizierung, wenn X eine Struktur (im Sinne von* Tukey*) von endlichen abgeschlossenen Überdeckungen hat, deren Überdeckungselemente sämtlich kompakt-zusammenhängend sind.*

Bemerkung 10. Man kann in den Theoremen 8 und 9 auch noch zusätzlich verlangen, daß das Gewicht der gesuchten Kompaktifizierung cX gleich dem Gewicht des Ausgangsraumes X ist und darüber hinaus noch $\dim cX \leqq 1 + \dim X$ gilt.

Bemerkung 11. Die Bedingungen der Endlichkeit und der Abgeschlossenheit für die in Theorem 9 auftretenden Überdeckungen sind wesentlich. Es gibt nämlich eine ebene zusammenhängende und lokal zusammenhängende Menge mit den folgenden Eigenschaften:

1. Sie hat eine Struktur von endlichen offenen Überdeckungen, deren Elemente sämtlich kompakt-zusammenhängend sind.
2. Sie hat eine Struktur von lokal endlichen (bzw. unendlichen) offenen (bzw. abgeschlossenen) Überdeckungen, deren Elemente sämtlich zusammenhängend sind.
3. Sie hat jedoch keine lokal zusammenhängende Kompaktifizierung.

Bemerkung 12. Man kann zur Konstruktion von lokal zusammenhängenden Kompaktifizierungen den entsprechend modifizierten Satz F nicht anwenden. Es gibt nämlich eine ebene zusammenhängende und lokal zusammenhängende Menge P mit den folgenden Eigenschaften:

1. Sie besitzt eine Struktur aus endlichen offenen (abgeschlossenen) Überdeckungen, deren Elemente sämtlich zusammenhängend sind.
2. Die Abschließung bP von P in der Ebene ist kompakt, aber nicht lokal-zusammenhängend.
3. Das Adjunkt $bP - P$ ist zusammenhängend und lokal-zusammenhängend. (Dazu ändere man leicht das in Bemerkung 9 gewählte Beispiel ab.)

Das Interesse an den Problemen, welche wir hier lösten, entstand bei mir in Greifswald durch Gespräche mit W. Rinow und J. Flachsmeyer. Das Theorem 9 ist eine Antwort auf eine Frage von J. Flachsmeyer. Meine Freunde A. S. Parchomenko (von Parchomenko kam die Frage nach der minimalen Dimension der gesuchten Kompaktifizierung), O. W. Lokuziewski und B. T. Lewschenko unterstützten mich in den schweren Stunden meiner Arbeit. Die Gespräche mit ihnen waren mir wertvoll. Allen sage ich meinen herzlichen Dank.

Literatur

[1] E. Čech, On bicompact spaces, Ann. Math. **38** (1937), 823–844.

[2] Yu. M. Smirnov, On dimensional properties of infinite-dimensional spaces, Proc. First Symposium on General Topology, Prague 1961; Prague 1962, p. 334–336.

[3] Ю. М. Смирнов, О размерности наростов бикомпактных расширений близостных и топологических пространств II, Матем. сборник **71** (1966), 454–482.

[4] J. Tukey, Convergence and uniformity in topology, Princeton 1940.

ZERLEGUNG METRISCHER RÄUME IN NIRGENDS DICHTE MENGEN

PETR ŠTĚPÁNEK und PETR VOPĚNKA (Praha)

In der vorliegenden Arbeit benutzen wir einige Resultate aus der Mengenlehre, nämlich die über die sogenannten ∇-Modelle. Diese Resultate sind in [1] angegeben.

Definition 1. Wir sagen, daß ein metrischer Raum $\langle X, \mathscr{T} \rangle$ *nirgends separabel* ist, wenn die folgende Bedingung gilt: Für jede offene nichtleere Menge $o \subset X$ ist der Unterraum $\langle o, \mathscr{T} \rangle$ nicht separabel.

Das Hauptresultat formulieren wir im folgenden

Satz 1. *Es sei* $\langle X, \mathscr{T} \rangle$ *ein metrischer nirgends separabler Raum. Dann gibt es ein System von Mengen* $\{F_\lambda\}_{\lambda \in \omega_1}$, *für das die folgenden Bedingungen gelten:*

(1) *Für jede Ordnungszahl* $\lambda \in \omega_1$ *ist* F_λ *eine abgeschlossene nirgends dichte Menge in* $\langle X, \mathscr{T} \rangle$.

(2) *Wenn* $\lambda_1 \in \lambda_2 \in \omega_1$ *gilt, dann gilt* $F_{\lambda_1} \subset F_{\lambda_2}$.

(3) $X = \bigcup_{\lambda \in \omega_1} F_\lambda$.

Folgerung. Es sei $\langle X, \mathscr{T} \rangle$ ein linearer metrischer Raum, der nicht separabel ist. Dann gibt es ein System von Mengen $\{F_\lambda\}_{\lambda \in \omega_1}$ mit den Eigenschaften (1), (2), (3).

Die Zerlegung eines allgemeinen metrischen Raumes hängt, wie wir gezeigt haben, von der Kontinuumshypothese ab.

Literatur

[1] P. VOPĚNKA, General theory of ∇-models, Comment. Math. Univ. Carolinae 8 (1967), 145—170

[2] P. ŠTĚPÁNEK and P. VOPĚNKA, Decomposition of metric spaces into nowhere dense sets, Comment. Math. Univ. Carolinae 8 (1967), 387—404.

THE ROLE OF COMPACTIFICATIONS IN THE THEORY OF TYCHONOFF SPACES

HISAHIRO TAMANO (Fort Worth, Tex./U.S.A.)

The existence of compactification is a characteristic property of Tychonoff spaces, and the effective utilization of compactification may be helpful in developing the theory of Tychonoff spaces.

Let us call a subset of $\beta X \setminus X$ a virtual set. Let $\mathfrak{O} = \{O_\alpha \mid \alpha \in A\}$ be a covering of X. Put $O_\alpha^\varepsilon = C_{\beta X}(\mathrm{cl}_{\beta X}(C_X(O_\alpha)))$, and call $C(\mathfrak{O}) = C_{\beta X}(\bigcup \{O_\alpha^\varepsilon \mid \alpha \in A\})$ the co-cover for $\mathfrak{O}$. Every closed set is a co-cover for some open covering $\mathfrak{O}$ of X. For the given open covering $\mathfrak{O} = \{O_\alpha \mid \alpha \in A\}$, we can associate another virtual set $C^*(\mathfrak{O})$ which is defined as follows:

Let A^* be the subset of A with the minimal cardinality such that $\{O_\alpha \mid \alpha \in A\}$ covers X. Well order the index set A^* in such a way that $\bigcup \{O_\alpha \mid \alpha < \beta\} \neq X$ for each $\beta \in A^*$. Put $F_\alpha = C_X(\bigcup \{O_\gamma \mid \gamma < \alpha\})$ and let $C^*(\mathfrak{O}) = \bigcap \{\mathrm{cl}_{\beta X}(F_\alpha) \mid \alpha \in A\}$. We shall call $C^*(\mathfrak{O})$ the central co-cover for $\mathfrak{O}$. Clearly $C(\mathfrak{O}) \supset C^*(\mathfrak{O})$ for each $\mathfrak{O}$. The paracompactness of X is characterized by the property that central co-covers are embedded in βX.

A descending chain $\mathscr{U} = \{U_\lambda \mid \lambda \in \Lambda\}$ of subsets of βX is said to be a neighbourhood chain of C if $\bigcap \{U_\mu \mid \mu < \lambda\}$ is a neighbourhood of C for each $\lambda \in \Lambda$. $\mathscr{U}$ is said to be relatively free if $\bigcap \{\mathrm{cl}_X (U_\lambda \cap X) \mid \lambda \in \Lambda\} = \emptyset$. Let $\mathscr{U} = \{U_\lambda \mid \lambda \in \Lambda\}$, $\mathscr{V} = \{V_\lambda \mid \lambda \in \Lambda\}$ be two descending chains. Define $\mathscr{V} < \mathscr{U}$ provided that $\bigcap \{\mathrm{cl}_{\beta X}(U_\mu) \mid \mu < \lambda\} \subset \mathrm{Int}_{\beta X} (\bigcap \{V_\mu \mid \mu < \lambda\})$.

Theorem. *X is paracompact if and only if the following conditions are satisfied for each central co-cover $C \subset \beta X \setminus X$:*

1. *C has a relatively free neighbourhood chain $\mathscr{U} = \{U_\lambda \mid \lambda \in \Lambda\}$.*
2. *Given a relatively free neighbourhood chain $\mathscr{U} = \{U_\lambda \mid \lambda \in \Lambda\}$ of C, there is a relatively free neighbourhood chain $\mathscr{U} = \{V_\lambda \mid \lambda \in \Lambda\}$ such that $\mathscr{V} < \mathscr{U}$.*
3. *Given two relatively free neighbourhood chains $\mathscr{U} = \{U_\lambda \mid \lambda \in \Lambda\}$ and $\mathscr{V} = \{V_\lambda \mid \lambda \in \Lambda\}$ such that $\mathscr{V} < \mathscr{U}$, there is a relatively free neighbourhood chain $\mathscr{W} = \{W_\lambda \mid \lambda \in \Lambda\}$ such that $\mathscr{V} < \mathscr{W} < \mathscr{U}$.*

Corollary. *X is paracompact if and only if every open covering has a linearly cushioned open refinement.*

Here, a covering $\mathfrak{R} = \{R_\sigma \mid \sigma \in \Sigma\}$, with a well ordered index set Σ, is said to be a linearly cushioned refinement of a covering $\mathfrak{O} = \{O_\alpha \mid \alpha \in A\}$ if there is a mapping

$\varphi: \Sigma \to A$ and the following condition is satisfied for each bounded subset Σ^* of Σ:

$$\overline{\bigcup \{R_\sigma \mid \sigma \in \Sigma^*\}} \subset \bigcup \{O_\alpha \mid \alpha \in \varphi(\Sigma^*)\}.$$

This corollary is a generalization of a well known result due to E. MICHAEL asserting that X is paracompact if and only if every open covering of X has a σ-cushioned open refinement.

THE MARTIN BOUNDARY AND ADJOINT HARMONIC FUNCTIONS

J. C. Taylor (Montreal/Can.)

In [4] Constantinescu and Cornea gave a construction of the Martin boundary which made no use of the Green's function. The main purpose of this note is to show how this construction can be extended to the axiomatic setting of Brelot.

1. Let Ω denote a locally compact space and let Φ be a collection of functions $f: \Omega \to \overline{R}$, f continuous on the complement of a compact set K_f. Then there is a unique compactification $\overline{\Omega}$ of Ω for which:

(1) each function in Φ extends continuously to $\overline{\Omega}$; and

(2) the extended functions separate the points of $\overline{\Omega} \setminus \Omega$.

This compactification will be said to *be determined by* Φ. The arguments given in [4] for the existence of the Q-compactification can be modified to prove this result.

2. Let Ω now denote a bounded domain in R^n $(n \geqq 2)$ and let $G(x, y)$ be the Green's function for Ω. Fix $y_0 \in \Omega$ and set

$$K(x, y) = \begin{cases} 1 & \text{if } x = y = y_0, \\ \dfrac{G(x, y)}{G(x, y_0)} & \text{otherwise.} \end{cases}$$

The compactification of Ω determined by the functions $x \rightsquigarrow K(x, y)$, $y \in \Omega$ is called the *Martin compactification* and the ideal boundary is called the *Martin boundary*.

The Martin compactification can be defined in the same way for any hyperbolic Riemann surface or more generally for any locally compact space Ω on which a sheaf $\mathscr{H}$ of vector spaces of continuous real-valued functions is given that satisfies the basic axioms of Brelot [2], [3] and certain other more technical axioms.

Given such a sheaf $\mathscr{H}$, Mme Hervé showed that a lower semicontinuous function G can be defined on $\Omega \times \Omega$ with properties analogous to those of a Green's function (see proposition 18.1 in [6]). Such a function will be referred to as a *Green's function for* $\mathscr{H}$. With the aid of a Green's function G a Martin compactification can be defined. Since it is independent of the choice of G it can be called the *Martin compactification determined by* $\mathscr{H}$. Presumably, as the sheaf $\mathscr{H}$ varies so does the compactification. There seem to be no results known that give information about the dependence of the compactification on the sheaf. The main result of this note is used to show that the compactification does not change if the sheaf is "altered on a compact set" (theorem 3).

3. Let Ω be a hyperbolic Riemann surface. Denote by M the set of bounded continuous functions f on Ω such that outside a compact non polar set A (depending on f) $f = H(f, \complement A) / H(1, \complement A)$ where $H(f, \complement A)$ is the solution of the so-called normed Dirichlet problem for $\complement A$ with boundary value f on ∂A and 0 at infinity. In [4] CONSTANTINESCU and CORNEA showed that the Martin compactification of Ω is the compactification determined by M. This compactification is also the same as the compactification determined by the non-negative functions in M.

It is worth noting that a bounded continuous non-negative function f is in M if and only if, for some compact non-polar set A, $f R_1^A = R_f^A$ on $\complement A$, where $R_f^A = \inf \{V \mid V \geqq f \text{ on } A, V \text{ superharmonic on } \Omega\}$.

Let $\mathscr{H}$ be a harmonic sheaf, that is a sheaf satisfying BRELOT's axioms. Define $M^+(\mathscr{H})$ to be the set of bounded continuous functions f on Ω for which there exists a compact set A with $\mathring{A} \neq \emptyset$ and $f R_1^A = R_f^A$ on $\complement A$, the reduced function R_f^A being defined as above.

4. Let now $\mathscr{H}$ be a sheaf for which a Green's kernel G can be defined. While $y \rightsquigarrow G(x, y)$ is superharmonic it is not true in general that $x \rightsquigarrow G(x, y)$ is also superharmonic. However, if $\mathscr{H}$ is required to satisfy a further restriction then Mme HERVÉ showed that a sheaf $\mathscr{H}^*$ could be defined for which $x \rightsquigarrow G(x, y)$ is superharmonic (see Chapter VI in [6]). This sheaf, the sheaf of adjoint harmonic functions, depends on G.

Theorem 1. *Let $\mathscr{H}$ be a sheaf on Ω for which a Green's kernel G can be defined and for which G defines an adjoint sheaf $\mathscr{H}^*$. Then the Martin compactification of Ω is the compactification determined by $M^+(\mathscr{H}^*)$.*

Since for the sheaf $\mathscr{H}$ of harmonic functions on a hyperbolic Riemann surface $\mathscr{H}^* = \mathscr{H}$ this theorem extends the result of CONSTANTINESCU and CORNEA.

5. Two harmonic sheaves $\mathscr{H}_1$ and $\mathscr{H}_2$ are said to be *equivalent* (LOEB [7]) if there is a compact set A with $\mathscr{H}_1 \mid \complement A = \mathscr{H}_2 \mid \complement A$.

Theorem 2. *Let $\mathscr{H}_1$ and $\mathscr{H}_2$ be two sheaves that satisfy the conditions of theorem 1. If they are equivalent then there are Green's functions G_1 and G_2 such that the corresponding adjoint sheaves $\mathscr{H}_1^*$ and $\mathscr{H}_2^*$ are equivalent.*

Proposition. *If $\mathscr{H}_1$ and $\mathscr{H}_2$ are equivalent then $M^+(\mathscr{H}_1)$ and $M^+(\mathscr{H}_2)$ define the same compactification of Ω.*

Combining these two results with theorem 1 gives

Theorem 3. *If two sheaves satisfy the conditions of theorem 1 and are equivalent then the Martin compactifications of Ω that they define coincide.*

6. Let G be a Green's kernel for $\mathscr{H}$ and let $G^*(x, y) = G(y, x)$. Set

$$K^*(x, y) = \begin{cases} 1 & \text{if } x = y = y_0, \\ \dfrac{G^*(x, y)}{G^*(x, y_0)} & \text{otherwise}. \end{cases}$$

If G defines an adjoint sheaf $\mathscr{H}^*$ then G^* is a Green's function for $\mathscr{H}^*$. Hence, the Martin compactification defined by $\mathscr{H}^*$ is the compactification defined by $M^+(\mathscr{H})$.

However, even if $\mathscr{H}^*$ fails to exist the arguments used to prove theorem 1 show that the compactification defined by $M^+(\mathscr{H})$ coincides with the one defined by the functions $x \rightsquigarrow K^*(x, y)$, $y \in \Omega$.

By direct analogy with the work of Doob [5] the boundary of the compactification defined by $M^+(\mathscr{H})$ will be called the *entrance boundary for* $\mathscr{H}$. The Martin boundary, when it is defined, is then the *exit boundary for* $\mathscr{H}$.

7. The cone $M^+(\mathscr{H})$ can be defined not only for sheaves satisfying the axioms of Brelot, but also for those that satisfy the weaker axioms of Bauer [1]. Consequently, for such sheaves an entrance boundary can be defined.

References

[1] H. Bauer, Harmonische Räume und ihre Potentialtheorie, Berlin 1966.
[2] M. Brelot, Seminaire de theorie du potentiel, 2e annee 1958, Paris 1959.
[3] M. Brelot, Lectures on potential theory, Tata Inst. Fund. Research, Bombay 1960.
[4] C. Constantinescu und A. Corneau, Ideale Ränder Riemannscher Flächen, Berlin 1963.
[5] J. L. Doob, Discrete potential theory and boundaries, J. Math. Mech. **8** (1959), 433—458.
[6] Mme. R. M. Hervé, Recherches axiomatiques sur la theorie des fonctions surharmoniques et du potentiel, Ann. Inst. Fourier **12** (1962), 415—571.
[7] P. Loeb, An axiomatic treatment of pairs of elliptic differential equations, Ann. Inst. Fourier **16** (1966), 167—208.

ON SOME COVERING PROPERTIES OF METRIC SPACES

R. TELGÁRSKY (Wrocław)

It is known that metric spaces which admit isometric embeddings into compact metric spaces are exactly those which are totally bounded. Moreover, for totally bounded metric spaces complete extensions coincide with compact extensions. In what follows I shall discuss the following metric property weaker than that of total boundedness: for each $\varepsilon > 0$ there is a countable cover $\alpha = \alpha(\varepsilon)$ of a space such that $\delta(A) < \varepsilon$ for $A \in \alpha$ and for each $\mu > 0$ the set $\{A \in \alpha : \delta(A) > \mu\}$ is finite. Such a cover (or open base) we shall call zero ε-cover (or zero base resp.). Clearly, each totally bounded metric space has for each $\varepsilon > 0$ a zero ε-cover. It is easy to see that a σ-totally bounded metric space also has for each $\varepsilon > 0$ a zero ε-cover. (By a σ-totally bounded space we mean a metric space which is the union of countably many totally bounded subspaces.)

Theorem 1 (DUDA and TELGÁRSKY [1]). *A metric space has a zero base iff it has for each $\varepsilon > 0$ a zero ε-cover.*

However, there exists a complete metric space B_0 such that B_0 is not σ-totally bounded, but still has a zero base. Moreover, $B_0 \times B_0$ with pythagorean metric even for $\varepsilon = \delta(B_0 \times B_0)$ has no zero ε-cover and hence a fortiori, $B_0 \times B_0$ has no zero base (for a proof see [1]).

Theorem 2 (DUDA and TELGÁRSKY [1]). *A metric space (X, ϱ) has a zero base iff there exists a sequence of finite sets $N_2, N_1, \ldots$ such that for each $x \in X$ and for each $\varepsilon > 0$ there are infinitely many k such that $\varrho(x, N_k) < \varepsilon$.*

It is easy to see that a metric space has a zero base iff each open cover has a refinement which is a zero cover.

MYCIELSKI has pointed out that a Baire space of sequences B even for $\varepsilon = \delta(B) = 1$ has no zero ε-cover and therefore B also has no zero base (see [1]). Hilbert space l^2 has not a zero base. LELEK shows in [5] that the space of irrational numbers which has a zero base possesses also another base which does not contain any zero base. LEKKERKERKER [4] constructs a metrizable separable space which has an open base β such that β does not contain a zero base in any metric compatible with the topology.

Theorem 3 (LELEK [6]). *If X is a metrizable space then the following conditions are equivalent:*

1. *For each metric ϱ there is a zero ε-cover of X such that $\varepsilon = \delta(X)$.*
2. *For each metric ϱ there is a zero base in X.*

Now let us consider the following conditions:

I. For each metric ϱ, X has a zero base.

II. For each metric ϱ, X is σ-totally bounded.

III. X is σ-compact.

Clearly III $\rightarrow$ II $\rightarrow$ I. As follows from results of LELEK [6] and SIERPIŃSKI (in [2]) I $\nrightarrow$ II.

Theorem 4 (HUREWICZ [3]). *If X is an analytic set in some complete metric space then X is in each metric σ-totally bounded iff it is σ-compact.*

The question of the necessity of this proposition on X is still an open problem of HUREWICZ. The following results seem to be related to it:

Let X be any metrizable space. Then

1. X is compact iff X is totally bounded in each metric;
2. X is locally compact iff X is locally totally bounded in each metric.

References

[1] R. DUDA and R. TELGÁRSKY, On some covering properties of metric spaces, Czechoslovak. Math. J. **18** (93) (1968), 66—82.

[2] W. HUREWICZ, Über Folgen stetiger Funktionen, Fund. Math. **9** (1927), 193—204.

[3] W. HUREWICZ, Über eine Verallgemeinerung des Borelschen Theorems, Math. Z. **24** (1926), 401—421.

[4] C. G. LEKKERKERKER, On metric properties of bases for separable metric space, Nieuw Archief voor Wiskunde **13** (1965), 192—199.

[5] A. LELEK, On strongly Lindelöf metric spaces (mimeographed).

[6] A. LELEK, Some cover properties of space (in print in Fund. Math.)

KOMPAKTE MENGEN UND NICHTFORTSETZBARKEIT VON INTEGRALEN

FRANK TERPE (Greifswald)

1. Maximale eingelagerte absolutkonvergente Integrale

Definition 1. *Eingelagerter Vektorverband.* Es sei $\mathfrak{V}$ ein Vektorteilverband des σ-Vektorverbandes $\mathfrak{M}$. $\mathfrak{V}$ heißt eingelagert in $\mathfrak{M}$, wenn es zu jedem $0 \leqq f \in \mathfrak{M} - \mathfrak{V}$ eine Folge $0 \leqq v_1 \leqq v_2 \leqq \ldots \leqq f, v_i \in \mathfrak{V}$ $(i = 1, 2, \ldots)$, gibt, so daß $\sup\limits_i v_i \in \mathfrak{M} - \mathfrak{V}$ ist.

Definition 2. *Eingelagertes absolutkonvergentes Integral.* Es sei $\mathfrak{V}$ ein eingelagerter Vektorteilverband des σ-Vektorverbandes $\mathfrak{M}$; $\mathfrak{W}$ sei ein bedingt vollständiger halbgeordneter Vektorraum. Sie bilden das Paar $(\mathfrak{M}, \mathfrak{W})$. Ferner sei I eine lineare, positive und stetige Abbildung von $\mathfrak{V}$ in $\mathfrak{W}$. Stetigkeit der Abbildung I bedeutet: Aus $0 \leqq v_1 \leqq v_2 \leqq \ldots, f \in \mathfrak{M}, v_0 \leqq f, v_i \in \mathfrak{V}$ $(i = 0, 1, 2, \ldots)$ folgt stets $I(v_0) \leqq \sup\limits_i I(v_i)$. Das Paar $(I, \mathfrak{V})$ — wir schreiben dafür $I/\mathfrak{V}$ — heißt dann ein eingelagertes absolutkonvergentes Integral in dem Paar $(\mathfrak{M}, \mathfrak{W})$.

Definition 3. *Maximales eingelagertes absolutkonvergentes Integral.* Es sei $I/\mathfrak{V}$ ein eingelagertes absolutkonvergentes Integral in dem Paar $(\mathfrak{M}, \mathfrak{W})$. $I/\mathfrak{V}$ heißt maximal, wenn es auf einen beliebigen Vektorteilraum $\mathfrak{K}$ von $\mathfrak{M}$ mit $\mathfrak{V} \subset \mathfrak{K} \subseteqq \mathfrak{M}$ entweder gar keine oder mehr als eine lineare, positive und stetige Fortsetzung von $I/\mathfrak{V}$ gibt.

Vgl. hierzu [3]. Dort wurden auch die allgemeinen Eigenschaften maximaler eingelagerter absolutkonvergenter Integrale hergeleitet. Es ist nun wichtig zu wissen, wie sich die konstruktiv definierten Integrale in das Begriffsschema der in [3] begonnenen deskriptiven Theorie einordnen.

Der Vortrag bringt keine Beweise zu den Sätzen. Es wird an den entsprechenden Stellen gesagt, wo diese Beweise zu finden sind.

2. Das zu einem Maßraum gehörige Integral als maximales eingelagertes absolutkonvergentes Integral

Es sei $(\Omega, \mathfrak{A}, m)$ ein Maßraum, d. h., Ω ist eine Menge, $\mathfrak{A}$ ein σ-Mengenkörper von Teilmengen von Ω und m ein Maß auf $\mathfrak{A}$, also eine nichtnegative, σ-additive Mengenfunktion mit dem Definitionsbereich $\mathfrak{A}$, für die $m(\emptyset) = 0$ ist ($+ \infty$ als Wert für m ist zugelassen!). Es sei $I_m/\mathfrak{S}_m$ das zu dem Maßraum $(\Omega, \mathfrak{A}, m)$ gehörige Integral im Sinne von [2].

Es ergibt sich nun die Frage: Für genau welche Maßräume $(\Omega, \mathfrak{A}, m)$ ist $I_m/\mathfrak{S}_m$ ein maximales eingelagertes absolutkonvergentes Integral in dem Paar $(\mathfrak{M}_m, R)$, wobei $\mathfrak{M}_m$ der σ-Vektorverband aller bezüglich $(\Omega, \mathfrak{A}, m)$ meßbaren reellen Funktionen auf Ω und R der Vektorverband der reellen Zahlen ist.

Eine Antwort gibt der

Satz 1. *$I_m/\mathfrak{S}_m$ ist genau dann maximales eingelagertes absolutkonvergentes Integral in dem Paar $(\mathfrak{M}_m, R)$ wenn m schwach σ-endlich ist.*

Dabei nennen wir *m schwach σ-endlich*, wenn es zu jeder Menge $A \in \mathfrak{A}$ mit $m(A) = +\infty$ eine Folge $A_1 \subseteqq A_2 \subseteqq \ldots \subseteqq A$ von Mengen $A_i \in \mathfrak{A}$ $(i = 1, 2, \ldots)$ gibt, so daß $m(A_i) < +\infty$ $(i = 1, 2, \ldots)$ und $m(\bigcup_{i=1}^{\infty} A_i) = +\infty$ ist.

Zusatz. Äquivalent zur schwachen σ-Endlichkeit ist die folgende Bedingung: Zu jeder Menge $A \in \mathfrak{A}$ mit $m(A) = +\infty$ existiert eine Menge $A^* \in \mathfrak{A}$, $A^* \subseteqq W$, so daß $0 < m(A^*) < +\infty$ ist.

Beweis. Vgl. [4] oder [5].

Es gelten ferner:

Satz 2. *$I_m/\mathfrak{S}_m$ ist genau dann maximales eingelagertes absolutkonvergentes Integral in $(\mathfrak{M}_m, R)$, wenn $\mathfrak{S}_m$ eingelagert in $\mathfrak{M}_m$ ist.*

Satz 3. *$I_m/\mathfrak{S}_m$ ist genau dann maximales eingelagertes absolutkonvergentes Integral in $(\mathfrak{M}_m, R)$, wenn $\mathfrak{T}_m$ eingelagert ist in $\mathfrak{M}_m$.*

Dabei ist $\mathfrak{T}_m$ der Vektorverband der erweiterten m-Treppenfunktionen, d. h., $f \in \mathfrak{M}_m$ gehört genau dann zu $\mathfrak{T}_m$, wenn $f = \sum_{i=1}^{\infty} a_i \cdot \chi_{A_i}$ gilt, wobei $A_i \in \mathfrak{A}$, $A_i \cap A_j = \emptyset$ $(i \neq j)$ und $\sum_{i=1}^{\infty} |a_i| \cdot m(A_i) < +\infty$ ist.

Beweis. Vgl. [4].

Beispiel eines Maßraumes $(\Omega, \mathfrak{A}, m)$, für den $I_m/\mathfrak{S}_m$ nicht maximal ist in $(\mathfrak{M}_m, R)$, für den es also einen Vektorzwischenraum $\mathfrak{K}$, $\mathfrak{S}_m \subset \mathfrak{K} \subseteqq \mathfrak{M}_m$ gibt, so daß $I_m/\mathfrak{S}_m$ auf $\mathfrak{K}$ auf genau eine Weise linear, positiv und stetig fortgesetzt werden kann:

Wir setzen $\Omega := [0, 1]$, $\mathfrak{A} := \mathfrak{P}(\Omega)$, wobei $\mathfrak{P}(\Omega)$ die Potenzmenge von Ω ist. Ferner sei $m(A) := 0$ für jede höchstens abzählbare Menge $A \subseteqq \Omega$, $m(A) := +\infty$ für jede überabzählbare Menge $A \subseteqq \Omega$. $\mathfrak{M}_m$ ist dann gleich $\mathfrak{H}$, dem Vektorverband aller reellen Funktionen auf $[0, 1]$. $\mathfrak{S}_m$ besteht aus genau denjenigen Funktionen $f \in \mathfrak{M}_m$, die an höchstens abzählbar vielen Punkten von 0 verschieden sind. Ferner gilt offenbar $I_m(f) = 0$ für jedes $f \in \mathfrak{S}_m$.

Wir behaupten nun: Auf $\mathfrak{K} = \mathfrak{M}_m$ kann $I_m/\mathfrak{S}_m$ auf genau eine Weise linear, positiv und stetig fortgesetzt werden. Es sei $I/\mathfrak{M}_m$ eine lineare, positive und stetige Fortsetzung von $I_m/\mathfrak{S}_m$. Wir setzen für jede Menge $A \subseteqq [0, 1]$

$$m_I(A) := I(\chi_A);$$

m_I ist dann offenbar ein Maß auf dem σ-Mengenkörper $\mathfrak{A}$ aller Teilmengen von $[0, 1]$ und hat die folgende Eigenschaft: $m_I(\{x\}) = 0$ für jede einpunktige Teilmenge von Ω. Nach einem Satz von C. Kuratowski [1] folgt hieraus $m_I(A) = 0$ für jede Teilmenge A von $[0, 1]$. Daraus folgt aber $I(f) = 0$ für jede Funktion $f \in \mathfrak{M}_m$. Andererseits ist diese Funktion auch wirklich eine lineare, positive und stetige Fortsetzung von I_m.

3. Das Bourbaki-Integral als maximales eingelagertes absolutkonvergentes Integral

Es sei jetzt Ω ein lokalkompakter topologischer Raum, $\mathfrak{E}$ der Vektorverband der auf Ω definierten stetigen reellen Funktionen mit kompaktem Träger. Ein auf $\mathfrak{E}$ definiertes lineares und positives (und damit auch stetiges) Funktional E nennt man ein Radon-Maß auf $\mathfrak{E}$, in Zeichen $E/\mathfrak{E}$. Wir sagen dazu auch Bourbaki-Elementar-Integral. Es bezeichne $\mathfrak{S}_E$ den zu $E/\mathfrak{E}$ gehörigen Vektorverband der summierbaren reellen Funktionen auf Ω, $\mathfrak{M}_E$ den σ-Vektorverband der zu $E/\mathfrak{E}$ gehörigen meßbaren reellen Funktionen auf Ω und I_E das zu $E/\mathfrak{E}$ gehörige Bourbaki-Integral auf $\mathfrak{S}_E$.

Die Fragestellung dieses Abschnitts lautet nun:

Für genau welche Elementar-Integrale $E/\mathfrak{E}$ ist das zugehörige Bourbaki-Integral $I_E/\mathfrak{S}_E$ ein maximales eingelagertes absolut-konvergentes Integral in dem Paar $(\mathfrak{M}_E, R)$?

Es ist also auch hierbei wieder wesentlich, daß über die Maximalität des Integrals am Ausgangsobjekt der Konstruktion desselben — hier am Bourbaki-Elementar-Integral — entschieden werden soll.

Es gilt der folgende

Satz 4. *Die beiden folgenden Bedingungen sind äquivalent:*

(A) *Das zu $E/\mathfrak{E}$ gehörige Bourbaki-Integral $I_E/\mathfrak{S}_E$ ist ein maximales eingelagertes absolutkonvergentes Integral in dem Paar $(\mathfrak{M}_E, R)$.*

(B) *Ist $A \subseteqq \Omega$ und existiert zu jeder kompakten Menge $K \subseteqq \Omega$ und jedem $\varepsilon > 0$ eine Folge $0 \leqq e_1^{(K)} \leqq e_2^{(K)} \leqq \ldots, e_i^{(K)} \in \mathfrak{E}$ $(i = 1, 2, \ldots)$, so daß $\chi_{A \cap K} \leqq \sup_i e_i^{(K)}$ und $\sup_i E(e_i^{(K)}) < \varepsilon$ ist, dann existiert eine Folge $0 \leqq e_1 \leqq e_2 \leqq \ldots, e_i \in \mathfrak{E}$ $(i = 1, 2, \ldots)$, so daß $\chi_A \leqq \sup_i e_i$ gilt.*

Beweis. Vgl. [4].

Beispiele. In den folgenden Fällen von Satz 4 ist die Bedingung (B) von Satz 4 erfüllt:

(1) Ω ist kompakt,

(2) Ω ist abzählbar im Unendlichen.

Bei diesen Räumen ist also für die Maximalität von $I_E/\mathfrak{S}_E$ das Funktional E gar nicht verantwortlich, sondern nur die Topologie auf Ω.

4. Das Stone-Integral als maximales eingelagertes absolutkonvergentes Integral

Es sei jetzt Ω eine nichtleere Menge, $\mathfrak{E}$ sei ein Funktionenvektorverband von reellen Funktionen mit dem Definitionsbereich Ω, E sei ein lineares, positives und stetiges Funktional auf $\mathfrak{E}$. $E/\mathfrak{E}$ heißt dann ein Stone-Elementar-Integral auf Ω.

Durch Normvervollständigung gelangt man bekanntlich von $E/\mathfrak{E}$ zum Vektorverband $\mathfrak{S}_E$ der zugehörigen summierbaren reellen Funktionen auf Ω und durch stetige Fortsetzung zu dem zugehörigen Stone-Integral $S_E/\mathfrak{S}_E$. $\mathfrak{M}_E$ bezeichne den σ-Vektorverband der zugehörigen reellen meßbaren Funktionen auf Ω.

Die Fragestellung dieses Abschnitts lautet:

Für genau welche elementaren Integrale $E/\mathfrak{E}$ ist das zugehörige Stone-Integral $S_E/\mathfrak{S}_E$ ein maximales eingelagertes absolutkonvergentes Integral in dem Paar $(\mathfrak{M}_E, R)$?

Bei der entsprechenden Fragestellung für das Bourbaki-Integral spielten bei der Beantwortung die kompakten Teilmengen von Ω eine wichtige Rolle; vgl. Satz 4. Hier haben wir kompakte Mengen nicht zur Verfügung. Wir schaffen uns einen Ersatz für diese Mengen durch die folgende

Definition 4. *Zu $E/\mathfrak{E}$ gehörige „kompakte" Mengen.* Es sei $\mathfrak{K}_\mathfrak{E}$ das System aller Teilmengen K von $\mathfrak{E}$ mit der folgenden Eigenschaft: Es existiert ein $0 \leqq e \in \mathfrak{E}$, und es gibt zwei Zahlen $c_1 > c_2 > 0$, so daß $K = \{x; x \in \Omega \text{ und } c_1 \geqq e(x) \geqq c_2\}$ ist. Die Mengen K aus $\mathfrak{K}_\mathfrak{E}$ heißen die zu $E/\mathfrak{E}$ gehörigen „kompakten" Mengen.

Es gilt nun der folgende

Satz 5.

Voraussetzung: *$\min(1, e) \in \mathfrak{E}$ für jedes $e \in \mathfrak{E}$.*

Behauptung: *Die beiden folgenden Bedingungen sind äquivalent:*

(A) *$S_E/\mathfrak{S}_E$ ist ein maximales eingelagertes absolutkonvergentes Integral in dem Paar $(\mathfrak{M}_E, R)$.*

(C) *Ist $A \subseteqq \Omega$ und existiert zu jeder „kompakten" Menge $K \in \mathfrak{K}_\mathfrak{E}$ und jedem $\varepsilon > 0$ eine Folge $0 \leqq e_1^{(K)} \leqq e_2^{(K)} \leqq \ldots, e_i^{(K)} \in \mathfrak{E}$, so daß $\chi_{A \cap K} \leqq \sup\limits_i e_i^{(K)}$ und $\sup\limits_i E(e_i^{(K)}) < \varepsilon$ ist, so existiert eine Folge $0 \leqq e_1 \leqq e_2 \leqq \ldots, e_i \in \mathfrak{E}$, so daß $\chi_A \leqq \sup\limits_i e_i$ gilt.*

Beweis. Vgl. [6].

Beispiele. In den folgenden Fällen ist die Bedingung (C) von Satz 5 erfüllt:

(1) $1 := \chi_\Omega \in \mathfrak{E}$.

(2) Es gibt eine Folge von Funktionen $0 \leqq e_1 \leqq e_2 \leqq \ldots, e_i \in \mathfrak{E}$, so daß $\sup\limits_i e_i(x) = +\infty$ für alle $x \in \Omega$ ist.

Beispiel eines Stone-Elementar-Integrals $E/\mathfrak{E}$, für das $\min(1, e) \in \mathfrak{E}$ für jedes $e \in \mathfrak{E}$ gilt, das aber die Bedingung (C) von Satz 5 nicht erfüllt, für das also das zugehörige Stone-Integral $S_E/\mathfrak{S}_E$ kein maximales eingelagertes absolutkonvergentes Integral in $(\mathfrak{M}_E, R)$ ist:

Es sei $\Omega := [0, 1]$. $\mathfrak{E}$ sei das System der reellen Funktionen auf Ω mit den folgenden Eigenschaften:

(a) $e/[0, 1/2]$ ist stetig; (b) $e(x) = 0$ für jedes $x \in (1/2, 1]$. Wir setzen $E(e) := \int\limits_0^1 e(x)\,dx$, wobei rechts das Lebesgue-Integral steht. $E/\mathfrak{E}$ ist dann offenbar ein Stone-Elementar-Integral. Ferner gilt offenbar $\min(1, e) \in \mathfrak{E}$ für jedes $e \in \mathfrak{E}$. Es sei nun $x_0 \in (1/2, 1]$. Wir setzen $A := \{x_0\}$. Für jede Menge $K \in \mathfrak{K}_\mathfrak{E}$ gilt dann $A \cap K = \emptyset$. Denn aus $K \in \mathfrak{K}_\mathfrak{E}$ folgt $K = \{x; x \in \Omega \text{ und } c_1 \geqq \tilde{e}(x) \geqq c_2\}$ für eine gewisse Funktion $\tilde{e}$ aus $\mathfrak{E}$ und gewisse Zahlen $c_1 > c_2 > 0$. Wegen $\tilde{e}(x_0) = 0$ folgt $x_0 \notin K$, also $A \cap K = \emptyset$. Also gilt $0 \leqq \chi_{A \cap K} \leqq \sup e_i$ für jede Folge $0 \leqq e_1 \leqq e_2 \leqq \ldots, e_i \in \mathfrak{E}$ $(i = 1, 2, \ldots)$, also auch für die Folge $e_1^{(K)} \leqq e_2^{(K)} \leqq \ldots$, für die $e_i^{(K)} = 0$ für alle $x \in [0, 1]$ ist. Es gilt $E(e_i^{(K)}) = 0$ für jedes $i = 1, 2, \ldots$ und jedes $\varepsilon > 0$. Damit ist der erste

Teil der Bedingung (C) erfüllt. Jedoch existiert keine Folge $0 \leqq e_1 \leqq e_2 \leqq \ldots, e_i \in \mathfrak{E}$ $(i = 1, 2, \ldots)$, so daß $\chi_A \leqq \sup_i e_i$ gilt, weil $e(x_0) = 0$ für jedes $e \in \mathfrak{E}$ ist.

Literatur

[1] St. Banach et C. Kuratowski, Sur une généralisation du problème de la mesure, Fund. Math. **14** (1929), 127–131.
[2] St. Saks, Theory of the integral, Warschau 1938.
[3] F. Terpe, Maximale eingelagerte absolutkonvergente Integrale, Math. Nachr. **28** (1965), 257–274.
[4] F. Terpe, Theorie des maximalen Integrals, Habilitationsschrift, Greifswald 1966.
[5] F. Terpe, Das zu einem Maßraum gehörige Integral als maximales Integral, Math. Nachr. (im Druck).
[6] F. Terpe, Das Stone-Integral als maximales eingelagertes absolutkonvergentes Integral, Math. Z. **107** (1968), 59–66.

ÜBER EINE LOKALKONVEXE ERWEITERUNG VON TOPOLOGISCHEN PRODUKTEN

STANISLAV TOMÁŠEK (Liberec)

In der vorliegenden Arbeit beschäftigen wir uns mit natürlichen Erweiterungen von Stetigkeitsstrukturen, insbesondere werden einige topologische Erweiterungen von kartesischen Produkten untersucht.

Es sei X eine nicht leere Menge. Der Vektorraum $E(X)$ aller endlichen linearen Kombinationen $\Sigma \lambda_i x_i$ ($x_i \in X$; λ_i Zahlen), mit einer lokalkonvexen Topologie versehen, heißt nach M. KATĚTOV eine Λ-Struktur über X (vgl. [5]).

Jede Λ-Struktur induziert in wohlbekannter Weise auf X eine Uniformität; in [10] wurde gezeigt, daß auch umgekehrt jede Uniformität durch eine geeignete Λ-Struktur erzeugt werden kann. Daraus ergibt sich die folgende Hierarchie der Stetigkeitsstrukturen: Λ-Strukturen $\to$ uniforme Räume $\to$ vollständig reguläre Räume.

Ist X ein vollständig regulärer Raum, so können wir X in den topologischen Dualraum $C^*(X)$ in wohlbekannter Weise topologisch einbetten. Also kann man den Dualraum $C^*(X)$ als eine topologische Erweiterungsstruktur des Raumes X betrachten.

Für uniforme Räume ist der Sachverhalt kompliziert durch die Tatsache, daß eine Uniformität nicht durch den Dualraum $P_0(X)$ (bzw. $P(X)$) aller gleichmäßig stetigen (bzw. beschränkten und gleichmäßig stetigen) Funktionen definiert ist. Deshalb ist es zweckmäßig, als eine natürliche Erweiterungsstruktur eines uniformen Raumes gerade die Λ-Struktur zu betrachten.

Als Illustration dieser Überlegung wollen wir eine Verallgemeinerung des Stone-Banachschen Satzes anführen.

Im folgenden schließen wir uns weitgehend der Terminologie und Bezeichnung N. BOURBAKIS an. Für einen uniformen Raum bezeichnen wir mit t (bzw. t_0) die Topologie auf $E(X)$ der gleichmäßigen Konvergenz auf der Gesamtheit aller gleichmäßig beschränkten (bzw. $\sigma(P(X), X)$-beschränkten) und gleichmäßig gleichstetigen Teilmengen in $P(X)$ (bzw. in $P_0(X)$). Ist E ein lokalkonvexer Raum, so schreiben wir E^* für den topologischen Dualraum. Es gilt der

Satz 1. *Sind X und Y zwei uniforme Räume, u eine topologische Isomorphie von $(E(X), t)$ auf $(E(Y), t)$, dann sind die folgenden Aussagen äquivalent:*

(a) *Die adjungierte Abbildung t_u ist eine lineare Isometrie von $P(Y)$ auf $P(X)$.*

(b) *Es existiert eine Funktion $\alpha(x)$ auf X, $|\alpha(x)| = 1$ für alle $x \in X$, so daß*

$$v(x) = \alpha(x) \cdot u(x)$$

eine uniforme Isomorphie von X auf Y ist.

Bemerkung 1. Ist u eine Isomorphie (schwache Isomorphie) von $(\hat{E}(X), t)$ auf $(\hat{E}(Y), t)$, so folgt aus der Voraussetzung (a), daß die vollständigen Hüllen $\hat{X}$ und $\hat{Y}$ uniform isomorph (homöomorph) sind. Sind insbesondere X und Y zwei kompakte vollständig reguläre Räume und ist u eine Isometrie von $C(Y)$ auf $C(X)$, dann ist t_u eine schwache Isomorphie von $C^*(X)$ auf $C^*(Y)$. Auf Grund der Beziehung $(\hat{E}(X), t_c) = C^*(X)$ (vgl. [7]) folgt hieraus die Behauptung des klassischen Stone-Banachschen Satzes.

Bemerkung 2. Der Beweis des Satzes 1 stützt sich wesentlich auf den Satz 1 von [12]. Ebensogut kann man den Satz 1 mit Hilfe der Ordnungsstruktur in $P(X)$ modifizieren (vgl. [4]). Dazu muß man die duale Charakterisierung der vollständigen Hülle eines uniformen Raumes aus [1] verwenden.

Von großer Bedeutung ist die Frage, unter welchen Voraussetzungen die vollständigen Hüllen $(\hat{E}(X), t)$ bzw. $(\hat{E}(X), t_c)$ (t_c ist auf $E(X)$ die Topologie der gleichmäßigen Konvergenz auf der Gesamtheit aller gleichmäßig beschränkten und gleichstetigen Teilmengen in $C(X)$) dem Dualraum $P^*(X)$ bzw. $C^*(X)$ isomorph ist. Diese Frage, die mit einem Problem von V. Pták (vgl. [8]) äquivalent ist, wurde in [14], [12] gelöst.

Ist X ein pseudokompakter Raum, so sind die positiven Elemente der vollständigen Hülle $(\hat{E}(X), t_c)$ mit der Gesamtheit aller Daniellschen Integrale auf X identisch (vgl. [14]). In [14] wurde bewiesen, daß für einen lokalkompakten und σ-kompakten Raum X die Elemente der Menge $(\hat{E}(X), t_{0c})$ mit der Gesamtheit aller Radonschen Maße, die einen kompakten Träger besitzen, identisch sind. Dabei ist t_{0c} auf $E(X)$ die Topologie der gleichmäßigen Konvergenz auf der Gesamtheit aller gleichstetigen und $\sigma(C_0(X), X)$-beschränkten Teilmengen in $C_0(X)$; $C_0(X)$ ist der Vektorraum aller in X definierten und stetigen Funktionen.

Eine analoge Situation liegt vor, wenn man den Funktionenraum $C(X)$ durch einen lokalkonvexen (bzw. pseudotopologischen) Vektorraum $\mathfrak{F}(X)$ von stetigen, in X definierten Funktionen ersetzt. Wir betrachten die folgenden Beispiele:

I. Es sei X ein lokalkompakter Raum, $\mathscr{K}(X)$ der Vektorraum aller auf X stetigen Funktionen, die einen kompakten Träger besitzen. Für jede kompakte Teilmenge $K \subseteqq X$ bezeichnen wir mit $\mathscr{C}_K$ die Gesamtheit aller abgeschlossenen und absolutkonvexen Hüllen der Nullfolgen in $\mathscr{K}(K, X)$. Die Topologie $T(\mathscr{C}_1)$ auf $E(X)$ wird in dem üblichen Sinne durch das System $\mathscr{C}_1 = \bigcup \mathscr{C}_K$ definiert.

Satz 2.

(a) *Die kanonische Einbettung* $\mathscr{W}: X \to (E(X), T(\mathscr{C}_1))$ *ist eine Homöomorphie.*

(b) *Der topologische Dualraum* $(E(X), T(\mathscr{C}_1))^*$ *ist mit dem Funktionenraum* $\mathscr{K}(X)$ *kanonisch identisch (im algebraischen Sinne).*

(c) *Die vollständige Hülle* $(\hat{E}(X), T(\mathscr{C}_1))$ *ist mit dem Vektorraum* $\mathscr{M}(X)$ *aller Radonschen Maße auf* X *identisch.*

II. Es sei $X = R^n$, $\mathscr{D}$ der lokalkonvexe Vektorraum von beliebig oft differenzierbaren Funktionen, die einen kompakten Träger besitzen (vgl. [11]). Ausgehend von der Gesamtheit $\mathscr{C}_2$ aller abgeschlossenen und absolutkonvexen Hüllen der Nullfolgen in $\mathscr{D}$ kann man auf $E(X)$ die Topologie $T(\mathscr{C}_2)$ betrachten.

Satz 3.

(a) *Die kanonische Einbettung* $\mathscr{W}$ *ist eine homöomorphe Abbildung von* X *in* $(E(X), T(\mathscr{C}_2))$.

(b) *Der topologische Dualraum* $(E(X), T(\mathscr{C}_2))^*$ *ist mit* $\mathscr{D}$ *kanonisch isomorph.*

(c) *Die vollständige Hülle* $(\hat{E}(X), T(\mathscr{C}_2))$ *ist mit dem Vektorraum* $\mathscr{D}^*$ *aller Distributionen über* X *identisch.*

III. Für $X = R^n$ bezeichnen wir mit $\mathscr{E}$ den Vektorraum aller beliebig oft differenzierbaren Funktionen auf X. Die Gesamtheit $\mathscr{C}_3$ ist analog definiert wie im Fall II. Dann gilt der

Satz 4. *Die vollständige Hülle* $(\hat{E}(X), T(\mathscr{C}_3))$ *ist identisch mit der Gesamtheit aller Distributionen über* X*, die einen kompakten Träger besitzen. Außerdem bestehen die analogen Behauptungen* (a) *und* (b) *wie im Fall* II.

Bemerkung 3. Das oben erwähnte Verfahren kann man auch für die Funktionenräume $K(M_p)$ (vgl. [2]) verwenden.

Sind X und Y zwei topologische (uniforme) Räume, so läßt sich die Λ-Struktur $E(X \times Y) = E(X) \otimes E(Y)$ mit der Topologie t (bzw. t_c, t_{0c}) definieren. Entsprechend kann man die Frage nach weiteren geeigneten Erweiterungsstrukturen aufwerfen, für die die kanonische Einbettung von $X \times Y$ gewisse Stetigkeitseigenschaften besitzt. Zuerst wollen wir uns mit denjenigen Erweiterungsstrukturen befassen, die mit dem Extension-Theorem (vgl. [9]) verbunden sind.

Definition. Ein lokalkonvexer Raum E heißt $(\mathscr{D}\mathscr{M})$-Raum (und wird mit $(E, \mathscr{B})$ bezeichnet), wenn eine Gesamtheit $\mathscr{B} = \{B_\alpha, \alpha \in \Omega\}$ von beschränkten Teilmengen in E existiert mit den folgenden Eigenschaften:

(a) Für jede beschränkte Teilmenge $B \subseteqq E$ gibt es ein $\alpha \in \Omega$ und eine natürliche Zahl n derart, daß $B \subseteqq n \ulcorner B_\alpha$ ist.

(b) Eine lineare Abbildung u von E in einen beliebigen lokalkonvexen Raum F ist dann und nur dann stetig, wenn die Beschränkung u_B auf beliebigen $B \in \mathscr{B}$ stetig ist.

Satz 5. *Es sei* X *ein lokalkompakter und zugleich ein parakompakter topologischer Raum.*

(a) *Eine Teilmenge* $B \subseteqq (E(X), t_{0c})$ *ist beschränkt dann und nur dann, wenn eine kompakte Teilmenge* $K \subseteqq X$ *existiert, so daß für ein geeignetes* n *die Beziehung* $B \subseteqq n \ulcorner K$ *besteht.*

(b) *Die* Λ*-Struktur* $(E(X), t_{0c})$ *ist ein* $(\mathscr{D}\mathscr{M})$*-Raum.*

Eine sapariert stetige bilineare Funktion $f(x, y)$ auf dem kartesischen Produkt $E \times F$ von $(\mathscr{D}\mathscr{M})$-Räumen $E = (E, \mathscr{B}_1)$, $F = (F, \mathscr{B}_2)$, heißt schwach kompakt (vgl. [3]), wenn $u(B)$ eine relativ $\sigma(E^*, E^{**})$-kompakte Teilmenge von E^* ist. Dabei ist u durch die Beziehung $f(x, y) = \langle x, u(y)\rangle$ bestimmt.

Satz 6. *Es sei* $f(x, y)$ *eine separiert stetige bilineare Funktion in der schwachen Topologie auf dem kartesischen Produkt* $E \times F$ *von* $(\mathscr{D}\mathscr{M})$*-Räumen. Dann sind die folgenden Aussagen äquivalent:*

(a) f *ist schwach kompakt.*

(b) *Es gibt eine separiert stetige und bilineare Erweiterung auf* $E^{**} \times F^{**}$ (*die bidualen Räume sind betrachtet in der schwachen Topologie*).

Folgerung. Es seien X und Y zwei lokalkompakte und zugleich parakompakte Räume, f eine separiert stetige Funktion auf $X \times Y$. Ist $\mathscr{K}$ die Gesamtheit aller kompakten Teilmengen in Y und ist die Abbildung u durch die Beziehung $f(x, y) = \langle x, u(y) \rangle$ bestimmt, so sind die folgenden Aussagen äquivalent.:

(a) Für jedes $K \in \mathscr{K}$ ist $u(K)$ relativ schwach kompakt in $C_0(X)$.

(b) Es gibt eine separiert schwach stetige bilineare Erweiterung der Funktion f auf $C_0^*(X) \times C_0^*(Y)$ (dabei sind die Räume $C_0(X)$ und $C_0(Y)$ mit der Topologie der kompakten Konvergenz versehen).

Bemerkung 4. Analog zu der vorliegenden Definition des $(\mathscr{D}\mathscr{M})$-Raumes kann man auch durch ähnliche Eigenschaften einen $(\mathscr{D}\mathscr{B})$-Raum definieren. Für diese Räume, die eine gewisse Verallgemeinerung der Λ-Struktur $(E(X), t)$ sind, besteht ebenfalls die Behauptung des Satzes 6. Daraus folgt das Extension-Theorem von V. Pták (vgl. [9], [14]).

Ist X ein uniformer Raum und A eine Teilmenge in X, so heißt A beschränkt in X, wenn A eine beschränkte Teilmenge des Raumes $(E(X), t_0(X))$ ist (vgl. [10]).

Es sei jetzt $\mathfrak{S}$ bzw. $\mathfrak{T}$ eine Gesamtheit von beschränkten Teilmengen im uniformen Raum X bzw. Y. Dann bezeichnen wir mit $R(\mathfrak{S}, \mathfrak{T})$ den Vektorraum aller uniform $\mathfrak{S}$-$\mathfrak{T}$-hypostetigen Funktionen auf $X \times Y$. Die Gesamtheit $\mathscr{N} = \mathscr{N}(\mathfrak{S}, \mathfrak{T})$ aller $\mathfrak{S}$-$\mathfrak{T}$-hypogleichstetigen Teilmengen von $R(\mathfrak{S}, \mathfrak{T})$ bestimmt auf $E(X \times Y)$ eine lokalkonvexe Topologie $\mathscr{T}(\mathfrak{S}, \mathfrak{T})$. Es gilt der

Satz 7. *Unter den oben erwähnten Voraussetzungen ist $\mathscr{T}(\mathfrak{S}, \mathfrak{T})$ die einzige lokalkonvexe Topologie auf $E(X \times Y)$ mit den folgenden Eigenschaften:*

(a) *Die kanonische Einbettung von $X \times Y$ in $(E(X \times Y), \mathscr{T}(\mathfrak{S}, \mathfrak{T}))$ ist eine $\mathfrak{S}$-$\mathfrak{T}$-hypostetige Abbildung.*

(b) *Ist u eine $\mathfrak{S}$-$\mathfrak{T}$-hypostetige Abbildung von $X \times Y$ in einen lokalkonvexen Raum F, dann ist die lineare Erweiterung von u auf $E(X \times Y)$ eine stetige Abbildung in der Topologie $\mathscr{T}(\mathfrak{S}, \mathfrak{T})$.*

Ist $\mathfrak{S}_K$ bzw. $\mathfrak{T}_K$ die Gesamtheit aller beschränkten Teilmengen in X bzw. in Y, so nennen wir die zugehörige Topologie $\mathscr{T}_K$ die Katětovsche Topologie auf $E(X \times Y)$. Sie löst das von M. Katětov aufgestellte Problem (vgl. [5], [6]). Es gilt nämlich $P_0(X) \otimes P_0(Y) \subset R(\mathfrak{S}_K, \mathfrak{T}_K)$. Die Bedeutung dieser Topologie besteht darin, daß auf jedem Produkt $M \times N$ (M und N beschränkte Teilmengen in X und Y) die Beschränkung der kanonischen Einbettung eine uniforme Isomorphie darstellt. Insbesondere ist für lokalpräkompakte und uniforme Räume X und Y die kanonische Einbettung eine Homöomorphie (vgl. [15]).

Literatur

[1] V. P. Fiodorova, Eine duale Charakterisierung der vollständigen Hülle und der Vollständigkeit eines uniformen Raumes (russ.), Mat. Sbornik **64** (1964), 631—639.

[2] I. M. Gelfand und G. E. Schilow, Verallgemeinerte Funktionen, Bd. 2, Berlin 1962 (Übersetzung aus dem Russischen).

[3] A. Grothendieck, Produits tensoriels topologiques et espaces nucléaires, Memoirs Amer. Math. Soc. Nr. 16 (1955), 1—191, 1—140.

[4] S. Kakutani, Concrete representation of abstract (M)-spaces, Ann. Math. **42** (1941), 994—1024.

[5] M. Katětov, On a category of spaces, Proc. First Symposium on General Topology, Prague 1961; Prague 1962, p. 226—229.

[6] M. KATĚTOV, Allgemeine Stetigkeitsstrukturen, Proc. Internat. Congress Math. 1962, p. 473—479.

[7] M. KATĚTOV, On certain projectively generated continuity structures, Celebrazioni archimedee del secolo XX, Simposio di topologia 1964, p. 47—50.

[8] V. PTÁK, Weak compactness in convex topological linear spaces, Czechoslovak Math. J. **4** (1954), 175—186.

[9] V. PTÁK, An extension theorem for separately continuous functions and its application to functional analysis, Czechoslovak Math. J. **89** (1964), 562—581.

[10] D. A. RAIKOW, Freie lokalkonvexe Räume der uniformen Räume (russ.), Mat. Sbornik **63** (1964), 582—590.

[11] L. SCHWARTZ, Théorie des distributions, Paris 1950/51.

[12] S. TOMÁŠEK, Über eine Klasse lokalkonvexer Räume, Proc. Second Symposium on General Topology, Prague 1966; Prague 1967, p. 353—355.

[13] S. TOMÁŠEK, On a certain class of Λ-structures I (erscheint in Czechoslovak Math. J.).

[14] S. TOMÁŠEK, On a certain class of Λ-structures II (erscheint in Czechoslovak Math. J.).

[15] S. TOMÁŠEK, On a certain class of Λ-structures III (eingesandt an Comment Math. Univ. Carolinae).

ON COMPLETION OF A UNIFORM SPACE BY LOCAL CLUSTERS

B. D. WARRACK and S. A. NAIMPALLY[1]) (Edmonton/Can.)

Given a uniform space X, we shall work only with the family $\mathcal{U}$ consisting of all open symmetric members of the uniformity; in fact $\mathcal{U}$ is a base for the uniformity (KELLEY [1], p. 179). A uniform space is complete if and only if every Cauchy filter in the space has a cluster point (since a Cauchy filter converges to its cluster point). There is an associated proximity relation δ on X induced by $\mathcal{U}$, namely:

$A \, \delta B$ iff $(A \times B) \cap U \neq \emptyset$ for every $U \in \mathcal{U}$.

We have shown in [2] that every ultrafilter in a proximity space generates a cluster and that given a set A in a cluster σ, there exists an ultrafilter containing A which generates σ. It is therefore natural to call a cluster *local* if it is generated by a Cauchy ultrafilter. One can readily convince oneself that every local cluster is a point cluster, i.e. one which is determined by a point of X or of its completion. The neighbourhood system of the point will contain arbitrarily "small" subsets which intersect every member of the cluster. This, then, leads to the following definition which is equivalent to the above (as will be seen in the concluding remarks) but is easier to work with:

1. Definition. A cluster σ in $(X, \mathcal{U}, \delta)$ is *local* iff there exists a filter $\mathcal{M} \subset \sigma$ such that for each $U \in \mathcal{U}$, there exists an $M \in \mathcal{M}$ such that $M \times M \subset U$ and $M \cap C \neq \emptyset$ for every $C \in \sigma$.

Two obvious facts should be noted here:

(a) If a cluster contains a point, then it is local.

(b) If a cluster is local, then *every* ultrafilter which generates it is Cauchy.

2. Definition. $(X, \mathcal{U}, \delta)$ is *complete* iff every local cluster has a point.

3. Lemma. *A closed subspace Y of a complete space $(X, \mathcal{U}, \delta)$ is complete.*

Proof. The trace $\mathcal{U}_Y = \{U \cap (Y \times Y) \colon U \in \mathcal{U}\}$ of $\mathcal{U}$ on Y is a base for the subspace uniformity of Y. If σ_1 is any local cluster in Y, then a slight modification of the proof of Theorem 6 in [2] shows that σ_1 is a subclass of a unique local cluster σ_2 in X. Since X is complete, σ_2 contains a point x so that $\{x\} \, \delta B$ for every $B \in \sigma_1$. But Y is closed, implying $x \in Y$ and $\{x\} \in \sigma_1$.

Let f be the mapping which associates with each point $x \in X$, the cluster σ_x consisting of all subsets of X which are near x. Then f is a one-one mapping of X onto the

---

[1]) This author was supported by a research grant from N. R. C. (Canada).

space $f(X)$ of all clusters in X containing a point. Let X^* denote the set of all local clusters in X. From the remarks following Definition 1, $f(X) \subset X^*$. Let $\mathscr{M}(\sigma)$ be a filter in σ satisfying Definition 1. For each $U \in \mathscr{U}$ define $U^* = \{(\sigma_1, \sigma_2) \in X^* \times X^*$: there exists $M \in \mathscr{M}(\sigma_1)$, $N \in \mathscr{M}(\sigma_2)$ such that $M \times N \subset U\}$.

4. Lemma. *$\mathscr{U}^* = \{U^* : U \in \mathscr{U}\}$ is a uniformity base on X^*.*

Proof. Every U^* obviously contains the diagonal and $(U \cap V)^* \subset U^* \cap V^*$. Given $U^* \in \mathscr{U}^*$, there exists a $V \in \mathscr{U}$ such that $V \circ V \subset U$. That $V^* \circ V^* \subset U^*$ follows from the following argument: If $(\sigma_1, \sigma_2) \in V^* \circ V^*$, then there exists a σ_3 such that $(\sigma_1, \sigma_3) \in V^*$ and $(\sigma_3, \sigma_2) \in V^*$. Hence there exists an $A \in \mathscr{M}(\sigma_1)$, $B \in \mathscr{M}(\sigma_2)$ and $C', C'' \in \mathscr{M}(\sigma_3)$ such that $A \times C' \subset V$ and $C'' \times B \subset V$. Letting $C = C' \cap \cap C'' \in \mathscr{M}(\sigma_3)$ we have $A \times C \subset V$ and $C \times B \subset V$. Hence $A \times B \subset V \circ V \subset U$ which implies $(\sigma_1, \sigma_2) \in U^*$.

5. Lemma. *$f(X)$ is a dense subset of X^*.*

Proof. Given any $\sigma \in X^*$ and any $U^* \in \mathscr{U}^*$, we must show that $(f(X) \times \sigma) \cap U^* \neq \emptyset$. Choose $V \in \mathscr{U}$ such that $V \circ V \circ V \subset U$. Since σ is local, there exists an $M \in \mathscr{M}(\sigma)$ such that $M \times M \subset V$. Then $V[M] \times V[M] \subset U$. Since $V[M]$ is open (recall V is open and symmetric) we can choose a point $p \in V[M]$ and a $W \in \mathscr{U}$ such that $W[p] \subset V[M]$. Then $W[p] \times W[p] \subset U$ where $W[p] \in \mathscr{M}(\sigma_p)$ and $V[M] \in \in \mathscr{M}(\sigma)$. Therefore $(\sigma_p, \sigma) \in U^*$ where $\sigma_p \in f(X)$.

Let δ^* be the natural proximity induced by $\mathscr{U}^*$ on X^*. The restriction $\mathscr{U}_f^*$ of $\mathscr{U}^*$ to $f(X)$ is a uniformity base on $f(X)$ and so induces the natural proximity δ_f^* on $f(X)$.

6. Lemma. *$(X, \mathscr{U}, \delta)$ and $(f(X), \mathscr{U}_f^*, \delta_f^*)$ are proximally isomorphic.*

Proof. Clearly f is one-one and onto. Suppose $A \delta B$. Given U_f^* we must show that $(f(A) \times f(B)) \cap U_f^* \neq \emptyset$. Now there exists $a \in A$, $b \in B$ such that $(a, b) \in V$. Then $V[a] \times V[b] \subset U$ and the point clusters σ_a and σ_b are such that $(\sigma_a, \sigma_b) \in U_f^*$. On the other hand, if $f(A)\, \delta_f^*\, f(B)$ then for each U_f^* there exists a $(\sigma_a, \sigma_b) \in U_f^*$ where $\sigma_a \in f(A)$ and $\sigma_b \in f(B)$. So $(a, b) \in U$, which means $(A \times B) \cap U \neq \emptyset$ for all $U \in \mathscr{U}$.

It may be similarly proven that $(X, \mathscr{U})$ and $(f(X), \mathscr{U}_f^*)$ are uniformly isomorphic.

7. Lemma. *Every local cluster in $(X^*, \mathscr{U}^*, \delta^*)$ has a point.*

Proof. Let σ^* be any local cluster in X^*. Since $f(X)$ is dense in X^*, a slight modification of the proof of Theorem 7 [2] shows that σ^* determines a unique local cluster σ' in $f(X)$ such that $\sigma' \subset \sigma^*$. But σ' is isomorphic to a local cluster σ in X. By Theorem 6 [2], in order to show that $\sigma \in \sigma^*$ it is sufficient to verify that for each $U^* \in \mathscr{U}^*$ and each $M \in \sigma'$, $(\sigma \times M) \cap U^* \neq \emptyset$. Given $U^* \in \mathscr{U}^*$, there exists a $V \in \mathscr{U}$ and $C \in \mathscr{M}(\sigma)$ such that $V \circ V \circ V \subset U$ and $C \times C \subset V$. Then $V[C] \times V[C] \subset U$. Letting $M_0 = V[C] \cap f^{-1}(M)$ we have $M_0 \in \sigma$ since $V[C] \in \mathscr{M}(\sigma)$, $f^{-1}(M) \in \sigma$ and we can find an ultrafilter containing both $V[C]$ and $f^{-1}(M)$ which generates σ. Choose a point $p \in M_0$. Since $V[C]$ is open, there exists a $W \in \mathscr{U}$ such that $W[p] \subset V[C]$. So we have $W[p] \times V[C] \subset U$ where $W[p] \in \mathscr{M}(\sigma_p)$, $V[C] \in \mathscr{M}(\sigma)$ and $\sigma_p \in M$. Hence $(\sigma_p, \sigma) \in \in U^*$ and $(\sigma \times M) \cap U^* \neq \emptyset$.

We can now conclude from the foregoing considerations that $(X^*, \mathscr{U}^*, \delta^*)$ is complete. If $\mathscr{F}$ is any Cauchy filter in X^*, then $\mathscr{F}$ is contained in a Cauchy ultrafilter. This ultrafilter generates a local cluster which, by Lemma 7, must contain some point x_0. Clearly x_0 is a cluster point of the Cauchy filter $\mathscr{F}$, so that $\mathscr{F}$ converges to x_0.

Finally we remark that every local cluster in X is generated by the Cauchy ultrafilter containing the neighbourhood filter of a point which is either in X or in X^*. Hence the Definition 1 is equivalent to: a cluster is local iff it is generated by a Cauchy ultrafilter.

References

[1] J. L. Kelley, General topology, Princeton 1955.
[2] B. D. Warrack and S. A. Naimpally, Clusters and ultrafilters, Publ. Inst. Math. 8 (22) (1968), 100—101.

ON THE STRENGTHENING OF ALEXANDER'S THEOREM

E. Wattel (Amsterdam)

The notion of compactness is important in topology, and in this lecture we will consider families of compact subsets. Every topological space $(X, \mathcal{O})$ contains a family of subsets, such that a subset is compact if and only if it is a member of the family. This family we will call the family of compact subsets. We will try to strengthen the topology $\mathcal{O}$, in such a way, that the family of compact subsets does not change.

Alexander's theorem implies that the collection of compact subsets in the topological space $(X, \mathcal{O})$ is exactly equal to the collection of subsets of X, whose members are compact relative to some given subbase $\mathcal{B}$ of the topology, and so we will try to strengthen a subbase of a topology too, in such a way, that the family of compact subsets does not change.

It has turned out to be convenient to consider closed subbases instead of open subbases, and hence we will use systems with the finite intersection property instead of covers. To avoid confusion we will define compactness complementary.

Definition. A subset A of a set X is *compact* relative to a collection of subsets $\mathcal{S}$, if and only if for every subcollection $\mathcal{S}'$ of $\mathcal{S}$ with the finite intersection property in the set A, it is true that $(\bigcap \mathcal{S}') \cap A \neq \emptyset$.

Definition. The *compactness operator* ϱ is an operator, defined on the power-set of the power-set of a set X, and it assigns to every collection of subsets $\mathcal{S}$ of X, the collection $\varrho\,\mathcal{S}$ of compact sets relative to $\mathcal{S}$.

The collection $\varrho\mathcal{S}$ is again a family of subsets of X, and hence ϱ assigns to this collection another collection of subsets of X. This family of sets will be called the *square compact* family, relative to $\mathcal{S}$. It will be denoted by $\varrho^2\mathcal{S}$, and from this definition we can derive our main theorem.

Theorem. *For every family of subsets $\mathcal{S}$ of a set X, the family of compact sets relative to $\mathcal{S}$ is exactly equal to the family of compact sets relative to $(\mathcal{S} \cup \varrho^2\mathcal{S})$.*

It is obvious that this theorem can be restated for the topology generated by $\mathcal{S} \cup \varrho^2\mathcal{S}$. We still have two other propositions concerning our question.

Proposition. *If X is a set, and $\mathcal{S}$ and $\mathcal{T}$ are collections of subsets of X, such that* $\varrho\mathcal{S} = \varrho\mathcal{T}$, then $\varrho(\mathcal{S} \cup \mathcal{T}) = \varrho\mathcal{S}$.

Proposition. *Let X be a set, and let $\mathcal{S}$ be a collection of subsets. Let $\varrho\mathcal{S}$ be the family of compact sets, relative to $\mathcal{S}$, and let $\mathcal{T}$ be the collection of sets, that has a com-*

pact intersection with every compact set, then there exists a maximal family $\tilde{\mathscr{S}}$, *such that* $\varrho\tilde{\mathscr{S}} = \varrho\mathscr{S}$, *if and only if* $\varrho\mathscr{S} = \varrho\mathscr{T}$. *In that case* $\tilde{\mathscr{S}} = \mathscr{T}$.

From this last proposition it follows, that for many topological spaces there is no strongest topology with the same system of compact sets as the original topological space, and so there is no best solution to our problem.

References

[1] J. DE GROOT, An isomorphism principle in general topology, Bull. Amer. Math. Soc. **73** (1967), 465–467.

[2] J. DE GROOT, G. E. STRECKER and E. WATTEL, The compactness operator in general topology, Proc. Second Symposium on General Topology, Prague 1966.

[3] G. E. STRECKER, E. WATTEL, H. HERRLICH and J. DE GROOT, Strengthening Alexander's subbase theorem (issued for publication).

[4] E. WATTEL, The compactness operator in set theory and topology, Tract 21, Math. Centre Amsterdam 1968.

ON $\mathscr{W}$-CONVERGENCE SPACES AND THEIR $\mathscr{W}$-ENVELOPES

KAREL WICHTERLE (Praha)

Let $\mathscr{W}$ be any class of directed sets which is non-empty and closed under cofinal subsets. $\mathscr{W}$-net denotes a net whose domain is an element of $\mathscr{W}$. $\mathscr{W}$-space denotes a closure space whose closure is determined by a convergence of $\mathscr{W}$-nets. Closure space will be called $\mathscr{W}$-regular iff the converging of the nets $f \circ N$ to fx for all bounded continuous functions f is sufficient for the converging of any $\mathscr{W}$-net N to a point x in $\mathscr{P}$. $\mathscr{W}$-envelope of a $\mathscr{W}$-regular $\mathscr{W}$-space $\mathscr{P}$ is a maximal $\mathscr{W}$-regular $\mathscr{W}$-space $\langle Q, v\rangle$ such that $\mathscr{P}$ is a subspace of $\langle Q, v\rangle$, $v^\alpha\,|\mathscr{P}| = Q$ for some ordinal α, all points of $Q - P$ are v-closed and every bounded continuous function on $\mathscr{P}$ has a continuous extension to $\langle Q, v\rangle$. $\mathscr{W}$-envelope of any $\mathscr{W}$-regular $\mathscr{W}$-space $\mathscr{P}$ exists and is determined up to homeomorphisms identical on $|\mathscr{P}|$; it can be constructed by the successive addition of $\mathscr{W}$-nets remarkable in $\mathscr{P}$ or with help of Čech-Stone compactification.

If $\mathscr{W}$ contains countable sets only then $\mathscr{W}$-spaces ($\mathscr{W}$-regular spaces, $\mathscr{W}$-envelope) coincide with sequential convergence spaces (sequentially regular spaces, sequential envelope resp.). If $\mathscr{P}$ is a $\mathscr{W}$-regular space and $\mathscr{W}$ is large enough then $\mathscr{P}$ is a uniformisable $\mathscr{W}$-space and its $\mathscr{W}$-envelope coincides with Čech-Stone compactification of $\mathscr{P}$.

The product of two $\mathscr{W}$-spaces need not generally be a $\mathscr{W}$-space.

References

[1] E. ČECH, Topological spaces, Prague 1966.

[2] V. KOUTNÍK, On sequence regular convergence spaces, Czechoslovak Math. J. **17** (1967), 232–247.

[3] J. NOVÁK, On convergence spaces and their sequential envelopes, Czechoslovak Math. J. **15** (1965), 74–100; or Proc. First Symposium on General Topology, Prague 1961.

[4] K. WICHTERLE, On $\mathscr{W}$-convergence spaces (will be published in Czechoslovak Math. J.).

LOCALLY CONNECTED STONE-ČECH COMPACTIFICATIONS[1])

D. E. Wulbert (Lausanne)

We present here a normed linear lattice characterization of $C(X)$ for completely regular spaces X which have locally connected Stone-Čech compactifications. This characterization provides an elementary proof for the theorem, due to Banaschewski (for the sufficiency) and Henriksen and Isbell (for the necessity), that a completely regular space has a locally connected Stone-Čech compactification if and only if it is both pseudo-compact and locally connected. This abstract is an announcement of a result from [3].

Let E be a normed linear lattice. A subset $\{p_i: i = 1, 2, \ldots, n\}$ of E is a *decomposition* of a point x in E if $|p_i| \wedge |p_j| = 0$ for $i \neq j$ and $\sum_{i=1}^{n} p_i = x$. A point x in E is *well behaved* if for every $r > 0$, x admits a decomposition $\{p_i: i = 1, 2, \ldots, n\}$ such that for $i = 1, 2, \ldots, n-1$, p_i admits no proper decomposition, and $\|p_n\| < r$. If every point in E is well behaved we say that E is well behaved.

Let X be a completely regular Hausdorff space, and let $C(X)$ denote the normed linear lattice of all bounded, continuous, real-valued functions on X with the supremum norm and the usual pointwise operations.

Theorem. *The following are equivalent*: (1) *$C(X)$ is a well behaved normed linear lattice*, (2) *X is pseudo-compact and locally connected*, (3) *the Stone-Čech compactification of X is locally connected.*

Proof. The equivalence of (1) and (3) follows as a special case of the equivalence of (1) and (2). To prove that (1) implies (2), assume that $C(X)$ is well behaved. If X is not pseudo-compact there is an infinite family F of open subsets of X such that each x in X has a neighborhood which meets at most one member of F. Hence there is a continuous function of norm 1 which attains its norm on each member of F, and which achieves all its non-zero values on the union of the sets in F. Such a function can not be well behaved.

If U is a neighborhood of a point x in X, then — since $C(X)$ is well behaved — there is a continuous function f of norm 1 which is 1 at x, vanishes of U, and admits no proper decomposition. It follows that $\{y \text{ in } X : f(y) \neq \emptyset\}$ is a connected neighbourhood of x contained in U. Hence (1) implies (2).

---

[1]) This research was sponsored by the Air Force Office of Scientific Research, Office of Aerospace Research, United States Air Force under AESOR Grant No. 1109—66.

To show that (2) implies (1) let f be in $C(X)$. If X is locally connected, the components of $B = \{x \text{ in } X: f(x) \neq 0\}$ are open. For any $r > 0$ the family of open sets $F = \{G \cap \{x \text{ in } X: |f(x)| > r\}: G \text{ a component of } B\}$ has the property that every x in X has a neighbourhood which meets at most one member of F. If X is pseudocompact, F can only contain a finite number of non-empty sets. It follows that f — and thus $C(X)$ — is well behaved.

References

[1] B. BANASCHEWSKI, Local connectedness of extension spaces, Canadian J. Math. 8 (1956), 395–398.

[2] M. HENRIKSEN and J. R. ISBELL, Local connectedness in the Stone-Čech compactification, Illinois J. Math. 1 (1957), 574–582.

[3] D. E. WULBERT, A characterization of $C(X)$ for locally connected X, Proc. Amer. Math. Soc. (to appear).

МЕТОД ТЕОРИИ КОЛЕЦ ФУНКЦИЙ В КОНСТРУКЦИИ БИКОМПАКТНЫХ РАСШИРЕНИЙ

А. В. Зарелуа (Новосибирск)

В настоящем сообщении освещаются связи между некоторыми характеристиками вполне регулярных топологических пространств X и свойствами колец непрерывных ограниченных вещественных функций $C(X)$.

Основные общие связи вытекают здесь из теории Гельфанда-Шилова [1]: существует взаимнооднозначное соответствие между замкнутыми подкольцами с единицей кольца $C(X)$ и бикомпактными расширениями непрерывных образов пространства X. Бикомпактным расширениям пространства X соответствуют замкнутые подкольца K с единицей, для которых выполняется следующее свойство регулярности: если $x_1, x_2 \in X$, $x_1 \neq x_2$, то существует функция $f \in K$ такая, что $f(x_1) \neq f(x_2)$.

Часто бывает полезной следующая явная конструкция пространства $\mathfrak{M}(K)$, соответствующего в этой теории замкнутому подкольцу с единицей $K \subseteqq C(X)$. Если $K = \{f_\lambda\}_{\lambda \in \Lambda}$, то $\mathfrak{M}(K) = \overline{F_K(X)}$, где $F_K = \prod_{\lambda \in \Lambda} f_\lambda$ есть произведение отображений $f_\lambda\colon X \to I_\lambda$, $I_\lambda = [\inf f_\lambda, \sup f_\lambda]$. Таким образом $\mathfrak{M}(K)$ можно рассматривать как подмножество тихоновского кирпича $T = \prod_{\lambda \in \Lambda} I_\lambda$. Обратное соответствие: бикомпактному расширению непрерывного образа $F(X)$, $\alpha[F(X)]$, — замкнутое подкольцо с единицей $K \subseteqq C(X)$, — определяется сопоставлением бикомпакту $\alpha[F(X)]$ подкольца K функций на пространстве X вида $g \circ F$, где $g \in C(\alpha[F(X)])$. После этого естественно напрашивается мысль рассматривать произвольные семейства функций $M \subseteqq C(X)$, непрерывное отображение $F_M = \prod_{f \in M} f$ в тихоновский кирпич и бикомпакт $B_M = \overline{F_M(X)}$. Нетрудно видеть, используя теорему Стона-Вейерштрасса, что бикомпакт B_M соответствует минимальному замкнутому подкольцу с единицей $[M]$ кольца $C(X)$, содержащему множество M, т. е. подкольцу $[M]$, полученному замыканием в $C(X)$ кольца многочленов $R[M]$ с вещественными коэффициентами от функций $f \in M$. Например, если (X, Δ) пространство близости и M семейство (кольцо) всех ограниченных Δ-функций, то B_M есть бикомпактное расширение пространства X, соответствующее в теории Ю. М. Смирнова пространству близости (X, Δ) (С. В. Фомин [2], Ю. М. Смирнов [3]).

Кстати, эта конструкция позволяет свести доказательство теоремы Стона-Вейерштрасса к классическому случаю — теореме Вейерштрасса для функций многих переменных. В самом деле, из неё следует, что достаточно доказать эту теорему для случая тихоновского кирпича $T = \prod_\lambda I_\lambda$ и подкольца кольца $C(T)$, порожденного проекциями $T \to I_\lambda$. Но из описания топологии в T легко видеть, что непрерывные функции на T равномерно аппроксимируются фунциями, значения которых зависят только от конечного числа координат. Отсюда и из классической теоремы Вейерштрасса следует утверждение.

В задачах, связанных с проблемами связи веса пространства X и веса расширений его непрерывных образов, полезно следующее дополнительное замечание: если M семейство функций такое, что $M = Q[M]$ ($Q[M]$ — множество многочленов от функций семейства M с рациональными коэффициентами), то M всюду плотно в $C(B_M)$; здесь M рассматривается, естественным образом, как подмножество кольца $C(B_M)$. Это замечание есть почти очевидное следствие плотности множества рациональных чисел в R. Заметим также, что для бикомпакта X вес его есть вес кольца $C(X)$, если под последним понимать наименьшую бесконечную мощность семейств E, порождающих все кольцо, т. е. $[E] = C(X)$.

1. Продолжение отображений

Рассмотрим такую задачу: дано семейство $F = \{F_\lambda\}$ отображений пространства X в бикомпакты Y_λ; построить бикомпактное расширение αX, на которое продолжались бы все эти отображения. Ясно, это по крайней мере одно бикомпактное расширение с этим свойством существует — таким будет, например, чеховское расширение βX. Ясно также, что в общем случае вес αX должен быть приблизительно равным $\tau_F = \max\{\text{Вес } X, \text{мощность } F \times \max\{\text{Вес } Y_\lambda\}\}$. Эта задача продолжения отображений на расширение $\alpha_F X$ веса $\leqq \tau_F$, легко решается следующим образом: $\alpha_F X = \overline{\Psi X}$, где Ψ равно произведению отображений $\Psi = 1_X \times \prod F_\lambda$, $\Psi: X \to X \times \prod_\lambda Y_\lambda$. Отображения, продолжающие F_λ будут тогда просто проекциями множества $\overline{\Psi(X)}$ на сомножители Y_λ. С точки зрения кольца $C(X)$, эта конструкция соответствует рассмотрению замкнутого подкольца с единицей кольца $C(X)$, порожденного регулярной системой функций мощности, равной весу пространства X и системами E_λ функций минимальной мощности среди всех систем порождающих подкольца, изоморфные образам кольца $C(Y_\lambda)$ при встречных гомоморфизмах F_λ^*: $C(Y_\lambda) \to C(X)$.

Близкая к этой задача рассматривалась R. Engelking'ом [4]: дано семейство F отображений F_λ: $X \to X$; построить бикомпактное расширение αX такое, что все отображения F_λ продолжаются до отображений $\tilde{F}_\lambda$: $\alpha X \to \alpha X$. Для её решения достаточно взять регулярное семейство функций $\{\pi_\alpha\}$, рассмотреть семейство Φ функций вида $\pi_\alpha \circ F_{\lambda_1} \circ F_{\lambda_2} \circ \ldots \circ F_{\lambda_k}$ и бикомпакт B_Φ; $\tilde{F}_\lambda$ есть отображение, соответствующее отображению семейства Φ в себя, которое определяется простой суперпозицией: $\pi_\alpha \circ F_{\lambda_1} \circ F_{\lambda_2} \circ \ldots \circ F_{\lambda_k} \to \pi_\alpha \circ F_{\lambda_1} \circ F_{\lambda_2} \circ \ldots \circ F_{\lambda_k} \circ F_\lambda$.

2. Продолжение отображений на расширения со специальными размерностными свойствами и теоремы факторизации

Хорошо известна следующая характеристика размерности нормального пространства X, принадлежащая П. С. Александрову: $\dim X \leqq n$ если, и только если, каждое непрерывное отображение замкнутого подмножества $F \subseteqq X$ в сферу S^n можно продолжить на все пространство X. С другой стороны, для конечных или счетных групп G и паракомпактного пространства X результаты P. J. Huber'a [5] и лемма Борсука показывают, что если определить когомологическую размерность $\mathrm{cdim}_G X$ как наименьшее такое n, что $\check{H}^i(X, F; G) = 0$ для всех $i > n$ и всех замкнутых $F \subseteqq X$ ($\check{H}^i(X, F; G)$ — обозначает спектральную группу когомологий пары (X, F) Александрова-Чеха), то $\mathrm{cdim}_G X \leqq n$ тогда и только тогда, когда каждое отображение каждого замкнутого множества $F \subseteqq X$ в комплекс Эйленберга-Маклейна $K(G, n)$ можно продолжить на все X. Определим $\dim_G X$ нормального пространства X как $\mathrm{cdim}_G \beta X$; $\dim_G X$ можно дать и внутреннюю характеристику с помощью когомологий нервов конечных открытых покрытий пространства X. Отметим, что $\dim_G X = \mathrm{cdim}_G X$, если X бикомпакт, или если X паракомпактно, $\dim X < \infty$ и группа конечно порождена; последнее следует из того, что в случае конечно порожденной группы G каждый остов конечной размерности комплекса $K(G, n)$ есть конечный полиэдр.

Общая теорема о бикомпактных расширениях. Пусть задано семейство $\{X_\lambda\}$ мощности $\leqq \tau$ замкнутых подмножеств нормального пространства X, семейство отображений $\{F_\alpha\}$ мощности $\leqq \tau$ пространства X в бикомпакты Y_α веса $\leqq \tau$ семейство преобразований $T_\omega: X \to X$ мощности $\leqq \tau$ и числа $n_{\lambda,\sigma}$ — размерности множества X_λ по счетным или конечным группам G_σ; мощность семейства $\{G_\sigma\}$ также предполагается $\leqq \tau$. Тогда за каждым бикомпактным расширением bX пространства X следует бикомпактное расширение aX пространства X веса $\leqq \max$ {вес bX, τ} такое, что

1. отображения F_α: $X \to Y_\alpha$ продолжаются до отображений $\tilde{F}_\alpha$: $aX \to Y_\alpha$,

2. преобразования T_ω: $X \to X$ продолжаются до преобразований $\tilde{T}_\omega$: $aX \to$ $\to aX$,

3. размерности замыкания $\dim_{G_\sigma} aX[X_\lambda] = n_{\lambda,\sigma}$,

4. $\dim aX[X_\lambda] = \dim X_\lambda$.

Общая теорема о факторизации. В предположениях общей теоремы о бикомпактных расширениях существует бикомпакт B веса $\leqq \tau$, отображение F: $X \to B$, отображения G_α: $B \to Y_\alpha$ и преобразования U_ω: $B \to B$ такие, что

1. $G_\alpha \circ F = F_\alpha$,

2. $U_\omega \circ F = F \circ T_\omega$,

3. $\dim_{G_\sigma} B[FX_\lambda] = n_{\lambda,\sigma}$,

4. $\dim B[FX_\lambda] = \dim X_\lambda$.

Сделаем несколько комментариев и приведем несколько следствий этих теорем.

1. Близкие результаты в этом же направлении независимо и частично раньше получены И. А. Шведовым.

2. Вторая теорема сильнее первой: если во второй теореме к системе $\{F_\alpha\}$ прибавить еще отображение вложения $X \to bX$ то бикомпакт B будет искомым aX.

3. Эти теоремы, если исключить вопросы, связанные с пунктами 2) и 3) были доказаны автором в [6].

4. Для пространства X со счетной базой и счетного семейства $\{X_i\}$ его замкнутых подмножеств существует компактное расширение aX такое, что $\dim aX[X_i] = \dim X_i$. Это — классическая теорема Гуревича.

5. Каждое нормальное пространство с выделенным счетным семейством $\{X_i\}$ его замкнутых подмножеств имеет бикомпактное расширение aX того же веса, что и X и такое, что $\dim aX[X_i] = \dim X_i$ (Е. Г. Скляренко [7]).

6. Если взять в теореме о расширениях $\{X_\lambda\} = \{X\}$ и пустые семейства $\{F_\alpha\}$ и $\{G_\sigma\}$ то получим результаты R. Engelking'а и Е. Г. Скляренко [8].

7. Если взять в теореме о факторизации $\{X_\lambda\} = \{X\}$, $\{Y_\alpha\} = \{Y\}$, семейства $\{T_\omega\}$ и $\{G_\sigma\}$ пустыми, то получим известную теорему S. Mardešića [9].

8. Теорема A. B. Forge'а [10] также является следствием теоремы о расширениях.

Мы приведем доказательство второй теоремы как иллюстрирующее вышесказанное. Положим $K_{\sigma,\lambda} = K(G_\sigma, n_{\lambda,\sigma})$ и пусть $P_{\sigma,\lambda}{}^s$ семейство (очевидно, счетное) всех конечных полиэдров, являющихся суммой конечного числа клеток CW-комплекса $K_{\sigma,\lambda}$. Полиэдры $P_{\sigma,\lambda}{}^s$ будем считать лежащими в евклидовом пространстве $E^{N(s,\sigma,\lambda)}$ подходящей размерности. Возьмем в этом евклидовом пространстве окрестность $U_{\sigma,\lambda}{}^s$ полиэдра $P_{\sigma,\lambda}{}^s$ для которой существует деформационная ретракция $\mathrm{Ret}_{\sigma,\lambda}{}^s \colon \bar{U}_{\sigma,\lambda}{}^s \to P_{\sigma,\lambda}{}^s$. Аналогично, пусть $\mathrm{Ret}_\lambda \colon \bar{U}_\lambda \to S^{\dim X_\lambda}$ ретракция замыкания некоторой окрестности $\bar{U}_\lambda$ сферы $S^{\dim X_\lambda}$. Выберем в Y_α регулярное семейство функций минимальной мощности и через M_α обозначим его образ в $C(X)$ при отображении $F_\alpha{}^* \colon C(Y_\alpha) \to C(X)$. Через $T(A)$, где $T = \{T_\omega\}$, $A \subset C(X)$, будем обозначать множество всевозможных конечных суперпозиций вида $a \circ T_{\omega_1} \circ \ldots \circ T_{\omega_k}$, $a \in A$. Положим $M^1 = Q[T(\bigcup_\alpha M_\alpha)]$. По индукции построим семейство функций M^j со следующими свойствами: А) $M_{j'} \subseteqq M_{j''}$, если $j' \leqq j''$; Б) $Q[M^j] = M^j$; В) $T(M^j) = M^j$; Г) для каждого отображения имеющего вид $\mathrm{Ret}_{\sigma,\lambda}{}^s \circ \Omega | \Phi$, где компоненты отображения Ω принадлежат M^{j-1}, замкнутого $\Phi \subseteqq X_\lambda$ в один из полиэдров $P_{\sigma,\lambda}{}^s$ существует отображение всего X в некоторое $R^{N(s',\sigma\lambda)}$, которое на X_λ есть отображение X_λ в $K_{\sigma,\lambda}{}^{s'}$ и компоненты которого принадлежат M^j; Д) для каждого отображения, имеющего вид $\mathrm{Ret}_\lambda \circ \Omega | \Phi$, где компоненты Ω принадлежат M^{j-1}, замкнутого $\Phi \subseteqq X_\lambda$ в сферу $S^{\dim X_\lambda}$, существует отображение всего X в $E^{\dim X_\lambda + 1}$, продолжающее $\mathrm{Ret}_\lambda \circ \Omega$ на X_λ и компоненты которого принадлежат M^j; Е) мощность $M^j \leqq \tau$. Если $M^1 \subseteqq \ldots \subseteqq M^i$ уже построены, то прибавим к M^i множество функций N из элементов которого можно составить отображения в евклидовы пространства, удовлетворяющие требованиям Г) и Д). Такие функции для Г) на X_λ всегда можно найти, т. к. по предположению $\dim_{G_\sigma} X_\lambda = \dim_{G_\sigma} \beta X_\lambda = n_{\lambda,\sigma}$ (см. характеристику размерности возможностью продолжения отображений), а затем достарочно продолжить эти функции на все X. Здесь мы пользуемся известным фактом, что бикомпактные подмножества CW-комплекса $K_{\sigma,\lambda}$ пересекаются только с конечным числом клеток, и в частности образ βX_λ при продолженном отображении лежит в одном из $P_{\sigma,\lambda}{}^s$. Функции для Д) отыскиваются аналогично, используя критерий П. С. Александрова. После этого полагаем $M^{i+1} = Q[T(M^i \cup N)]$. Положим $M = \bigcup_{j=1}^{\infty} M^j$; M обладает всеми свойствами Б) — Е), если вместо M^j и M^{j-1} взять M. Кроме того, $M \supseteqq M^1$. Покажем, что $B = B_M$ обладает почти всеми нужными свойствами. Прежде всего выделим в $C(B)$ множество M' изоморфное M; если положить $F = F_M$, то соответствие между $f' \in M'$ и $f \in M$ дается равенством $f = f' \circ F$. Пусть $G_\alpha = \prod_{f' \in M_\alpha'} f'$, а преобразование U_ω: $B \to B$ определяется преобразованием U_ω': $M' \to M'$, $U_\omega'(m) = m \circ T_\omega$. Тогда свойства 1), 2) теоремы и неравенство вес $B \leqq \tau$ очевидны. Пусть теперь Φ замкнутое подмножество бикомпакта $B[F X_\lambda]$ и Ω отображение Φ в $K_{\sigma,\nu}$; Ω можно считать отображением в один из полиэдров $P_{\sigma,\lambda}{}^s$. В силу плотности $M' = Q[M']$ в $C(B)$ существует отображение Ω' некоторой замкнутой окрестности $\overline{V}$ множества Φ в $U_{\sigma,\lambda}{}^s$, компоненты которого принадлежат M, такое, что $\mathrm{Ret}_{\sigma,\lambda}{}^s \circ \Omega'$ гомотопно Ω. Согласно Г) существует продолжение ξ на X_λ отображения $\mathrm{Ret}_{\sigma,\lambda}{}^s \circ \Omega' | F X_\lambda$ (или, в терминах $C(X)$, продолжение отображения $\mathrm{Ret}_{\sigma,\lambda}{}^s \circ \Omega' \circ F | F^{-1}(\overline{V} \cap F X))$ в другой полиэдр $P_{\sigma,\lambda}{}^{s'} \subseteqq K_{\sigma,\lambda}$, компоненты которого принадлежат M'; в частности это отображение ξ автоматически породолжается на $B[F X_\lambda]$. Так как $\xi | \Phi$ равное $\mathrm{Ret}_{\sigma,\lambda}{}^s \circ \Omega' | \Phi$ гомотопно Ω, то по лемме Борсука существует и продолжение отображения Ω. Этим доказано, что $\dim_{G_\sigma} B[F X_\lambda] \leqq n_{\lambda,\sigma}$. Аналогично доказывается, что $\dim B[F X_\lambda] \leqq$ $\leqq \dim X_\lambda$. Наконец, равенства легко добиться, если с самого начала включить в семейство $\bigcup_\alpha M_\alpha$ отображения, ограничения которых на некоторые замкнутые подмножества $\Phi_\lambda \subseteqq X_\lambda$ задают отображения в $K(G_\sigma, n_{\lambda,\sigma} - 1)$ и в $S^{\dim X_\lambda - 1}$, которые не продолжаются на все X_λ. Теорема доказана.

3. Сравнение с другими конструкциями бикомпактных расширений

А. Если μ равномерная структура на пространстве X, обладающая базисом из конечных открытых покрытий, то бикомпактное расширение пространства X — пополнение по этой равномерной структуре есть, с точки зрения кольца $C(X)$, расширение, определенное кольцом равномерно непрерывных относительно μ функций на X.

Б. Если расширение αX получается как предел обратного спектра бикомпактов B_λ то, с точки зрения кольца $C(X)$ этому спектру соответствует частично упорядоченное по включению множество замкнутых подколец $C_\lambda = \pi_\lambda{}^* C(\overline{\pi_\lambda X})$, где π_λ: $X \to B_\lambda$ каноническая проекция, причем для каждых λ и μ существует $\nu \geqq \lambda, \mu$, для которого $C_\lambda \cup C_\mu \subseteqq C_\nu$. Кольцо $C(\alpha X) \subseteqq C(X)$ есть просто замыкание $\overline{\bigcup_\lambda C_\lambda}$. Это замечание позволяет, при желании, существенно упростить доказательство многих теорем, основанные на технике спектров.

Заметим также, что структура (в смысле теории частично упорядоченных множеств) всех бикомпактных расширений изоморфна структуре всех замкнутых регулярных подколец с единицей кольца $C(X)$: $C((\alpha X) \wedge (\alpha' X)) =$ $= C(\alpha(X)) \cap C(\alpha'(X))$, $C(\alpha X \wedge \alpha' X)$ есть минимальное замкнутое подкольцо, содержащее $C(\alpha X) \cup C(\alpha' X)$.

4. Пространства действительных идеалов

Для произвольного вещественного нормированного кольца C с единицей будем называть, следуя [11] действительным идеалом (h-идеалом в терминологии [12]) каждый идеал I фактор по которому изоморфен нормированному полю вещественных чисел R. Отметим, что мы не требуем полноты кольца G. Каждый действительный идеал максимален; обратное неверно. В множестве $\mathfrak{M}(C)$ всех действительных идеалов вводится естественная топология, в которой $\mathfrak{M}(C)$ становится бикомпактом [12]. Например, для свободного нормированного кольца G от τ неизвестных, представляющего кольцо многочленов, норма в котором определяется как сумма модулей коэффициентов, пространство $\mathfrak{M}(C)$ есть тихоновский кирпич веса τ. Основные факты о пространствах действительных идеалов, изложенные в [12] схожи с аналогичными утверждениями для пространств максимальных идеалов Гельфанда-Шилова [1]. Например, гомоморфизму $C \to C'$ соответствует отображение $\mathfrak{M}(C') \to \mathfrak{M}(C)$; это отображение будет вложением, если образ кольца C всюду плотен в C'. В частности, тот факт, что свободное кольцо можно гомоморфно отобразить на каждое кольцо означает, что бикомпакт веса $\leqq \tau$ вкладывается в тихоновский кирпич веса τ.

Использование пространства действительных идеалов часто позволяет пользоваться алгебраическими и функционально-аналитическими конструкциями для построения бикомпактов с нужными свойствами. Для этого необходимо иметь описание этих свойств в достаточно простых терминах.

Назовем, следуя М. Катетову подкольцо $A \subseteqq C$ алгебраически замкнутым в C, если из $x^n + a_1 x^{n-1} + \cdots + a_n = 0$, где $a_i \in A$, $x \in C$, следует, что $x \in A$. Оказывается, что если кольцо C изоморфно подкольцу $C(\mathfrak{M}(C))$, то A алгебраически замкнуто в C тогда и только тогда, когда соответствующее отображение $\mathfrak{M}(C) \to \mathfrak{M}(A)$ нульмерно в том смысле, что $\dim f^{-1} y \leqq 0$ для всех y. Эти результаты могут быть полезны для отыскания новых подходов к известным проблемам Хопфа и Уайлдера об открытых нульмерных отображениях n-мерного куба Q^n, так как $Q^n = \mathfrak{M}(C_n)$, где C_n-свободное нормированное кольцо от n переменных.

Мы дадим здесь только два приложения — это будут теоремы, доказанные первоначально Б. А. Пасынковым.

А. Пусть X бикомпакт, $\pi = \{\pi_\lambda\}$ регулярная сустема функций мощности, равной весу X. Для каждого $\tau \geqq$ веса X и для каждой функции $\varphi(\pi) \in Q[\pi_\lambda]$ возьмём τ символов $\tilde{\varphi}_\omega$. Рассмотрим свободное нормированное кольцо $\tilde{C}$ от символов $\{\tilde{\pi}_\lambda\}$, $\{\tilde{\varphi}_\omega\}$, считая $\|\tilde{\pi}_\lambda\| = \|\pi_\lambda\|$, $\|\tilde{\varphi}_\omega\| = \|\varphi(\pi)\|$. Если I замкнутый идеал, порождённый элементами вида $\tilde{\varphi}_\omega{}^2 - \tilde{\varphi}_\omega \varphi(\tilde{\pi})$ и $C = \tilde{C}/I$, то $\mathfrak{M}(C)$ есть универсальное пространство в классе всех бикомпактов веса $\leqq \tau$, допускающих нульмерное отображение в бикомпакт X.

Б. Пусть C' свободное нормированное кольцо от символов f, π_λ, φ_λ; мощность множества индексов равна τ. Пусть I замкнутый идеал, порождённый элементами вида $\varphi_\lambda{}^2 - \varphi_\lambda \pi_\lambda$ и $\pi_\lambda{}^2 - \pi_\lambda f$, и $C = C'/I$. Тогда $\mathfrak{M}(C)$ есть одномерный бикомпакт, отображающийся нульмерным и открытым образом на тихоновский кирпич веса τ, $T = \mathfrak{M}(\overline{C})$, где $\overline{C}$ — свободное нормированное кольцо, порождённое символами $\{\pi_\lambda\}$. В частности, получаем следующую замечательную теорему Б. А. Пасынкова: каждое вполне регулярное пространство есть открыто-замкнутый образ одномерного пространства при совершенном отображении.

Литература

[1] И. М. Гельфанд, Д. А. Райков и Г. Е. Шилов, Коммутативные нормированные кольца, Москва 1960 (I. M. Gelfand, D. A. Raikow und G. E. Schilow, Kommutative normierte Algebren, Berlin 1964).

[2] С. В. Фомин, К вопросу о связи между пространствами близости и бикомпактными расширениями, Доклады АН СССР **121** (1958), 236—238.

[3] Ю. М. Смирнов, Обобщение теоремы Вейерштрасса-Стона на пространства близости, Чехосл. Мат. Ж. **10** (1960), 493—500.
[4] R. Engelking, Sur la compactification des espaces métriques, Fund. Math. **48** (1960), 321—324.
[5] P. J. Huber, Homotopical cohomology and Čech cohomology, Math. Ann. **144** (1961), 73—76.
[6] А. В. Зарелуа, О продолжении отображений на расширения, обладающие некоторыми специальными свойствами, Сибирск. Мат. Ж. **5** (1964), 532—548.
[7] Е. Г. Скляренко, О вложении нормальных пространств в бикомпакты того же веса и той же размерности, Доклады АН СССР **123** (1958), 36—39.
[8] R. Engelking and E. G. Sklyarenko, On compactifications allowing extensions of mappings, Fund. Math. **53** (1963), 65—80.
[9] S. Mardešić, On covering dimension and inverse limits of compact spaces, Illinois J. Math. **4** (1960), 278—291.
[10] A. B. Forge, Dimension preserving compactifications allowing extensions of continuous functions, Duke Math. J. **28** (1961), 625—627.
[11] L. Gillman and M. Jerison, Rings of continuous functions, Princeton 1960.
[12] А. В. Зарелуа, Универсальный бикомпакт данного веса и данной размерности, Доклады АН СССР **154** (1964), 1015—1018.

Summary

The method of the theory of rings of functions for the construction of compact extensions

A. V. Zarelua (Novosibirsk)

Following Gelfand-Šilov we shall construct compact extensions of a given completely regular space by the space of maximal ideals of a suitable ring of continuous bounded real valued functions. The main results are the following:

A general extension theorem

For a given normal space X let $(X_\lambda)_{\lambda \in \Lambda}$ be a family of closed subsets with power of $\Lambda \leqq \tau$; $(F_\alpha)_{\alpha \in A}$ a family of mappings of the space X into compact Hausdorff spaces Y_α (weight $Y_\alpha \leqq \tau$) with power of $A \leqq \tau$; a family of transformations $T_\omega: X \to X$ $(\omega \in W)$ with power of $W \leqq \tau$. Furtheron let $n_{\lambda,\sigma}$ denote the dimension numbers of the subsets X_σ with respect to given finite or countable groups G_σ, $\sigma \in S$, with power of $S \leqq \tau$.

Then for each compact extension bX of the space X exists a compact extension aX greater then bX with weight $\leqq \max\{\text{weight } bX, \tau\}$ such that:

1. the mappings $F_\alpha: X \to Y_\alpha$ can be extended to $\tilde{F}_\alpha: aX \to Y_\alpha$,

2. the transformations $T_\omega: X \to X$ can be extended to $\tilde{T}_\omega: aX \to aX$,

3. the dimension number of the closure of X_λ in aX with respect to the groups G_σ is identical with $n_{\lambda,\sigma}$: $\dim_{G_\sigma} \overline{X}_\lambda{}^{aX} = n_{\lambda,\sigma}$,

4. $\dim \overline{X}_\lambda{}^{aX} = \dim X_\lambda$.

A general factorisation theorem

Under the assumptions of the first theorem it can be stated the existence of a compact Hausdorff space B which weight $\leqq \tau$ and a mapping $F: X \to B$ and mappings $H_\alpha: B \to Y_\alpha$ and transformations $U_\omega: B \to B$ thus that:

1) $H_\alpha \circ F = F_\alpha$,

2) $U_\omega \circ F = F \circ T_\omega$,

3) $\dim_{G_\sigma} \overline{FX_\lambda}^B = n_{\lambda,\sigma}$,

4) $\dim \overline{FX_\lambda}^B = \dim X_\lambda$.

РАСШИРЕНИЯ ТОПОЛОГИЧЕСКИХ СТРУКТУР И МЕТРИЧЕСКИЕ СВОЙСТВА ОТОБРАЖЕНИЙ

Г. Д. Суворов (Донецк)

Мы приводим здесь краткий обзор основных результатов, полученных автором и его учениками при изучении метрических свойств плоских и пространственных отображений замкнутых областей евклидовых и некоторых других пространств. В наших исследованиях замыкание областей происходит присоединением граничных элементов, определяемых по-разному в разных ситуациях. Используется методика, в основном восходящая к известной работе К. Каратеодори [1] о простых концах односвязной области, дополненная подходящей метризацией замкнутых областей с помощью ,,относительных" расстояний. Впервые граница К. Каратеодори была метризована, видимо, С. Мазуркевичем [2], а первая оценка искажения ,,относительных" расстояний при конформных отображениях замкнутого круга на замкнутую односвязную область принадлежит М. А. Лаврентьеву [3]. В описываемых работах эти идеи систематически используются и в некоторых направлениях обобщаются. Исследуются классы отображений, выделение и изучение которых является, по нашему мнению, следующим шагом после изучения квазиконформных отображений, плоских и пространственных. Значение результатов — в новых фактах теории функций. С топологической точки зрения работы содержат разве что удобные в приложениях конкретные реализации сравнительно простых расширений топологических структур. Однако эти работы вновь показывают, что общее топологическое понятие границы, восходящее к К. Каратеодори и систематически изученное и обобщенное на общие топологические структуры в работах А. Д. Мышкиса [4], [5], находит применение и в современной метрической теории отображений, причем, по мере дальнейшего ее развития неизбежно вовлечение в обиход метрической теории все более общих топологических концепций. Это и дает нам некоторые основания для помещения нашего обзора в трудах топологического Симпозиума.

Не ставя себе цели перечислить все результаты в полных формулировках, мы ограничимся общим описанием тематики и выявлением основных направлений проводимых исследований. Приводимая библиография не полна.

1. Общая постановка задачи

Нас интересуют преимущественно метрические свойства отображений в ,,замкнутых" областях, причем, первоначально отображения задаются только внутри областей. Следовательно, первым является вопрос о возможности продолжения отображения на границу области, в частности, вопрос о соответствии границ, если отображение гомеоморфное. Он имеет два аспекта: топологический — вопрос о введении граничных элементов в области и метрический — действительно ли для данного отображения соответствие границ осуществляется по a priori введенным граничным элементам. При этом естественно, для начала, ограничиться задачей о выделении тех классов отображений, для которых в допустимых парах областей (то есть в областях, которые можно отобразить друг на друга функцией из данного класса) возможно единообразное введение граничных элементов, так чтобы соответствие границ в пределах класса осуществлялось именно по этим элементам. Таким образом, нужно согласованное выделение объекта: класса отображений и граничных элементов в допустимых областях. Такая ,,согласованность" обеспечена, если для конкретного класса отображений удается реализовать следующее построение.

Пусть A — область произвольного компакта (M, r) (M — множество элементов, r — расстояние), B — область другого компакта (N, ϱ) и $T(A) = B$ — топологическое отображение. В A вводим новое (относительное) расстояние r_A, в области B — расстояние ϱ_B, причем так, чтобы относительные метрики в A и B были эквивалентны (в малом) метрикам объемлющих пространств r и ϱ соответственно. Пусть $\tilde{A}$ — пополнение A по r_A и $\tilde{B}$ — пополнение B по ϱ_B. Присоединяемые к A и B ,,граничные" элементы суть классы эквивалентных фундаментальных последовательностей в пространствах (A, r_A) и (B, ϱ_B).

Если известны функции $\varphi_j(\alpha)$ $(j = 1, 2)$, $\varphi_j(\alpha) \to 0$ при $\alpha \to 0$, такие что для любых, достаточно близких по r_A точек x', $x'' \in A$ будет:

$$\varphi_1[r_A(x', x'')] \leqq \varrho_B[T(x'), T(x'')] \leqq \varphi_2[r_A(x', x'')] \tag{1}$$

то, очевидно, T можно продолжить до гомеоморфизма $T(\tilde{A}) = \tilde{B}$ (вопрос о соответствии границ решен) и (1) будет справедливо и в ,,замкнутой" области:

$$\varphi_1[r_A(e_1, e_2)] \leqq \varrho_B[T(e_1), T(e_2)] \leqq \varphi_2[r_A(e_1, e_2)], \tag{2}$$

где e_j — элементы $\tilde{A}$.

Двусторонняя оценка (2), в особенности если φ_j и ,,интервал", на котором (2) имеет место, одни и те же для отображений некоторого класса, содержит в себе информацию, достаточную для обнаружения ряда основных метрических свойств отображений (выявлению этой информации в общем случае посвящена готовящаяся к печати работа В. П. Луференко и Г. Д. Суворова). Поэтому поиски ,,согласованных" объектов, для которых имеет место (2) (или хотя бы односторонняя оценка) является основной задачей описываемых дальше исследований.

2. Классы отображений

Пусть E^n — n-мерное евклидово пространство в прямоугольной системе координат (x): $x = \{x_1, \ldots, x_n\}$, и $y \equiv T(x) = \{f_1(x), f_2(x), \ldots, f_p(x)\}$, — отображение области $D \subset E^n$ в E^p; $\mu = \mu(y)$, $y = \{y_1, \ldots, y_p\}$, непрерывная и неотрицательная функция, определенная для весх $y \in \Delta$, где Δ — подмногообразие E^p, которому принадлежат образы областей D при отображениях T определяемого дальше класса.

Пусть $\alpha \geqq 1$. При $\alpha > 1$ предполагается, что

$$\int_{\bar{\Delta}_1} \mu^{-\frac{1}{1-\alpha}}(y)\, dy < +\infty$$

для любой ограниченной замкнутой подобласти $\bar{\Delta}_1 \subset \Delta$, а при $\alpha = 1$ считаем, что $\mu(y) \neq 0$ в Δ.

Отображение T принадлежит классу $BL_k^\alpha(\mu)$ в D относительно системы координат (x), если f_j $(j = 1, \ldots, p)$, непрерывны в D, имеют обобщенные частные производные первого порядка по всем x_i в смысле С. Л. Соболева, причем, для любой замкнутой ограниченной подобласти $\bar{D}_1 \subset D$

$$\int_{\bar{D}_1} \lambda(x, T)\, dx < \infty,$$

где

$$\lambda(x, T) = \sum_{i=1}^{n} \sum_{j=1}^{P} \left(\frac{\partial f_i}{\partial x_i}\right), \qquad dx = dx_1, \cdots dx_n,$$

и, кроме того,

$$\int_D \mu[T(x)]\, \lambda^\alpha(x, T)\, dx \leqq \boldsymbol{k}.$$

$T \in BL^\alpha(\mu)$ в D, если $T \in BL_k^\alpha(\mu)$ при некотором k. При $\mu \equiv 1$ и $\alpha = n/2$ соответствующие классы обозначаем $BL_k^{n/2}$ и $BL^{n/2}$. Если $\mu \equiv 1$, $\alpha = 1$, $n = p = 2$, получаем классы BL_k и BL, а если $\mu = \dfrac{1}{\left(1 + \sum_{j=1}^{2} f_j^2\right)^2}$, $\alpha = 1$, $n = p = 2$, — классы $\widetilde{BL}_k$ и $\widetilde{BL}$.

Существенно, что класс $BL_k^\alpha(\mu)$ отображений области D замкнут относительно равномерной сходимости внутри D (М. В. Бакланов и Г. Д. Суворов [6]).

3. Основные неравенства метода

Единственным пока методом изучения метрических свойств отображений некоторых из выше определенных классов является метод, основанный на использовании неравенств типа „принципа длины и площади“, известного в теории аналитических финкций.

Рассмотрим непрерывное отображение $w = T(z)$, $w = f_1 + if_2$, $z = x + iy$, области $D \subset E^2$ в E^2. В плоскости z рассматривается сферическая метрика (R), получаемся стереографическим проектированием плоскости z на сферу Римана радиуса R, касающуюся плоскости в начале координат. Аналогично в плоскости w рассматривается сферическая метрика (r) (в общем случае $R \neq r$).

Пусть $F \subset E^2$ — замкнутое множество, $\varrho_R(z)$ — сферическое расстояние от $z \in E^2$ до F, $\Gamma_t = \{z: \varrho_R(z) = t\} \cap D$ — часть множества сферического „уровня t“ функции ϱ_R, принадлежащая D, $q \geqq 1$, и пусть f_j $(j = 1, 2)$ имеют обобщенные в смысле С. Л. Соболева производные в D первого порядка и дифференцируемы почти всюду в D (последнее условие можно заменить условием открытости отображения T). Тогда

$$\int_{\tau_1}^{\tau_2} \frac{L_r^q[T(\Gamma_t)]}{L_R^{q-1}(\Gamma_t)} \, dt \leqq \iint_{D_{\tau_1 \tau_2}} \mu_r^{q/2}[T(z)] \lambda^{q/2}(z, T) \, \mu_R^{(2-q)/2}(z) \, dx \, dy, \tag{3}$$

где τ_1, τ_2 — числа, выбранные так, что для $t \in [\tau_1, \tau_2]$ Γ_t не пусто, $L_R(\Gamma_t)$ — длина по Хаусдорфу, определяемая на основе сферической метрики, $L_r[T(\Gamma_t)]$ для почти всех t есть сумма сферических (в метрике (r)) длин образов составляющих дуг множества Γ_t, $D_{\tau_1 \tau_2}$ — подмножество D, заметаемое Γ_t при изменении t и

$$\mu r(T) = \frac{1}{\left(1 + \left|\frac{T}{2r}\right|^2\right)^2}, \quad \mu_R(z) = \frac{1}{\left(1 + \left|\frac{z}{2R}\right|^2\right)^2}.$$

Впрочем в (3) вместо длины по Хаусдорфу $L_R(\Gamma_t)$ можно брать просто сферическую длину в метрике (R) (см. работы В. К. Ионина и Г. Д. Суворова [7], Б. П. Куфарева и Н. Г. Никулиной [8]).

Если F — точка, $q = 2$ и $T \in \widetilde{BL}$ в D, то из (3) получаем:

$$\int_{\tau_1}^{\tau_2} L_r^2[T(\Gamma_t)] \frac{dt}{t} \leqq 2\pi \iint_{D_{\tau_1 \tau_2}} \mu[T(z)] \lambda(z, T) \, dx \, dy \tag{4}$$

— неравенство в классе BL, получившее пока что наибольшее число приложений (J. Lelong-Ferrand [9], Г. Д. Суворов [10], [11]). Более общий результат (3) получен Б. П. Куфаревым [12], [22].

Имеются уточнения неравенства (4) для Q-квазиконформных топологических отображений и в несколько видоизмененном виде — для внутренних Q-квазиконформных отображений [10]. Для внутренних Q-квазиконформных отображений аналог неравенства (3) имеется в работе [12].

Неравенство, являющееся аналогом (4) для трехмерного случая $(n = p = 3)$ установлено И. С. Овчинниковым и Г. Д. Суворовым в [13], а для произвольных $n \geqq 3$ получено И. С. Овчинниковым в [14] как следствие установленного им же общего метрико-геометрического неравенства, имеющего ,,изопрометрический" характер. Приведем наиболее общий результат $(n \geqq 3)$ из [14]:

Пусть $T \in BL^{n/2}$ в D, $\{S_t\}$ — семейство концентрических сфер в E^n с центром в точке a, $a < \tau_1 \leqq t \leqq \tau_2$, и для этого семейства множества $S_t' = S_t \cap D$ не пусты. Обозначим через K_t открытый сферический круг сферического радиуса $R(t) \leqq \frac{\pi t}{2}$, $K_t \subset S_t'$. Предположим, что на $[\tau_1, \tau_2]$ определены измеримые функции $\Omega(t)$ и $\beta(t)$ такие, что для почти всех t

$$\Omega(t) \leqq \omega(K_t, T), \ \beta(t) \geqq \frac{2R(t)}{\pi t},$$

где ω — колебание T на K_t.

Тогда

$$\int_{\tau_1}^{\tau_2} \frac{\Omega^n(t)}{t\,\beta(t)}\,dt \leqq M_n \int_{D_{\tau_1 \tau_2}} \lambda^{n/2}(x, T)\,dx\,, \tag{5}$$

где

$$D_{\tau_1,\tau_2} = \bigcup_{t \in [\tau_1, \tau_2]} S_t', \qquad M_n = \frac{1}{2}\,\pi^n\,\Gamma\left(\frac{n-1}{2}\right)\left[\frac{\Gamma\left(\frac{1}{2(n-1)}\right)}{\Gamma\left(\frac{n}{2(n-1)}\right)}\right]^{n-1},$$

Γ — гамма-функция Эйлера.

4. Резултаты в случае $n = p = 2$

Построение, общая схема которого приведена в п. 1 для этого случая полностью осуществлено [10]. Как мы уже отметили, начало здесь было положено М. А. Лаврентьевым [3].

Неравенство (4) служит для получения основных оценок (1). Компакты (M, r), (N, ϱ) — плоскости, пополненные бесконечностью, допустимые области — произвольные односвязные плоские области с границей, содержащей более одной точки, $\{T\}$ — класс $\widetilde{BL}$ (или BL) причем обратные отображения должны принадлежать тем же классам. r_A (и ϱ_B) — относительные расстояния, вводимые на основе сферической или евклидовой метрик. В первом случае определение таково: Пусть односвязная область $A \subset E^2$ содержит точку O и $x', x'' \in A$, $x', x'' \neq 0$ — точки. Тогда

$$\varrho_A(x', x'') = \min(\varrho_1, \varrho_2),$$

где ϱ_1 — точная нижняя грань сферических диаметров дуг, соединяющих x' и x'' в A, а ϱ_2 — точная нижняя грань сферических диаметров сечений A, отделяющих $x' \cup x''$ от O. Пополнение A по ϱ_A присоединяет точку O и „граничные" элементы, которые можно отождествить с простыми концами К. Каратеодори. Функции φ_j в (1) определяются: $\varphi_2(\alpha) = K \ln^{-\frac{1}{2}} \frac{1}{\alpha}$ и $\varphi_1 \equiv \varphi_2^{-1}$ (обратная к φ_2 функция), K — константа в случае классов $\widetilde{BL}_k$ (или BL_k), т. е. φ_j — одни и те же для всех отображений класса. Не зависит от отображений и интервал, на котором имеют место оценки (2), то есть для классов $\widetilde{BL}_k$ и BL_k (при некоторых естественных дополнительных условиях нормировки) оценки носят равностепенный характер.

Установленные оценки (2) для этих классов позволяют оценить порядки равностепенной равномерной непрерывности и открытости в замкнутых областях (по относительным метрикам), порядки равномерной непрерывности и открытости внутри областей (уже в терминах сферических или евклидовых расстояний), оценить искажение множеств уровня расстояний r_A и r до границы области, искажение площадей пограничных колец, граничных дуг и т. д. (см. [10], [11]). Классы $\widetilde{BL}_k$ и BL_k содержат конформные, квазиконформные и более общие отображения, причем полученные результаты оказались новыми даже для конформных отображений.

Распространение основных результатов на случай конечно-связных областей содержится в работе В. Н. Лукина [15], а на случай областей произвольной связности в готовящейся к печати работе В. П. Луференко и В. М. Миклюкова.

Аналогичное исследование было проведено в случае, когда компакты — ограниченная часть плоскости Лобачевского, r и ϱ — гиперболические расстояния, а r_A (и ϱ_B) вводятся на их основе (М. В. Бакланов, Г. Д. Суворов [16]). В плане реализации схемы п. 1 рассмотрен общий класс плоских отображений таких, что соответствие границ носит более общий характер (не по простым концам (М. В. Бакланов [17])).

Отображения одного общего класса, переводящие всю конечную плоскость в такую же плоскость (случай исключаемый в других работах) рассмотрен Ю. К. Устиновым в [18].

Мы описали результаты для случаев плоских отображений классов BL_k и $\widetilde{BL}_k$, т. е. для случая $\alpha = 1$. При $\alpha > 1$ классы

$$BL_k^\alpha(1) \subset BL_k \quad \text{и} \quad BL_k^\alpha(\mu) \subset \widetilde{BL}_k, \qquad \mu = (1 + \sum f_j^2)^{-1},$$

сужаются. Как следует из теорем вложения С. Л. Соболева отображения этих классов областей с достаточно гладкими границами можно продолжать по непрерывносты на границу, и в замкнутых (по евклидовому расстоянию) областях имеет место верхняя оценка (2) с $\varphi_2(t) \equiv kt^\beta$ где $0 < \beta \leqq 1$ и β зависит от k. Следовательно, если отображение — гомеоморфизм, то все простые концы области — образа содержат всегда только одну точку. Значит, не любые две односвязные области отобразимы друг на друга в пределах этого класса. Другие свойства, специфические для этих классов неизвестны.

При $0 < \alpha < 1$ классы $BL_k^\alpha(1) \supset BL_k$, $BL_k^\alpha(\mu) \supset \widetilde{BL}_k$ существенно расширяются. Ведение граничных элементов a priori в допустимых областях как показал на примере И. С. Овчинников невозможно. Оценки типа (2) равностепенные по классу невозможны, равностепенная непрерывность класса не имеет места. Дальнейшие свойства этих классов не изучены.

В случае $\alpha = 1$ И. С. Овчинников на примере показал точность порядка оценок (2) с φ_j, указанными выше. По-видимому оценки точны и для подкласса конформных отображений односвязных областей с произвольными границами, хотя соответствующие примеры нам не известны.

Отметим еще одно обобщение неравенства (4), полученное В. М. Миклюковым: Пусть $w = T(z)$ — непрерывное в области D отображение, имеющее обобщенные частные производные первого порядка, суммируемые с квадратом на любом компакте $F \subset D$. Предположим, что существует дважды непрерывно дифференцируемая неотрицательная вещественная функция $\Phi(x)$, выпуклая вниз (т. е. $\Phi''(x) > 0$) такая, что

$$\iint_D \Phi\left[\sqrt{\lambda(z,\, T)}\right] dx\, dy < \infty .$$

Тогда для отображений этого класса имеет место неравенство

$$\int_{\tau_1}^{\tau_2} \Phi\left[\frac{L[T(\Gamma_t)]}{2\pi t}\right] t dt \leqq \iint_{D_{\tau_1 \tau_2}} \Phi\left[\sqrt{\lambda(z,\, T)}\right] dx\, dy, \tag{6}$$

где L — обычная длина, а остальные обозначения те же, что и выше.

При $\Phi(x) \equiv x^2$ получаем класс BL и (6) переходит в (4).

Если интеграл $\int\limits_0^a \Phi\left(\frac{1}{r}\right) r\,dr$ расходится, то существуют функции $\varphi_j (j = 1, 2)$, удовлетворяющие условиям п. 1 такие, что оценки (1), (2) искажения относительных расстояний при гомеоморфизмах указанного класса имеют место с этими функциями, причем φ_2 уже не обязательно выражается через логарифмы. С помощью этих оценок результаты, установленные для классов BL, BL_k с помощью оценки (2) распространяются и на этот более широкий класс отображений.

Известно, что уже для Q-квазиконформных отображений круга на круг их продолжения на границу не обязательно абсолютно непрерывны на граничной окружности. Поэтому для таких и для более общих отображений интересно выделить такие множества простых концов или других каких-то граничных образований области, которые при отображении области, например, на круг переходили бы во множество лебеговой меры нуль на окружности. Два результата для отображений $T \in BL$, $T^{-1} \in BL$ (или для класса $\widetilde{BL}$), содержащие достаточные условия, получены Г. Д. Суворовым [20], исходя из неравенства (4) и Б. П. Куфаревым [21] с помощью неравенства (3), однако вопрос этот нельзя считать исчерпанным.

Большинство полученных резултатов, по нашему мнению, выявляет основные метрические свойства отображений. Например, свойства равностепенной непрерывности и открытости внутри областей дают (в сочетании с одной общей метрико-топологической теоремой из [10]) достаточные условия для существования связи между равномерной сходимостью последовательности отображений внутри области и сходимостью к ядру последовательности областей — образов [10], связи, вполне аналогичной той, которая имеется в случае конформных отображений (Теорема К. Каратеодори). Еще пример: свойства равностепенной равномерной непрерывности и открытости отображений в замкнутых областях обеспечивает возможность решения вопроса о соответствии границ при отображениях областей с переменными границами, а именно, обеспечивается применимость теории простых концов последовательности областей, сходящейся к невырожденному ядру, развитой сначала для конформных отображений [19], и к отображениям класса $\widetilde{BL}_k$, если и $T^{-1} \in \widetilde{BL}_k$ в соответствующих областях [10].

Мы приведем здесь основную теорему о соответствии границ при отображении областей с переменными границами. Предварительно напомним, как вводится основное понятие соответствующей теории — понятие простого конца последовательности областей [10].

Пусть последовательность $B(B_0) = \{B_n\}$ плоских односвязных областей B_n сходится относительно начала координат к невырожденному ядру B_0 (в смысле К. Каратеодори), граница которого содержит более одной точки.

Последовательность $\{\beta_n\} = \beta\{\beta_0\}$ жордановых сечений лежит над сечением β_0 ядра B_0, если $\operatorname{lt} \beta_n = \beta_0$ (топологический предел) и точки $P' \in B_0$, $P'' \in B_0$, разделяемые сечением β_0 в B_0 разделяются и β_n в B_n при $n > n(P', P'')$. Такая последовательность определяет (с точностью до конечного числа членов) последовательности $b(b_0') = \{b_n'\}$ и $b(b_0'') = \{b_n''\}$ компонент связности $B_n \setminus \beta_n$, содержащих, соответственно, P' и P''. Эти последовательности называются „элементами“, лежащими, соответственно, над компонентами b_0' и b_0'' связности множества

$B_0 \setminus \beta_0$. Цепью элементов называется последовательность $\{b(b_0^k)\}$ элементов, лежащих соответственно над членами цепи (в смысле теории простых концов К. Каратеодори) подобластей $b_0^1 \supset b_0^2 \supset \cdots \supset b_0^k \supset \cdots$ ядра B_0. Цепь $\{b(b_0^k)\}$ входит в элемент $a(a_0)$, если для некоторых k_1 и n_1 будет $b_n^{k_1} \subset a_n$, для всех $n \geqq n_1$, и — входит в цепь $\{a(a_0^k)\}$, если входит в каждый $a(a_0^k)$.

Две цепи, входящие друг в друга, считаются эквивалентными, а класс эквивалентности цепей называется концом последовательности областей $B(B_0)$. Понятие делимости концов и понятие простого конца $B(B_0)$ вводятся по К. Каратеодори. Между простыми концами B_0 и простыми концами $B(B_0)$ естественно устанавливается взаимнооднозначное соответствие, так что простые концы $B(B_0)$ можно обозначить как $e_b(e_{b_0})$, где e_{b_0} — соответствующий простой конец ядра B_0.

Соотнесенной точкой $(e, n) \equiv e_n$ области B_n называем пару из внутренней точки $e \in B_n$ (или простого конца e области B_n) и числа n; $(e, n) = (e', n')$ в том и только в том случае, если $e = e'$ и $n = n'$. Последовательность соотнесенных точек называется правильной, если в ней содержится не более одного простого конца (или внутренней точки) каждой из областей последовательности $B(B_0)$.

Правильная последовательность $\{e_{n_i}\}$ сходится к простому концу $e_b(e_{b_0})$, если e_{n_i} входит в каждый элемент цепи $\{b(b_0^k)\}$, определяющей $e_b(e_{b_0})$, т.е. если начиная с некоторого $i(k)$ e_{n_i}, входит в $b_n{}^k$, где $b_{n_i}{}^k$ — одна из областей, образующих $b(b_0^k)$.

Доказывается, что из всякой правильной последовательности можно выбрать подпоследовательность, сходящуюся к простому концу $B(B_0)$ или к точке ядра B_0.

Основной результат для случая отображений класса $\widetilde{BL}_k$ формулируется так:

Рассматривается последовательность $A(A_0) = \{A_n\}$ (соответственно $B(B_0) = \{B_n\}$) $(n = 1, 2, \ldots)$ плоских односвязных областей плоскости z (соответственно плоскости w), не содержащих внутри бесконечно удаленной точки, сходящаяся к невырожденному ядру $A_0 \ni O$ (соответственно, к $B_0 \ni O$). Предполагается, что найдется число $\gamma_0 > 0$ такое, что сферические диаметры в метрике $\left(\frac{1}{2}\right)$ границ всех областей не меньше γ_0.

Пусть $w = T_n(z)$, $T_n(0) = 0$ $(n = 1, 2, \ldots)$ — последовательность топологических отображений замкнутых простыми концами областей последовательности $A(A_0)$ на области последовательности $B(B_0)$, $\tilde{B}_n = T_n(\tilde{A}_n)$, причем $T_n \in \widetilde{BL}_k$ в A_n, $T_n^{-1} \in \widetilde{BL}_k$ в B_n и k — не зависит от n.

Предполагается так же, что последовательность $\{T_n\}$ (последовательность $\{T_n^{-1}\}$) сходится равномерно внутри области A_0 (области B_0) к топологическому отображению T_0 (T_0^{-1}) области A_0 на B_0 (области B_0 на A_0).

Тогда между простыми концами последовательности $A(A_0)$ и простыми концами последовательности $B(B_0)$ существует взаимнооднозначное соответствие, устанавливаемое предельным отображением T_0, $\tilde{B}_0 = T_0(\tilde{A}_0)$, обладающее следующими свойствами:

Если бесконечная последовательность $\{e^z_{n_i}\}$ ($e^z_{n_i}$ — внутренняя точка или простой конец области A_{n_i}) и бесконечная последовательность $\{e^w_{n_i}\}$ ($e^w_{n_i}$ — внутренняя точка или простой конец области B_{n_i}) связаны равенствами

$$T_{n_i}(e^z_{n_i}) = e^w_{n_i},$$

то из сходимости последовательности $\{e^z_{n_i}\}$ к простому концу $e_a(e_{a_0})$ последовательности $A(A_0)$ следует сходимость последовательности $\{e^w_{n_i}\}$ к простому концу

$e_b(e_{b_0})$ последовательности $B(B_0)$, причем $e_{b_0} = T_0(e_{a_0})$, и обратно, из сходимости $\{e^w_{n_i}\}$ к $e_b(e_{b_0})$ следует сходимость $\{e^z_{n_i}\}$ к $e_a(e_{a_0})$, причем $e_{a_0} = T_0^{-1}(e_{b_0})$.

Заметим, что топологическое содержание теории простых концов последовательности $B(B_0)$ сводится к введению границы во множестве B всех соотнесенных точек последовательности $B(B_0)$ (которое можно превратить в топологическое пространство) двумя эквивалентными способами — один раз — с помощью некоторых семейств открытых множеств соотнесенных точек, (и это обеспечивает геометрическую наглядность и удобство приложений) и второй раз — с помощью некоторых семейств последовательностей соотнесенных точек (что и позволяет применять теорию к изучению свойств последовательностей отображений). Точки ядра B_0 и простые концы последовательности $B(B_0)$ суть граничные элементы топологического пространства B, совокупность их есть граница B „в узком смысле" по А. Д. Мышкису [4], [5], а в целом, построение вполне аналогично построению К. Каратеодори (теория простых концов). Приведенная выше теорема устанавливает гомеоморфизм пополненных пространств $\tilde{A}$ и $\tilde{B}$ при отображениях $\{T_n\}$. В [10] даны многочисленные приложения этой теоремы к вопросам сходимости последовательностей однолистных отображений. Кроме того в [10] и в ряде других работ систематически развивается чисто топологически теория простых концов последовательности областей, которая оказывается достаточно содержательной.

Вот еще один, неопубликованный пока результат (Г. Д. Суворов), устанавливающий (с использованием вышеупомянутой основной теоремы) равностепенную устойчивость конформных отображений замкнутых областей в классе $\widetilde{BL_k}$.[1])

Рассматривается семейство $\{T\}$ плоских топологических отображений односвязных замкнутых (простыми концами К. Каратеодори) областей $\{\tilde{D}_T\}$ на замкнутые области $\{\tilde{\Delta}_T\}$, $T(\tilde{D}_T) = \tilde{\Delta}_T$, $T(O) = O$, $T, T^{-1} \in \widetilde{BL_k}$. Пусть для всех $T \equiv U + iV \in \{T\}$

$$\iint\limits_{D_T} \frac{(U_x \mp V_y)^2 + (U_y \pm V_x)^2}{(1 + |T|^2)^2}\, dx\, dy \leqq \varepsilon,$$

где знаки выбираются верхние (нижние), если T сохраняет (меняет) ориентацию. Семейства $\{D_T\}$ и $\{\Delta_T\}$ имеют невырожденные ядра относительно точки O, и сферические диаметры границ всех областей ограничены снизу одним и тем же положительным числом.

В каждой области D_T фиксируется по одному простому концу e^{D_T} и рассматривается семейство $\{\Phi_T\}$ конформных отображений 1-го или 2-го рода, $\Phi_T(\tilde{D}_T) = \Delta_T$, $\Phi_T(O) = O$, $\Phi_T(e^{D_T}) = T(e^{D_T})$, ориентированных так же, как и соответствующие T. Тогда существуют функции $\lambda_j(\varepsilon)$, $\lambda_j \to 0$ при $\varepsilon \to 0$ $(j = 1, 2)$ такие, что для всех $T \in \{T\}$ будет

$$\varrho\left[T(e),\ \Phi_T(e);\ \tilde{\Delta}_T;\ \frac{1}{2}\right] \leqq \lambda_1(\varepsilon), \qquad \varrho\left[T^{-1}(e),\ \Phi_T^{-1}(e);\ \tilde{D}_T;\ \frac{1}{2}\right] \leqq \lambda_2(\varepsilon),$$

причем, оба неравенства имеют место в замкнутых областях $\tilde{D}_T$ и $\tilde{\Delta}_T$ соответственно.

[1]) Примечание при корректуре: Результат опубликован, см. Укр. Матем. Ж. **20** 1968), 78—84.

Метод исследования в плоском случае, а так же решенные здесь задачи, послужили образцом для поисков аналогов в случае пространственных отображений. Этот же метод годится и для изучения неоднолистных плоских отображений, например, монотонных, или внутренних. Имеющиеся здесь возможности далеко не исчерпаны.

5. Случай $n \geqq 3$

Основное неравенство метода — неравенство (5). Первоначально был рассмотрен случай $n = p = 3$ (И. С. Овчинников, Г. Д. Суворов [13]). Полученные в [13] результаты, с добавлением новых, были перенесены и на случай $n > 3$ И. С. Овчинниковым [14]. Займемся кратким перечислением этих результатов в той общности, которую им придал И. С. Овчинников:

Получена оценка сверху искажения евклидового расстояния внутри произвольных областей для монотонных отображений класса $BL^{n/2}$. Для класса $BL_k^{n/2}$ эта оценка носит равностепенных характер, стало быть определяется порядок равностепенной непрерывности внутри области этого класса отображений. Рассмотрены вопросы компактности класса, установлена, в частности, его нормальность. Доказано, что не существует монотонных отображений класса $BL^{n/2}$, отличных от константы, заданных во всем пространстве E^n (аналог теоремы Лиувилля) и что изолированные особенности гомеоморфизмов этого класса всегда устранимы так, что, например, n-мерный шар с выброшенным центром нельзя гомеоморфно отобразить на область E^n, граница которой состоит из двух компонент, отличных от точек. Указан порядок роста отображений для случая отображений шара.

В плане реализации построения п. 1 установлено следующее: Пусть D — область E^n, содержащая начало координат O. Относительным (в $D \setminus O$) расстоянием точками x', $x'' \in D \setminus O$ называется число

$$\varrho(x', x''; D \setminus O) = \inf d(K), \tag{7}$$

где d — евклидов диаметр множества, inf берется по всевозможным относительным континуумам $K \subset D \setminus O$, удовлетворяющим условиям: а) $\bar{K} \not\ni O$, б) $K \ni (x' \cup x'')$; или, если $K \not\ni (x' \cup x'')$, то $\bar{K} \cap \partial D$ не пусто и O принаднежит той компоненте множества $D \setminus K$, которая не содержит точек x' и x''.

Расстояние (7) оказывается метрическим. Пополнение метрического пространства $D \setminus O$ по расстоянию (7) присоединяет точку O и „граничные элементы" — классы эквивалентных фундаментальных последовательностей в $D \setminus O$ не сходящихся в $D \setminus O$. Пусть $\widetilde{\partial D}$ — множество этих граничных элементов, $\tilde{D} = D \cup \widetilde{\partial D}$ обычным образом превращается в полное (но не обязательно компактное) метрическое пространство с расстоянием $\varrho(e_1, e_2; \tilde{D})$, которое в случае плоской односвязной и ограниченной области численно совпадает с относительным расстоянием п. 4.

Доказана следующая теорема: Если $y = T(x)$ гомеоморфное отображение класса $BL^{n/2}$ шара D: $|x| < 1$ на область Δ, $T(0) = 0$, то T можно доопределить до непрерывного в $\bar{D}$, так что $T(\bar{D}) = \tilde{\Delta}$ и каждой точке $x \in \bar{D} \setminus D$ при отображении T отвечает единственный граничный элемент области $\tilde{\Delta}$, причем, если x', x'' — любые точки $\overline{D}$ при условии $0 < |x' - x''| < 1/2$, то

$$\varrho[T(x'),\ T(x'');\ \tilde{\Delta}] < \varphi_2(|x' - x''|), \tag{8}$$

где

$$\varphi_2(\alpha) = \left[4M_n \int_D \lambda^{n/2}\ (x,\ T)\, dx\right]^{1/n} \ln^{-1/2}\ \frac{1}{2\,\alpha}.$$

Следовательно, для отображений класса $BL_k^{n/2}$ оценка носит равностепенных характер. Отсюда же следует, что необходимым условием возможности отображения шара на область с помощью гомеоморфного отображения класса $BL^{n/2}$ является компактность пополнения области по относительному расстоянию. Это простое замечание позволяет легко строить примеры областей, гомеоморфных шару, на которые шар не отображается с помощью гомеоморфизмов класса $BL^{n/2}$ (значит и с помощью Q-квазиконформных отображений).

Следствием (8) является и двусторонняя оценка (типа оценок (1), (2)) искажения евклидовых расстояний при отображениях двух шаров друг на друга, так что гомеоморфизм T, $T^{-1} \in BL^{n/2}$ шара на шар доопределяется до гомеоморфизмов замкнутых шаров.

В работе [13] приведены два примера (И. С. Овчинников и В. М. Миклюков). Первый показывает невозможность нетривиальной оценки снизу искажения относительных расстояний при гомеоморфизмах класса $BL^{n/2}$ замкнутых жордановых областей, второй — невозможность оценки сверху в той же общей ситуации. Следовательно, результат о гомеоморфизме шаров, упомянутый выше, нельзя распространить даже на гомеоморфизмы жордановых областей. Эти же примеры показывают, что такие гомеоморфизмы класса $BL^{n/2}$ не осуществляют граничного соответствия по точкам. Этот факт выявляет существенное отличие пространственного случая от плоского, а тэк же случая пространственных отображений класса $BL^{n/2}$ от пространственных Q-квазиконформных отображений. Более того, В. М. Миклюков построил пример двух гомеоморфных отображений класса $BL^{3/2}$ шара на одну и ту же жорданову область Δ так, что полным прообразом некоторой точки $y_0 \in \partial\Delta$ является в одном случае единственная точка, в другом — целый континуум на границе шара. Пример существенный, ибо он показывает невозможность введения в допустимых областях граничных элементов a priori, он же выявляет в известном смысле законченность результатов в [13], относящихся к выяснению общего характера соответствия границ при топологических отображениях класса $BL^{3/2}$.

Приведенные примеры показывают, что класс $BL^{n/2}$ шире класса отображений, рассмотренных В. А. Зоричем. Заметим попутно, что В. А. Зорич[2]) полностью решил вопрос о соответствии границ для пространственных Q-квазиконформных отображений шара на область (см. [24]—[26]).

Как и в плоском случае в областях пространства E^n можно ввести простые концы по аналогии с теорией К. Каратеодори в плоском случае. Однако сразу же ясно, что пополнение областей такими граничными элементами в общем случае не будет компактным, что и привело к тому, что в пространственном случае схема К. Каратеодори была забракована (Б. Кауфман [27]). И. С. Овчинников [23], [28], тем не менее провел такое построение и показал, что для некоторого класса областей (в него входят, например, все односвязные ограниченные области компактные по относительному расстоянию) это пополнение оказывается ком-

[2]) В. А. Зорич — ученик Б. В. Шабата.

пактным и что для этого класса областей простые концы можно отождествить с граничными элементами по относительному расстоянию. В отличие от плоского случая оказалось, что в областях, гомеоморфных шару и компактных по отпосительному расстоянию могут существовать простые концы ,,пятого типа" (у К. Каратеодори в плоском случае 4 типа простых концов), которые имеют несвязное замкнутое множество главных точек. Однако область, имеющая такие простые концы, не может быть гомеоморфизмом шара класса $BL^{n/2}$, поскольку И. С. Овчинников [29] показал, что при таких гомеоморфизмах предельное множество по любому некасательному пути в шаре, идущему в граничную точку A, совпадает с множеством главных точек простого конца, $e = T(A)$ (аналог теоремы Линделефа).

Класс областей, имеющих простые концы пятого типа, является довольно широким. Например, если рассмотреть на грани H некоторого куба произвольное замкнутое несвязное множество F, то можно построить такую область, гомеоморфную шару и компактную по относительному расстоянию, что она будет содержать простой конец, тело которого есть множество H, а множество главных точек этого простого конца будет совпадать с множеством F.

Всякое гомеоморфное отображение класса $BL^{n/2}$ шара на область можно доопределить до непрерывного отображения в замкнутом шаре так, что каждой граничной точке шара будет соответствовать единственный простой конец области. Если дополнительно предположить, что обратное отображение принадлежит классу $BL^{n/2}$, то при $n = 2$ соответствие границ при отображении будет взаимнооднозначное по простым концам, а при $n \geqq 3$, как показывают примеры, соответствие границ уже может не быть взаимнооднозначным. Если рассмотреть более узкий класс квазиконформных отображений шара, то соответствие границ как и в плоском случае будет взаимнооднозначным соответствием по простым концам [24], [26].

Получены и другие признаки областей, компактных по относительному расстоянию, не являющихся гомеоморфизмами шара класса $BL^{n/2}$. Такими областями будут, например, области, имеющие простой конец, разбивающий границу области и не имеющий достижимых точек (В. А. Жуков, В. М. Миклюков [30]). Замечено так же, что если простой конец разбивает границу области на две компоненты, то возможность или невозможность гомеоморфного отображения T шара на такую область, T, $T^{-1} \in BL^{3/2}$ зависит от порядка касания этих компонент (А. М. Лапко, И. С. Овчинников [31]).

В. М. Миклюков в работе [32] для монотонных отображений класса $BL^{3/2}$ с непрерывными производными первого порядка доказал, что если отображение T шара имеет предельное значение в точке границы вдоль некоторого пути, то это же значение имеет и в качестве углового граничного значения, и что T почти везде на границе шара имеет конечные угловые граничные значения. В работе [30] второй результат усилен: аналогичное заключение установлено для монотонных отображений класса $BL^{\alpha}(1)$ $(\alpha > 1)$ трехмерного шара в E^3.

Мы уже отметили выше, что для гомеоморфных отображений класса $BL^{n/2}$ построение п. 1 реализовать нельзя, если иметь целью получить двусторонние оценки (2), причем такие, чтобы был содержательно рассмотрен и ворпос о соответствии границ, поскольку последний вопрос в плане п. 1 вообще решен быть не может. Между тем многие результаты метрического характера (например, аналог теоремы К. Каратеодори, см. п. 1) могут быть получены лишь при наличии двусторонних оценок. Однако остаётся некоторый произвол в выборе относительного расстояния. Этим и воспользовался И. С. Овчинников [33], [34], определив новое относительное расстояние, пополнение по которому превращает произвольную область в компакт. Приведём его определение:

Пусть $x', x'' \in D$, $D \ni O$. Положим

$$\sigma(x', x''; D) = \min\,[\varrho(x', x''), \inf \sup_{x \in F} \varrho(x, \partial D)],$$

где ϱ — евклидово расстояние, inf берется по всевозможным замкнутым относительно D множествам F, отделяющим точки x', x'' от O в D и таким, что если $\bar{F} \cap \partial D$ пусто, то F отделяет $x' \cup x''$ ещё и от ∂D в $\bar{D}$ (∂D предполагается не пустой). σ — метрическое расстояние. Пусть $\tilde{D}$ — пополнение D по σ. Тогда $\tilde{D} \setminus D = \widetilde{\partial D}$ оказывается одной точкой в метрике σ, и эту „точку" можно отождествить с обычной границей ∂D. Однако σ удовлетворяет всем требованиям п. 1 и в отличие от выше приведенной метрики $\varrho(x', x''; \tilde{D})$ получение оценок типа (2) для нового расстояния оказалось возможной с

$$\varphi_2(\alpha) = [4\, M_n \int_D \lambda^{n/2}(x, T)\, dx]^{1/n} \ln^{-1/2} \frac{1}{\alpha} \quad \text{и} \quad \varphi_1 = \varphi_2^{-1},$$

причем для отображений класса $BL_k^{n/2}$ оценки равностепенные.

Конечно, заключение о соответствии границ при отображениях, следующее из этих оценок (точнее — из оценок (1)) совершенно тривиально: обычная граница переходит в обычную границу и только, но поскольку оценка (2) оказывается верной вплоть до границы, можно оценивать скорость приближения к границе области точки-образа в зависимости от скорости приближения к границе области точки-прообраза. Это позволяет установить ряд существенных метрических свойств классов $BL^{n/2}$ и $BL_k^{n/2}$, следуя методике плоского случая. Получены двусторонние оценки искажения множеств уровня по относительному и евклидовому расстояниям (равностепенные в классе $BL_k^{n/2}$), установлены двусторонние оценки искажения евклидовых расстояний внутри областей, при отображениях произвольных областей, следствиями которых являются свойства равностепенной непрерывности и равностепенной открытости (относительно начала координат, если $T(O) = O$) в смысле определений в [10], аналог теоремы К. Каратеодори об отображениях областей с переменными границами.

6. Заключительные замечания

Описанные работы можно условно разделить на три группы, в зависимости от трех возникающих топологических ситуаций: Объемлющие компакты, рассматриваемые области и относительные расстояния таковы, что 1) пополнения $\tilde{A}$ компактны и $\widetilde{\partial A} = \tilde{A} \setminus A$ не сводятся к одному элементу, 2) $\tilde{A}$ — компактны, но $\widetilde{\partial A}$ — одноэлементные множества, 3) $\tilde{A}$ в общем случае не компактны, но $\widetilde{\partial A}$ содержит более одного элемента. Следует заметить, что использование той или другой ситуации определяется сутью дела, так что эти ситуации не взаимно заменимы, если оставаться на позициях априорного введения граничных элементов в областях, единообразного для всех отображений выделяемых классов.

В работе Б. Кауфмана [27] в пространственных областях вводятся граничные элементы — простые концы, причем пополнение областей такими граничными элементами — компактно. Однако, к сожалению, до сих пор не выделено класса отображений, для которого соответствие границ осуществлялось бы по простым концам Б. Кауфмана. Поэтому изложенные в п. 5 результаты остаются пока что наиболее общими.

Литература

[1] C. Caratheodory, Über die Begrenzung einfach zusammenhängender Gebiete, Math. Annalen **73** (1913), 323—370.

[2] S. Mazurkiewicz, Über die Definition der Primenden, Fund. Math. Varsovie **6** (1936), 272—279.

[3] М. А. Лаврентьев, Sur une classe de représentations continues, Матем. сб. **42** (1935), 407—423.

[4] А. Д. Мышкис, К понятию границы, Матем. сб. **25** (67) (1949), 384—414.

[5] А. Д. Мышкис, Об эквивалентности некоторых способов введения границы, Матем. сб. **26** (68) (1950), 228—236.

[6] М. В. Бакланов и Г. Д. Суворов, О замкнутости некоторых классов отображений относительно равномерной сходимости, Труды ТГУ (Томск), серия мех.-матем., **182** (1965), 3—14.

[7] В. К. Ионин и Г. Д. Суворов, О компонентах множеств уровня функции-расстояния до плоского континуума, Доклады АН СССР **129** (1959), 496—498.

[8] Н. Г. Никулина и Б. П. Куфарев, Мера Лебега подмножеств евклидова пространства, как старшая вариация функции-расстояния до замкнутого множества, Доклады АН СССР **160** (1965), 1004—1006.

[9] J. Lelong-Ferrand, Représentation conforme et transformations à intégrale de Dirichlet bornée, Paris 1955.

[10] Г. Д. Суворов, Семейства плоских топологических отображений, Новосибирск 1965.

[11] Г. Д. Суворов, Метрические свойства плоских однолистных отображений замкнутых областей, Труды ТГУ (Томск), серия мех.-матем., **182** (1965), 46—58.

[12] Б. П. Куфарев, Соотношения типа „принципа длины и площади", Доклады АН СССР **170** (1966), 268—270.

[13] И. С. Овчинников и Г. Д. Суворов, Преобразования интеграла Дирихле и пространственные отображения, Сибирск. Матем. Ж. **6** (1965), 1292—1314.

[14] И. С. Овчинников, Неравенство типа „принципа длины и площади" для n-мерного пространства, Труды ТГУ (Томск), серия мех.-матем., **189** (печатается).

[15] В. Н. Лукин, Метрические свойства некоторого класса отображений плоских конечносвязных областей, Труды ТГУ (Томск), серия мех.-матем., **189** (печатается).

[16] М. В. Бакланов и Г. Д. Суворов, Искажение относительных расстояний в замкнутых областях при топологических отображениях класса в конформно-инвариантной метрике, Труды ТГУ (Томск), серия мех.-матем., **182** (1965), 15—26.

[17] М. В. Бакланов, О некоторых классах топологических отображений плоских областей с граничным соответствием не по простым концам, Труды ТГУ (Томск), серия мех.-матем., **189** (печатается).

[18] Ю. К. Устинов, Об одном классе плоских отображений, Труды ТГУ (Томск), серия мех.-матем., **189** (печатается).

[19] Г. Д. Суворов, Простые концы последовательности плоских областей, сходящейся к ядру, Матем. сб. **33** (75) (1953), 73—100.

[20] Г. Д. Суворов, Однолистные отображения плоских областей и множества простых концов области обобщенной меры нуль, Доклады АН СССР **152** (1963), 296—298.

[21] Б. П. Куфарев, Нуль-множества и гомеоморфизмы с конечным интегралом Дирихле, Доклады АН СССР (печатается).

[22] Б. П. Куфарев, К теории плоских отображений некоторых классов, Канд. диссертация, Томск 1966.

[23] И. С. Овчинников, Некоторые метрические свойства пространственных отображений, Канд. диссертация, Томск **1966**.
[24] В. А. Зорич, О соответствии границ при Q-квазиконформных отображениях шара, Доклады АН СССР **145** (1962), 31—34.
[25] В. А. Зорич, Граничные свойства одного класса отображений в пространстве, Доклады АН СССР **153** (1963), 23—26.
[26] В. А. Зорич, Определение граничных элементов посредством сечений, Доклады АН СССР **164** (1965), 736—739.
[27] B. KAUFMANN, Über die Berandung ebener und räumlicher Gebiete, Math. Annalen **103** (1930), 70—144.
[28] И. С. Овчинников, Простые концы одного класса пространственных областей, Труды ТГУ (Томск), серия мех.-матем., **189** (печатается).
[29] И. С. Овчинников, О несуществовании гомеоморфных отображений некоторого класса шара на область, имеющего простые концы с несвязным множеством главных точек, Труды ТГУ (Томск), серия мех.-матем. (печатается).
[30] В. А. Жуков **и** В. М. Миклюков, Об угловых граничных значениях пространственных отображений, Труды ТГУ (Томск), серия мех.-матем. (печатается).
[31] А. М. Лапко и И. С. Овчинников, О несуществовании отображений некоторого класса шара на область, Труды ТГУ (Томск), серия мех.-матем. (печатается).
[32] В. М. Миклюков, О граничных свойствах одного класса отображений в пространстве, Труды ТГУ (Томск), серия мех.-матем., **189** (печатается).
[33] И. С. Овчинников, Метрические свойства отображений класса $BL^{3/2}$, Доклады АН СССР **161** (1965), 526—529.
[34] И. С. Овчинников, Метрические свойства отображений класса $BL^{3/2}$, Труды ТГУ (Томск), серия мех.-матем., **182** (1965), 32—45.

Resümee

Erweiterungen von topologischen Strukturen und metrische Eigenschaften von Abbildungen

G. D. SUWOROW (Donezk)

Sei A ein Gebiet eines Kompaktums (M, r) und B ein Gebiet eines anderen Kompaktums (N, ϱ). In A führen wir eine neue (relative) Distanz r_A und in B eine Distanz ϱ_B ein, und zwar so, daß die relativen Metriken in A und B im kleinen den Metriken r und ϱ äquivalent sind. Seien $\tilde{A}$ und $\tilde{B}$ die Vervollständigungen von A und B in bezug auf r_A bzw. ϱ_B. Sei T eine topologische Abbildung von A auf B. Es gebe Funktionen $\varphi_j(\alpha)$ $(j = 1, 2)$ mit $\varphi_j(\alpha) \to 0$ für $\alpha \to 0$ und mit folgender Eigenschaft: Für alle bezüglich r_A genügend nahen Punkte $x', x'' \in A$ ist

$$\varphi_1(r_A(x', x'')) \leqq \varrho_B(T(x'), T(x'')) \leqq \varphi_2(r_A(x', x'')). \tag{1}$$

Dann kann man T offensichtlich (unter Erhaltung von (1)) zu einem Homöomorphismus $T(\tilde{A}) = \tilde{B}$ fortsetzen.

Die Abschätzung (1) liefert in vielen Fällen genügend viel Information, um eine Reihe von grundlegenden metrischen Eigenschaften von Abbildungen herzuleiten (gleichgradige Stetigkeit und Offenheit in abgeschlossenen Gebieten und innerhalb von Gebieten, Fragen der Kompaktheit und Normalität, Abschätzungen für die Verzerrung verschiedener Größen, Stabilitätsfragen für gewisse Klassen von Abbildungen u. a.). Insbesondere ist das der Fall, wenn die Abbildungen φ_j und der Gültigkeitsbereich von (1) für alle Abbildungen einer gewissen Klasse einheitlich gewählt werden können.

Der Vortrag ist einer Übersicht über Arbeiten gewidmet, in denen die grundlegenden metrischen Eigenschaften gewisser Klassen von topologischen (und z. T. noch allgemeineren) Abbildungen von abgeschlossenen Gebieten in euklidischen und gewissen anderen Räumen untersucht werden. Dabei sind diese Klassen von Abbildungen durch bestimmte Differenzierbarkeitseigenschaften gekennzeichnet, und die Hauptaufgabe der Untersuchungen ist das Auffinden von „passenden" Objekten, für die die oben beschriebene topologische Situation mit der Abschätzung (1) oder zumindest mit einer einseitigen Abschätzung eintritt.

Diese Arbeiten kann man in Abhängigkeit von den drei dabei auftretenden Fällen zunächst ungefähr wie folgt einteilen: Sie betreffen Kompakta, die die betrachteten Gebiete enthalten, zulässige Gebiete und relative Distanzfunktionen mit folgenden Eigenschaften:

1. Die $\tilde{A}$ sind kompakt, und $\partial A = \tilde{A} - A$ bestehen nicht nur aus einem Element.
2. Die $\tilde{A}$ sind kompakt, aber die ∂A sind einelementig.
3. Die $\tilde{A}$ sind nicht kompakt, und ∂A enthält mehr als ein Element.

In den Arbeiten der ersten Gruppe werden hauptsächlich Abbildungen in der komplexen Ebene (konforme, quasikonforme, solche mit beschränktem Dirichletschen Integral usw.) untersucht. Die ∂A sind in diesem Fall (auf verschiedene Art und Weise) metrisierte Mengen von Primenden von C. Caratheodory (oder Mengen von Intervallen von solchen Primenden). Wir merken an, daß M. A. Lawrentjew als Erster eine Abschätzung der Gestalt (1) für konforme Abbildungen des Kreises auf einfach zusammenhängende Gebiete erhielt. Zu der gleichen Gruppe gehören Arbeiten, in denen die Ränderzuordnung bei Abbildungen ebener Gebiete mit „variablen Grenzen" studiert wird.

Außer dem oben angeführten Verfahren der Vervollständigung von Gebieten und den Abschätzungen der Form (1) werden hier noch folgende Konstruktionen herangezogen: die beiden topologisch äquivalenten Arten der Vervollständigung durch Adjunktion von gewissen Klassen von Punktfolgen und der Vervollständigung durch Adjunktion von gewissen Klassen von offenen Mengen. Damit folgen wir demselben Plan, nach dem Caratheodory seine bekannte Theorie der Primenden eines einfach zusammenhängenden ebenen Gebiets aufbaute. Es sei noch bemerkt, daß der systematische Ausbau und die Verallgemeinerung dieser Methode auf allgemeine topologische Strukturen von A. D. Myschkis durchgeführt wurde.

In den Arbeiten der zweiten und dritten Gruppe werden einige Klassen von räumlichen Abbildungen (quasikonforme, solche mit beschränktem Dirichletschen Integral u. a.) betrachtet. In den Arbeiten der zweiten Gruppe, wo also ∂A aus einem Element besteht und sich demzufolge die Ränderzuordnung selbstverständlich völlig trivial beschreiben läßt, liefert aber das Bestehen der Abschätzung (1) einschließlich des Randes viele wesentliche metrische Eigenschaften der betrachteten Klassen von Abbildungen.

In den Arbeiten der dritten Gruppe werden solche Untersuchungsobjekte abgegrenzt, für die man die metrisierten Mengen ∂A mit den Primenden von räumlichen Gebieten identifizieren kann. Diese Primenden werden nach Analogie mit der Theorie von Caratheodory für den ebenen Fall eingeführt; und zwar wird $\tilde{A}$ genau dann ein Kompaktum, wenn A durch eine Funktion der ausgezeichneten Klasse auf das Innere einer Vollkugel abgebildet werden kann. Auf diese Weise behält die Methode von Caratheodory für ebene Gebiete ihre Bedeutung, obwohl sie sich für den allgemeinen räumlichen Fall als völlig ungeeignet herausgestellt hatte (in der bekannten Arbeit von B. Kaufmann auf Grund der Nichtkompaktheit der Vervollständigung von Gebieten durch solche Primenden).

Wir unterstreichen, daß das Vorliegen einer der drei angeführten Situationen der Natur der Sache entspricht: Beim Studium von besonderen Klassen von Abbildungen lassen sich diese Situationen nicht gegeneinander austauschen, wenn man festhält an der a-priori-Einführung von Randelementen in für alle Abbildungen der Klasse einheitlich gewählten Gebieten, um eine inhaltsreiche Untersuchung der metrischen Eigenschaften von Abbildungen in abgeschlossenen Gebieten zu gewährleisten.

Die Bedeutung der hier betrachteten Arbeiten liegt in neuen Ergebnissen der Funktionentheorie. Vom topologischen Standpunkt aus enthalten sie geometrisch anschauliche, für die Anwendungen handliche konkrete Realisierungen von verhältnismäßig einfachen Erweiterungen topologischer Strukturen. Dessen ungeachtet zeigen diese Arbeiten von neuem, daß die allgemeinen topologischen Begriffe des Randes, die ihren Ursprung in der Arbeit von C. Caratheodory haben, auch in der modernen metrischen Abbildungstheorie Anwendungen finden, wobei im Laufe der weiteren Entwicklung die metrische Theorie immer allgemeinere topologische Begriffsbildungen wird heranziehen müssen.

ПСЕВДОМЕТРИКИ ПРОСТРАНСТВ БЛИЗОСТИ

Николай Хаджииванов (София)

Говорим, что $p(x, y)$ есть δ-псевдометрика пространства близости (X, δ), тогда и только тогда, когда $A\,\delta\,B$ влечет $p(A, B) = 0$. Называем псевдометрику $p(x, y)$ разномерно непрерывной относительно равномерной структуры $(X, \mathfrak{R})$, тогда и только тогда, когда $U_{p,\varepsilon} \in \mathfrak{R} \quad \forall \varepsilon > 0$. $(U_{p,\varepsilon} = \{(x, y) \mid p(x, y) < \varepsilon\})$.

Каждое равномерное пространство $(X, \mathfrak{R})$ порождает близость $\delta_{\mathfrak{R}}$ следующим образом:

$$A\,\delta_{\mathfrak{R}}\,B \Leftrightarrow \forall\, U \in \mathfrak{R} \,:\, U \cap (A \times B) \neq \emptyset\,.$$

$\mathfrak{R}$ называем допустимой равномерной структурой близостного пространства (X, δ), когда $\delta_{\mathfrak{R}} = \delta$.

Пусть $P = \{p_\alpha\}_{\alpha \in \mathscr{A}}$ фамилия псевдометрик множества X, разделяющяя точки. В X естественным образом можно ввести равномерную структуру $\mathfrak{R}_P$ с псевдобазой $\{U_{p_\alpha,\varepsilon}\}_{\substack{\alpha \in \mathscr{A} \\ \varepsilon > 0}}$. (Близость, порождаемую структурой $\mathfrak{R}_P$, будем обозначать $\delta_{\mathfrak{R}_P}$ или δ_P.) Отметим, что таким образом можно получить каждую равномерную структуру. И действительно, если $\mathfrak{R}$ равномерная структура, то для каждого $U \in \mathfrak{R}$ существует псевдометрика p_u такая, что $U_{p_u,\varepsilon} \in \mathfrak{R}$ и $U_{p_u,1} \subset U$ [1]. Имеем $\mathfrak{R}_P = \mathfrak{R}$ где $P = \{p_u\}_{u \in \mathfrak{R}}$.

Говорим, что действительная функция f есть δ-функция пространства близости (X, δ), когда $A\,\delta\,B$ влечет $\varrho(fA, fB) = 0$, где $\varrho(U, V) = |U - V|$. Ефремович в [2] доказывает, что если $A\,\overline{\delta}\,B$ существует δ-функция f для которой $fA = 0$, $fB = 1$, $\quad 0 \leqq fx \leqq 1$.

Когда f действительная функция в X, тогда $p_f(x, y) = |fx - fy|$ псевдометрика. Когда f δ-функция, тогда p_f δ-псевдометрика и обратно. Следовательно, если $A\,\overline{\delta}\,B$ существует δ-псевдометрика p_f, для которой $p_f(A, B) > 0$.

Теорема 1. *Пусть дано пространство близости* (X, δ) *и пусть* $P = \{p_\alpha\}_{\alpha \in \mathscr{A}}$ *фамилия псевдометрик, разделяющая точки. Она порождает близость* δ *тогда и только тогда, когда*:

1. *Сумма произвольного конечного числа псевдометрик от* P *есть* δ-*псевдометрика.*

2. *Если* $A\,\overline{\delta}\,B$, *то существует конечное число псевдометрик от* P, *сумма которых разделяет* A *и* B (*расстояние между* A *и* B *относительно этой суммы положительно*).

Теорема 2. *Пусть* (X, δ) *пространство близости*, $p(x, y)$ *вполне ограниченная* δ-*псевдометрика, а* $q(x, y)$ δ-*псевдометрика. Тогда* $r(x, y) = p(x, y) + q(x, y)$ *есть* δ-*псевдометрика. Если* $q(x, y)$ *тоже вполне ограничена, тогда* $r(x, y)$ *вполне ограничена.*

Через P_0 будем обозначать фамилию всех псевдометрик вида p_f, где f ограниченная δ-функция. Нетрудно доказать, что все p_f вполне ограничены δ-псевдометрики.

Как следствие из первых двух теорем получаем:

Теорема 3. *Пусть* $P = P' \cup P_0$, *где* P' *фамилия псевдометрик.* $\delta_P = \delta$ *тогда и только тогда, когда сумма конечного числа псевдометрик от* P' *есть* δ-*псевдометрика.*

Следствие 1. P_0 порождает близость δ.

Следствие 2. Пусть P фамилия вполне ограниченных δ-псевдометрик, разделяющая далекие множества. Тогда $\delta_P = \delta$.

Следствие 3. Пусть P фамилия вполне ограниченных δ-псевдометрик, содержащая P_0. Тогда P порождает близость δ.

Следствие 4. Пусть p δ-псевдометрика. Тогда существует равномерная структура, порождающая δ, относительно которой p равномерно непрерывна. Такова, например, структура, порожденная $P = P_0 \cup \{p\}$.

Следствие 5. Если f δ-функция, то существует равномерная структура, порождающая δ, относительно которой f равномерно непрерывна.

Теорема 4. *Пусть* (X, δ) *пространство близости и* P *фамилия вполне ограниченных* δ-*псевдометрик, порождающая близость* δ. *Тогда равномерная структура* P *минимальна в множестве равномерных структур, порождающих* δ.

Следствие 6. Каждые две вполне ограниченные равномерные структуры, цорождающие одну и ту же близость δ, совпадают.

Следствие 7. Каждая вполне ограниченная δ-псевдометрика равномерно непрерывна относительно произвольной равномерной структуры, порождающей δ.

Следствие 8. Если p δ-псевдометрика, то равномерная структура, порожденная $P = P_0 \cup \{p\}$, есть минимальная равномерная структура, порождающая δ, для которой p равномерно непрерывна.

Некоторые из полученных выше результатов можно объединить в одну теорему.

Теорема 5. *Пусть* (X, δ) *пространство близости. Тогда* $\mathfrak{R}_{P_0}$ *есть минимальная и единственная вполне ограниченная структура, порождающая* δ.

Пространство близости называется правильным тогда и только тогда, когда оно имеет максимальную допустимую равномерную структуру.

Через P_1 будем обозначать совокупность всех δ-псевдометрик.

Теорема 6. *Пусть* (X, δ) *пространство близости. Следующие утверждения эквивалентны:*

1. *Пространство правильно.*
2. *Сумма двух* δ-*псевдометрик есть* δ-*псевдометрика* [3].

3. *Близость, порожденная P_1 совпадает с δ.*

4. *Для каждой фамилии δ-псевдометрик, содержащую P_0 имеем $\delta_P = \delta$.*

5. *Если фамилия псевдометрик P порождает δ и $P' \supset P$ есть фамилия псевдометрик, содержащаяся в P_1, то $\delta_{P'} = \delta$.*

6. *Существует равномерная структура, порождающая δ, относительно которой каждая δ-псевдометрика равномерно непрерывна (максимальная допустимая равномерная структура).*

7. *Верхняя грань произвольной фамилии допустимых равномерных структур есть допустимая равномерная структура.*

8. *Для каждых двух равномерных структур, порождающих δ, существует равномерная структура, содержащая их и порождающая δ* [4].

Примечание. Каждая фамилия равномерных структур, порождающая δ, имеет для нижней грани равномерную структуру, тоже порождающую δ, несмотря на то, (X, δ) правильно или нет.

Теорема 7 ([5]). *Если (X, ϱ) метрическое пространство, то оно правильно и максимальная равномерная структура та, которая порождается метрикой.*

Пространство (X, δ) называется вполне ограниченным тогда и только тогда, когда каждая δ-псевдометрика вполне ограничена.

Теорема 8. *(X, δ) вполне ограничено тогда и только тогда, когда оно правильно и минимальные и максимальные допустимые структуры совпадают, т. е. когда имеют точно одну допустимую равномерную структуру.*

Теорема 9. *Если (X, δ) вполне ограничено, то каждая δ-функция ограничена.*

Обратное неверно даже для метрических пространств.

Пусть (X, δ) пространство близости и $M \subset X$. Говорим, что M дискретно тогда и только тогда, когда каждые два непересекающиеся подмножества множества M далеки. (X, δ) называется близостно ограниченной, если не содержит безконечное дискретное подмножество.

Теорема 10. *Если (X, δ) близостно ограничено, то оно вполне ограничено.*

Обратное утверждение неверно.

Пусть γ непразное множество точек $X \times X$, которое вместе с каждой своей точкой (x, y) содержит и точку (y, x). Будем горить, что γ есть система с малыми относительно равномерной структуры X, $\mathfrak{R}$ тогда и только тогда, когда $\gamma \cap U \neq \emptyset \ \forall U \in \mathfrak{R}$.

Пусть p псевдометрика. Через T_p будем обозначать совокупность тех γ, для которых $p(\gamma) = 0$ $\left(p(\gamma) = \inf_{(x,y) \in \gamma} p(x, y)\right)$.

Теорема 11. *γ система с малыми относительно равномерной структуры $\mathfrak{R}$ тогда и только тогда, когда $\gamma \in T_p$ для каждой равномерно непрерывной псевдометрики p.*

Теорема 12. *Пусть (X, δ) пространство близости. Тогда:*

1. *γ есть система с малыми относительно каждой допустимой равномерной структуры точно тогда, когда $p(\gamma) = 0$ для каждой δ-псевдометрики p.*

2. *γ не есть система с малыми относительно никакой допустимой равномерной структуры точно тогда, когда существует вполне ограниченная δ-псевдометрика p, для которой* $p(\gamma) > 0$.

Первая часть этой теоремы содержится без доказательства в [4]. Указание, данное там, нам неясно.

Теорема 13. *γ система с малыми относительно X, $\mathfrak{R}$ тогда и только тогда, когда* $X \times X \setminus \gamma \notin \mathfrak{R}$.

Пусть $\Gamma_{\mathfrak{R}}$ означает совокупность систем с малыми относительно равномерной структуры $\mathfrak{R}$. Тогда верны следующие утверждения:

1) $\{(x, y), (y, x)\}$ есть система с малыми только тогда, когда $x = y$.

2) Пусть $\gamma = \gamma_1 \cup \gamma_2$. $\gamma \notin \Gamma_{\mathfrak{R}}$ точно тогда, когда $\gamma_1 \notin \Gamma_{\mathfrak{R}}$ и $\gamma_2 \notin \Gamma_{\mathfrak{R}'}$.

3) Пусть $\gamma \notin \Gamma_{\mathfrak{R}}$. Тогда существует такое $\gamma' \notin \mathfrak{R}$, что если $(x, y) \notin \gamma'$ и $(y, z) \notin \gamma'$, то $(x, z) \notin \gamma$.

Будем говорить, что Γ есть структура с малыми, если элементы γ подмножества произведений $X \times X$, симметричные относительно диагонали и удовлетворяющие аксиомам 1, 2, 3.

Как мы убедились, каждая равномерная структура $\mathfrak{R}$ порождает структуру с малыми $\Gamma_{\mathfrak{R}}$. Обратно, если дана структура с малыми Γ и мы положим $U \notin \mathfrak{R}_\Gamma$ точно тогда, когда $X \times X \setminus U \notin \Gamma$, получаем равномерную структуру $\mathfrak{R}_\Gamma$. Можно легко убедиться, что $\Gamma = \Gamma_{\mathfrak{R}_\Gamma}$ и $\mathfrak{R} = \mathfrak{R}_{\Gamma_{\mathfrak{R}}}$. Кроме того $\Gamma_1 \subsetneqq \Gamma_2$ тогда и только тогда, когда $\mathfrak{R}_{\Gamma_1} \supsetneqq \mathfrak{R}_{\Gamma_2}$. Легко проверяется тоже, что $A\, \delta_{\mathfrak{R}_\Gamma} B$ точно тогда, когда $\gamma_{A,B} \in \Gamma$ $(\gamma_{A,B} = A \times B \cup B \times A)$.

Будем говорить, что γ полусемейство, если γ система с малыми относительно минимальной равномерной структуры, порождающей δ, однако не система с малыми относительно хотя одной равномерной структуры, порождающей δ.

Теорема 14 ([4]). *(X, δ) правильно тогда и только тогда, когда сумма двух полусемейств есть полусемейство.*

Отметим, что предложенный выше способ вседения структур с малыми значительно проще, чем у Сандберга [6] и у Мордковича [4].

Литература

[1] N. BOURBAKI, Topologie générale, 2. éd., Paris 1958, ch. 9.
[2] В. А. Ефремович, Геометрия близости **I**, Матем. сб. **31** (73) (1952), 189—200.
[3] В. З. Поляков, Правильность, произведение и спектры пространств близости, Доклады АН СССР **154** (1964), 51—54.
[4] А. Г. Мордкович, Системы с малыми и пространства близости, Матем. сб. **67** (109) (1965), 474—480.
[5] Ю. М. Смирнов, О пространствах близости, Матем. сб. **31** (73) (1952), 543—574.
[6] В. Ю. Сандберг, Новое определение равномерных пространств, Доклады АН СССР **135** (1960), 535—537.

Summary

Pseudometrics of proximity spaces

N. Hadzhivanov (Sofia)

Let (X, δ) be a proximity space; a pseudometric $p(x, y)$ on X we call a δ-pseudometric, iff $A \delta B$ implies $p(A, B) = 0$. We study proximity spaces and uniform spaces by families of δ-pseudometrics. For example our first theorem says that for a proximity space (X, δ) a family P of pseudometrics, separating the points of X, generates δ iff

1. the sum of a finite number of elements of P is a δ-pseudometric;
2. for $A \bar{\delta} B$ there exists a finite number of elements of P, the sum of which separates A and B.